Welcome to the second edition of the enhanced Racing Post Guide to the Flat, which now, like its acclaimed sister jumps edition, incorporates the highly-valued Horses to Follow.

The combined power of these two potent publications is much needed muscle in the struggle to find winners and make a profit from betting, and at the same time boost your chances of success in the Tote Ten to Follow competition. We are confident that again the whole of what we have produced greatly exceeds the sum of the parts of the previous two stand-alone titles.

The very best of luck with the Tote Ten to Follow competition. In this book is all you could need to land the pot. Beyond that, the Guide to the Flat's acclaimed in-depth trainer interviews, the views of Racing Post experts and statistical content should further improve your chances of successfully chasing winners through the summer and at the season's festival high points.

Very close to the deadline for printing this Guide to the Flat edition, the resident designer's wife gave birth to a baby girl. If that doesn't bode well for a year blessed with good fortune I don't know what would.

**Colin Cameron,**
**Editor**

racingpost.com

## Contributors

Colin Boag
Jocelyn De Moubray
Dave Edwards
Dylan Hill
Brian Morgan
Nick Pulford
Tom Segal
Nancy Sexton
Alan Sweetman
Alan Thatcher
Simon Turner
Mark Winstanley

Published in 2011 by Racing Post Books
Raceform, High Street, Compton, Newbury, Berkshire, RG20 6NL

Copyright © Raceform Ltd 2011

All rights reserved. No part of this publication may be reproduced, stored in a retrieval system, or transmitted in any form or by any means, electronic, mechanical, photocopying, recording, or otherwise, without the prior written permission of the publishers.

The Racing Post specifies that post-press changes may occur to any information given in this publication.

A catalogue record for this book is available from the British Library.

ISBN: 978-1-906820-56-5

Edited by **Colin Cameron**
Designed by **David Dew**
Printed in the UK by Buxton Press

# Contents

## INTERVIEWS
| | |
|---|---|
| Ralph Beckett | 4 |
| Henry Cecil | 10 |
| Roger Charlton | 20 |
| Luca Cumani | 27 |
| Godolphin | 34 |
| John Gosden | 43 |
| Mark Johnston | 51 |
| Sir Michael Stoute | 59 |
| Trainers' picks and dark horses | 66 |

## TEN TO FOLLOW
| | |
|---|---|
| Colin Boag's Ten to Follow | 68 |
| View from Ireland | 70 |
| Irish Ten to Follow | 74 |
| View from France | 76 |
| French Ten to Follow | 78 |
| Quiet Achievers | 80 |
| Pedigree Ten to Follow | 84 |
| Mark Winstanley's TV Ten to Follow | 86 |
| Topspeed Ten to Follow | 88 |
| Topspeed ratings | 90 |
| Racing Post Ratings Ten to Follow | 96 |
| Racing Post Ratings | 98 |
| Pricewise Logic | 104 |
| Tote Ten to Follow explained | 106 |
| Tote Ten to Follow contenders | 112 |

## STATISTICS
| | |
|---|---|
| Leading trainers in numbers | 158 |
| Top trainers 2010 | 169 |
| Top jockeys 2010 | 170 |
| Top owners 2010 | 171 |
| Fixtures 2011 | 172 |
| Index | 175 |

# Set for record-breaking season from new yard

RALPH BECKETT's training career was already a progressive one, but Look Here's Oaks win in 2008 gave it the impetus to move to a new level, as his tally of 70 wins last season shows. His recent move to Kimpton Down Stables near Andover has given him space for around 100 horses and they're finally all on one site after a number of years in which he's had to manage several yards.

In an excellent season for the stable, **Puff** must have been a major disappointment. The season started so well with her win in the Group 3 Fred Darling, but after that nothing went right.

'We declared her for the 1,000 Guineas and took her out on the day, but then we had a few issues just before the French Guineas that meant she couldn't run. That was a major disappointment, as I felt that was the right race for her – I felt that even more after the race. That's life, isn't it? She then went to Ascot and I'm not 100 per cent convinced she got the stiff mile there.

'The track didn't suit her at Goodwood and she ran well under her Group 3 penalty in that Ascot Listed race. We were thinking of Dubai but she slipped on some ice around Christmas time and got a tiny hairline fracture. She won't come back into training until April, so it will be the second half of the season before she runs. I think we'll stick to seven furlongs for now or maybe even come back to six.

'**Tropical Treat** did well last season. I was delighted with her Listed win and her second in a York Group 3 – the winner definitely got the run of the race that day. Our horses weren't at their best in August and September – we hit the buffers in terms of results – and she was one who didn't really perform.

'I'd ignore those runs and my aim this season is to frame her campaign around the Summer Stakes at York, the race where she finished second last season. There's also a fillies' six-furlong race at Leopardstown in June that we might consider and I hope she'll be ready to run first at Nottingham in May.

'Five and six furlongs come alike to her and I hope she can win a Group race before tackling the boys again – I think she has a decent race in her. She's certainly a stronger filly this year.

'**Ceilidh House** didn't handle Epsom in last season's Oaks; did you know only three of the 14 fillies behind the winner managed to win a race and two of those were the ones who finished last and second last? Anyway, I was delighted to win the fillies' Listed race at Doncaster at the end of the year – she doesn't have a wind problem but I feel the tongue-tie I fitted there helped her. She benefits from some give in the ground and a possible early target is the Group 3 Blue Wind Stakes over a mile and a quarters at Naas in May.'

**Oasis Dancer** won a conditions race at Newbury in July, but seemed to go off the boil afterwards. 'Yes, he did. I'm going to drop him back to six furlongs for now and, if I'm right in thinking that will suit him, then the Wokingham would be the obvious race for him.

'**Agony And Ecstasy** ran well to finish second in a Listed race at Saint-Cloud in November and I wish we'd kept her going

**Oasis Dancer (left)**

after that, as the third and fourth went on to win similar contests before the end of the year. Soft ground is the key to her and the hope is to win in Listed company.

'**Ashbrittle** was a very immature horse last year. I was very pleased with his win at Doncaster on his final start and I think he can turn out to be a progressive four-year-old – I'm hopeful about his prospects. He needs some give in the ground and the plan initially is to go for a staying 0-95 handicap at Salisbury on Guineas weekend. He'll stay further than that without any problem.'

**Moretta Blanche** started last season well, winning a Newbury maiden and then following up in a Salisbury fillies' handicap off 78. She ran less well in a Newmarket event in July and wasn't seen out again.

'She's fine and is a filly who looked very promising last season, only to go off the boil. There wasn't anything wrong with her, but she was extremely immature and I decided to send her home for a decent break so that she could grow into her frame. She's back now and is much more the finished article – my hope is that she can progress into Pattern races.

'You should include **Vulcanite**, who won five races for us last season. Although he's gone up a long way in the weights, I hope he'll progress into a useful stayer this year.'

It seems as though last season's juveniles were a pretty decent bunch and the hope has to be that they will progress to become a good crop of three-year-olds. As with most yards there are a number of 'could be anythings' among them, many with all-weather form to their names. ▸▸

**Tropical Treat (left, blue cap)**

'**Echo Ridge** won at Kempton at the end of November and she might turn into a nice filly. It was an ordinary maiden that she won, but she was an immature two-year-old. She goes well and I'm open-minded about whether she can progress into a proper filly – I like her.

'**Charleston Lady** is a nice filly who has done a lot of growing up over the winter and I hope she'll continue to go the right way. I haven't given her any fancy entries, but she's from a good family, and her sire, Hurricane Run, ran only once as a juvenile and his first crop of two-year-olds have done well. I'm sure she's going to progress.

'**Ruby Brook** is okay. It wasn't a great race that he won, but he got the hang of things late on. He's a hard one to weigh up but I like him and I think he's potentially a nice ten-furlong handicapper.

'**Western Prize** was a huge, weak two-year-old who came late into training, having had an injury as a yearling. He's done really well to come as far as he has, and to win over a mile with his pedigree – I wouldn't have been afraid to start him out at a mile and a quarter. He's an uncomplicated horse and I really like him – it's just a question of how far he can progress. I hope he's really nice.

'We ran **Matula** in a Listed race at Newmarket, which was a big step up from her success in a Ffos Las maiden. She was a weak filly last season but I like her. She didn't thrive as well as some of the others over the winter, so she will take a bit of time but I hope that she'll be all right.

'Although **Encore Une Annee** won only a Southwell maiden, I hope she's decent. She's by Hernando, who doesn't have too many two-year-old winners, so that's in her favour.

I like her a lot and she has done very well over the winter. I'm optimistic about her prospects and she'll probably start out in an Oaks trial.

'**Ishbelle** won twice and then ran well in the Dick Poole Fillies' Stakes, a Salisbury Listed contest – the form of that race has worked out well. She was a May foal and was a backward filly last season. A big filly, we put her away early and she has had a nice, long break – I can see her making a leap forward this season. I think she's probably a seven-furlong filly, but I may well run her in a Guineas trial if she's working well.

'I think quite a lot of **Miss Diagnosis**. I don't know if you've seen the video of the race at Nottingham when she finished second – it's a horror show! She comes to win her race and then gets lonely out in front – if you stop the tape at the furlong point you think "Goodness, she could be all right", but then she idles and gets pipped. She's from a late-maturing family, and we like her – I hope I'm right about her. She'll start at a mile and a quarter but will get a mile and a half.'

**The first year in a new yard can be a tricky time, as a trainer gets to grip with the new facilities, but Ralph Beckett's team looks strong and one would have to be optimistic that last season's progress can be continued. Expect a steady stream of winners to flow from Kimpton Down over the coming months.**
[Colin Boag]

**Horse to follow** Tropical Treat
**Dark horse** Miss Diagnosis

# RALPH BECKETT
## KIMPTON, HANTS

|  | No. of Hrs | Races Run | 1st | 2nd | 3rd | Unpl | Per cent | £1 Level Stake |
|---|---|---|---|---|---|---|---|---|
| 2-y-o | 50 | 165 | 24 | 22 | 26 | 93 | 14.5 | +77.84 |
| 3-y-o | 41 | 195 | 42 | 18 | 20 | 114 | 21.5 | +61.23 |
| 4-y-o+ | 12 | 40 | 4 | 4 | 4 | 28 | 10.0 | -25.68 |
| Totals | 103 | 400 | 70 | 44 | 50 | 235 | 17.5 | +113.39 |
| 2009 | 101 | 394 | 58 | 43 | 48 | 244 | 14.7 | -1.50 |
| 2008 | 85 | 334 | 42 | 41 | 36 | 214 | 12.6 | -9.09 |

## BY MONTH

| 2-y-o | W-R | Per cent | £1 Level Stake | 3-y-o | W-R | Per cent | £1 Level Stake |
|---|---|---|---|---|---|---|---|
| January | 0-0 | 0.0 | 0.00 | January | 4-6 | 66.7 | +7.88 |
| February | 0-0 | 0.0 | 0.00 | February | 2-5 | 40.0 | -0.02 |
| March | 0-0 | 0.0 | 0.00 | March | 2-4 | 50.0 | +2.50 |
| April | 0-2 | 0.0 | -2.00 | April | 3-13 | 23.1 | +20.00 |
| May | 1-6 | 16.7 | +4.00 | May | 8-33 | 24.2 | +27.03 |
| June | 1-10 | 10.0 | -6.00 | June | 9-28 | 32.1 | +12.60 |
| July | 4-26 | 15.4 | +29.91 | July | 7-38 | 18.4 | -5.25 |
| August | 5-28 | 17.9 | +11.25 | August | 0-16 | 0.0 | -16.00 |
| September | 4-42 | 9.5 | -26.42 | September | 1-28 | 3.6 | -21.50 |
| October | 7-38 | 18.4 | +74.07 | October | 3-18 | 16.7 | +3.50 |
| November | 2-11 | 18.2 | -4.97 | November | 2-5 | 40.0 | +29.00 |
| December | 0-2 | 0.0 | -2.00 | December | 1-1 | 100.0 | +1.50 |

| 4-y-o+ | W-R | Per cent | £1 Level Stake | Totals | W-R | Per cent | £1 Level Stake |
|---|---|---|---|---|---|---|---|
| January | 0-4 | 0.0 | -4.00 | January | 4-10 | 40.0 | +3.88 |
| February | 1-3 | 33.3 | +1.00 | February | 3-8 | 37.5 | +0.98 |
| March | 0-1 | 0.0 | -1.00 | March | 2-5 | 40.0 | +1.50 |
| April | 0-1 | 0.0 | -1.00 | April | 3-16 | 18.8 | +17.00 |
| May | 0-4 | 0.0 | -4.00 | May | 9-43 | 20.9 | +27.03 |
| June | 0-9 | 0.0 | -9.00 | June | 10-47 | 21.3 | -2.40 |
| July | 2-8 | 25.0 | -0.93 | July | 13-72 | 18.1 | +23.73 |
| August | 1-6 | 16.7 | -2.75 | August | 6-50 | 12.0 | -7.50 |
| September | 0-3 | 0.0 | -3.00 | September | 5-73 | 6.8 | -50.92 |
| October | 0-1 | 0.0 | -1.00 | October | 10-57 | 17.5 | +76.57 |
| November | 0-0 | 0.0 | 0.00 | November | 4-16 | 25.0 | +29.00 |
| December | 0-0 | 0.0 | 0.00 | December | 1-3 | 33.3 | +1.50 |

## DISTANCE

| 2-y-o | W-R | Per cent | £1 Level Stake | 3-y-o | W-R | Per cent | £1 Level Stake |
|---|---|---|---|---|---|---|---|
| 5f-6f | 17-103 | 16.5 | +98.44 | 5f-6f | 6-33 | 18.2 | -4.88 |
| 7f-8f | 7-61 | 11.5 | -19.59 | 7f-8f | 17-83 | 20.5 | +34.88 |
| 9f-13f | 0-1 | 0.0 | -1.00 | 9f-13f | 18-74 | 24.3 | +28.23 |
| 14f+ | 0-0 | 0.0 | 0.00 | 14f+ | 1-5 | 20.0 | +3.00 |

| 4-y-o+ | W-R | Per cent | £1 Level Stake | Totals | W-R | Per cent | £1 Level Stake |
|---|---|---|---|---|---|---|---|
| 5f-6f | 1-10 | 10.0 | -4.50 | 5f-6f | 24-146 | 16.4 | +89.06 |
| 7f-8f | 0-8 | 0.0 | -8.00 | 7f-8f | 24-152 | 15.8 | +7.29 |
| 9f-13f | 3-20 | 15.0 | -11.18 | 9f-13f | 21-95 | 22.1 | +16.05 |
| 14f+ | 0-2 | 0.0 | -2.00 | 14f+ | 1-7 | 14.3 | +1.00 |

## TYPE OF RACE

| Non-Handicaps | W-R | Per cent | £1 Level Stake | Handicaps | W-R | Per cent | £1 Level Stake |
|---|---|---|---|---|---|---|---|
| 2-y-o | 21-140 | 15.0 | +80.09 | 2-y-o | 3-25 | 12.0 | -2.25 |
| 3-y-o | 23-79 | 29.1 | +60.42 | 3-y-o | 19-116 | 16.4 | +0.81 |
| 4-y-o+ | 1-5 | 20.0 | -1.00 | 4-y-o+ | 3-35 | 8.6 | -24.68 |

## RACE CLASS

| | W-R | Per cent | £1 Level Stake | FIRST TIME OUT | W-R | Per cent | £1 Level Stake |
|---|---|---|---|---|---|---|---|
| Class 1 | 3-35 | 8.6 | +5.50 | 2-y-o | 6-50 | 12.0 | -10.00 |
| Class 2 | 6-34 | 17.6 | +3.25 | 3-y-o | 11-41 | 26.8 | +42.50 |
| Class 3 | 3-39 | 7.7 | -25.25 | 4-y-o+ | 1-12 | 8.3 | -8.00 |
| Class 4 | 17-110 | 15.5 | +74.19 | | | | |
| Class 5 | 33-152 | 21.7 | +39.96 | Totals | 18-103 | 17.5 | +24.50 |
| Class 6 | 8-30 | 26.7 | +16.75 | | | | |
| Class 7 | 0-0 | 0.0 | 0.00 | | | | |

## RALPH BECKETT

Making his debut in the Guide to the Flat, Ralph Beckett is a trainer on the up. There are good and bad aspects of that for punters. The positive side is that the bookies might just be a tad off the pace in assessing the chances of the yard's runners, but against that patterns are still emerging, which makes life difficult.

The past two seasons have seen great level-stakes profits, as did two of the preceding four. That will have hurt the bookies and they're sure to react – don't expect the pattern to be repeated. However, the two-year-olds and three-year-olds outside of handicap company are well worth a second glance – Beckett places them well and they can go in at decent odds.

Beckett uses the all-weather extensively and each of the three tracks showed a strike-rate in excess of 20 per cent. Chepstow was a staggering six from 12 last season and it will be interesting to watch Beckett-trained runners there to see if the run can be maintained. Runners sent north seem to be well worth respect and that's another angle to watch out for.

Jim Crowley is very much the main man in the saddle and showed a decent profit from his mounts. However, last season was a breakthrough one for the yard and, as Beckett consolidates his place at the top table of Flat racing, his runners' prices will contract.

The best advice with this stable is simple: it needs to be closely followed. If the horses are running well and things seem to be on track to repeat last year's successes, then it's worth following. Equally, it's too early to make definitive statements about profitable patterns. *[CB]* ■

# Frankel tops team out to impress in championship

FIFTH place in the trainers' list and more than £2.25 million in prize-money made 2010 Henry Cecil's best season since 1999. The dark days of the middle of the last decade seem a long way away and the cries of 'Well done 'Enry' are being heard more and more after big-race wins. Hugely popular with racegoers and punters, Henry starts this season with a potential superstar in his Warren Place yard.

As the song puts it: 'What's that coming over the hill, is it a monster?' Every so often a horse appears that looks so outstanding it's frightening, and so it is with Prince Khalid Abdullah's **Frankel**. So good was Frankel as a juvenile that there has been serious discussion about Henry Cecil mounting a major challenge for the trainers' title.

Frankel, a son of Galileo, is unbeaten in his four visits to the racecourse. He landed a maiden at Newmarket in effortless style, followed by an even more impressive win in a Doncaster conditions race, and then scored devastating victories in the Royal Lodge over a mile and the Dewhurst at a furlong shorter. There appear to be no flaws in the form of his wins and it's little wonder he is a short-priced Guineas favourite. He's also favourite for the Derby, but that's just bookmaker hype as the colt is far from certain to stay the trip or even to make it to post.

'He's strengthened and grown and is settling well at home. At this stage I'm very happy with him and the aim is the Guineas. I'd like him to run in a trial before that – he could well go to Newbury for the Greenham. I intend to feel my way with him and we'll see whether he'll stay beyond a mile – there's a lot of speed on the dam's side of his pedigree. When he grows up I can see him eventually getting a mile and a quarter, but I wouldn't know whether he'd get a mile and a half.

'We'll let him tell us which way to go and he'll be entered everywhere. If I was worried about him getting an extended trip he could even be a St James's Palace horse and stay at a mile – who knows? The main thing is that I'm happy with him.'

**Picture Editor** won a maiden at Doncaster and then a conditions race over a mile and a quarter at Leicester, before disappointing when only third in the Zetland Stakes.

'He was a late foal and immature last season. He was over the top on his last start – he'd worked very well but nature then just said enough and he ran very flat. That wasn't his form at all. He's not that big, but he has strengthened and I like him – he's big enough. We'll start him out over a mile and a quarter at Newbury or Newmarket and I'm confident that he'll get a mile and a half.'

**Specific Gravity** was fourth in a Yarmouth maiden in mid-September and then showed the experience wasn't wasted on him when he won a more valuable maiden at Nottingham three weeks later. That win was by a long-looking six lengths and he just galloped clear.

'He's a likeable horse, although he's not over-big. He needs to go on improving, but on his pedigree there's no reason why he shouldn't do that. I think we'll run him in a conditions race and go on from there – he'll definitely stay at least a mile and a quarter and maybe a mile and a half. ▶▶

Dansili's progeny usually stay and he's pretty good.'

**First Mohican** is firmly in the 'could be anything' camp. Winner of his only start so far, a seven-furlong maiden at Yarmouth, he did it in fine style, getting the message late on and forging ahead of his rivals to win by a couple of lengths.

'He's a good mover. Looking at his family, most of them are fillies, although there have been a couple of colts. He's a masculine colt and he could be all right. At the back end of last season he was ready for a race and he won, so he has done nothing wrong so far – I think there's quite a lot of improvement in him. I'll probably start him off in mile handicaps at a decent track and take it from there.'

**Glencadam Gold** was second on his debut, and then went on to win a Redcar maiden.

'He's improving and has done well physically. I liked the way he won at Redcar and he's a nice horse who could stay well.

'Of the other colts, **I like Air Traffic**, who is a brother to Aviate. A great big horse, he could be worth watching – he's settling mentally now and could come out in the Wood Ditton Stakes.

'**Aldedash** ran second on the all-weather and he could be worth watching.

'There's a horse who I liked last year, but then he had a hairline fracture, **Flash Of Intuition**, by Mingun – he could be all right.

'**Late Telegraph**, who is by Montjeu, was very immature last year, but I like him. Similar comments apply to **Ravindra**, who is by Red Ransom.

'Finally among the colts, **World Domination**, who is by Empire Maker out of Reams Of Verse, is another I like. He needs to go the right way, of course.

'Moving to the three-year-old fillies, I liked **All Time** last year, but she was very immature and I couldn't get a race into her – I had about 50 two-year-olds who didn't run.'

'There's one called **Arizona Jewel**, by Dansili out of Rainbow Lake. She ran once, at Yarmouth at the back end, but was very backward – both she and All Time could be mile-and-a-half fillies.

'**Millennium Star** is a complete unknown but I like her – she could be worth watching. It's the time of year when you hope all of your ugly ducklings will turn into swans – of course you also hope that some of your swans won't turn into ugly ducklings.'

Moving to the older horses the star turn is **Twice Over**, who started last season in disappointing fashion in the Dubai World Cup, but once he was back home he had a tremendous year.

He began his campaign by finishing second in the Prince of Wales's Stakes at Royal Ascot and then added another Group 1 to his tally when landing the Eclipse. Second place in the Juddmonte and third in the Irish Champion were commendable efforts, and he then put in a grand performance when winning the Champion Stakes at Newmarket for the second consecutive year.

'It will be very similar to last season – the top mile-and-a-quarter races. He's won almost £2 million in prize-money already and I hope he can add to that this season. A stiff finish at a mile and a quarter, such as the ones at Newmarket and Sandown, really seems to suit.'

The admirable filly **Midday** stays in training at five. She won two Group 1s last season, the Nassau at Goodwood and the Prix Vermeille at Longchamp, and finished up with second in the Breeders' Cup Filly & Mare Turf, where she ran a few pounds below her best.

'She looks very well and has strengthened since last year. She did very little wrong last season. In America it was a very tight track and they went very slowly, with the Japanese filly holding her in all the way, and

**Midday**

it became a sprint over the final furlong – she tried her best but that isn't her way of running. If they'd gone a better gallop it might have been a very different story. We can't run her on very fast ground as she'll jar up, so she might end up having to take on the colts.'

**Manifest** started last season well, winning the Group 2 Yorkshire Cup after running second in the John Porter. His final run of the season was in the Gold Cup at Royal Ascot, where he seemingly didn't stay.

'He's done very well – he was very backward last season and got jarred up at York. I tried to get him back for the Gold Cup but it didn't work. What that race showed us is there is a limit to his stamina – I think he'll get two miles but probably not further. Now that he's stronger there's every chance he'll be running at a mile and a half. If he shows ▸▸

Jacqueline Quest (green cap) gets the better of Special Duty before being disqualified and placed second in the 2,000 Guineas

me he's right he could start out again in the John Porter, but he will probably have major entries at a mile and a half. I wouldn't be worried by taking him to the Yorkshire Cup again and then bringing him back in trip.'

Last season's 1,000 Guineas was 'won' by the 66-1 outsider **Jacqueline Quest**, only for the Newmarket stewards to break owner Noel Martin's heart by disqualifying the filly. Most people thought the decision was the right one and Martin took the decision in a sporting manner.

After Newmarket Jacqueline Quest didn't quite manage to live up to her Guineas performance, finishing third in the Coronation Stakes and then fifth in a Goodwood Group 3, not being seen out again after the end of July.

'She got jarred up on the fast ground last year – everything seemed to suffer on it. She's well now. I thought she was saving herself a little bit on the quick ground at Goodwood – she came through nicely to win her race but then couldn't quite go through with her effort. She has done well physically and we'll be looking at the decent mile races with her.'

**Timepiece** stays in training at four and showed in her final start last season that she's a useful filly. Second in the Lingfield Oaks Trial, she was said not to have handled the hill at Epsom in the big one but, dropped in class, she won the Sandringham Handicap at Royal Ascot.

'I think a mile and a quarter is her best trip and I'm pleased with her at present. She's a big filly who seems to be much stronger this year and she could do with a little bit of give in the ground. I think she'll be a decent filly this season and will be aimed at Pattern races.

'There's a filly who maybe isn't as obvious as some of the others, but whom I like. **Vita Nova** ran twice last year, winning both of her races, but was very backward. She has done very well and I hope she will be nice this season – I think she's possible Pattern class.

'**Diescentric** won the Wood Ditton last season but got jarred up and never properly came back to form. He seems to be in good form now – he's an unknown quantity but he's a pretty nice horse.'

**Henry starts this season with around 140 horses, about 80 of which are three-year-olds, many of them unexposed. Assuming they stay healthy it's hard to visualise anything other than another great season for the racing legend that is Henry Cecil. Maybe the quotes about him landing an eleventh trainers' championship are over-optimistic, but if Frankel can deliver, who knows?** [CB]

**Horse to follow** Frankel
**Dark horse** Vita Nova

## HENRY CECIL

It was as if the tough times for Warren Place were simply a bad dream. A total of 62 British winners and a strike-rate of 21 per cent last year were an excellent result, but Cecil's reputation is such that those pesky bookmakers ran scared and the result was a modest, overall level-stakes loss.

The advice remains the same: buy The Racing Post and look at Today's Trainers – if Cecil's strike-rate is around the 25 per cent mark, which it was in several months last season, get stuck in. Profits won't be huge but that's infinitely better than a loss.

On the jockey front, Tom Queally is the number one man, but Cecil strongly promoted Ian Mongan last season and has announced him as his number two. The pair will take the lion's share of the yard's mounts.

There was a priceless Breeders' Cup moment when an American hack asked Cecil about Wolverhampton, saying that he'd never been there. Quick as a flash, Cecil said: 'Neither have I.' However, the Warren Place horses know their way around there and last season six of the 13 who went there won. Newmarket's Rowley Mile and July Course, plus Newbury, continue to feature strongly in his way of working – he sends a lot of his better two and three-year-olds there but level-stakes support would have shown a loss last season. The best advice remains to watch the stable's form and then step in.

When Cecil runs two horses in the same race, as he does from time with his maidens, don't neglect the one at the bigger price – it's an old system with the yard's runners but it still works from time to time.

In a strange way this yard is still in a period of transition as the good times roll again after the dark years of the middle of the last decade. Numbers are on the increase and that makes spotting patterns difficult. However, when the yard is running hot, Cecil's runners are worth following wherever he chooses to run them and I can do no better than to repeat previous advice – the man's a genius! [CB] ■

Henry Cecil

# HENRY CECIL
## NEWMARKET, SUFFOLK

|       | No. of Hrs | Races Run | 1st | 2nd | 3rd | Unpl | Per cent | £1 Level Stake |
|-------|-----------|-----------|-----|-----|-----|------|----------|----------------|
| 2-y-o | 21        | 44        | 11  | 9   | 5   | 19   | 25.0     | +6.20          |
| 3-y-o | 50        | 206       | 38  | 33  | 28  | 107  | 18.4     | -9.95          |
| 4-y-o+| 14        | 48        | 13  | 8   | 2   | 25   | 27.1     | -3.34          |
| Totals| 85        | 298       | 62  | 50  | 35  | 151  | 20.8     | -7.09          |
| 2009  | 94        | 324       | 63  | 54  | 47  | 160  | 19.4     | +2.82          |
| 2008  | 71        | 282       | 52  | 43  | 37  | 150  | 18.4     | +6.71          |

### BY MONTH

| 2-y-o | W-R | Per cent | £1 Level Stake | 3-y-o | W-R | Per cent | £1 Level Stake |
|-------|------|----------|----------------|-------|------|----------|----------------|
| January  | 0-0 | 0.0  | 0.00  | January  | 0-0  | 0.0  | 0.00   |
| February | 0-0 | 0.0  | 0.00  | February | 0-0  | 0.0  | 0.00   |
| March    | 0-0 | 0.0  | 0.00  | March    | 0-0  | 0.0  | 0.00   |
| April    | 0-0 | 0.0  | 0.00  | April    | 4-32 | 12.5 | -16.00 |
| May      | 0-1 | 0.0  | -1.00 | May      | 11-38| 28.9 | +18.88 |
| June     | 0-3 | 0.0  | -3.00 | June     | 4-28 | 14.3 | +5.67  |
| July     | 1-2 | 50.0 | +3.00 | July     | 5-26 | 19.2 | +4.48  |
| August   | 2-5 | 40.0 | +2.75 | August   | 6-26 | 23.1 | +0.75  |
| September| 3-13| 23.1 | +0.80 | September| 4-30 | 13.3 | -9.67  |
| October  | 5-16| 31.3 | +7.65 | October  | 4-23 | 17.4 | -11.05 |
| November | 0-2 | 0.0  | -2.00 | November | 0-2  | 0.0  | -2.00  |
| December | 0-2 | 0.0  | -2.00 | December | 0-1  | 0.0  | -1.00  |

| 4-y-o+ | W-R | Per cent | £1 Level Stake | Totals | W-R | Per cent | £1 Level Stake |
|--------|------|----------|----------------|--------|------|----------|----------------|
| January  | 1-1 | 100.0 | +3.33  | January  | 1-1   | 100.0 | +3.33  |
| February | 0-1 | 0.0   | -1.00  | February | 0-1   | 0.0   | -1.00  |
| March    | 1-1 | 100.0 | +1.38  | March    | 1-1   | 100.0 | +1.38  |
| April    | 0-8 | 0.0   | -8.00  | April    | 4-40  | 10.0  | -24.00 |
| May      | 3-12| 25.0  | -3.50  | May      | 14-51 | 27.5  | +14.38 |
| June     | 1-6 | 16.7  | -1.67  | June     | 5-37  | 13.5  | +1.00  |
| July     | 4-7 | 57.1  | +7.62  | July     | 10-35 | 28.6  | +15.10 |
| August   | 1-4 | 25.0  | -0.25  | August   | 9-35  | 25.7  | +3.25  |
| September| 0-5 | 0.0   | -5.00  | September| 7-48  | 14.6  | -13.87 |
| October  | 2-3 | 66.7  | +3.75  | October  | 11-42 | 26.2  | +0.35  |
| November | 0-0 | 0.0   | 0.00   | November | 0-4   | 0.0   | -2.00  |
| December | 0-0 | 0.0   | 0.00   | December | 0-3   | 0.0   | -1.00  |

### DISTANCE

| 2-y-o | W-R | Per cent | £1 Level Stake | 3-y-o | W-R | Per cent | £1 Level Stake |
|-------|------|----------|----------------|-------|------|----------|----------------|
| 5f-6f  | 1-9  | 11.1 | -4.00  | 5f-6f  | 0-14   | 0.0  | -14.00 |
| 7f-8f  | 9-33 | 27.3 | +11.13 | 7f-8f  | 13-55  | 23.6 | +23.00 |
| 9f-13f | 1-2  | 50.0 | -0.93  | 9f-13f | 25-130 | 19.2 | -11.95 |
| 14f+   | 0-0  | 0.0  | 0.00   | 14f+   | 0-7    | 0.0  | -7.00  |

| 4-y-o | W-R | Per cent | £1 Level Stake | Totals | W-R | Per cent | £1 Level Stake |
|-------|------|----------|----------------|--------|------|----------|----------------|
| 5f-6f  | 2-3  | 66.7 | +4.33 | 5f-6f  | 3-26   | 11.5 | -13.67 |
| 7f-8f  | 2-8  | 25.0 | +1.12 | 7f-8f  | 24-96  | 25.0 | +35.25 |
| 9f-13f | 7-27 | 25.9 | -3.67 | 9f-13f | 33-159 | 20.8 | -16.55 |
| 14f+   | 2-10 | 20.0 | -5.13 | 14f+   | 2-17   | 11.8 | -12.13 |

### TYPE OF RACE

| Non-Handicaps | W-R | Per cent | £1 Level Stake | Handicaps | W-R | Per cent | £1 Level Stake |
|---------------|------|----------|----------------|-----------|------|----------|----------------|
| 2-y-o  | 11-41  | 26.8 | +9.20  | 2-y-o  | 0-3   | 0.0  | -3.00  |
| 3-y-o  | 26-132 | 19.7 | +4.97  | 3-y-o  | 12-74 | 16.2 | -14.92 |
| 4-y-o+ | 10-30  | 33.3 | +86.00 | 4-y-o+ | 3-18  | 16.7 | -7.79  |

### RACE CLASS / FIRST TIME OUT

| RACE CLASS | W-R | Per cent | £1 Level Stake | FIRST TIME OUT | W-R | Per cent | £1 Level Stake |
|------------|------|----------|----------------|----------------|------|----------|----------------|
| Class 1 | 16-66 | 24.2 | -8.67   |         |       |      |        |
| Class 2 | 1-21  | 4.8  | -19.50  | 2-y-o   | 4-21  | 19.0 | +10.75 |
| Class 3 | 8-34  | 23.5 | -0.18   | 3-y-o   | 8-50  | 16.0 | +3.50  |
| Class 4 | 13-74 | 17.6 | -15.88  | 4-y-o+  | 3-14  | 21.4 | -4.29  |
| Class 5 | 22-93 | 23.7 | +36.22  | Totals  | 15-85 | 17.6 | +9.96  |
| Class 6 | 2-10  | 20.0 | +0.91   |         |       |      |        |
| Class 7 | 0-0   | 0.0  | 0.00    |         |       |      |        |

# THE RACING INDUSTRY'S BIBLE

The 2011 edition of the number one racing annual, *Horses in Training*, is due out on 4th March. Now in its 121st year of publication, it is the must have companion for professionals and punters alike, containing:

- A-Z listing of 695 racehorse trainers and their strings from the UK and leading trainers in Ireland and France
- Over 17,600 horses listed with their breeding and owner's details Foaling dates of two year olds
- Complete alphabetical index
- 200 page statistical section covering everthing from big-race winners, leading trainer tables to fixtures and racecourse information

**SAVE £1**

**SPECIAL OFFER £17.99**

**ORDER NOW RACINGPOST.com/shop**
**ORDERLINE 01933 304858** Quote ref: HITCH11

racingpost.com

# All-age team to maintain impressive strike-rate

IN terms of the number of winners, last season was Roger Charlton's best since 2003 and the strike-rate at 20 per cent was also the best since then.

Among the older horses, the star is **Cityscape**. He missed most of 2009 after finishing sore in the 2,000 Guineas, but he showed last season he has considerable ability and promise. He won twice: a Haydock Listed contest and the Group 3 Joel Stakes over a mile at Newmarket in October, when his jockey felt he had become unbalanced going into the Dip.

'That's possibly the case. It is quite a noticeable dip as they run downhill and maybe it didn't suit a big horse like him, but we hadn't got many options at that time of year. I think he wants to run a mile at this stage in his career and he wants good-to-soft ground. For that kind of horse an uphill finish suits and he needs to aim at a Group 2, so the Sandown Mile is an obvious starting point – then if it came up soft in the Lockinge, who knows? As a son of Selkirk one can be optimistic about there being more improvement to come from him.'

**Bated Breath** is Cityscape's half-brother and he won his first three starts last season: a maiden at Pontefract and then six-furlong handicaps off 90 and 95. He was then third off his new mark of 105, before finishing with fourth place in a Doncaster Listed contest.

'He's a lovely, big, strong horse who I've never thought wanted firm ground, but I really don't know what his ideal ground is. He probably should have won his second last race – the gap just didn't come when it needed to – and it had been touch and go whether he ran at Doncaster as he'd had an abscess on his near fore. Off 107 now, he's effectively out of handicaps, so it will be Listed races and hopefully Group company after that.'

**Definightly** had a good four-year-old season, after a tough time at three. He started with a win in a Goodwood handicap off 85, won another handicap off 88 and also managed to land both a Listed and a Group 3 contest, all of his wins coming at six furlongs.

'I think the key to him is soft ground. We've always thought good or softer, but if it is a really strong contest then I think the softer the better – it was very bad ground when he won his Group 3 in France and not bad enough on his final start, in Italy.

'The way he ran in the Ayr Silver Cup would also serve to illustrate that – he had a lot of weight in hand but ran no race at all, for no apparent reason. He was beaten so easily, and by so far, that it just had to be the ground. There are very few races for him in the spring and after May the ground will probably have gone so, realistically, he won't be able to have a proper crack at a decent prize until the autumn.

'Therefore the Prix l'Abbaye is a sensible target for him. It's over five furlongs but it's marginally uphill and they go a real good gallop, so you almost need a six-furlong horse to win it – as, of course, was Patavellian. He's off 114 so he isn't out of it on class – it's just a question of whether he's fit and well, whether the ground is soft enough and whether we've looked after him well through the season. I think he's

**Definightly**

probably a Group 3 horse, but some of those win Group 1 sprints, so who knows?'

**Sea Of Heartbreak** won her first three starts of the season, in a conditions race and in handicaps off 78 and 85. She ran poorly off 92 in a decent Goodwood event but rounded off her season with a cracking effort to finish fourth in a Newmarket Listed contest.

'Something was clearly wrong at Goodwood as she didn't come down the hill – it just didn't suit. That apart, her form was progressive and good all the way through. I think it's important with four-year-old fillies to try to get black type, as owners like to breed from them and it adds a lot of value to them. Listed contests at a mile and a quarter will be on the cards.

'**Genki** ran pretty well throughout last season, bar the Stewards' Cup, although the ground was pretty poor that day, as it can be at the end of a busy week. When the ▶▶

**Clowance**

ground is loose he doesn't run very well although he goes on pretty well any ground, he's one of those who doesn't really get a purchase when it's loose on top. The same applies to him as it does with Definightly – you meet the same horses in handicaps and in Group races. You'd expect a Group 1 sprinter to be rated over 120, but they're often rated quite a way below that. Off the mark he now has, I think he'll be better off running in an eight-runner Group race than a 28-runner handicap.

'**High Constable** has just come back – he missed most of last season with a stress fracture. It's early days and it's the same proviso as it is with many others, but if he stays sound he has the potential to progress. The dream would be to win the Royal Hunt Cup – I've never won the race and, as he's owned by Her Majesty, winning at Royal Ascot would be very special.

'**Clowance** could be worth a mention. She is going to be covered by Oasis Dream but she is currently in training. Soft ground determines where she runs and it could be here or in France. We're concentrating mainly on April and May and the John Porter would be a possibility if the ground was right.

Moving to the three-year-olds, **Al Kazeem** is an interesting prospect. He showed promise in his maiden at Newbury but then won nicely at the same track a fortnight later, both of those races being at a mile.

'He's an exciting prospect. He's an attractive colt by Dubawi, who is turning out to be a good stallion. Al Kazeem was always big and backward as a two-year-old and when we started to do some work with him, he showed promise. In his first race he ran pretty well, as I expected him to, and got tired, but he then exceeded my expectations on his next start. Let's assume there's no reason why he can't improve again. He looks like a staying horse, but he's not guaranteed to get a mile and a half, so the Derby isn't in the equation at this stage. I hope he's up to Listed and Group class, so the obvious starting point is a conditions race.

'**Pontenuovo** has arrived from France and has settled in very well. She seems very relaxed and sensible. Her form in France is pretty good, and she has rather slipped under the radar here in Britain. As with all fillies, it's a case of whether she has trained on and we won't know that until she runs. Is she a six- seven- or eight-furlong filly? If she's a miler that's useful, but if she only stays six furlongs then life is more difficult as she has a Group penalty. She has to improve to be considered a Classic contender, but if she's in good form we'll probably go for a Guineas trial – perhaps the Fred Darling.'

Charlton's horses tend to improve considerably for their first run, so it was encouraging that Primevere was able to win on her debut.

'It was her class that saw her through at Kempton. I always felt she should be a winning two-year-old, but she had niggling problems with sore shins that prevented her running sooner. She overcame some trouble in running and won in good style, going away at the finish, in what was seemingly a decent time. She's a big filly and, being by Singspiel, you'd think she will be better at three, and that she would stay.

She starts off a mark of 83 and is an unknown quantity. The handicapper put Al Kazeem on 95 and there's a lot of guesswork involved – maybe Primevere should be 95 and Al Kazeem 83, nobody knows yet.'

As with all major yards, there are any number of well-bred but unraced horses and Charlton singled out a few to look out for.

'**Deck Walk** is out of a half-sister to the dam of Cityscape. She's a huge filly who has always shown promise but hasn't been entirely straightforward to train. A totally unknown quantity, she might struggle to win or she might turn out to be very useful – time will tell, although she hasn't been allowed into fourth gear yet.

'**Federation** is a half-sister to Attraction by Motivator. She's a bit buzzy but is a nice, big, scopey filly. I quite like her, but whether she's an 80-rated filly or a 95-plus one is impossible to tell – we'll find out when she goes into fast work.

'**Korithi** is an attractive filly from a good family and her sire, Oasis Dream, is doing very well. Again it's hard to tell at this stage but I'll be disappointed if she can't win her races.

'**Thistle Bird** was about to run last year and literally the day before had a setback, but she seems to be over that now. I see her as more of a sprinting than staying Selkirk filly – her mother was a six- and seven-furlong winner. I hope she'll be all right.'

**Charlton starts the new season with a strong-looking team. With the likes of Cityscape and Definightly, there have to be hopes that some major prizes will come the way of Beckhampton in the coming months and it wouldn't be the biggest surprise if one or two of the three-year-olds became stars by the end of the year.** *[CB]*

**Horse to follow** Cityscape
**Dark horse** Pontenuovo

## ROGER CHARLTON

It's not a definitive rule, but in general terms when Roger Charlton's strike-rate creeps above the 20 per cent mark, his is a profitable team to follow. Last year saw it hit that figure and a sizeable profit followed.

Follow Today's Trainers closely in the Racing Post – when the yard is in form and the strike-rate hits 20 per cent, step in. If you can apply a measure of selectivity, so much the better.

Charlton places his horses with great care, rarely running them out of their class, and when he steps one up in class, it's because it's ready to cope with it. That makes the Charlton team a good one to follow. The older horses are kept in training for a purpose – they're always worth a second look.

Steve Drowne takes most of the mounts and gets most of the winners, but outside bookings of big names are worth watching – last season Richard Hughes and Jimmy Fortune were significant.

You won't make a mint following the horses going off as favourite, but there are profits to be made with this system.

This team tends to hit top form in mid-summer – watch out for that. Courses that have been favoured over the years include Newmarket's July Course and, although Newbury is the local track, don't discount runners there – it was very profitable last season. Bath has long been a happy hunting ground and anything sent to Brighton is well worth a close look.

Finally, if Charlton runs two horses in a maiden, don't disregard the one less-fancied one. They're both there with a chance and modest each-way support can be worthwhile. *[CB]* ∎

# ROGER CHARLTON
## BECKHAMPTON, WILTS

|       | No. of Hrs | Races Run | 1st | 2nd | 3rd | Unpl | Per cent | £1 Level Stake |
|-------|------------|-----------|-----|-----|-----|------|----------|----------------|
| 2-y-o | 21         | 58        | 10  | 3   | 5   | 40   | 17.2     | -1.24          |
| 3-y-o | 28         | 109       | 27  | 9   | 10  | 63   | 24.8     | +24.09         |
| 4-y-o+| 15         | 72        | 11  | 7   | 6   | 48   | 15.3     | +28.63         |
| Totals| 64         | 239       | 48  | 19  | 21  | 151  | 20.1     | +51.48         |
| 2009  | 67         | 240       | 35  | 28  | 43  | 134  | 14.6     | -1.00          |
| 2008  | 76         | 281       | 33  | 30  | 31  | 186  | 11.7     | -10.25         |

### BY MONTH

| 2-y-o     | W-R  | Per cent | £1 Level Stake | 3-y-o     | W-R  | Per cent | £1 Level Stake |
|-----------|------|----------|----------------|-----------|------|----------|----------------|
| January   | 0-0  | 0.0      | 0.00           | January   | 1-1  | 100.0    | +0.67          |
| February  | 0-0  | 0.0      | 0.00           | February  | 0-1  | 0.0      | -1.00          |
| March     | 0-0  | 0.0      | 0.00           | March     | 0-3  | 0.0      | -3.00          |
| April     | 0-0  | 0.0      | 0.00           | April     | 1-17 | 5.9      | -13.50         |
| May       | 1-2  | 50.0     | +0.20          | May       | 5-21 | 23.8     | +7.50          |
| June      | 2-7  | 28.6     | +0.58          | June      | 9-21 | 42.9     | +22.67         |
| July      | 0-5  | 0.0      | -5.00          | July      | 6-14 | 42.9     | +6.38          |
| August    | 2-11 | 18.2     | +1.73          | August    | 0-9  | 0.0      | -9.00          |
| September | 2-14 | 14.3     | -5.00          | September | 4-12 | 33.3     | +20.38         |
| October   | 2-17 | 11.8     | +6.00          | October   | 1-8  | 12.5     | -5.00          |
| November  | 0-1  | 0.0      | -1.00          | November  | 0-2  | 0.0      | -2.00          |
| December  | 1-1  | 100.0    | +1.25          | December  | 0-0  | 0.0      | 0.00           |

| 4-y-o+    | W-R  | Per cent | £1 Level Stake | Totals    | W-R   | Per cent | £1 Level Stake |
|-----------|------|----------|----------------|-----------|-------|----------|----------------|
| January   | 0-0  | 0.0      | 0.00           | January   | 1-1   | 100.0    | +0.67          |
| February  | 0-0  | 0.0      | 0.00           | February  | 0-1   | 0.0      | -1.00          |
| March     | 0-0  | 0.0      | 0.00           | March     | 0-3   | 0.0      | -3.00          |
| April     | 1-11 | 9.1      | +30.00         | April     | 2-28  | 7.1      | +16.50         |
| May       | 2-10 | 20.0     | +5.00          | May       | 8-33  | 24.2     | +12.70         |
| June      | 1-11 | 9.1      | -1.00          | June      | 12-39 | 30.8     | +22.25         |
| July      | 2-10 | 20.0     | -3.38          | July      | 8-29  | 27.6     | -2.00          |
| August    | 1-9  | 11.1     | -0.50          | August    | 3-29  | 10.3     | -7.77          |
| September | 2-8  | 25.0     | +2.00          | September | 8-34  | 23.5     | +17.38         |
| October   | 2-10 | 20.0     | -0.50          | October   | 5-35  | 14.3     | +0.50          |
| November  | 0-3  | 0.0      | -3.00          | November  | 0-6   | 0.0      | -5.00          |
| December  | 0-0  | 0.0      | 0.00           | December  | 1-1   | 100.0    | 0.00           |

### DISTANCE

| 2-y-o  | W-R  | Per cent | £1 Level Stake | 3-y-o  | W-R   | Per cent | £1 Level Stake |
|--------|------|----------|----------------|--------|-------|----------|----------------|
| 5f-6f  | 5-24 | 20.8     | -5.22          | 5f-6f  | 5-16  | 31.3     | +1.97          |
| 7f-8f  | 5-33 | 15.2     | +4.98          | 7f-8f  | 6-43  | 14.0     | -12.86         |
| 9f-13f | 0-1  | 0.0      | -1.00          | 9f-13f | 16-48 | 33.3     | +36.98         |
| 14f+   | 0-0  | 0.0      | 0.00           | 14f+   | 0-2   | 0.0      | -2.00          |

| 4-y-o  | W-R  | Per cent | £1 Level Stake | Totals | W-R    | Per cent | £1 Level Stake |
|--------|------|----------|----------------|--------|--------|----------|----------------|
| 5f-6f  | 4-23 | 17.4     | +2.63          | 5f-6f  | 14-63  | 22.2     | -0.62          |
| 7f-8f  | 6-31 | 19.4     | +39.50         | 7f-8f  | 17-107 | 15.9     | +31.62         |
| 9f-13f | 1-16 | 6.3      | -11.50         | 9f-13f | 17-65  | 26.2     | +24.48         |
| 14f+   | 0-2  | 0.0      | -2.00          | 14f+   | 0-4    | 0.0      | -4.00          |

### TYPE OF RACE

| Non-Handicaps | W-R  | Per cent | £1 Level Stake | Handicaps | W-R   | Per cent | £1 Level Stake |
|---------------|------|----------|----------------|-----------|-------|----------|----------------|
| 2-y-o         | 8-48 | 16.7     | -0.24          | 2-y-o     | 2-10  | 20.0     | -1.00          |
| 3-y-o         | 6-33 | 18.2     | -13.33         | 3-y-o     | 21-76 | 27.6     | +37.42         |
| 4-y-o+        | 5-12 | 41.7     | +33.00         | 4-y-o+    | 6-60  | 10.0     | +18.50         |

### RACE CLASS / FIRST TIME OUT

| Race Class | W-R   | Per cent | £1 Level Stake | First Time Out | W-R  | Per cent | £1 Level Stake |
|------------|-------|----------|----------------|----------------|------|----------|----------------|
| Class 1    | 4-16  | 25.0     | +3.50          | 2-y-o          | 3-21 | 14.3     | +11.33         |
| Class 2    | 6-33  | 18.2     | +46.17         | 3-y-o          | 4-28 | 14.3     | -14.83         |
| Class 3    | 4-20  | 20.0     | +0.17          | 4-y-o+         | 2-15 | 13.3     | +36.00         |
| Class 4    | 13-71 | 18.3     | +12.60         |                |      |          |                |
| Class 5    | 19-84 | 22.6     | -11.22         | Totals         | 9-64 | 14.1     | +32.50         |
| Class 6    | 2-15  | 13.3     | +0.25          |                |      |          |                |
| Class 7    | 0-0   | 0.0      | 0.00           |                |      |          |                |

# High hopes for success both home and away

Presvis

LUCA CUMANI trained 66 British winners and earned almost £1 million in prize-money last year, but that's far from the whole story. More than most trainers, Cumani sends his horses far and wide in search of rich foreign pickings, as his as yet unrequited love affair with the Melbourne Cup shows.

**Bauer** was one of his contenders in 'the race that stops a nation' back in 2008, being beaten by just a nose. Off the track until September of last season, he made the trip back to Flemington, only to be withdrawn on the eve of the race with a bruised hoof.

'He was in very good form and then after his final gallop he had a little problem and we had to take him out of the race. He's eight now, so he's an old boy – let's hope there are a couple of nice races left in him. The plan will be for him to have a British campaign this season.'

**Manighar** was Cumani's only runner in the Melbourne Cup last year, finishing a creditable seventh, and he could arguably have finished closer with a bit more luck in running. The best of his European runs was when beaten just a short head by Americain, the eventual Melbourne Cup winner, in the Prix Kergorlay over 1m7f at Deauville.

'The prerequisite for him is that he needs some cut in the ground. As long as he gets that he'll be aimed at the good staying events, the Cup races and so on. We'll probably consider another crack at the Melbourne Cup with him.'

**Presvis** illustrates the point about the international nature of the Cumani stable. The Form Book shows that in Britain last ▶▶

year he ran just once, when finishing ninth in the Prince of Wales's Stakes at Royal Ascot. However, he also won more than £90,000 in the Jebel Hatta in Dubai and his fifth place in the Singapore Airlines Cup and the QE II Cup in Hong Kong added another £60,000. Presvis again added to his earnings in Dubai at the start of this year but what would be the plan for the spring and summer?

'If all is well it will be the same again: Hong Kong and then back to Singapore. I don't foresee him having a British campaign.'

**Summit Surge** started his year in Dubai, then was second in an Italian Group 3 before winning the Group 2 York Stakes when stepped up to a mile and a quarter for the first time. He then went to America, where he finished fifth in the Arlington Million, and rounded off his season when he was runner-up in a Listed race at Lingfield.

'He was due to go to Hong Kong late last year but had a setback and missed the trip. It will be a similar story to last year, decent ten-furlong races at home and abroad. He seemed to be suited by the step up to a mile and a quarter.'

**Drunken Sailor** began both last year and this year in Dubai. On his return last season he started out over a mile and a quarter in a Goodwood Listed race and was stepped right up to two miles for the Northumberland Plate, where he finished a gallant second, having encountered some trouble in running. After that it was staying trips all the way, with the best of his British runs being his Listed win in the March Stakes at Goodwood. He had an Australian campaign at the back end before heading once again to Dubai.

'The plan will be similar – staying races at Listed and Group 3 level. We now know he gets two miles well.'

**Bourne** had an interrupted but successful

Forte Dei Marmi (5) in action at Goodwood

season. The winner of a Nottingham handicap off 72 in May, he was off for more than five months before ending his campaign with a win in a similar race at Doncaster off 77. That was, in itself, fairly modest handicap form, but he gave the impression there was a lot more to come if his trainer got a clear run with him.

'Sadly it was a stop-and-go season with him, so let's hope we get an uninterrupted campaign this time. He's still off a reasonable mark and the hope is that he can work up through the handicap ranks – I think he'll stay a mile and a half.'

**Forte Dei Marmi** was gelded over the winter before last season and was a revelation. He won four handicaps, off 81, 92, 98 and 102, collecting around £120,000 in the process.

'He was very progressive last season. In particular his final two wins, at Sandown and in the Dubai Duty Free at Newbury, were very good – let's hope he can carry on in that vein. He's effectively out of handicaps now, so he'll be stepping up in class and hopefully will make up into a Group horse.'

**Afsare** had a great season, winning three races and ending up by landing the Listed Hampton Court Stakes at Royal Ascot.

'He's done very well and is another who has to make the transition from Listed to Group company, but I'm hopeful he will. He likes a galloping track and, although a mile and a quarter is as far as he has gone yet, I'm confident he'll stay a mile and a half.'

There were high hopes for **Seta** before the start of last season and, although she ended up winning three races, two at Listed level, there must have been a feeling of some disappointment she hadn't done even better.

'She has to step up on what she has achieved and win at Group level. Her final start, in the Sun Chariot, showed she wasn't up to it at

that point in her career. I'm hoping that a year on she might manage that – she is a filly who has always had the physical scope to be even better at four.'

**Never Forget** is a fascinating addition to Cumani's team. Formerly trained in France by Elie Lellouche, she won at Listed and Group 2 level last season. Her form seemed to tail off a bit after that and she was last seen out in the Prix Vermeille, where she never made much of a show behind Midday.

'She's by Westerner, so she should stay further if that's the way we go. She's a useful addition to the team of older horses.'

The last of Cumani's strong team of older horses is the filly **Contredanse**, the winner of the Italian Oaks last year.

'She was very progressive last season and I was pleased to win the race in Italy. She's in a tough division with fillies such as Snow Fairy and Midday still around, so we'll have to pick and choose her races carefully. I think a mile and a quarter is her trip.

'We've received a nice addition to our team in the three-year-old filly **Mohedian Lady**. We haven't had her very long, but I like what I've seen so far.'

Mohedian Lady was trained last season by Michael Bell, for whom she won a Yarmouth maiden fillies' event. That was over a mile and she's bred to get a mile and a half this season.

Moving to the three-year-olds, **Khor Sheed** was very useful at two. She broke her duck in a Listed race at Newmarket – a clue in itself that she is well regarded – and went on to win the valuable Tattersalls Millions Fillies' Auction race, having finished third in the Group 3 Sweet Solera in the meantime. She then ran in the Cheveley Park Stakes but disappointed.

'She was over the top by then, so I would disregard that form. Sadly, she will have it tough this year as her trip is six furlongs and there aren't many targets for three-year-old sprinting fillies.

'**Fulgur** ran two very good races when placed in decent maidens at Newmarket and then won well at Newbury – he'd learned a lot from his previous runs and settled a lot better. If he can carry on learning he should continue to improve. He's bred to stay a mile and a half and he'll probably start out at a mile and a quarter.'

**Naqshabban's** record is one run, one win, placing this gelded son of Street Cry in the 'could be anything' category.

'I was very pleased he won first time out at Leicester, showing a good turn of foot. He was gelded early on as a two-year-old and he's potentially nice.

'**Chill** won his maiden at Warwick – it wasn't the greatest race in the world but he did it well and handled the soft ground okay. He can continue to improve and make his mark in handicap company.

'**Lyric Street** ran well at Newmarket over seven furlongs, which is a trip that's too short for him. He'll come into his own once we start stretching him a bit.

'**Kirthill** managed a very promising run at Doncaster. He was still a weak horse last year and the hope is that he'll be stronger this season – a mile and a quarter will probably be the limit of his stamina.'

**In addition to the horses mentioned, there are a lot of unraced three-year-olds in Cumani's team and some useful types are bound to be unleashed in the early weeks of this season. With the television racing channels now showing more and more of the big races abroad, it's much easier for punters to keep an eye on foreign affairs, so keep a close eye out for the stable's international travellers.** [CB]

**Horse to follow** Forte Dei Marmi
**Dark horse** Naqshabban

# LUCA CUMANI
## ARUNDEL, W SUSSEX

|  | No. of Hrs | Races Run | 1st | 2nd | 3rd | Unpl | Per cent | £1 Level Stake |
|---|---|---|---|---|---|---|---|---|
| 2-y-o | 26 | 65 | 9 | 8 | 11 | 37 | 13.8 | -25.45 |
| 3-y-o | 39 | 151 | 35 | 15 | 13 | 87 | 23.2 | +42.09 |
| 4-y-o+ | 29 | 117 | 22 | 20 | 12 | 62 | 18.8 | -2.08 |
| **Totals** | 94 | 333 | 66 | 43 | 36 | 186 | 19.8 | +14.56 |
| 2009 | 87 | 320 | 48 | 50 | 31 | 190 | 15.0 | -7.05 |
| 2008 | 89 | 351 | 60 | 52 | 48 | 191 | 17.1 | -1.91 |

### BY MONTH

| 2-y-o | W-R | Per cent | £1 Level Stake | 3-y-o | W-R | Per cent | £1 Level Stake |
|---|---|---|---|---|---|---|---|
| January | 0-0 | 0.0 | 0.00 | January | 0-4 | 0.0 | -4.00 |
| February | 0-0 | 0.0 | 0.00 | February | 0-1 | 0.0 | -1.00 |
| March | 0-0 | 0.0 | 0.00 | March | 0-0 | 0.0 | 0.00 |
| April | 0-0 | 0.0 | 0.00 | April | 2-7 | 28.6 | +0.25 |
| May | 0-0 | 0.0 | 0.00 | May | 8-27 | 29.6 | +57.86 |
| June | 1-3 | 33.3 | +1.00 | June | 6-19 | 31.6 | +3.41 |
| July | 0-5 | 0.0 | -5.00 | July | 4-28 | 14.3 | -11.18 |
| August | 2-9 | 22.2 | +0.80 | August | 4-17 | 23.5 | -1.80 |
| September | 3-14 | 21.4 | -4.00 | September | 3-25 | 12.0 | -7.75 |
| October | 3-23 | 13.0 | -7.25 | October | 3-13 | 23.1 | -6.33 |
| November | 0-11 | 0.0 | -11.00 | November | 4-8 | 50.0 | +12.00 |
| December | 0-0 | 0.0 | 0.00 | December | 1-2 | 50.0 | +0.63 |

| 4-y-o+ | W-R | Per cent | £1 Level Stake | Totals | W-R | Per cent | £1 Level Stake |
|---|---|---|---|---|---|---|---|
| January | 0-2 | 0.0 | -2.00 | January | 0-6 | 0.0 | -6.00 |
| February | 0-0 | 0.0 | 0.00 | February | 0-1 | 0.0 | -1.00 |
| March | 0-1 | 0.0 | -1.00 | March | 0-1 | 0.0 | -1.00 |
| April | 2-6 | 33.3 | +1.58 | April | 4-13 | 30.8 | +1.83 |
| May | 4-19 | 21.1 | -0.67 | May | 12-46 | 26.1 | +57.19 |
| June | 4-22 | 18.2 | +4.25 | June | 11-44 | 25.0 | +8.66 |
| July | 3-21 | 14.3 | -3.50 | July | 7-54 | 13.0 | -19.68 |
| August | 6-17 | 35.3 | +15.58 | August | 12-43 | 27.9 | +14.58 |
| September | 2-18 | 11.1 | -11.33 | September | 8-57 | 14.0 | -23.08 |
| October | 1-7 | 14.3 | -1.00 | October | 7-43 | 16.3 | -14.58 |
| November | 0-4 | 0.0 | -4.00 | November | 4-23 | 17.4 | +8.00 |
| December | 0-0 | 0.0 | 0.00 | December | 1-2 | 50.0 | +0.63 |

### DISTANCE

| 2-y-o | W-R | Per cent | £1 Level Stake | 3-y-o | W-R | Per cent | £1 Level Stake |
|---|---|---|---|---|---|---|---|
| 5f-6f | 3-22 | 13.6 | -10.63 | 5f-6f | 2-8 | 25.0 | -0.83 |
| 7f-8f | 6-43 | 14.0 | -14.82 | 7f-8f | 15-65 | 23.1 | +24.27 |
| 9f-13f | 0-0 | 0.0 | 0.00 | 9f-13f | 18-78 | 23.1 | +18.65 |
| 14f+ | 0-0 | 0.0 | 0.00 | 14f+ | 0-0 | 0.0 | 0.00 |

| 4-y-o | W-R | Per cent | £1 Level Stake | Totals | W-R | Per cent | £1 Level Stake |
|---|---|---|---|---|---|---|---|
| 5f-6f | 0-0 | 0.0 | 0.00 | 5f-6f | 5-30 | 16.7 | -11.46 |
| 7f-8f | 6-38 | 15.8 | -10.33 | 7f-8f | 27-146 | 18.5 | -0.88 |
| 9f-13f | 13-67 | 19.4 | +13.00 | 9f-13f | 31-145 | 21.4 | +31.65 |
| 14f+ | 3-12 | 25.0 | -4.75 | 14f+ | 3-12 | 25.0 | -4.75 |

### TYPE OF RACE

| Non-Handicaps | W-R | Per cent | £1 Level Stake | Handicaps | W-R | Per cent | £1 Level Stake |
|---|---|---|---|---|---|---|---|
| 2-y-o | 7-57 | 12.3 | -27.25 | 2-y-o | 2-8 | 25.0 | +1.80 |
| 3-y-o | 17-78 | 21.8 | +37.02 | 3-y-o | 18-73 | 24.7 | +5.08 |
| 4-y-o+ | 3-36 | 8.3 | -16.00 | 4-y-o+ | 19-81 | 23.5 | +17.67 |

### RACE CLASS

| | W-R | Per cent | £1 Level Stake |
|---|---|---|---|
| Class 1 | 9-51 | 17.6 | +20.16 |
| Class 2 | 10-40 | 25.0 | +15.83 |
| Class 3 | 3-28 | 10.7 | -13.75 |
| Class 4 | 19-79 | 24.1 | +23.33 |
| Class 5 | 23-120 | 19.2 | -25.02 |
| Class 6 | 2-15 | 13.3 | -5.00 |
| Class 7 | 0-0 | 0.0 | 0.00 |

### FIRST TIME OUT

| | W-R | Per cent | £1 Level Stake |
|---|---|---|---|
| 2-y-o | 1-26 | 3.8 | -16.00 |
| 3-y-o | 6-39 | 15.4 | +3.45 |
| 4-y-o+ | 5-29 | 17.2 | -1.58 |
| Totals | 12-94 | 12.8 | -14.13 |

## LUCA CUMANI

A total of 66 winners at a 20 per cent strike-rate meant 2010 was a cracking year for Luca Cumani's team and there was a lot more prize-money earned overseas for the yard.

Overall level-stakes backing would have produced a modest loss, but in five months the strike-rate nudged above 25 per cent and then level-stakes support, while maybe not advisable, would have shown a profit.

With 2010 a better season for the yard, the old angle of following favourites worked again. This stable knows the time of day with its favourites, but the bookies also know that and cut their prices accordingly. However, if the Cumani horses are going well, it's an angle to follow.

Kieren Fallon rode most of the yard's winners, but his mounts showed a sizeable level-stakes loss. The excellent Jean-Pierre Guillambert rode most of the rest and following him showed a decent profit – however, goodness knows whether that can be repeated in 2011.

Don't rely on course statistics with the Cumani team as things seem to vary from year to year. Having said that, Doncaster has seemed to be in favour for the past couple of seasons and is worth keeping a close eye on.

Cumani's three-year-old handicappers have been the stuff of legend over the years and were 18 from 74 last season, producing a modest profit – they're worth looking out for. Don't back them blindly, but with a degree of selectivity – the stable in form, prominent in the market are the signs – there should be profits to be made.

Overall, the best advice is to follow the stable's form: if it's in form then focus on its runners, if it's out of form then give them the swerve. *[CB]* ∎

Guide to the Flat 2011

# Double-handed team has strength in depth

THE big change last season was the appointment of Mahmood Al Zarooni alongside Saeed Bin Suroor as a Godolphin trainer. The question that has occupied the minds of observers is how the allocation of horses will work. Simon Crisford, the Godolphin racing manager, explained how the pair will operate together.

'Sheikh Mohammed discusses it with me and the rest of the team and then he makes the decision. It largely depends on which trainer has which horses in their string at any given time. What Sheikh Mohammed is trying to do is to keep it as even and fair as possible.'

The Godolphin team is huge. Always helpful, Crisford took me through the main hopes among the horses who will be based in Britain this year.

'Let's start with **Poet's Voice**. He's been running in Dubai and what has been pleasing is how relaxed he was – that's the key with him. He'll be targeted at all of the top mile and ten-furlong races.'

Last season Poet's Voice won the Group 2 Celebration Mile at Goodwood and then the Group 1 Queen Elizabeth II Stakes at Ascot. He was tried over a mile and a quarter but, with a very slow pace, he pulled hard and wrecked his chances. Crisford's comments suggest there is confidence he can stay a mile and a quarter.

**Rewilding** was third in the Derby and then won the Great Voltigeur before running less well in the St Leger.

'He'll be running in the top middle-distance races, possibly starting out at Epsom in the Coronation Cup.'

**Mastery**, the 2009 St Leger winner, wasn't seen out in Europe until October, when finishing third over an inadequate trip in a Kempton Listed race, although he'd had one run in Dubai over the winter. He then won a Kempton Listed event over a more suitable mile and a half, before jetting off to Hong Kong to land the Group 1 Hong Kong Vase, also over a mile and a half.

'He's done very well, but he needs time after a big effort in a championship race. The plan is geared towards the second half of the season: he'll have an entry in the Melbourne Cup and we'll think about Hong Kong again, or maybe Canada. Of course, he might even run in England too, but he's one for much later on in the year.

'The same applies to **Rio De La Plata**: he won't be out early. He stays in training with a view to building on his impressive portfolio – he won two Group 1s in Italy at the end of last year. He's effective at anywhere between a mile and a mile and a quarter.

'**Prince Bishop** won at Group 3 and Group 2 level last season for Andre Fabre. It looks as though he's a mile-and-a-half horse and he has the potential to step up on his Group 2 form and become a player in the bigger European races.

'**Antara** won the Princess Elizabeth at Epsom last season [Group 3, fillies, 1m] and ran well in Group 1 events, notably the Nassau and the Prix Jean Romanet. It will be a similar campaign this season, primarily at a mile and a quarter, although she has the pace to be competitive at a shorter trip.

**Campanologist** finally got a well-deserved Group 1 win last season in Hamburg and immediately followed up with another, this time in Cologne. He finished his season with a disappointing effort in the Melbourne Cup.

'He stays in training and will be running in Europe in Pattern company. Of course, he has a Group 1 penalty and that might hinder him in lesser races, so it may be that you'll have to wait until the second half of the season, when his penalty has expired, before you see him at his best.' ▶▶

Poet's Voice (blue) is a contender for top races over a mile and a mile and a quarter

'**Delegator** was second to Sea The Stars in the 2,000 Guineas of 2009 and it has never been entirely clear what his best trip is. At a mile he sometimes seems to stay and on other occasions looks as though he doesn't. In last year's Guide to the Flat, Crisford intimated that he'd be tried over sprint trips, but in the end Delegator was not seen out until September, when he won a Listed race over seven furlongs, and rounded off his season when he ran down the field in the Breeders' Cup Mile.

'Delegator stays in training. We'll probably go sprinting with him, possibly starting out in the Duke of York in May.'

'**Monterosso** won last season's King Edward VII Stakes at Royal Ascot for Mark Johnston and landed a Group 2 at Meydan in March on his first run for Godolphin.

'That was a very gratifying win as, after his fourth in the Irish Derby, his form tailed off a bit. He'll be competing in good mile-and-a-half races.

'**Cavalryman** has had a good break over the winter with a view to freshening him up – he had a busy time of it last year and was also busy over the previous winter as well as the season before that. Again, he's a candidate for the top mile-and-a-half races in Europe.

'**Opinion Poll** joined us from Michael Jarvis and has done well out here in Dubai. He'll run in decent staying races.

'**Rainfall** is the ex-Mark Johnston filly who won the Jersey Stakes last year – she's with Saeed Bin Suroor. We're looking forward to seeing her in some of the feature races for fillies at seven furlongs and a mile.'

Moving to the three-year-olds, **Casamento** ran in Sheikh Mohammed's colours for Irish trainer Michael Halford last season. His best effort was when winning the Racing Post Trophy. That win was by three-quarters of a length from Aidan O'Brien's Seville, but Casamento left the strong impression he had a bit more up his sleeve if required.

'He'll run in either the 2,000 Guineas or the Dante. The decision will be made based on how he's training, how much speed he's showing, and so on, but he'll be ready to run at the beginning of May.'

'**Saamidd** won the Champagne Stakes at Doncaster but was then disappointing in the Dewhurst. For some reason he just wasn't himself that day, getting very worked up beforehand, plus he didn't like the soft ground. He's done well over the winter and is being prepared for the 2,000 Guineas – if everything goes to plan, that will be his first target.

'**Dubai Prince** won his Group 3 very impressively in Ireland [for Dermot Weld] last season. He's an interesting horse, we like him a lot, and he's coming along very well. Again, he's in the Guineas and nearer the time we're going to have to pick and choose our team – they'll all be entered and will all be ready to run at that time of the year.

'The same applies to **French Navy**, an ex-French horse, formerly trained by Andre Fabre. He's entered for Newmarket but is also in the French Guineas, so we'll have to see.

'It's definitely worth mentioning **Neebras**. He was a very competitive early-season colt last year, coming second in the July Stakes at Newmarket. He's doing well and we're looking to run him in the sales race over six furlongs at the Craven meeting.

'Another colt to mention is **Splash Point**, the winner of the UAE Guineas. He'll be running in decent races in Europe. Although, at this stage, he hasn't got the form of the 2,000 Guineas horses, there's scope for improvement and he's a very nice horse.

'Moving to the fillies, we like **Khawlah**. She was placed in the Oh So Sharp Stakes last season and won the UAE Oaks. We haven't decided whether she'll run again in Dubai, but in any event she'll go for the Musidora. She has a 1,000 Guineas entry but we see her as more of a staying type – we think she's Oaks material rather than a Guineas filly.

**Saamidd**

'**White Moonstone** is a nice, big, tall filly who has had a good winter and is doing everything right at present. She'll go straight for the Guineas and then we'll make a plan, but as an unbeaten filly, and the winner of the May Hill and the Fillies' Mile, she belongs in the race. She has high-class credentials and we're pleased with her.

'I think we should mention **Zoowraa**. Michael Jarvis trained this filly last year and she won the Listed Radley Stakes for him. She's a nice filly who is doing everything right and probably goes best with a bit of cut in the ground – or at any rate, we know she handles soft ground. Any races where she's likely to get those conditions are possibilities – such as, for example, the French 1,000 Guineas. ▸▸

'I think those are the key older horses and three-year-old colts and fillies that we have in Dubai, but of those who have wintered in Europe you should mention the four-year-old filly, **Anna Salai**. She was second in last year's Irish 1,000 Guineas, but had a setback after that and needed time off. She's going well now, so she stays in training.

'Among the three-year-olds is **Blue Bunting**. She won the Listed Montrose Stakes at Newmarket and is a nice filly who has some good entries. We have high hopes for her.

'**Farhh** won very well first time out at Newmarket and then went to Doncaster for the conditions race won by Frankel, but he reared up in the stalls and hurt himself quite badly. As a result we left him in England for the winter, but he showed so much potential first time out that we're very hopeful. We haven't given him a Guineas entry as we want to give him as much time as he needs – he won't be rushed and will probably start out in a Listed race towards the end of May. Hopefully he will develop into a promising stakes-race performer.'

**The Godolphin team is a huge one and Crisford has done us proud by giving us his thoughts on the key horses that will make up their European team this season. In particular, the three-year-olds look especially intriguing this time and both of the Godolphin trainers will have a formidable array of talent with which to contest the season's best races.** *[CB]*

**Horse to follow** Rio De La Plata
**Dark horse** Splash Point

Anna Salai (right)

# SAEED BIN SUROOR
## NEWMARKET, SUFFOLK

|         | No. of Hrs | Races Run | 1st | 2nd | 3rd | Unpl | Per cent | £1 Level Stake |
|---------|------------|-----------|-----|-----|-----|------|----------|----------------|
| 2-y-o   | 43         | 115       | 40  | 20  | 14  | 41   | 34.8     | -8.47          |
| 3-y-o   | 41         | 124       | 28  | 20  | 8   | 68   | 22.6     | +8.68          |
| 4-y-o+  | 48         | 161       | 22  | 22  | 21  | 96   | 13.7     | -41.97         |
| Totals  | 132        | 400       | 90  | 62  | 43  | 205  | 22.5     | -41.76         |
| 2009    | 182        | 530       | 148 | 83  | 70  | 228  | 27.9     | -9.03          |
| 2008    | 115        | 313       | 58  | 60  | 47  | 148  | 18.5     | -16.41         |

### BY MONTH

| 2-y-o     | W-R    | Per cent | £1 Level Stake | 3-y-o     | W-R    | Per cent | £1 Level Stake |
|-----------|--------|----------|----------------|-----------|--------|----------|----------------|
| January   | 0-0    | 0.0      | 0.00           | January   | 0-0    | 0.0      | 0.00           |
| February  | 0-0    | 0.0      | 0.00           | February  | 0-0    | 0.0      | 0.00           |
| March     | 0-0    | 0.0      | 0.00           | March     | 0-0    | 0.0      | 0.00           |
| April     | 0-0    | 0.0      | 0.00           | April     | 0-4    | 0.0      | -4.00          |
| May       | 0-3    | 0.0      | -3.00          | May       | 2-18   | 11.1     | -13.05         |
| June      | 4-12   | 33.3     | -3.43          | June      | 3-8    | 37.5     | +3.25          |
| July      | 5-14   | 35.7     | +6.88          | July      | 3-19   | 15.8     | -1.00          |
| August    | 11-20  | 55.0     | +6.54          | August    | 5-29   | 17.2     | -5.10          |
| September | 10-27  | 37.0     | -6.79          | September | 9-22   | 40.9     | +23.75         |
| October   | 8-29   | 27.6     | -3.92          | October   | 6-20   | 30.0     | +8.83          |
| November  | 2-10   | 20.0     | -4.75          | November  | 0-4    | 0.0      | -4.00          |
| December  | 0-0    | 0.0      | 0.00           | December  | 0-0    | 0.0      | 0.00           |

| 4-y-o+    | W-R    | Per cent | £1 Level Stake | Totals    | W-R    | Per cent | £1 Level Stake |
|-----------|--------|----------|----------------|-----------|--------|----------|----------------|
| January   | 0-0    | 0.0      | 0.00           | January   | 0-0    | 0.0      | 0.00           |
| February  | 0-0    | 0.0      | 0.00           | February  | 0-0    | 0.0      | 0.00           |
| March     | 0-0    | 0.0      | 0.00           | March     | 0-0    | 0.0      | 0.00           |
| April     | 0-0    | 0.0      | 0.00           | April     | 0-4    | 0.0      | -4.00          |
| May       | 0-19   | 0.0      | -19.00         | May       | 2-40   | 5.0      | -35.05         |
| June      | 4-22   | 18.2     | +16.38         | June      | 11-42  | 26.2     | +16.20         |
| July      | 4-31   | 12.9     | -21.09         | July      | 12-64  | 18.8     | -15.21         |
| August    | 5-29   | 17.2     | +4.04          | August    | 21-78  | 26.9     | +5.48          |
| September | 4-26   | 15.4     | +4.10          | September | 23-75  | 30.7     | +21.06         |
| October   | 4-24   | 16.7     | -16.90         | October   | 18-73  | 24.7     | -11.99         |
| November  | 1-10   | 10.0     | -9.50          | November  | 3-24   | 12.5     | -13.50         |
| December  | 0-0    | 0.0      | 0.00           | December  | 0-0    | 0.0      | 0.00           |

### DISTANCE

| 2-y-o  | W-R    | Per cent | £1 Level Stake | 3-y-o  | W-R    | Per cent | £1 Level Stake |
|--------|--------|----------|----------------|--------|--------|----------|----------------|
| 5f-6f  | 14-40  | 35.0     | -0.55          | 5f-6f  | 4-8    | 50.0     | +10.65         |
| 7f-8f  | 26-72  | 36.1     | -4.92          | 7f-8f  | 13-48  | 27.1     | +8.93          |
| 9f-13f | 0-3    | 0.0      | -3.00          | 9f-13f | 11-66  | 16.7     | -8.90          |
| 14f+   | 0-0    | 0.0      | 0.00           | 14f+   | 0-2    | 0.0      | -2.00          |

| 4-y-o  | W-R    | Per cent | £1 Level Stake | Totals | W-R     | Per cent | £1 Level Stake |
|--------|--------|----------|----------------|--------|---------|----------|----------------|
| 5f-6f  | 1-11   | 9.1      | -9.50          | 5f-6f  | 19-59   | 32.2     | +0.60          |
| 7f-8f  | 11-50  | 22.0     | +31.85         | 7f-8f  | 50-170  | 29.4     | +35.86         |
| 9f-13f | 10-79  | 12.7     | -43.32         | 9f-13f | 21-148  | 14.2     | -55.22         |
| 14f+   | 0-21   | 0.0      | -21.00         | 14f+   | 0-23    | 0.0      | -23.00         |

### TYPE OF RACE

| Non-Handicaps | W-R     | Per cent | £1 Level Stake | Handicaps | W-R    | Per cent | £1 Level Stake |
|---------------|---------|----------|----------------|-----------|--------|----------|----------------|
| 2-y-o         | 36-102  | 35.3     | -12.07         | 2-y-o     | 4-13   | 30.8     | +3.60          |
| 3-y-o         | 15-65   | 23.1     | +2.10          | 3-y-o     | 13-59  | 22.0     | +6.58          |
| 4-y-o+        | 19-133  | 14.3     | +8.00          | 4-y-o+    | 3-28   | 10.7     | +26.00         |

### RACE CLASS / FIRST TIME OUT

| RACE CLASS | W-R    | Per cent | £1 Level Stake | FIRST TIME OUT | W-R    | Per cent | £1 Level Stake |
|------------|--------|----------|----------------|----------------|--------|----------|----------------|
| Class 1    | 25-160 | 15.6     | -35.81         | 2-y-o          | 10-43  | 23.3     | -10.40         |
| Class 2    | 12-69  | 17.4     | +17.60         | 3-y-o          | 11-41  | 26.8     | +1.20          |
| Class 3    | 13-61  | 21.3     | -17.07         | 4-y-o+         | 7-48   | 14.6     | -26.47         |
| Class 4    | 22-56  | 39.3     | +7.46          |                |        |          |                |
| Class 5    | 17-53  | 32.1     | -11.67         | Totals         | 28-132 | 21.2     | -35.67         |
| Class 6    | 1-1    | 100.0    | +0.73          |                |        |          |                |
| Class 7    | 0-0    | 0.0      | 0.00           |                |        |          |                |

## GODOLPHIN

Things just got a lot more complicated with the boys in blue. No longer is Saeed Bin Suroor the only trainer, as they have added Mahmood Al Zarooni to their roster. How the horses will be split between the two remains to be seen, as will whether patterns change. There are some constants: the quality of the stock with which their trainers work will remain high, as will Sheikh Monhammed's relentless desire for success.

Last season Suroor trained 90 winners and Al Zarooni 43 *(pictured)*, with the more established man winning the strike-rate battle. However, the two teams are likely to be more evenly matched this season, judging by Simon Crisford's comments about fairness. So what's a punter to do?

My advice is to carry on as if nothing was different. The big imponderable with Godolphin is what happens immediately after their return to these shores. Sometimes they come back firing and in other years it takes time for things to settle down. The Racing Post Today's Trainers is your friend – follow it closely.

When the strike-rate is close to 25 per cent, profits tend to flow – watch out for that.

Ahmed Ajtebi seems to be Al Zarooni's man, but when Frankie Dettori takes over the tip was worth taking last season – we need to see how that pans out this time around. Conversely, Frankie's the man on the Suroor-trained horses, but if Ajtebi rides one then last year that was significant.

Course statistics are up in the air with this yard – sometimes Ascot's are great and in other years dreadful, as it all depends on how the yard is firing.

The Godolphin runners need careful watching: when they're bang in form strike-rates can go through the roof, but when they're slightly below their best the bookies' fear of them can lead to very unprofitable punting. No easy angles, I'm afraid, as a degree of hard work and study is required. *[CB]* ■

Godolphin

# LEGENDS OF HORSERACING

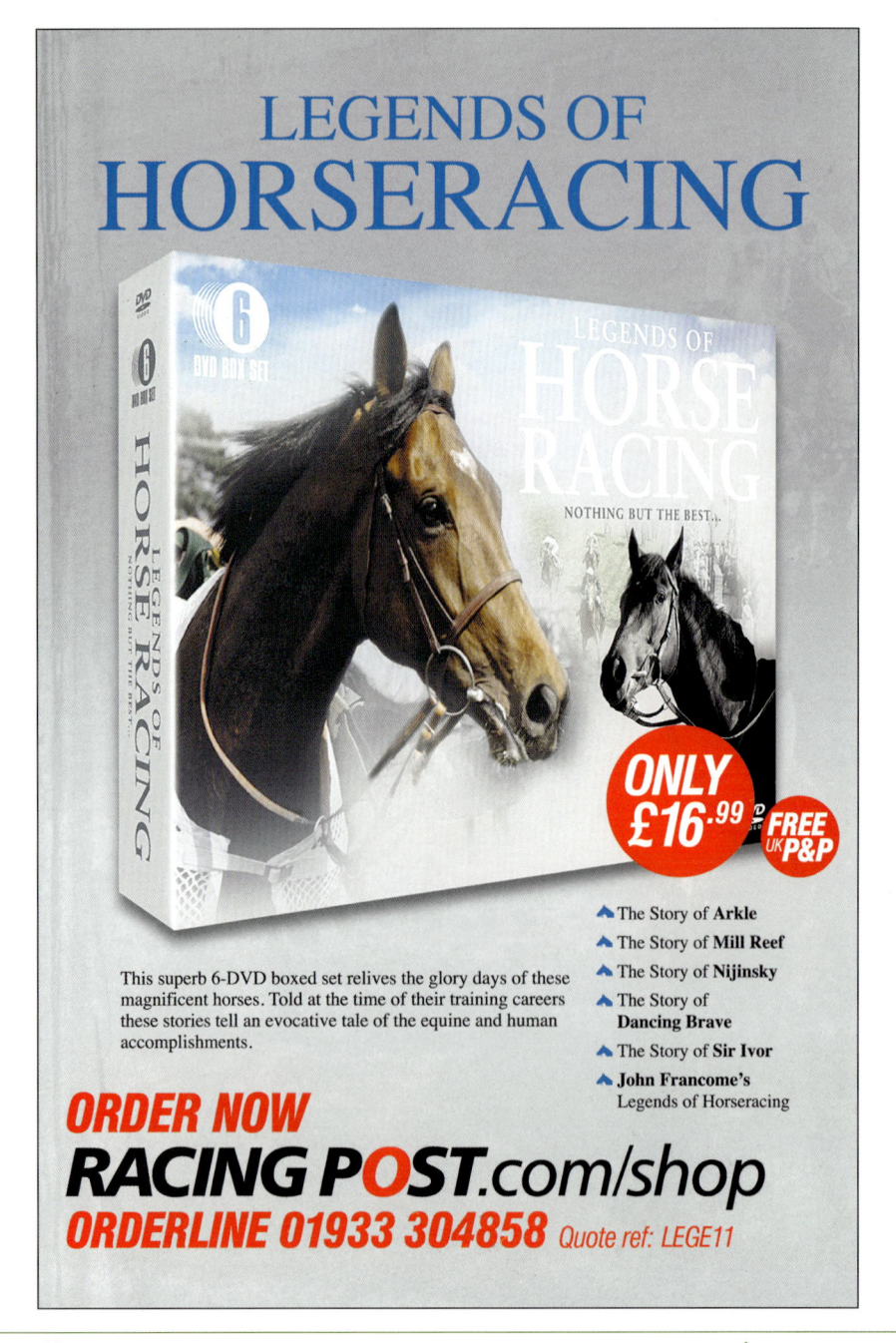

**ONLY £16.99** · FREE UK P&P

- The Story of **Arkle**
- The Story of **Mill Reef**
- The Story of **Nijinsky**
- The Story of **Dancing Brave**
- The Story of **Sir Ivor**
- **John Francome's** Legends of Horseracing

This superb 6-DVD boxed set relives the glory days of these magnificent horses. Told at the time of their training careers these stories tell an evocative tale of the equine and human accomplishments.

## ORDER NOW
## RACINGPOST.com/shop
### ORDERLINE 01933 304858 *Quote ref: LEGE11*

# A mature hand to play in seeking another ton

**W**HEN Arctic Cosmos stayed on up the Doncaster straight he gave John Gosden his third St Leger win, following on from Shantou and Lucarno. He also proved just how difficult it is for punters to spot the winner of the final Classic as back in May he was beaten off a mark of 78 in a Newbury handicap, having previously won the disgraceful amount of £1,774 for landing a Wolverhampton maiden.

Come June, however, **Arctic Cosmos** started to show loads of improvement: a handicap at Kempton off that mark of 78 was followed by a good second in the King Edward VII at Royal Ascot and third place in Goodwood's St Leger trial, the Gordon Stakes. Good though that form was, he still went off at 12-1 at Doncaster, but the application of blinkers brought about the necessary improvement to enable him to become a Classic winner.

'He's in great form at present. When we put the little visor on him at Doncaster it did the trick, so I think we'll continue with that. When William [Buick] got off him after the Leger he commented that he'd shown plenty of speed, and I wouldn't be afraid to run him in the top mile-and-a-half races – he'll have plenty of entries.'

After the Leger there was plenty of talk about Arctic Cosmos following in the footsteps of Moonax and becoming another winner of the race to try his hand over hurdles – fences were also mooted. Was that still in the plan?

'Not as a four-year-old – let's get this year out of the way and then the owners can consider their options.' ▶▶

**Arctic Cosmos**

**Gertrude Bell**

**Duncan** won the Prix Foy on Arc trials day at Longchamp and it was a deserved victory, as he hadn't had the best of luck in his earlier races. He lost a shoe on his seasonal debut, when second to Barshiba in an Ascot Listed contest, and then didn't have a clear run in the Hardwicke, although in any event he probably wouldn't have beaten Harbinger. He then disappointed in a Goodwood Group 3, although again he didn't have the clearest of runs.

In the Prix Foy new tactics were adopted and in a slowly run contest he was sent about his business, before fighting back bravely when headed two furlongs out. That earned him a tilt at the Arc, where he didn't ever look like getting into contention.

'You're right, he did deserve that win, and then he had a really rough passage in the Arc. My plan is to step him up in trip, initially to 1m6f and see how that suits him – a race like the Yorkshire Cup might be an obvious first target.'

**Caucus**, in the same ownership as Duncan, is a new arrival at the yard. Trained at three by Hughie Morrison, he won his maiden at Chepstow and then was placed in the King George V Handicap and in Group 3 and Listed company, before rounding off his season with a below-par effort when stepped up to 1m7f in the Group 2 Prix Chaudenay at the Arc meeting.

'He needs some time to furnish and develop, but I think he has the makings of a nice staying horse – he seems to have a grand attitude.'

**King Of Wands** wasn't seen out after finishing third in the Group 2 Lonsdale Cup at York's Ebor meeting. Prior to that he'd won a conditions event at Ripon and then a Sandown Listed event over two miles.

'He got a nasty bump from the winner at York, which probably affected his finishing effort – I think it was that rather than lack of stamina that found him out, even though the ground was softer than at Sandown. He's a very nice horse and I hope he's going to be up to acquitting himself well in the Cup races – that's certainly the plan.'

**Kansai Spirit** had a good four-year-old season, winning his final three starts, all in handicap company, off 74, 83 and 92. The last of those, in a valuable Heritage Handicap, the Old Borough Cup at Haydock, suggested he was well up to progressing beyond handicap company.

'He's off 98 now and was very progressive in the second half of last season. The plan will be to try him in at least one more handicap before stepping him up in grade. He seems to get 1m6f well, which gives us options.'

**Beachfire**, a progressive handicapper last season, stays in training at four. Apart from a blip at Goodwood in May, when inexperience seemed to catch him out, he was unbeaten in his other four starts, a maiden on the Polytrack at Lingfield and then three handicaps off 80, 85 and 91. He wasn't, however, seen out after July.

'He got kicked when training on Newmarket Heath and fractured a stifle. He seems fine now and I'd like to aim him at the Jubilee Handicap at Kempton on the Bank Holiday Monday of Easter.

'**Tazeez** is seven but still in good form. He won the Group 3 Dubai Duty Free at Newbury on his final start and will run in similar races this season.

'**Gertrude Bell** wasn't out after June last season, but is back and in good form. She'll be running in fillies' Group races at around a mile and a quarter and a mile and a half.'

Moving to the three-year-olds, Rainbow View's half-brother, **Utley**, is only a maiden winner, but he was thought good enough to run in Group 1 company in France and then be sent over to Kentucky for the Breeders' Cup Juvenile, where his trainer believed he had a great chance.

'In France the ground was very soft, which ▶▶

didn't ideally suit, as he likes a faster surface. The ground was a real problem in the Juvenile, as it was for a lot of horses – it was very slick and he just wasn't moving well until late in the race, after which he ran on well. A possibility is the Free Handicap. I think his form's pretty solid.'

**Splendid Light** was fourth in a Newmarket maiden, but there was something in Gosden's comments that tells us he's considered to be much better than that.

'I like him – he's a grand horse. I was impressed with the way he ran at Newmarket considering he was a backward juvenile. He has a good stride on him and he just became a bit unbalanced coming out of the Dip. We'll start him at a mile and a quarter and take it from there – I hope he has the class to progress from there.'

**Masked Marvel** won on his debut at Sandown and then was sixth in the Group 3 Autumn Stakes at Ascot in October on much softer ground than he'd encountered on his debut.

'He's another I like and I can see him starting out in the Sandown Classic Trial.'

**Rainbow View** is still a maiden, but her third in the Group 1 Prix Marcel Boussac marks her down as one of the best maidens in training.

'Her debut run at Doncaster was a good one – there was no disgrace in being beaten by Frankel. After that I couldn't find a suitable maiden for her and, as she was working so well, I let her take her chance at Longchamp – I thought she ran really well considering she was such an inexperienced filly. I think she'll stay a mile and a quarter and, by Selkirk, she handles the soft. I haven't got a campaign in mind yet, but France is certainly a possibility.'

**Devastation** won her maiden at Doncaster at the back end of the season, having previously finished second at Nottingham.

'Her race at Doncaster was one I like and she's possibly a tad unlucky not be unbeaten as she lost out on her debut only by a short head and ran green. She's a beautifully bred filly and I like her. She could well start out in the Pretty Polly over a mile and a quarter or maybe another of the Oaks trials.'

At Doncaster, Devastation still showed some signs of greenness when she idled in front and she was run close by her stablemate, **Izzi Top**. There were some who believed that had the runner-up been given a harder ride she might well have won, but Devastation looked likely to have found more had she been seriously challenged. That said, Izzi Top looked highly promising.

'She's a lovely filly who hadn't, in all honesty, shown me a great deal at home, so it was a pleasant surprise when she ran as well as she did. I'll give her a 1,000 Guineas entry and, like all of mine, wouldn't be afraid to run her in a trial if she was going well in the spring.'

**Maqaasid** won her first two starts and then was fourth and third behind Hooray in the Lowther and the Cheveley Park. The question with her is whether she's a sprinter or will stay further.

'She won the Queen Mary at Ascot and ran well on her other starts. All being well she'll go for a trial over seven furlongs and that will tell us more about the way her season will go.'

**Aneedah** won her maiden at Yarmouth and was beaten on her other three starts. However, she's clearly thought better than that, as she is considered to be a possible contender for the Nell Gwyn.

**Flood Plain** won on her debut and then was second in the Listed Radley Stakes, showing herself to be a promising filly. Sent for the Juvenile Fillies' Turf at the Breeders' Cup, she ran poorly but there were excuses.

'I should ignore that race as the horse next to her fell and was sadly killed – thankfully the jockey got up okay. The ground that day was pretty dreadful, with very little root growth – it was positively dangerous. I like Flood Plain and she'll have some good

**Treasury Devil**

entries – I think she's probably a miler.'

**Treasury Devil** won on his debut, in a Newbury maiden, and then followed up in the Sandown event, looking decent on both occasions. That he was held in high regard was confirmed when his final start of the season was in the Group 1 Grand Criterium on Arc weekend. That was run on very soft ground and he disappointed badly.

'He hated the ground. He's a very promising colt and I can see him staying a mile and a quarter in time, but I might just put him in the Guineas and we'll see how he is doing nearer the time.'

**Man Of God** showed promise in a Newmarket maiden over a mile and then won a similar event at Yarmouth – both those runs were on easy ground.

'I'm very pleased with him. He should stay well and I have the option of starting him out in handicap company, which is what I'll do. I think a mile and a half on soft ground will be right up his street.'

**Umseyat** was second at Goodwood in a maiden fillies' event and then broke her duck in a similar event at Haydock. It's hard to weigh up the form, so how good is she?

'It was a modest contest but she won nicely and is a tough and tenacious filly. She's off 83, so we have the option of starting out in handicaps and that will tell us a lot more about how she should be campaigned.'

**Seelo** falls into the 'could be anything' category. All we have to go on is that he won a modest Yarmouth maiden, the form of which seems nothing special.

'The ground was quite testing that day, and I thought he won well. Again, we'll start out on the handicap route and let him tell us where we should be going.'

**Last season's tally of 105 British winners was John Gosden's best since 1993 and he starts 2011 with a strong hand – his older horses look to have considerable strength in depth. With a fair wind he can notch up another century of winners and collect plenty more big-race wins along the way.** *[CB]*

**Horse to follow** Arctic Cosmos
**Dark horse** Splendid Light

## JOHN GOSDEN

A great season for John Gosden, with both the number of winners and the strike-rate up. The most modest of level-stakes losses was the result, with the older horses running in conditions races leading the way.

Favourites were worth following and 20 per cent seems to be the magic figure – get above that strike-rate in any month and the likelihood of a profit is high. Keep a close eye on stable form.

William Buick had a great first season as stable jockey but whether his level-stakes profit can be maintained has to be open to question – people have twigged just how good he is. Nicky Mackay's strike-rate was even better and his profit nearly as good, so he's worth looking out for. If Frankie Dettori gets the leg up on one for his old boss, take the hint – it's fancied.

In the previous two issues of Guide to the Flat, Lingfield's Polytrack has been nominated as a venue to avoid, with Kempton one to follow. You guessed it: last year Lingfield shone and Kempton bombed out. And the lesson is? There isn't a definitive pattern to the yard's course statistics, so take care. [CB]

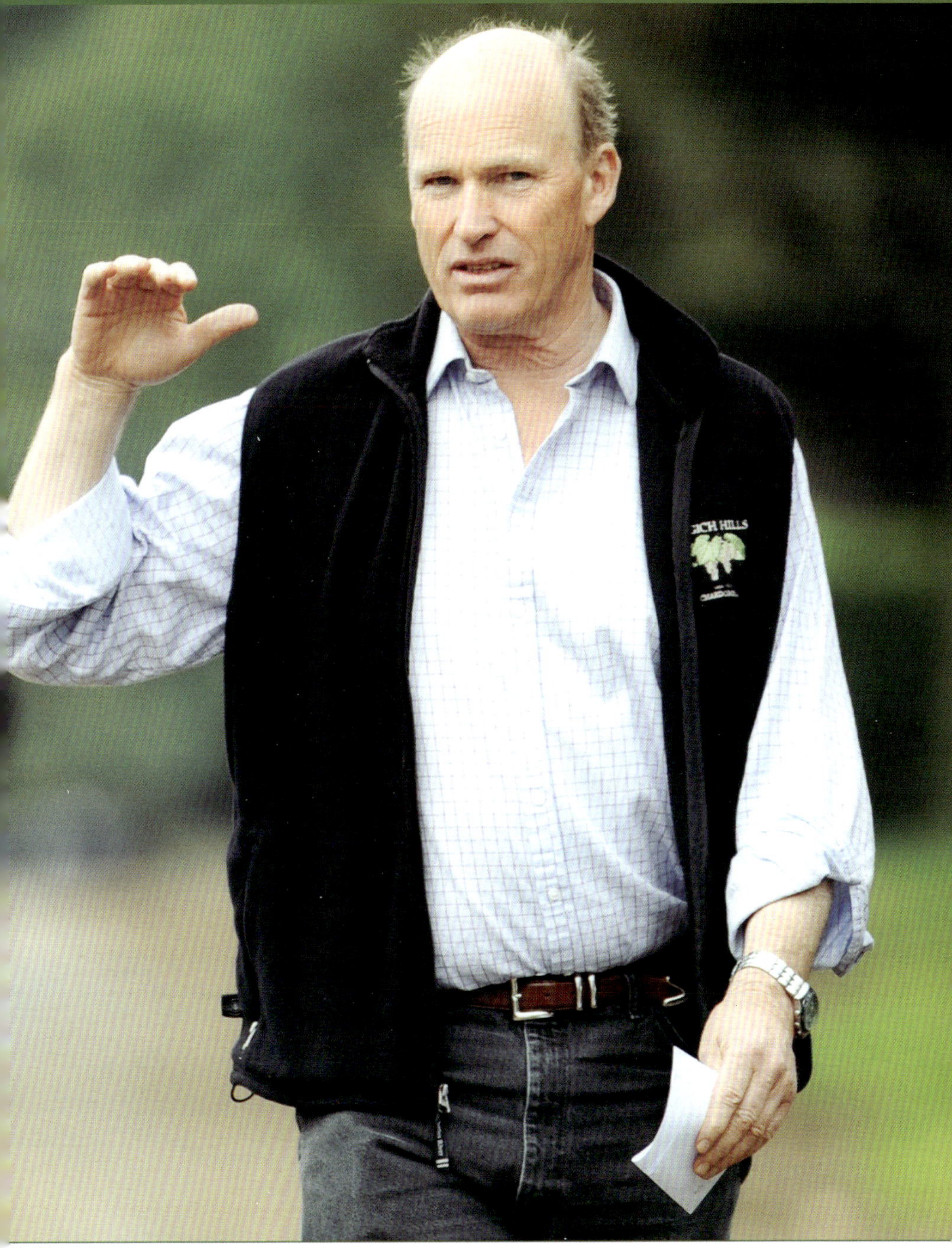

# JOHN GOSDEN
## ARUNDEL, W SUSSEX

|  | No. of Hrs | Races Run | 1st | 2nd | 3rd | Unpl | Per cent | £1 Level Stake |
|---|---|---|---|---|---|---|---|---|
| 2-y-o | 71 | 160 | 29 | 28 | 25 | 78 | 18.1 | -23.36 |
| 3-y-o | 71 | 301 | 64 | 41 | 34 | 162 | 21.3 | -20.39 |
| 4-y-o+ | 17 | 57 | 12 | 7 | 11 | 27 | 21.1 | +15.03 |
| Totals | 159 | 518 | 105 | 76 | 70 | 267 | 20.3 | -28.72 |
| 2009 | 159 | 516 | 88 | 79 | 65 | 284 | 17.1 | +16.50 |
| 2008 | 154 | 498 | 95 | 70 | 53 | 278 | 19.1 | +34.66 |

## BY MONTH

| 2-y-o | W-R | Per cent | £1 Level Stake | 3-y-o | W-R | Per cent | £1 Level Stake |
|---|---|---|---|---|---|---|---|
| January | 0-0 | 0.0 | 0.00 | January | 0-0 | 0.0 | 0.00 |
| February | 0-0 | 0.0 | 0.00 | February | 1-1 | 100.0 | +2.00 |
| March | 0-0 | 0.0 | 0.00 | March | 6-17 | 35.3 | +7.02 |
| April | 0-0 | 0.0 | 0.00 | April | 7-34 | 20.6 | +0.50 |
| May | 1-7 | 14.3 | -2.50 | May | 8-49 | 16.3 | -18.42 |
| June | 2-11 | 18.2 | +13.25 | June | 7-48 | 14.6 | -26.27 |
| July | 0-6 | 0.0 | -6.00 | July | 5-32 | 15.6 | -8.65 |
| August | 6-27 | 22.2 | +2.41 | August | 17-37 | 45.9 | +31.23 |
| September | 12-46 | 26.1 | +4.55 | September | 7-47 | 14.9 | -5.38 |
| October | 5-41 | 12.2 | -22.23 | October | 5-26 | 19.2 | +6.38 |
| November | 1-14 | 7.1 | -12.09 | November | 0-7 | 0.0 | -7.00 |
| December | 2-8 | 25.0 | -0.75 | December | 1-3 | 33.3 | -1.80 |

| 4-y-o+ | W-R | Per cent | £1 Level Stake | Totals | W-R | Per cent | £1 Level Stake |
|---|---|---|---|---|---|---|---|
| January | 0-3 | 0.0 | -3.00 | January | 0-3 | 0.0 | -3.00 |
| February | 0-1 | 0.0 | -1.00 | February | 1-2 | 50.0 | +1.00 |
| March | 0-1 | 0.0 | -1.00 | March | 6-18 | 33.3 | +6.02 |
| April | 3-7 | 42.9 | +7.70 | April | 10-41 | 24.4 | +8.20 |
| May | 1-8 | 12.5 | +4.00 | May | 10-64 | 15.6 | -16.92 |
| June | 1-10 | 10.0 | -7.50 | June | 10-69 | 14.5 | -20.52 |
| July | 2-9 | 22.2 | +11.00 | July | 7-47 | 14.9 | -3.65 |
| August | 1-6 | 16.7 | 0.00 | August | 24-70 | 34.3 | +33.64 |
| September | 3-7 | 42.9 | +5.83 | September | 22-100 | 22.0 | +5.00 |
| October | 1-5 | 20.0 | -1.00 | October | 11-72 | 15.3 | -16.85 |
| November | 0-0 | 0.0 | 0.00 | November | 1-21 | 4.8 | -7.00 |
| December | 0-0 | 0.0 | 0.00 | December | 3-11 | 27.3 | -1.80 |

## DISTANCE

| 2-y-o | W-R | Per cent | £1 Level Stake | 3-y-o | W-R | Per cent | £1 Level Stake |
|---|---|---|---|---|---|---|---|
| 5f-6f | 3-25 | 12.0 | -11.25 | 5f-6f | 2-11 | 18.2 | -3.00 |
| 7f-8f | 25-131 | 19.1 | -29.11 | 7f-8f | 22-111 | 19.8 | -23.56 |
| 9f-13f | 1-4 | 25.0 | +17.00 | 9f-13f | 38-167 | 22.8 | -0.82 |
| 14f+ | 0-0 | 0.0 | 0.00 | 14f+ | 2-12 | 16.7 | +7.00 |

| 4-y-o | W-R | Per cent | £1 Level Stake | Totals | W-R | Per cent | £1 Level Stake |
|---|---|---|---|---|---|---|---|
| 5f-6f | 0-8 | 0.0 | -8.00 | 5f-6f | 5-44 | 11.4 | -22.25 |
| 7f-8f | 2-14 | 14.3 | -1.50 | 7f-8f | 49-256 | 19.1 | -54.17 |
| 9f-13f | 7-29 | 24.1 | +10.53 | 9f-13f | 46-200 | 23.0 | +26.71 |
| 14f+ | 3-6 | 50.0 | +14.00 | 14f+ | 5-18 | 27.8 | +21.00 |

## TYPE OF RACE

| Non-Handicaps | W-R | Per cent | £1 Level Stake | Handicaps | W-R | Per cent | £1 Level Stake |
|---|---|---|---|---|---|---|---|
| 2-y-o | 26-140 | 18.6 | -33.74 | 2-y-o | 3-20 | 15.0 | +10.38 |
| 3-y-o | 39-168 | 23.2 | -20.97 | 3-y-o | 25-133 | 18.8 | +0.58 |
| 4-y-o+ | 9-35 | 25.7 | +37.00 | 4-y-o+ | 3-22 | 13.6 | -8.50 |

## RACE CLASS | FIRST TIME OUT

|  | W-R | Per cent | £1 Level Stake |  | W-R | Per cent | £1 Level Stake |
|---|---|---|---|---|---|---|---|
| Class 1 | 11-67 | 16.4 | +5.25 | 2-y-o | 8-71 | 11.3 | -27.13 |
| Class 2 | 6-64 | 9.4 | -34.88 | 3-y-o | 17-71 | 23.9 | +6.37 |
| Class 3 | 14-51 | 27.5 | +13.81 | 4-y-o+ | 3-17 | 17.6 | +7.50 |
| Class 4 | 29-138 | 21.0 | +37.78 |  |  |  |  |
| Class 5 | 39-183 | 21.3 | -47.42 | Totals | 28-159 | 17.6 | -13.26 |
| Class 6 | 6-15 | 40.0 | -3.27 |  |  |  |  |
| Class 7 | 0-0 | 0.0 | 0.00 |  |  |  |  |

Mark Johnston

# Juvenile fortunes the key to even better times

MARK JOHNSTON'S 2010 tally was 211 British winners and more than £2.4 million in prize-money, an admirable total by anyone's standards. It's not so many years ago that Johnston had 100 winners as one of his objectives for the year, but the past couple of seasons have seen the 200 barrier broken. That this was achieved last season despite a somewhat disappointing total for the juveniles makes the performance all the more remarkable, but more of that later.

Among the older horses **Jukebox Jury** wasn't seen out after July, but he still paid his way with a Group 2 success in the Jockey Club Stakes at Newmarket in May. Prior to that he'd run poorly on quick ground in the Sheema Classic in Dubai and subsequently he was below par in the Coronation Cup and in the Hardwicke. His final run was when fourth in a German Group 1.

'He's back and seems okay. There wasn't a major problem but he just didn't seem to be in love with the game and we think there was a minor injury involved. He's had a long time off, including quite a while when he got turned out every day, so he should be fresh and ready for the start of the season. I'm still not 100 per cent sure we have his trip right. He won over a mile and a half at Newmarket and I tend to be pushing them to stay further, but I just have a hunch he might be even better at a mile and a quarter.'

Johnston had high hopes for **Awzaan** at the start of last season, as the colt had been unbeaten at two, but he ran poorly in the 2,000 Guineas and wasn't seen out again until September.

'It was a huge disappointment to miss out on most of the season, but looked as though the ability was still there when he came back. ▶▶

Jukebox Jury

**Oceanway**

Although the jury is still out to some extent, we think he stays a mile. He's had a good rest and is an exciting horse for this year.'

**Bikini Babe** was on the go from February at Meydan through to Dundalk in November, taking in a couple of trips to Deauville along the way.

'She's a typically highly rated horse who is stuck between handicaps and Group races in this country and all of her significant earnings have come when she has run abroad. She's a very good horse and she deserves to win a good race.'

**English Summer** is a new arrival in the yard, having previously been trained by Andre Fabre in France.

'English Summer and **Exemplary** have been bought by Dr Marwan Koukash with the Chester Cup in mind. Exemplary has won his last two starts, one of them for Marwan – I don't know a lot about English Summer at this stage. However, they're both nice horses to have and it's just the sort of challenge I like.'

**Fox Hunt** didn't make his debut until the August of his three-year-old career, when he landed a maiden at Windsor in taking style. After that he ran well in three other handicaps off a mark of 91. What made him interesting was that he's bred to get further than a mile and a quarter and he looked the type to progress at four – his 2010 season lasted a mere seven weeks, which suggests he's not the easiest horse to train.

'When he came out as a four-year-old, in a Kempton conditions race, he ran well although he didn't settle, but the performance left the impression that he's still a horse of some promise.

'He isn't the easiest. We didn't have him very long as he didn't arrive until the middle of the year, but he's obviously a pretty nice horse and he isn't so hard to train that he won't win races this season. He's off 96, though, which makes life difficult.

'We could talk all day about our handicap system – I think it's the worst thing about British racing, even worse than the prize-money. The best horses don't win the most races and that's a sad flaw in the way the game is structured.'

The Johnston team's performance in 2010 was remarkable, and yet it conceals one worrying statistic. Johnston won 25 races with his two-year-olds last year, whereas the totals for the previous three seasons were 68, 58 and 64.

'There's no getting away from it, last year was a disastrous one for our two-year-olds – I think we only had one juvenile that won more than one race. A number of them started out well and then ran inexplicably badly after that. At the same time, the older horses were in great form, so it's hard to fathom out. I had 18 horses move to Godolphin, but not one of them was a two-year-old.

'**Stentorian** was probably the biggest disappointment among them. Even as late as the end of July, when he was second in the Group 2 Vintage Stakes, you'd still have said he was a top-class horse, but after that he ran very badly – last in the Solario and then second-last in the Tattersalls Million sales race. I could never find anything wrong with him and it was desperately disappointing.

'At the moment we're simply hoping that he, and some of the others, can come back. I'm the last person to be a believer in viruses or stable sicknesses, but whatever the reason that the two-year-olds ran so badly last year, some of the lesser horses that we ran over the winter have performed well and that's very encouraging.

'**Dordogne** fits the pattern too. He won on his debut over nine furlongs and looked very good, but he disappointed me a bit when only third in the Houghton Stakes back at a mile. It probably didn't help that we brought him back in trip. He's not a good mover, but we have always liked him – Kieren Fallon commented at Goodwood that he went down to the start very badly and he couldn't believe how well he came back.

'**Oceanway** is rated 87, so the handicapper doesn't think she's as good as Dordogne, but I still have high hopes for her. She has the scope to be better at three, and she should get a mile. She's by Street Cry and he seems to get them over all sorts of trips, so it's hard to say – I don't however, see her as an out-and-out stayer.

'**Falmouth Bay** didn't come until late on – he isn't one where we were sitting back and waiting to run. He won at Wolverhampton and let's hope he can progress.

'**Hurricane Higgins** is Jukebox Jury's half-brother and was very backward last season. Jukebox Jury cost €280,000 and even after he'd won a Group 1 I was able to buy Hurricane Higgins for €100,000, so there were plenty of people who didn't think he'd make it. He's huge and, while the race he won at Lingfield didn't amount to much, the further he goes the better he'll be, and he won despite being very green. So, all the hopes are still there.

'**Namibian** is another where we started with high hopes and then had a disappointment. He won his maiden on his second start and then ran in a nursery at Doncaster off a mark of 82 and finished third – I thought he was better than an 82-rated horse. Hopefully he can bounce back – we like him.

'It's exactly the same story with **State Opera**. He was so impressive when he won at Hamilton, but then I was disappointed with his run in the Tattersalls Million race at Newmarket. He was dropped back in trip, which maybe didn't help, the ground was soft and those sales races can be funny, but he was still disappointing. Again, we're hoping he can show us that the impression he made at Hamilton was the right one.

'**Son Vida** is an extremely backward horse and we'd never have expected him to be out early. I trained his half-brother, Ransom O'War, for a German owner and he kept asking me whether he would be a Group horse – when I said I didn't know he obviously thought I was being too negative because he took the horse away. Ransom O'War ended up winning a Group 1, so I was at pains to say to his owner, Jim McGrath, that Son Vida needed time and that whatever he showed us, he'd be far better later. Hence, he didn't start until January and we've been in no rush to run him again. He won nicely over a mile, but we think he needs further and he needs time.'

'**Sadler's Risk** was third on his debut, then stayed on nicely without getting into the Tattersalls Million sales race before winning a Leicester maiden over a mile.

'He's a lovely horse and didn't do much wrong. He spent the winter at his owner's and we haven't had him back long, but he'd be one of my more exciting prospects. He's rated only 82, so he can work his way up through the handicap route, and let's hope he can do that and maybe even progress beyond that. He'll stay a mile and a half.

'**Cape Of Dance** is a nice horse, but she got a fracture after winning at Hamilton. She's back and hopefully the time off will have done her no harm.

'**Art History** is a bit like Falmouth Bay in that he came to us late on, and with problems. So what he's done so far, by winning his maiden, is a bit of a bonus. We haven't got our sights set hugely high at this stage but, having said that, he's done very well.

'**Crown Counsel** has only just started out, showing promise at Wolverhampton and then just being caught late on in a maiden at Deauville.'

**On the face of it, with 18 of his better horses having gone to Godolphin, Johnston has a challenging season ahead, but it would be a brave person who bet against him having another hugely successful campaign. The mystery of the under-performing two-year-olds is worthy of Sherlock Holmes, but all the signs are that it was just an aberration. Who knows, it may even work to Johnston's advantage with the handicapper having less evidence than he might normally have had on which to assess the stable's three-year-olds. As Johnston said when talking about Exemplary and English Summer, he likes a challenge and my money is on him having yet another great season.** [CB]

**Horse to follow** Bikini Babe
**Dark horse** Sadler's Risk

# MARK JOHNSTON

**MIDDLEHAM MOOR, N YORKS**

|  | No. of Hrs | Races Run | 1st | 2nd | 3rd | Unpl | Per cent | £1 Level Stake |
|---|---|---|---|---|---|---|---|---|
| 2-y-o | 77 | 260 | 25 | 23 | 30 | 181 | 9.6 | -116.63 |
| 3-y-o | 140 | 857 | 139 | 107 | 95 | 514 | 16.2 | -173.38 |
| 4-y-o+ | 45 | 341 | 47 | 36 | 42 | 216 | 13.8 | -86.04 |
| Totals | 262 | 1458 | 211 | 166 | 167 | 911 | 14.5 | -376.05 |
| 2009 | 250 | 1227 | 216 | 161 | 138 | 707 | 17.6 | -32.01 |
| 2008 | 257 | 1145 | 164 | 146 | 137 | 696 | 14.3 | -17.13 |

## BY MONTH

| 2-y-o | W-R | Per cent | £1 Level Stake | 3-y-o | W-R | Per cent | £1 Level Stake |
|---|---|---|---|---|---|---|---|
| January | 0-0 | 0.0 | 0.00 | January | 11-25 | 44.0 | +3.16 |
| February | 0-0 | 0.0 | 0.00 | February | 16-38 | 42.1 | +7.85 |
| March | 0-0 | 0.0 | 0.00 | March | 10-52 | 19.2 | -6.67 |
| April | 0-1 | 0.0 | -1.00 | April | 14-77 | 18.2 | -18.25 |
| May | 0-7 | 0.0 | -7.00 | May | 12-108 | 11.1 | -50.51 |
| June | 1-19 | 5.3 | -10.50 | June | 10-116 | 8.6 | -62.07 |
| July | 3-29 | 10.3 | -11.75 | July | 30-156 | 19.2 | +26.86 |
| August | 5-41 | 12.2 | -7.38 | August | 17-100 | 17.0 | -1.00 |
| September | 8-58 | 13.8 | -10.25 | September | 10-113 | 8.8 | -63.75 |
| October | 5-62 | 8.1 | -38.00 | October | 5-55 | 9.1 | -16.00 |
| November | 2-28 | 7.1 | -22.25 | November | 1-7 | 14.3 | -3.00 |
| December | 1-15 | 6.7 | -8.50 | December | 3-10 | 30.0 | +10.00 |

| 4-y-o+ | W-R | Per cent | £1 Level Stake | Totals | W-R | Per cent | £1 Level Stake |
|---|---|---|---|---|---|---|---|
| January | 3-13 | 23.1 | -4.05 | January | 14-38 | 36.8 | -0.89 |
| February | 1-13 | 7.7 | -6.50 | February | 17-51 | 33.3 | +1.35 |
| March | 0-23 | 0.0 | -23.00 | March | 10-75 | 13.3 | -29.67 |
| April | 4-30 | 13.3 | -4.63 | April | 18-108 | 16.7 | -23.88 |
| May | 9-51 | 17.6 | -1.25 | May | 21-166 | 12.7 | -58.76 |
| June | 8-55 | 14.5 | -22.25 | June | 19-190 | 10.0 | -94.82 |
| July | 9-44 | 20.5 | +8.56 | July | 42-229 | 18.3 | +23.67 |
| August | 7-45 | 15.6 | -3.67 | August | 29-186 | 15.6 | -12.05 |
| September | 4-43 | 9.3 | -18.13 | September | 22-214 | 10.3 | -92.13 |
| October | 2-17 | 11.8 | -4.13 | October | 12-134 | 9.0 | -58.13 |
| November | 0-3 | 0.0 | -3.00 | November | 3-38 | 7.9 | -6.00 |
| December | 0-4 | 0.0 | -4.00 | December | 4-29 | 13.8 | +6.00 |

## DISTANCE

| 2-y-o | W-R | Per cent | £1 Level Stake | 3-y-o | W-R | Per cent | £1 Level Stake |
|---|---|---|---|---|---|---|---|
| 5f-6f | 5-96 | 5.2 | -76.00 | 5f-6f | 16-124 | 12.9 | -40.29 |
| 7f-8f | 19-158 | 12.0 | -45.63 | 7f-8f | 67-397 | 16.9 | -72.48 |
| 9f-13f | 1-6 | 16.7 | +5.00 | 9f-13f | 52-302 | 17.2 | -39.98 |
| 14f+ | 0-0 | 0.0 | 0.00 | 14f+ | 4-34 | 11.8 | -20.63 |

| 4-y-o+ | W-R | Per cent | £1 Level Stake | Totals | W-R | Per cent | £1 Level Stake |
|---|---|---|---|---|---|---|---|
| 5f-6f | 1-16 | 6.3 | -9.50 | 5f-6f | 22-236 | 9.3 | -125.79 |
| 7f-8f | 10-89 | 11.2 | -29.25 | 7f-8f | 96-644 | 14.9 | -147.36 |
| 9f-13f | 25-179 | 14.0 | -53.83 | 9f-13f | 78-487 | 16.0 | -88.81 |
| 14f+ | 11-57 | 19.3 | +6.54 | 14f+ | 15-91 | 16.5 | -14.09 |

## TYPE OF RACE

| Non-Handicaps | W-R | Per cent | £1 Level Stake | Handicaps | W-R | Per cent | £1 Level Stake |
|---|---|---|---|---|---|---|---|
| 2-y-o | 20-207 | 9.7 | -87.13 | 2-y-o | 5-53 | 9.4 | -29.50 |
| 3-y-o | 46-222 | 20.7 | -34.35 | 3-y-o | 93-635 | 14.6 | -139.03 |
| 4-y-o+ | 12-41 | 29.3 | +76.00 | 4-y-o+ | 35-300 | 11.7 | -112.23 |

## RACE CLASS      FIRST TIME OUT

| | W-R | Per cent | £1 Level Stake | | W-R | Per cent | £1 Level Stake |
|---|---|---|---|---|---|---|---|
| Class 1 | 13-65 | 20.0 | +15.88 | 2-y-o | 6-77 | 7.8 | -43.25 |
| Class 2 | 20-292 | 6.8 | -132.50 | 3-y-o | 26-140 | 18.6 | -36.57 |
| Class 3 | 32-217 | 14.7 | -20.59 | 4-y-o+ | 6-45 | 13.3 | -23.30 |
| Class 4 | 59-372 | 15.9 | -95.22 | | | | |
| Class 5 | 75-417 | 18.0 | -98.41 | Totals | 38-262 | 14.5 | -103.12 |
| Class 6 | 12-95 | 12.6 | -44.19 | | | | |
| Class 7 | 0-0 | 0.0 | 0.00 | | | | |

## MARK JOHNSTON

I can do no better than repeat last year's mantra: great trainer, fantastic season and a sure-fire route to the poorhouse if you'd blindly followed his horses.

Apart from a memorable January on the all-weather, the monthly stats are such that you can't make a level-stakes profit. In 2009 the three-year-olds running outside of handicap company were profitable and those who stayed on as four-year-olds ensured that category was profitable in 2010. This might be an angle for the future.

One hint for this year comes straight from the Johnston interview. The mysterious loss of form after a promising start among the juveniles must have been a nightmare for their trainer, but it could work in our favour. I am not saying blindly follow them – that would be disastrous – but keep a close eye on whether this season's three-year-olds start out a step ahead of the handicapper. I think that might just be the case.

On the jockey front, Joe Fanning is number one (big losses) and Greg Fairley number two (more losses). Frankie Dettori had a 22 per cent strike-rate (more losses). Royston Ffrench got a lot of mounts and, you guessed it, more losses. Watch out for Kieren Fallon being booked – that seems to be a clue in itself.

Course statistics aren't much help either, although Leicester and Goodwood are always worth watching.

Overall, from a trends perspective this is a yard to avoid. It's far better to study the form book and identify a runner that you fancy backing – that's where the Johnston motto 'Always Trying' comes into its own. *[CB]* ■

racing & football outlook
FLAT RACING GUIDE 2011
THE FLAT GUIDE YOU CAN'T AFFORD TO BE WITHOUT
Dave Nevison with his thoughts on the new season
Steve Mellish gives you five of the best
Sfeffan Edwards with his unrivalled ante-post service
Mark Nelson with his top time performers of last season
ONLY £7.99
FREE UK P&P
ORDER NOW
RACING POST.com/shop
ORDERLINE 01933 304858 Quote ref: RFOF11

Sir Michael Stoute

# Derby hero leads bid to reclaim trainer's crown

SIR MICHAEL STOUTE couldn't add to his tally of trainers' championships last season and, at 73, his tally of British winners was his lowest for ten years, but his prize-money total of more than £3 million was yet another outstanding achievement for the master of Freemason Lodge. The stars of the show were the brilliant but now-retired Harbinger and the wonderful Workforce, winner of the Derby and the Prix de l'Arc de Triomphe. The one disappointment was his below-par effort in the King George – that briefly cast doubt over the Derby form, but his Longchamp effort silenced any doubters.

'It's great that he stays in training at four, but I haven't yet discussed a programme with his owner, other than that, having taken him to Kentucky in November, we weren't then going to rush him back into action in Dubai in the spring. I'll talk with Prince Khalid and with his racing manager, Teddy Grimthorpe, and it might be that we consider starting him back at a mile and a quarter – I wouldn't be afraid to run him over that trip. He's a big, 16.2 horse who was still very unfurnished last year and who has had only five starts, so at this stage we're entitled to hope there's more to come from him. It would be nice if he could go back to Ascot for the King George and perform at his best.'

For everyone's sake, and for the good of racing, let's hope the decision to keep Workforce in training is rewarded with another good season – at his best the colt is one of the game's superstars.

**Total Command** started his season in good form, winning his maiden and then ▶▶

Workforce

racingpost.com 59

**Crystal Capella**

running well in the Queen's Vase. However, he put in a stinker in the Great Voltigeur and disappointed again in the St Leger.

'He baffled us last season. It was a very good run at Ascot and I just felt he emptied a bit at the end of the two miles, but after that race nothing went right. We couldn't find anything physical that could explain his disappointing runs, so we backed off and gelded him, and basically decided to start all over again this season. There is talent there but we just need to find the way to unlock it. We'll start him back steadily and I don't think he wants to be going any further then 1m6f at this stage.'

**Verdant** was progressive last season, winning three handicaps, off 80, 90 and 98. The last of his wins came at the end of July and he wasn't seen out again after that.

'He popped a splint and rather than mess about trying to get him ready to run in October we decided to give him time for it to settle down. He's now rated 103, so he'll have to go into stakes races – let's hope he progresses. We've always liked him – he's a handsome horse. He stays a mile and a half well and I wouldn't be in a hurry to send him beyond that trip.'

**Conduct** didn't make his racecourse debut until the September of his three-year-old season, but he made a big impression, winning both of his starts. He bolted up at Sandown in a maiden that has worked out very well and then won off 85 in a Newbury handicap where he again had a number of subsequent winners behind him. His form looks rock solid.

'He had a tendon injury as a two-year-old, so we gave him plenty of time. The problem is that he has run twice and is off 95. However, he has a lot of talent – he showed us that at two and he was almost ready for a run before he sustained that injury. We've been patient with him and hopefully he can progress again – he'd get further than a mile and a quarter if we asked him to.'

**Crystal Capella** is a useful mare but managed only two runs last season: winning the Group 2 Pride Stakes on her debut and then being unplaced in the Hong Kong Vase.

'She threw a splint on one limb and then on another limb. Apart from that she's a sound mare and we didn't envisage having a problem with her. She showed in the Pride she has all the talent in the world and then it all went wrong for her in Hong Kong – it's been very frustrating.

'She'll have a long life at stud, so we're going to give her one final fling and hope we get a clear run where she can show her true colours. I think a mile and a half is her best trip, but I wouldn't be worried about bringing her back to a mile and a quarter.

'**Eleanora Duse** is a tough filly and I just hope she can progress a little bit more. She's a delightful filly with a really good attitude. She got struck into on her final start in the Pride Stakes – she was cantering one moment and then went out like a light. She showed great tenacity when she won the Blandford Stakes at the Curragh on very bad ground – the bravest filly won that day. That was at a mile and a quarter but she'll stay a mile and a half.'

**Nouriya** won her maiden and then two Listed races, before finishing seventh in the Group 1 Prix de l'Opera on Arc weekend.

'We like her. She progressed well last season but didn't get much of a run in the Opera, where it all went wrong for her. Hopefully there's more to come from her – she doesn't want the ground to be too quick.'

Moving to Sir Michael's three-year-olds, Carlton House was second on his debut, on soft ground over a mile at Salisbury, and then bolted up at Newbury.

'He was very impressive at Newbury. I nearly pulled him out of the Salisbury race as the ground was desperate. We didn't fancy him on that surface, but it was late in the year and we were running out of time, so we let him take his chance and he ran creditably. I don't think the ground was ideal at Newbury but he handled it okay. It was the way he did it that impressed me; he had the race wrapped up a long way out, which is always a good sign. It's early days but he looks the part and he has a mile-and-a-half pedigree. The plan will be to start him out in a Derby trial and take it from there.' ▸▸

'**Dux Scholar** is a tough little horse who is just taking a little bit of time to become really professional. He just needs to pull himself together – he's hard to get fit, but I think he'll keep progressing. I'm sure he's a stakes horse, but quite how far he'll go I wouldn't know at this stage.

'For sure there's potential there and I'll give him the Guineas entry. He's a glutton for work and I'm not convinced I ever had him 100 per cent fit last season – if I can get him there I think we can win a Group race or two with him.'

**Sea Moon** was second on his debut, beaten a short head, but then won his maiden over a mile at Yarmouth right at the back end of the season.

'We like him and he has a lot of scope, with a good mind – he's a fine, big, athletic horse.

'We liked the way **Tazahum** won his race at Kempton on his debut and Richard Hills was adamant the ground was too soft when he finished second at Ascot – we think he's a good or fast ground horse He's a big, scopey sort who should improve and we like him.

'**Labarinto** won his maiden nicely at Warwick and we wanted to step him up in class, but he had sore shins so we had to put him away. He's a good-looking, useful type – he'll be all right.

'We don't know a lot about **Raahin**: he's by a decent sire [Oasis Dream] and he's a good-looking horse but we haven't got too far down the road with him yet. We do, however, believe he has potential.'

Among the fillies, **Havant** looks an exciting prospect. She won her maiden in effortless style at Newmarket and then landed the Group 3 Oh So Sharp Stakes in ready style, with her jockey not touching her with the whip.

'What we plan to do is give her the 1,000 Guineas entry and aim her for the race without a 'prep' run, in the hope she shows us enough to do that. Of course she'll also have an Oaks entry and there's every chance she can stay the Oaks trip, but we'll learn about her as we go along. It's still early days, but at this stage I'm happy with how she's doing.

'**Cape Dollar** is a bonny, tough, competitive little filly who showed a good attitude in winning the Group 2 Rockfel. She's not over-big but she's useful and I think she has the mind to go forward and train on – that's often more important than size. She's sure to get a mile, and probably a bit further, so we'll give her a Guineas entry and probably aim her at a trial.'

With a team the size and quality of Sir Michael's, there is always a host of 'dark' three-year-olds – the sort who could be anything or might not amount to much. The good ones are in there, but spotting them early in the season is a tough task. **Caraboss**, **Crystal Etoile** and **Rien Ne Vas Plus** all fall into that category, each having shown ability on their one run.

'We like them all. They showed promise and the main thing is that they weren't cut out to be two-year-olds. With luck they'll all progress, but as to how far, no-one knows at this stage.'

**It's impossible to imagine anything other than another excellent season for Sir Michael and his team. His select bunch of older horses, led by Workforce, looks to be particularly strong and the three-year-olds are as impressive as always. We can be pretty sure it will be a really good season and that he will be mounting another strong challenge for the trainers' title, but I just have a hunch that 2011 will turn out to be a vintage one for the Freemason Lodge team.** [CB]

**Horse to follow** Workforce
**Dark horse** Raahin

# SIR MICHAEL STOUTE
## NEWMARKET, SUFFOLK

|        | No. of Hrs | Races Run | 1st | 2nd | 3rd | Unpl | Per cent | £1 Level Stake |
|--------|------------|-----------|-----|-----|-----|------|----------|----------------|
| 2-y-o  | 43         | 115       | 40  | 20  | 14  | 41   | 34.8     | -8.47          |
| 3-y-o  | 41         | 124       | 28  | 20  | 8   | 68   | 22.6     | +8.68          |
| 4-y-o+ | 48         | 161       | 22  | 22  | 21  | 96   | 13.7     | -41.97         |
| Totals | 132        | 400       | 90  | 62  | 43  | 205  | 22.5     | -41.76         |
| 2009   | 182        | 530       | 148 | 83  | 70  | 228  | 27.9     | -9.03          |
| 2008   | 115        | 313       | 58  | 60  | 47  | 148  | 18.5     | -16.41         |

### BY MONTH

| 2-y-o     | W-R   | Per cent | £1 Level Stake | 3-y-o     | W-R   | Per cent | £1 Level Stake |
|-----------|-------|----------|----------------|-----------|-------|----------|----------------|
| January   | 0-0   | 0.0      | 0.00           | January   | 0-0   | 0.0      | 0.00           |
| February  | 0-0   | 0.0      | 0.00           | February  | 0-0   | 0.0      | 0.00           |
| March     | 0-0   | 0.0      | 0.00           | March     | 0-0   | 0.0      | 0.00           |
| April     | 0-0   | 0.0      | 0.00           | April     | 0-4   | 0.0      | -4.00          |
| May       | 0-3   | 0.0      | -3.00          | May       | 2-18  | 11.1     | -13.05         |
| June      | 4-12  | 33.3     | -3.43          | June      | 3-8   | 37.5     | +3.25          |
| July      | 5-14  | 35.7     | +6.88          | July      | 3-19  | 15.8     | -1.00          |
| August    | 11-20 | 55.0     | +6.54          | August    | 5-29  | 17.2     | -5.10          |
| September | 10-27 | 37.0     | -6.79          | September | 9-22  | 40.9     | +23.75         |
| October   | 8-29  | 27.6     | -3.92          | October   | 6-20  | 30.0     | +8.83          |
| November  | 2-10  | 20.0     | -4.75          | November  | 0-4   | 0.0      | -4.00          |
| December  | 0-0   | 0.0      | 0.00           | December  | 0-0   | 0.0      | 0.00           |

| 4-y-o+    | W-R   | Per cent | £1 Level Stake | Totals    | W-R   | Per cent | £1 Level Stake |
|-----------|-------|----------|----------------|-----------|-------|----------|----------------|
| January   | 0-0   | 0.0      | 0.00           | January   | 0-0   | 0.0      | 0.00           |
| February  | 0-0   | 0.0      | 0.00           | February  | 0-0   | 0.0      | 0.00           |
| March     | 0-0   | 0.0      | 0.00           | March     | 0-0   | 0.0      | 0.00           |
| April     | 0-0   | 0.0      | 0.00           | April     | 0-4   | 0.0      | -4.00          |
| May       | 0-19  | 0.0      | -19.00         | May       | 2-40  | 5.0      | -35.05         |
| June      | 4-22  | 18.2     | +16.38         | June      | 11-42 | 26.2     | +16.20         |
| July      | 4-31  | 12.9     | -21.09         | July      | 12-64 | 18.8     | -15.21         |
| August    | 5-29  | 17.2     | +4.04          | August    | 21-78 | 26.9     | +5.48          |
| September | 4-26  | 15.4     | +4.10          | September | 23-75 | 30.7     | +21.06         |
| October   | 4-24  | 16.7     | -16.90         | October   | 18-73 | 24.7     | -11.99         |
| November  | 1-10  | 10.0     | -9.50          | November  | 3-24  | 12.5     | -13.50         |
| December  | 0-0   | 0.0      | 0.00           | December  | 0-0   | 0.0      | 0.00           |

### DISTANCE

| 2-y-o  | W-R    | Per cent | £1 Level Stake | 3-y-o  | W-R     | Per cent | £1 Level Stake |
|--------|--------|----------|----------------|--------|---------|----------|----------------|
| 5f-6f  | 14-40  | 35.0     | -0.55          | 5f-6f  | 4-8     | 50.0     | +10.65         |
| 7f-8f  | 26-72  | 36.1     | -4.92          | 7f-8f  | 13-48   | 27.1     | +8.93          |
| 9f-13f | 0-3    | 0.0      | -3.00          | 9f-13f | 11-66   | 16.7     | -8.90          |
| 14f+   | 0-0    | 0.0      | 0.00           | 14f+   | 0-2     | 0.0      | -2.00          |

| 4-y-o  | W-R    | Per cent | £1 Level Stake | Totals | W-R     | Per cent | £1 Level Stake |
|--------|--------|----------|----------------|--------|---------|----------|----------------|
| 5f-6f  | 1-11   | 9.1      | -9.50          | 5f-6f  | 19-59   | 32.2     | +0.60          |
| 7f-8f  | 11-50  | 22.0     | +31.85         | 7f-8f  | 50-170  | 29.4     | +35.86         |
| 9f-13f | 10-79  | 12.7     | -43.32         | 9f-13f | 21-148  | 14.2     | -55.22         |
| 14f+   | 0-21   | 0.0      | -21.00         | 14f+   | 0-23    | 0.0      | -23.00         |

### TYPE OF RACE

| Non-Handicaps | W-R    | Per cent | £1 Level Stake | Handicaps | W-R   | Per cent | £1 Level Stake |
|---------------|--------|----------|----------------|-----------|-------|----------|----------------|
| 2-y-o         | 36-102 | 35.3     | -12.07         | 2-y-o     | 4-13  | 30.8     | +3.60          |
| 3-y-o         | 15-65  | 23.1     | +2.10          | 3-y-o     | 13-59 | 22.0     | +6.58          |
| 4-y-o+        | 19-133 | 14.3     | +8.00          | 4-y-o+    | 3-28  | 10.7     | +26.00         |

### RACE CLASS / FIRST TIME OUT

| Race Class | W-R    | Per cent | £1 Level Stake | First Time Out | W-R    | Per cent | £1 Level Stake |
|------------|--------|----------|----------------|----------------|--------|----------|----------------|
| Class 1    | 25-160 | 15.6     | -35.81         | 2-y-o          | 10-43  | 23.3     | -10.40         |
| Class 2    | 12-69  | 17.4     | +17.60         | 3-y-o          | 11-41  | 26.8     | +1.20          |
| Class 3    | 13-61  | 21.3     | -17.07         | 4-y-o+         | 7-48   | 14.6     | -26.47         |
| Class 4    | 22-56  | 39.3     | +7.46          |                |        |          |                |
| Class 5    | 17-53  | 32.1     | -11.67         | Totals         | 28-132 | 21.2     | -35.67         |
| Class 6    | 1-1    | 100.0    | +0.73          |                |        |          |                |
| Class 7    | 0-0    | 0.0      | 0.00           |                |        |          |                |

## SIR MICHAEL STOUTE

The bare statistics speak for themselves: second in the trainers' list with 73 winners and less than £200,000 behind the champion, Richard Hannon, who trained 137 winners more. The Sir Michael Stoute team is all about quality. The problem, however, is that it's not just you and me who've spotted that, and those nasty bookies squeeze the value out of Stoute-trained runners like a python with its prey.

Workforce and Harbinger apart, last season wasn't a vintage one for the yard and level-stakes losses were the norm across the board. Strike-rates were down, but this was an aberration. Let's stick with the usual advice: despite last year's blip, follow the older horses in non-handicap company – it generally works.

Ryan Moore is the stable jockey, but that meant losses last season, whereas former retained rider Kieren Fallon managed a decent profit from just 16 rides – watch out for his booking in the coming months.

Course statistics don't tend to help. Sir Michael treats each horse as an individual and places them accordingly, not in line with habit. That said, anything sent to the north is travelling for a reason – last year was an aberration in this trend too, but it won't deter me from looking out for future travellers.

The best thing to do is to follow individuals from the Stoute team. You know they'll be trained to the minute, that they'll be well placed by their handler – he hasn't been champion ten times just through good luck. Three-year-olds in valuable handicaps are a source of endless fascination – many's the time I've looked back and thought, with the benefit of hindsight, what a snip a subsequent Group winner must have been. *[CB]* ∎

Sir Michael Stoute

Guide to the Flat **2011**

# THE ONES

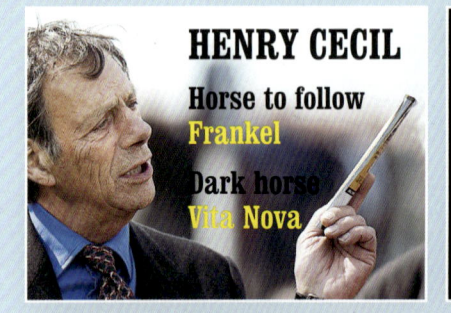

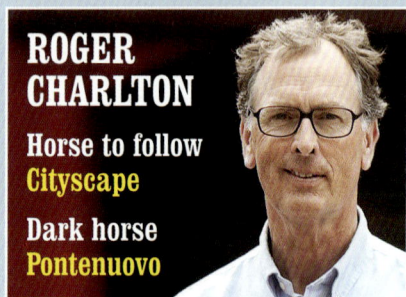

### HENRY CECIL
**Horse to follow**
Frankel

**Dark horse**
Vita Nova

### LUCA CUMANI
**Horse to follow**
Forte Dei Marmi

**Dark horse**
Naqshabban

### GODOLPHIN
**Horse to follow**
Rio De La Plata

**Dark horse**
Splash Point

### ROGER CHARLTON
**Horse to follow**
Cityscape

**Dark horse**
Pontenuovo

Dark horses

# TO WATCH

### MARK JOHNSTON
Horse to follow
**Bikini Babe**

Dark horse
**Sadler's Risk**

### JOHN GOSDEN
Horse to follow
**Arctic Cosmos**

Dark horse
**Splendid Light**

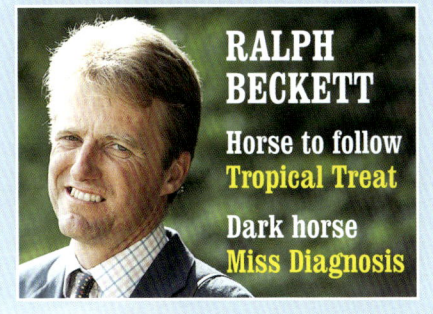

### RALPH BECKETT
Horse to follow
**Tropical Treat**

Dark horse
**Miss Diagnosis**

### SIR MICHAEL STOUTE
Horse to follow
**Workforce**

Dark horse
**Raahin**

# Stoute has know-how in Carlton Derby quest

**Colin Boag draws on in-depth conversations with our eight featured trainers and picks a crack team destined for success**

### Bourne Luca Cumani

Bourne, seemingly not much more than moderate at three, won over a mile and a quarter on both of his four-year old starts to put the previous year behind him. Assuming that he stands training, this gelded son of Linamix can progress through the handicap ranks, and in Luca Cumani he's trained by the right man for the job of winning while rising through the weights.

### Carlton House Sir Michael Stoute

Sir Michael Stoute trained the Derby winner last season and Carlton House is my speculative tip to do the job again for the stable, which has had such success in the race over the years. Bred to stay, this son of Street Cry is clearly well regarded by his trainer, and seems sure to win good races this season, maybe even the best of them all. That he is owned by the Queen means he would be a popular as well as profitable winner.

### Devastation John Gosden

Unlucky not to be unbeaten at two, this daughter of Attraction by Montjeu is seen by John Gosden as a possible Oaks candidate. Whichever trial she heads for, she's worthy of the greatest respect. She is in good hands to build on the potential she showed in her two runs at 1m as a juvenile.

### Farhh Saeed Bin Suroor

Inasmuch as any Godolphin horse can be a 'dark' one, Farhh appears to fit the bill. He looked extremely promising when winning his maiden in July but didn't run again, having injured himself in the stalls on his intended next start. In a manner that comes naturally to this most patient of yards, he has been given plenty of time off the track but is highly regarded in his powerful stable, which considering the firepower, is quite a status.

## Colin Boag's Ten to Follow

### Frankel Henry Cecil

Zero out of ten for originality, but anyone who omits Frankel from their list of horses to follow this season is likely to look foolish come the end of the year. The worthy favourite for the 2,000 Guineas, he could just be a special horse. And in the hands of Henry Cecil there is every reason to believe he will fulfil his undoubted potential as a three-year-old, even if he doesn't stay a mile and a half.

### Havant Sir Michael Stoute

When Sir Michael Stoute told me the plan was the 1,000 Guineas en route to the Oaks, it confirmed the view that this daughter of Halling is extremely well regarded at Freemason Lodge. She seems sure to win decent races this season and is with a trainer who has bucketloads of experience of handling top-class fillies.

### Pontenuovo Roger Charlton

We're taking a chance with this filly as even her trainer doesn't know how good she is. Trained in France last season she has joined Roger Charlton's team and it could well be that her French form will be under-rated by most people. In Charlton she is with an ideal trainer to tease out the ability of this unknown quantity. She has the potential to be successful in Britain and maybe back 'home' in France in due course.

### State Opera Mark Johnston

State Opera was one of many of Mark Johnston's two-year olds to underperform after a good start to his career. Whatever the reason for that, my hunch is that he can bounce back and confirm the good impression he made when winning a Hamilton maiden. The form of Johnston's juveniles last year is best ignored. But not the horses themselves.

### Vita Nova Henry Cecil

Unraced at two, this Galileo filly ran just twice as a three-year old, winning both of her starts. Those runs were over a mile and a half and, while the form is nothing special, Henry Cecil clearly likes her and thinks she's up to Group class. There should be sufficient opportunity for her to show her ability, then the challenge of the colts awaits.

### Western Prize Ralph Beckett

The winner of a modest Lingfield maiden on a bitterly cold January day, Western Prize was a proper winter warmer. Ralph Beckett clearly likes him and can place him to win in handicap company over middle distances. Beckett features in the Guide to the Flat for the first time and this could be the horse who shows he more than deserves to keep the company of Guide to the Flat perennials like Henry Cecil, Sir Michael Stoute and John Gosden. ■

*Frankel (right) is hard to exclude from any list*

# New faces expected to boost Irish prospects

### Alan Sweetman senses this is a season in which the older guard of trainers is likely to be joined by the next generation

CHANGE comes only slowly on the Irish Flat scene. For the past decade the familiar names have reigned supreme: O'Brien, Weld, Oxx and Bolger, with the evergreen Kevin Prendergast following close behind, along with the emerging David Wachman. Meanwhile others such as Ger Lyons and Michael Halford have carved out a niche, seeking to upgrade stable strength in order to join the elite group.

In 2010 Halford made a significant breakthrough thanks to **Casamento**, a Shamardal colt sent to him by Sheikh Mohammed as a result of a policy decision to spread the owner's raw-material more widely among Irish trainers. Casamento won three of his four races and gave Halford a memorable success in the Racing Post Trophy before departing to be prepared for a Classic campaign by Godolphin. He is a major loss to the Irish scene in 2011.

The only horse to beat Casamento was **Pathfork**, whose victory in the National Stakes was a triumph for Jessica Harrington, a more familiar influence as a trainer of jumpers and hitherto best known for her handling of the dual two-mile champion chaser Moscow Society. Pathfork was unbeaten in three races.

The American-bred colt looked very much at home on quickish ground in the Futurity Stakes at the Curragh in August before coping with deteriorating conditions in the National Stakes, the defining race of the domestic two-year-old campaign. He is a prime Classic contender who can consolidate Harrington's profile on the Flat in 2011.

There was a strong Irish flavour to two of Britain's principal juvenile races, with Casamento's Doncaster win achieved at the main expense of the Aidan O'Brien-trained pair Seville and Master Of Hounds. In addition, another Ballydoyle colt, **Roderic O'Connor**, was runner-up to Frankel in the Dewhurst in which the Jim Bolger-trained Glor Na Mara took third place, a performance that will entitle him to the status of Ireland's best three-year-old maiden at the start of the new season. His turn should not be long delayed.

There is clearly a respectable strength in depth among the Irish juveniles, although the standard for the Classic campaign is set by the Henry Cecil-trained Frankel.

The National Stakes form stacked up in domestic terms, as well as in the context of Casamento's Racing Post win. The Ballydoyle-trained **Zoffany**, who was five lengths behind Casamento in third in the Curragh Group 1, won five of his seven races. He atoned for his unplaced run behind Strong Suit in the Coventry Stakes by relegating the Richard Hannon-trained raider to third in the Group 1 Phoenix Stakes at the Curragh in August and will possibly lead O'Brien's 2,000 Guineas challenge at Newmarket.

By the end of the season Roderic O'Connor had surpassed Zoffany as O'Brien's leading three-year-old prospect. After a surprise

## View from Ireland

**Master Of Hounds**

win over his better-fancied stable companion **Master Of Hounds** in a maiden at the Curragh in June, the Galileo colt did not appear again until the Dewhurst in which he made the running until headed by Frankel a furlong out. Only just over a fortnight later he was sent to Saint-Cloud for the Criterium International and accounted for a field that included Maiguri, who had been beaten only narrowly by the British-trained Wootton Bassett in the Prix Jean-Luc Lagardere.

Master Of Hounds gained a bloodless victory in a maiden at Tipperary before finishing third to Casamento at Doncaster. Although he cut little ice in the Breeders' Cup Juvenile Turf on his final start, the Kingmambo colt, out of a Group 2-winning daughter of Sadler's Wells, looks capable of holding his own in smart company as a three-year-old.

While O'Brien failed to exert his customary dominance in the two-year-old category at home, the French Pattern helped him to finish the season on a high. After making a winning debut in a maiden over one mile at Navan in the fourth week of October, the French-bred Montjeu colt **Recital** emerged as a smart staying prospect with a five-length win in the Group 1 Criterium de Saint-Cloud.

A French Group 1 provided the stage for O'Brien's best juvenile filly, **Misty For Me**, to advertise her Classic prospects. After making all to win the Moyglare Stud Stakes on the fourth start of her career, the Galileo filly showed good battling qualities to beat the well-fancied Helleborine in the Prix Marcel Boussac. She deserves her prominent place in the ante-post market for the 1,000 Guineas at Newmarket and the Epsom Oaks.

Just in case anyone thought Pathfork's emergence was a one-off for Harrington, the filly **Laughing Lashes** also showed top-class juvenile form for the yard. The daughter of Mr Greeley captured Group 2 ▸▸

racingpost.com 71

honours when beating Misty For Me by one length in the Debutante Stakes at the Curragh but did not make quite the same progress as the runner-up, who beat her by the same margin in the Moyglare three weeks later.

Behind Misty For Me in the pecking order of fillies at Ballydoyle is the experienced **Together**, who finished fourth in the Moyglare before going down by only a neck to the unbeaten Godolphin filly White Moonstone in the Fillies' Mile at Ascot. The Galileo filly ran eight times, ending the campaign by finishing fifth in the Breeders' Cup Juvenile Fillies' Turf.

In finishing fifth in the Racing Post Trophy, Dunboyne Express was merely fourth-best of the Irish-trained runners, his cause not helped by a failure to settle effectively. However, the form of the two wins achieved on home territory by the Kevin Prendergast-trained Shamardal colt stands up to close scrutiny. The maiden in which he beat Master Of Hounds and Roderic O'Connor at Leopardstown in June was one of the best of the season and he trounced his three rivals in the Anglesey Stakes at the Curragh in July. He should do well at three and has the makings of an Irish 2,000 Guineas contender.

Prendergast also has promising fillies for 2011 in **Kissable**, a daughter of Danehill Dancer who looked in need of a bit further when staying on well to finish third to Misty For Me in the Moyglare, and **Handassa**, a Dubawi filly who was a strikingly emphatic debut winner of a maiden at the Curragh in June.

After a sensational 2009 season with Sea The Stars, last year was relatively quiet for John Oxx. Still, the stable has some interesting unexposed types going into the new campaign, including **Alanza**, an Aga Khan-owned Dubai Destination filly who won well first time out at Listowel.

Dermot Weld's most notable performer in 2010 was **Rite Of Passage**, who beat the O'Brien-trained Age Of Aquarius in the Ascot Gold Cup on his first run since finishing third in the Supreme Novices' Hurdle. Weld's decision to bypass a Champion Hurdle bid in 2011 confirmed that his priority will be the retention of the famed trophy, which has a strong record in terms of multiple winners.

O'Brien's team of older horses will be led by the former Bart Cummings-trained star **So You Think**, the New Zealand-bred High Chaparral colt who ended his career down-under by finishing third in the Melbourne Cup. An intriguing recruit to the European scene, he is reported to be settling in well in County Tipperary and will be aimed at the major middle-distance races.

It will be fascinating to see how So You Think measures up against the other top-class older horses retained at Ballydoyle: **Cape Blanco**, winner of the Irish Derby and the Irish Champion Stakes in 2010 and **Fame And Glory**, the 2009 Irish Derby winner who added two further Group 1 wins to his record as a four-year-old in the Tattersalls Gold Cup and Epsom's Coronation Cup before concluding his season with a hampered fifth in the Arc.

Cape Blanco's front-running defeat of stable companion Rip Van Winkle in the big Leopardstown race was one of the most memorable performance of the season, although his campaign ended with an anti-climax in the Arc.

O'Brien's team of older horses will be further strengthened if **St Nicholas Abbey** can retrieve the level of form that made those close to the stable identify him as a strong contender for last year's Derby before injury intervened.

With the retirement to stud of Starspangledbanner, the sprinting division, never the strongest in Ireland, has suffered a huge loss, but the Edward Lynam-trained **Sole Power**, who beat the star Australian import in the Nunthorpe, should continue to prosper on his favoured fast ground. If not, the new generation of emerging trainers may have something to unleash. ■

# THE DYNAMIC DUO

Official BHA results for the 2010 Flat season plus full horse index

Definitive A-Z of all the horses that ran on the Flat in 2010

**The Form Book® FLAT ANNUAL FOR 2011**
THE OFFICIAL FORM BOOK
ALL THE 2010 RETURNS
**£30**

**RACEHORSE RECORD FLAT 2011**
A-Z GUIDE TO HORSES THAT RAN DURING THE 2010 SEASON
**£26**

**UNBEATABLE OFFER**
**SAVE £11**
BUY BOTH FOR £45
plus FREE p&p for UK customers only

**ORDER NOW**
**RACING POST.com/shop**
ORDERLINE 01933 304858  Quote ref: FBFC11

# Brilliant Cape Blanco to prove a potent force

**With half of his select squad trained at Ballydoyle's stables, Alan Sweetman senses a bumper season for Aidan O'Brien**

### Cape Blanco Aidan O'Brien

One of a select group of older horses to remain in training at Ballydoyle, this brilliant winner of the Irish Champion Stakes will be a force to be reckoned with in Europe's major middle-distance events. Despite Cape Blanco's status as an Irish Derby winner, Aidan O'Brien believes the Galileo colt is best at a mile and a quarter and his demolition of now-retired stable companion Rip Van Winkle at Leopardstown lends credence to that theory. He met trouble in running and was eased down when down the field in the Arc on his final start, so disregard that form.

### Handassa Kevin Prendergast

Having been training since 1963, Kevin Prendergast passed a notable milestone last season when saddling his 2,000th winner. He shows no sign of slowing up and was responsible for several good juveniles in 2010. Anglesey Stakes winner Dunboyne Express was the most accomplished of them and the Hamdan Al Maktoum-owned Handassa is a once-raced filly who showed considerable potential. A well-supported favourite for a seven-furlong maiden at the Curragh in October on her only start, the daughter of Dubawi picked up well to record a wide-margin win. She gives the impression she will be suited by middle distances.

### Misty For Me Aidan O'Brien

Aidan O'Brien's best juvenile colts had to play second fiddle to Pathfork and Casamento but, after losing out to Pathfork's stable companion Laughing Lashes in the Debutante Stakes at the Curragh, Misty For Me turned the tables in the Moyglare. She ended the season on a high with a fine victory in the Prix Marcel Boussac, showing a healthy attitude for a battle in getting the better of the well-fancied Helleborine. The daughter of Galileo looks an authentic Classic contender.

### Pathfork Jessica Harrington

In the past few seasons Jessica Harrington's training operation has evolved significantly, moving from a situation whereby she was principally associated with jumpers to a stage at which she was an almost fifty-fifty split in her team. At the head of a 2010 juvenile squad that also included Moyglare Stud Stakes runner-up Laughing Lashes, the American-bred Pathfork gave the stable a first Group 1 success in the National Stakes. This form was significantly boosted by the runner-up Casamento winning the Beresford Stakes and the Racing Post Trophy. Pathfork is due to start off in the 2,000 Guineas and Harrington hopes he will relax well enough to get the Derby trip.

### Recital Aidan O'Brien

A winning favourite first time out at Navan in October, this Montjeu colt contributed to a good late-season haul for Aidan O'Brien's two-year-olds by winning the Group 1 Criterium de Saint-Cloud the following

## Irish Ten to Follow

month. Often run on heavy ground, as it was on this occasion, over a trip of nearly a mile and a quarter, it is not one of the stronger juveniles races in the European Pattern, but Recital won by an emphatic five lengths. A big colt with plenty of physical scope, he is a half-brother to a Prix Ganay winner and appeals as a type who could mature into an Irish Derby contender.

### Rite Of Passage Dermot Weld

Winner of the 2009 Leopardstown November Handicap in handsome style off a mark of 88, former top bumper horse Rite Of Passage embarked on a career over hurdles, ending last winter's campaign with third place in the Neptune at Cheltenham. It was all very satisfactory, but when Weld decided to prepare him for the Ascot Gold Cup it looked to many observers that this was a shade too ambitious. Not for the first time, Weld proved the doubters wrong when the Pat Smullen-ridden gelding outstayed the Aidan O'Brien-trained Age Of Aquarius for a famous victory. This time around the seven-year-old will be taken much more seriously and has realistic prospects of dominating the staying division.

### Roderic O'Connor Aidan O'Brien

A Curragh winner after making his debut in a Leopardstown maiden that was arguably the best of the entire season, the Galileo colt was no match for the Henry Cecil-trained Frankel in the Dewhurst. However, he emerged with a degree of credit that made his subsequent victory in the Criterium International at Saint-Cloud unsurprising. He boasts quality form involving Maiguri, who had been beaten only a nose in the Prix Jean-Luc Lagardere by the Richard Fahey-trained Wootton Bassett, an unbeaten winner of five races.

### Sole Power Edward Lynam

When Edward Lynam decided to send Sole Power for last season's Nunthorpe Stakes punters completely ignored the Kyllachy colt. It was hardly surprising, as his career record showed only two wins before he was sent to take on the big names of the sprinting division. However, taking advantage of his favoured fast ground, he produced a powerful display under Wayne Lordan to defeat the Golden Jubilee and July Cup winner Starspangledbanner. He is clearly ground-dependent but will be a legitimate Group 1 contender when conditions are right.

### So You Think Aidan O'Brien

Following his success last season with former Australian sprinter Starspangledbanner, Aidan O'Brien will aim for top European honours with this New Zealand-bred colt, who built a powerful reputation by winning the last two runnings of the Cox Plate for training legend Bart Cummings. A son of O'Brien's Derby winner High Chaparral, he added further lustre to a glowing reputation with wins in the Underwood Stakes, the Yalumba Stakes and the Mackinnon Stakes before finishing third behind the French-trained Americain in the Melbourne Cup.

### Zaminast Dermot Weld

Dermot Weld, who has lost his best 2010 juvenile Dubai Prince to Godolphin, has plenty to look forward to with Zaminast, a filly who made her debut in a Galway maiden that the trainer has used as an early stepping stone for a number of high-class types. Weld always places great store by previous experience when sending a two-year-old to Galway and it is significant that he made a rare exception with this daughter of Zamindar. Although it took a while for her to get to grips with a 50-1 outsider, she put in a strong finish to get on top and the form of the race worked out well. She is a half-sister to Famous Name, a prolific winner for the stable in Group 3 and Listed races. ■

# Goldikova to spearhead summer French charge

**Jocelyn de Moubray highlights strength in depth heading for Newmarket and Royal Ascot from across the Channel**

FRENCH-TRAINED fillies have won two of the last three 1,000 Guineas and Khalid Abdullah's Helleborine is likely to be a major contender this year. Helleborine is a sister to the Ladbrokes Sprint Cup winner African Rose and showed plenty of speed on her debut to beat Pontenuovo impressively over six furlongs. The daughter of Observatory was then asked to step up in trip and won a Listed race over seven furlongs and a Group 3 over a mile, without having to make any real effort on both occasions.

The local crowd expected Helleborine to win the Group 1, Prix Marcel Boussac on Arc day and for most of the 1m race she looked like doing so as she travelled easily behind the early leaders. At the top of the straight Helleborine drew alongside Misty For Me in a matter of strides when asked for her effort, but then couldn't get away from her rival and was headed again close home to be beaten a length.

The pair drew clear of the remainder and are both top-class fillies but there seems to be a doubt as to whether Helleborine was beaten by lack of stamina or perhaps by a lack of experience. Helleborine comes from a female family full of stayers; her dam was placed in the Lancashire Oaks, while her grand-dam won over a mile and six furlongs and is a half-sister to the American champion Vandlandingham, who won Grade 1s on dirt over a mile and a half. So you would certainly expect her to last out a mile.

Pontenuovo is a likely rival in the Newmarket Classic, although she is now trained by Roger Charlton having been sold at the end of her two-year-old career for €450,000.

A possible contender for the first fillies' Classic still in France is the Mikel Delzangles-trained **Dealbata**. The filly was not entered in the race at the early closing stage, but the same trainer's Makfi had to be supplemented for the 2,000 Guineas last year that he won. This daughter of Dubawi won impressively on her only start over a mile at Saint-Cloud in November.

None of the French-trained two-year-old colts would have been a match for Frankel and they are most unlikely to take on Khalid Abdullah's champion and other talent due to feature in the 2,000 Guineas at Newmarket. There are, however, several promising juvenile colts in France from last year who may be aimed at the Epsom Derby.

The Niarchos family's **Maxios** is a half-brother to the Arc winner Bago by Monsun and showed a great deal for a colt bred to be a top three-year-old over Classic distances. The last son of Monsun to win a Group race at two was Manduro. Indeed, these are the only two Monsun colts ever to win Pattern races as juveniles. The Jonathan Pease-trained colt won easily on his debut and then came from a long way behind to win a Group 3 over a mile, beating a useful stakes winner. If Maxios comes to hand early enough he could be a major contender at Epsom.

Two other French-trained colts with Epsom entries are the Aga Khan's **Vadamar** and Hamdan Al Maktoum's **Manhaj**. Neither has run in a stakes race but both have shown great promise. Vadamar broke his maiden on his second start over nine furlongs at Maisons-Laffitte and, although he only narrowly beat a well-exposed colt, he won with some style and is likely to improve over longer trips. The John Hammond-trained Manhaj has not run since early August but won both his starts and on the second of them beat some useful horses while giving away weight. Manhaj is by Medicean but comes from a German Classic family and is likely to be aimed at Epsom if everything goes to plan.

One French stable that looks to have plenty of Classic prospects is that of the Wertheimer brothers. Possible stars include **Moonyr**, a son of Hernando who beat Vadamar among others on his only start, **Salto**, a Pivotal colt who was second to Roderic O'Connor in a Group 1 at the end of the year, and **Galikova**, a half-sister to Goldikova.

None of these are likely to be asked to run in Britain before Royal Ascot but Galikova could well be a contender for the Coronation Stakes. An easy winner on her debut, this Freddie Head-trained daughter of Galileo finished fifth in the Marcel Boussac under a considerate ride from Olivier Peslier and at this stage could still be every bit as good as her older sister.

**Goldikova** herself stays in training again and could easily go for another win at Ascot. If she is as good as ever – and there seems no reason why she won't be – she will be hard to beat again.

**Sarafina** and **Lily Of The Valley**, the best two three-year-old fillies in France last year, both stay in training. They are likely to have the Prix Vermeille and the Arc as their principal targets, although both could run at Goodwood or York beforehand. Sarafina's Arc third was a small miracle as she was taken back to last place by a tiring pacemaker at the top of the straight and if she trains on the Aga Khan's filly will always be hard to beat.

The same owner's **Behkabad** also stays in training but his old rival **Planteur** looks more likely to be aimed at top races in Britain. Behkabad is a true middle-distance colt and is another whose campaign will revolve around the Arc, but the Wildenstein family's Planteur has shown on several occasions that he does not stay a mile and a half and his best opportunities to win Group 1s will be in Britain. The Elie Lellouche-trained son of Danehill Dancer is at his best in fast-run races over a mile and a quarter, of which there will be many more in Britain than in France. ■

Goldikova

# Maxios could take the Derby back to France

**Jocelyn de Moubray picks a French team that looks capable of plundering some of Britain's biggest prizes this summer**

### Maxios Jonathan Pease

A half-brother to the Arc winner Bago, Maxios was last year as good a two-year-old as any son of Monsun to date. After a promising juvenile season, he is likely to improve a great deal at three over Classic distances and holds an Epsom Derby entry. This race will suit him better than the French version over a mile and a quarter.

### Manhaj John Hammond

Unbeaten in two starts over six furlongs and a mile in the summer, Manhaj looked to have something special when coming from behind to win at Deauville when giving weight to horses who went on to run well in Group and stakes races. From a German Classic family, the colt is bred for races like the Epsom Derby and Irish Derby and connections have already entered for both these races to show their enthusiasm for hitting the road.

### Arizona Run Frederique Rossi

Arizona Run does not have the traditional profile of a Classic contender as he is trained in Marseille by a private trainer and his biggest successes on the track came at Marseille and at Salon de Provence. Nonetheless, he won his last start over a mile and a quarter by six lengths in a canter beating useful horses and looks to be a potential Group player, whatever his background and lodgings suggest.

### Galikova Freddie Head

This filly looked every bit as good at two as her outstanding half-sister Goldikova. After a brilliant debut victory, she managed to finish fifth in the Marcel Boussac, beaten only five lengths under a characteristically gentle ride from Olivier Peslier. Considering there was more to come on that day, she must be a leading contender for the French fillies' Classics and after that Royal Ascot and beyond.

### Golden Lilac Andre Fabre

Golden Lilac was an easy winner of her two starts over a mile at Saint-Cloud and will try to emulate her dam, who was placed in the Poule d'Essai des Pouliches and the Prix de Diane before winning the Prix du Moulin. She is with a trainer who knows all about success in the Classics and will have every chance if the talent is there.

### Footsteppy Stephan Wattel

Footsteppy came from too far off the pace to be second in a Group 3 over a mile on her last start in 2010. Before that she had looked promising over shorter distances and could compete with the best in a fast-run race over a mile or a mile and a quarter. Trained in Deauville, she could bring high-ranking success to the town at the big Paris tracks or across the water.

**Lily Of The Valley**

### Sarafina Alain de Royer-Dupre

The Aga Khan's older fillies failed to train on last year but Sarafina has had only five career starts and after winning the Diane easily was unlucky when only third in the Arc after being taken back to last place on the home turn by a weakening pacemaker. On this basis, she still has the potential to win the Arc or any of the top middle-distance races and we should expect her to make up for the Aga Khan's disappointments last season.

### Lily Of The Valley Jean-Claude Rouget

Lily Of The Valley won her last seven starts climbing from a seven-furlong race at Mont de Marsan to a Group 1 at Longchamp over a mile and a quarter. On the basis of this form, she will have a leading chance in all the top races for fillies and mares and could be good enough to win Group 1s against colts later in the summer.

### Planteur Elie Lellouche

Planteur was runner-up in the Prix du Jockey Club, Grand Prix de Paris and Prix Niel but will have his chance to win top races as a four-year-old when he is most likely to run over a mile and a quarter having been clearly outstayed over a mile and a half. Because of the pace of such races he would be suited to racing in Britain as he is at his best over a mile and a quarter in a fast-run race.

### Luminieux Andre Fabre

Luminieux looked like a top horse at the beginning of last year, winning brilliantly at Longchamp and Maisons-Laffitte and finishing sixth in the Jockey Club, despite nearly being pushed through the rails on the far side of the course. He disappointed afterwards but if he returns to his best could still be a Group 1 contender in 2011.

Guide to the Flat **2011**

# Blades has the cutting edge for final strides

**Brian Morgan casts his net beyond the big stables to identify the potential winners from some of Britain's smaller yards**

### Autumn Blades Alan Bailey

Cannily named (by Daggers Drawn out of September Tide), this six-year-old gelding is at home both on turf and sand, performing to about the same level on either and unusually boasting a double-figure percentage strike-rate at each of the four all-weather tracks. He stands his racing well, with more than 60 runs, and is capable of holding his own at up to Class Two level. In the past he's been called all sorts of things – 'monkey' being one of the kinder – and had the deadly Timeform squiggle against his name, but since strengthening up and gaining confidence he seems to have left his tearaway days behind him. All forms of racing aids have been employed in efforts to get the best out of Autumn Blades (visor, blinkers and cheekpieces), of which cheekpieces have worked best. He's now hugely consistent over seven furlongs and stays a mile, and appears to be best going left-handed, with a noticeably low success rate on straight tracks. All of his nine wins have been gained by half a length or less – once he gets his head in front he now hates to be denied and will fight all the way home.

### Denton Jeremy Gask

A New Zealand-bred son of Montjeu, Denton came to Britain from racing in Australia, where he had managed two places from seven races. After a lengthy gap of 18 months off the track, he was backed solidly on his British debut but disappointed. It wasn't long before he atoned and justified both the migration and the earlier confidence with five wins from his next eight appearances. He has the ability to travel sweetly in a fast-run event and probably stays a mile and a half – certainly his breeding would suggest so – while the current evidence is that a mile and a quarter is ideal. When not on Polytrack, he needs some juice in the ground. On his debut at Southwell it was maybe the mile trip more than the track that did for him and he'd be interesting on a return visit there. Denton has always been tongue-tied so far and, although he has yet to show he's up to winning in class three company, he may get there this year.

### Hanoverian Baron Tony Newcombe

This admirably consistent Green Desert gelding was campaigned at sprint and seven-furlong trips until joining his current yard, which invited him to test his stamina from race one. This has been the making of him and he's since won four and been placed twice from eight efforts over a mile and a quarter to the St Leger distance, which may have been a few hundred yards too far. It's difficult to know how far he gets at present. Over a mile and six furlongs he seemed to be travelling well, but when asked to make a move at the three pole he soon came under pressure and faded away, yet when winning a mile-and-a-half handicap at York he'd looked more than comfortable at the finish. His other unplaced run, at Haydock, is easily forgiven as he was struck into and lost his stride. Let's guess that a mile and a half is the optimum for now and see what happens. The

**Hillview Boy**

Baron acts on an artificial surface but is much better on turf, where he handles anything from soft through to firm, so there are sure to be plenty of options open to him this campaign. A game and genuine gelding, he has something about him that is reminiscent Sergeant Cecil.

### Hillview Boy Jim Goldie

A late developer, Hillview Boy has had only two seasons of racing and there's every chance of further improvement. His first four starts were in bumpers in the 2008-09 jumps season and he won the second of them, at Musselburgh, before contesting a Grade Two event on the last one. He seemed the type to take to hurdles but has yet to jump one in public. In May 2009 he was switched to the Flat and sprang a 22-1 surprise on his debut over nine furlongs at Hamilton, where his stamina gained him a cosy success. In eight further outings that season he managed a win and five places over ten to 12-furlong trips, on going ranging from good-to-firm to soft, and saw his mark rise to 90, which seemed pretty fair for a horse who had not finished growing. Lightly raced last season with just five appearances, he won a small Listed affair over a mile and a half at Hamilton, displaying again an ability to quicken from off the pace. A fourth-place finish in the John Smith's Cup at York, on unsuitably fast ground and over his minimum needed trip of a mile and a quarter, was followed by a respectable ninth in the Ebor off a mark of 99. He stays two miles at jumps pace but may not quite get a mile and six furlongs in Flat company – this coming campaign should tell us if he can. He shows a distinct preference for softer ground, boasts a 50 per cent strike-rate going right-handed but only eight per cent the other way, and has never been out of the frame for Daniel Tudhope. Whatever happens, he'll be a grand horse to campaign in the good middle-distance handicaps and may yet develop into a Group-class performer.

### Hoof It Mick Easterby

According to my speed ratings from the last Flat season, this is one who stands out as a great improver. Bred from good sprinting bloodlines, the £14,000 he has repaid his £14,000 price tag with interest, as he won ▸▸

on his final appearance of three as a juvenile and added four more victories to his tally in 2010, including a northern hat-trick in May. Hoof It has won twice on good going but has a 60 per cent strike-rate on good to firm and clearly handles soft too, judged on his penultimate start at Haydock, where he failed by just a short head to overcome Cheveton. He ended that first full season with another impressive performance, taking a competitive Doncaster Class Two handicap in some style and showed he can handle the hurly burly of a large field. We know he stays six furlongs and may indeed get seven with another year on his back, but he looks an out-and-out minimum-distance specialist, born with an impressive afterburner that could propel him into the higher echelons of sprinting in 2011. He's certainly in the right hands to live up to that billing.

### Life And Soul Amanda Perrett

Having finished second on each of his final two runs from three as a two-year-old, Life And Soul racked up two victories while finishing unplaced only three times in ten appearances last term. He lost his maiden tag over a mile and a quarter on the Polytrack at Lingfield off what now appears a generous mark of just 75 and was then placed twice at the same trip at Epsom and Sandown. The step up to a mile and a half looked sure to suit this Azamour colt, but it was hard to be sure on his first attempt as he got no sort of run in the King George V at Ascot. Next time out, at Goodwood, he confirmed that earlier impression, looking as if the track was more of a challenge for him than the distance. Only a short head then separated him from the winner Mister Angry at Ascot and Life And Soul was well supported at York when, racing out of his age group for the first time, he ran a thoroughly decent race to get within just over a length of The Fonz. Ignoring his penultimate appearance over an inadequate mile and a quarter, his last run was his best, back at Ascot and two furlongs up in trip, where he stayed on best on softened ground to beat Prompter and gain revenge on The Fonz. He displays a grand attitude, is thoroughly willing, and sticks to his task really well even if he sometimes lacks just a little bit of toe in the closing stages of a race.

### Medicean Man Jeremy Gask

This five-year-old gelding is certainly a character, often carrying his head high or awkwardly, and needs his effort timed to perfection as he seems to get lonely out in front. All forms of racing assistance have been tried to produce some consistency: cheekpieces worked once from five attempts, while blinkers and a visor were fitted once each without effect. He's equally at home on turf and all-weather and seems suited by genuinely good racing ground, while not minding a bit of cut. He has been found out just a bit so far in Class Two company, when his mark went through the 90 barrier, so either he needs to improve a few more pounds or wait until the handicapper drops him a few to be ideally weighted. He should get 7f on breeding and has done so on Polytrack, but on turf he's probably ideally suited by a stiff 6f on good or dead going. Strangely, my best rating for him last season wasn't given for either of his victories (at Wolverhampton over 5f from Gilt Edge Girl and Ascot over 6f from Wildcat Wizard) but instead for his third-last race when he tackled 7f back at Wolverhampton, where he was caught in the final strides by Hajoum. Medicean Man has a good cruising speed and, given some true-run races, should pay his way over the next few months.

### Noble Citizen David Simcock

It says a lot for the improved quality of all-weather racing in recent years that I now tend to use the term 'dual purpose' for a Flat horse that's as good (or even better) on the artificial surfaces as on turf, rather than the traditional Flat/jumps interpretation. This six-year-old gelding is a classic example of this. He has achieved seven placed efforts and some fine speed ratings in defeat. In class two company he has been placed four times but remains winless, so trim your stakes with this in mind. Noble Citizen has been tried at up to a mile and a quarter but all his wins have been over seven furlongs and his best runs last term were both at Ascot, with a staying-on fourth in the Victoria Cup and then a fast finish into the runner-up spot nine weeks later over the same seven furlongs. It's worth noting his 0-12 record going left-handed and the return of 0-17 in blinkers or eyeshield against 3-17 without. A 3-4lb drop from his current mark of 95 should enable him to claim a decent handicap or two at nice prices.

## Sharedah Sir Michael Stoute

Sharedah is an attractive four-year-old Pivotal filly (a half-sister to Maraahel) who didn't see the racecourse until May last year and has just six runs to her name, all of them over a mile and a quarter. So what do we know about her? She stays 10 furlongs at the very least, having made all in both of her wins, a Lingfield maiden and a 0-85 handicap at Newbury. She acts on going either side of good and handled Kempton's Polytrack well enough in November. Her wins both came on left-handed tracks but she's been placed going the other way. To use an old racing cliche, she could be anything. Looking at both her breeding, and her frame at three, Sharedah is highly likely to improve at four and may well get an extra furlong or two. She'll probably be at her best on good racing ground, perhaps even with a bit of moisture in it, and seems to enjoy bowling along at the head of affairs. Given Sir Michael's impeccable record with older horses Sharedah's career should be followed with great interest.

## Shifting Star Walter Swinburn

This quiet achiever is one of two this year to have been winless for two years. His last successes were a hat-trick over six furlongs in the summer of 2008, off marks of 81 to 92 on good and easy ground and on straight tracks. The handicapper dropped him to 89 last May and this Night Shift gelding ran a cracker at Newbury to finish just half a length adrift of Rileyskeepingfaith. His win and place record is better than 50 per cent when racing off 89 or less, so keep a close eye on his mark through the coming campaign. He acts on any going with good in the description but seems to prefer a shade of cut and has been finding Class Two a step too far for him – I believe that sticking to Class Three company whenever possible appears a better option. He's had nine outings in cheekpieces or a tongue strap and achieved just one third place with them, which appears to tell a story. Shifting Star has been asked to race only three times at any trip other than six furlongs, with each of the three over one furlong further and on quickish ground. His pedigree suggests he should get beyond six and he does seem to be getting outpaced rather often. He likes Kempton's all-weather circuit, so a step up in trip there would be interesting. ■

**Life And Soul**

# Carlton House is Derby hope fit for a Queen

**Racing Post bloodstock expert Nancy Sexton picks ten whose breeding suggests they will impress on the track this season**

### Carlton House Sir Michael Stoute

Carlton House entered many notebooks when taking a Newbury maiden by nine lengths from subsequent winner Yaseer. His sire, the Kentucky-based Dubai World Cup winner Street Cry, wasted little time in demonstrating a rare ability to sire top-class horses over a variety of distances worldwide, ranging from dirt performers Zenyatta and sprinter Street Boss in America to Sun Chariot Stakes winner Majestic Roi in Europe. Although Carlton House is a half-brother to a 5f winner, another sibling, the Listed winner Friston Forest, stayed 2m, which suggests the Queen's colt has the resolve for the Derby.

### Dream Ahead David Simcock

Dream Ahead defied his $11,000 yearling price tag by winning three races, including the Middle Park Stakes by nine lengths. The best runner by Godolphin's top-class 6-7f runner Diktat, Dream Ahead's female family offers mixed messages about his ability to stay the Guineas mile. Land Of Dreams won the Flying Childers Stakes and is the daughter of another fast juvenile in Molecomb Stakes winner Sahara Star. But Dream Ahead is a half-brother to four winners ranging from seven furlongs to a mile and a half including Listed winner Into A Dark, although he is admittedly by stamina influence Rainbow Quest.

### Frankel Henry Cecil

Last year's Dewhurst Stakes winner is yet another brilliant prospect by the dual Derby winner Galileo, whose stud record includes Derby winners such as Cape Blanco and New Approach as well as the Group 1-winning stayer Alandi. He is also another example of the powerful Galileo-Danehill cross, which also produced Cima De Triomphe, Roderic O'Connor and Teofilo. Doubts arise over Frankel's ability to stay a mile and a half from his female family: although his grand-dam, Rainbow Lake, won the Lancashire Oaks before producing the high-class middle-distance performer Powerscourt to Galileo's sire, Sadler's Wells, his dam, Kind, was a Listed winner between five and six furlongs. Frankel's three-parts brother, Bullet Train (by Sadler's Wells), stayed a mile and three furlongs well enough to win the Lingfield Derby Trial but Frankel's keen way of racing may see him prove best between a mile and a mile and a quarter.

### Havant Sir Michael Stoute

Havant appealed as a likely Oaks candidate when powering away to win the Oh So Sharp Stakes. Although not short of pace, she has a pedigree that suggests she'll be more at home over middle distances. By the top mile-and-a-quarter performer Halling, who is the sire of 15 Group winners over a mile and a quarter or further, she is a half-sister to mile-and-a-half Italian Group 1 winner Leadership as well as classy jumper Rougham and two-mile Flat winner Tuscan Gold. Providing she can cope with a faster surface – she has a noticeable knee action and won her Group 3 on good to soft – she should be a force in the leading middle-distance events.

## Pedigree Ten to Follow

### Hooray Sir Mark Prescott

Hooray showed relentless improvement once allowed to stride on in her races and won three Group races including the Cheveley Park Stud Stakes. Connections will be hoping she can defy her fast background and go two better than her close relation Dazzle in 1997. Haydock Sprint Cup winner Invincible Spirit produced Prix du Jockey Club winner Lawman in his first crop but generally sires horses in his mould, such as Fleeting Spirit and Zebedee.

### Misty For Me Aidan O'Brien

Misty For Me became the first juvenile filly by Galileo to win a Group 1 when landing the Moyglare Stud Stakes in August, a performance she later confirmed when taking the Prix Marcel Boussac. That she should show more precocity than the average Galileo probably stems from the fact her unraced dam is a half-sister to champion two-year-old Fasliyev (later a noted source of two-year-olds at stud) and a sister to seven-furlong Group 3 winner Kamarinskaya. Misty For Me deserves to be a leading candidate for the 1,000 Guineas but her female family raises questions whether she has the necessary stamina for the major middle-distance events.

### Pathfork Jessica Harrington

Victory in the National Stakes saw Pathfork become the first European Group 1 winner by leading American sire Distorted Humor. Distorted Humor was best over 7-9f on dirt and has since sired a number of top-class runners over even further, including Kentucky Derby winner Funny Cide and Belmont Stakes hero Drosselmeyer. However, while Pathfork is a half-brother to 1m4f winner Psi, his Listed-winning dam showed her best form over a mile and is half-sister to Irish 2,000 Guineas winner Spinning World. This is a strong Niarchos family replete with high-class milers.

### Specific Gravity Henry Cecil

The first indication that miler Dansili was an effective source of good 1m4f runners came when Rail Link took the 2006 Grand Prix de Paris and Arc. Five years on and the family tradition could be upheld by his relative Specific Gravity, who created a good impression when bolting up in a Nottingham maiden for Henry Cecil. Specific Gravity is likely to be seen to best effect over a mile and a quarter or further; out of a mile juvenile winner by noted stamina influence Alleged, he is a half-brother to Linda's Lad, who won the Criterium de Saint-Cloud over a mile and a quarter at two, and from the family of Dahlia.

### White Moonstone Godolphin

Dynaformer's progeny generally progress with age and it will be surprising if unbeaten Fillies Mile winner White Moonstone doesn't follow suit. While Rainbow View, another high-class European juvenile by the Kentucky-based Dynaformer, didn't go on as hoped, his record also contains Lucarno and Wiener Walzer, progressive types with a similar profile to many of his better American runners. White Moonstone is out of a five-and-a-half-furlong stakes winner, herself the daughter of Breeders' Cup Sprint winner Desert Gold. However, her sister, Towanda, was placed over a mile and a half (albeit at a low level) while White Moonstone is already proven over a mile, which bodes well for her Oaks prospects.

### Wootton Bassett Richard Fahey

The presence of several fast runners in the background of unbeaten Prix Jean-Luc Lagardere winner Wootton Bassett suggests he may struggle to get further than a mile. He is the flag-bearer of the record-breaking first crop by 7f Group 2 winner Iffraaj, while his dam is by the high-class sprint two-year-old and speed influence Primo Dominie. Although she was Listed-placed over a mile and a quarter, two of her three previous winners proved best over 6-7f including the Listed-placed sprinter Mister Hardy. ∎

Guide to the Flat **2011**

# Emiyna to thrive when stamina is at premium

**Mark Winstanley selects ten runners he believes are capable of providing profitable viewing during the summer months**

### Elrasheed John Dunlop

For many moons, John Dunlop has been sending out winners for Hamdan Al-Maktoum. This son of Red Ransom is a half-brother to Akmal, who was a decent stayer as a three-year-old when under the care of the Arundel trainer. When Frankel was earning all the plaudits when making a winning debut at Newmarket in August, I was taken by the way this colt ran back in seventh spot. That was his only outing as a youngster and I'm sure his master handler will give him two quiet runs before embarking on a handicap career over longer trips.

### Emiyna John Oxx

Every summer from now until eternity, we will be searching for the next Sea The Stars to emerge from Currabeg. This daughter of Maria's Mon saw a racecourse only once last season, when she ran a race full of promise to finish fifth of 17 over seven furlongs at Leopardstown in October. As her dam's side of the pedigree is packed with stamina, that was a cracking effort from the Aga Khan's filly. Emiyna won't come into her own until she runs over a mile and a half, so what chance she rocks up in the Galtres Stakes at York's Ebor meeting?

### Fair Trade Hughie Morrison

If there was an award given out for the most underrated trainer in Christendom, the East Ilsley handler would get my vote. This four-year-old started off last season by taking a warm maiden over a mile at Newbury on Greenham day in April, but he failed to win another race. David Elsworth trained the gelding last season, so it will be interesting to see how the horse gets on in his new surroundings. Rated 110, he will get all the allowances in Listed and Group affairs, as he has only a maiden success.

### Hurricane Higgins Mark Johnston

When you name a horse after one of the most iconic sporting figures of the past 40 years, he had better be good. Owner Alan Spence made a bold decision to call this son of Hurricane Run after the Northern Ireland snooker legend, but before he made his racecourse bow in a mile-and-a-quarter maiden at Lingfield in January, he was backed off the boards. I received a phone call from my best contact at Middleham very early that Saturday morning urging me to lump on and, despite running greener than a Jolly Giant, Hurricane Higgins obliged comfortably. Spence loves to have a winner at Sandown, so keep an eye out for this exciting three-year-old in the Classic Trial run at the Esher venue in late April.

### Mahayogin Henry Cecil

It was the beast Frankel who got everyone talking about the great times returning to Warren Place last summer and it warmed the cockels of the heart to see the master of Warren Place back in the big time, I remember going into a Deptford betting shop

## Mark Winstanley's TV ten

as an ugly teenager – I'm now an ugly middle-aged fat bloke – when Steve Cauthen was riding, and having my last, and only, pound on an unraced juvenile at Yarmouth. It made all and, from that day until now, HRAC has been a God. Mahayogin was too backward to run as a juvenile, but this colt is out of Shiva, whom Henry trained to win a Group 1 contest in 1999. He could make his debut at the Craven meeting, just like Commander In Chief, who obliged on his debut for Cecil before landing the Derbies at Epsom and the Curragh.

### Primevere Roger Charlton

You don't expect to see a Classic horse on parade on a cold October night at Kempton – although Ghanaati landed a maiden here before capturing the 1,000 Guineas – but the turn of foot this one produced to mow down her nine rivals suggested she is a talented lady. Not many daughters of Singspiel have enough pace to score as a juvenile, so the fact the Beckhampton filly quickened up in such great style bodes well for her three-year-old career. The Oaks trip should be within her compass, with maybe a tilt at the 1,000 Guineas as a good starting point.

### Sea Moon Sir Michael Stoute

When it comes to winning Epsom Derbies, the master of Beech Hurst and Freemason Lodge can teach Aidan O'Brien a thing or two. While many of the lads in the yard believe Carlton House will turn out to be the stable's number one middle-distance colt, I have a gut feeling this Beat Hollow offspring will turn out the real deal. Heavily backed to make a successful debut at Leicester in mid-October, he was given too much to do by Ryan Moore and went under by a short head to a rival with much more race knowledge. Sea Moon made no mistake on his last outing at Yarmouth a fortnight later and, as his dam Eva Luna landed the Park Hill, Sea Moon has every chance of staying the St Leger trip. After he has scored at Epsom in June, of course.

### Signor Verdi Brian Meehan

The master of Manton showed what he can do with an improving four-year-old handicapper last season, when Dangerous Midge ended up winning the Breeders' Cup Turf, having started the campaign on a mark of 88. This horse has a similar profile, as he begins this summer rated 86, having landed a Thirsk handicap in late July off 80. Could lightning strike twice and will this superbly named son of Green Tune be up to winning Group races this season? I will be surprised if Signor Verdi doesn't pick up a lucrative mile handicap, like the Royal Hunt Cup at Ascot in June, on his favoured fast ground.

### Slumber Barry Hills

For many moons, Khalid Abdullah has been sending horses to the legendary Lambourn handler and, according to a good source who lives in the village, this once-raced colt has really thickened up and done well during the winter. The Cacique offspring fell out of the stalls on his only trip to the belts and braces at Newbury last term and he wasn't knocked about at any stage. My news is that Slumber will take in a maiden at the Craven meeting, when his handler loves to put one over his Newmarket counterparts.

### Yaseer Marcus Tregoning

This son of Dansili is from one of Hamdan Al-Maktoum's best families and is related to top-class performers Nayef, Unfuwain and Ghanaati. It's well known that the Lambourn handler never rushes his juveniles, so it was no surprise to see the colt sent off a 40-1 shot on his racecourse bow. But despite looking in need of the run, he chased home the more experienced Carlton House, with 16 horses behind him. Tregoning gave him plenty of time to recover from those exertions and we next saw Yaseer at Lingfield in December, when he was backed as if defeat was no option. It wasn't, and he hacked up. Bred to stay at least a mile and a quarter, Yaseer is expected to make up into a Group performer at the very least. ■

# Gravity can reach Derby heights this summer

**Dave Edwards (Topspeed) selects ten who, according to his figures, have time on their side and can make their mark**

### Alainmaar Roger Varian

Although a five-year-old, Alainmaar has raced only five times but won four of them and is more than capable of adding to his tally. The colt earned Pattern-standard time figures when he romped home under a bumper burden in a valuable mile-and-a-quarter handicap at Epsom in April and followed up with authority in a conditions contest at Lingfield a fortnight later. Pencilled in for a tilt at the Hardwicke at Royal Ascot, he unfortunately suffered a hairline fracture of a pastern, which put paid to that. He is likely to relish a strongly run 1m4f on his return and with some deserved luck could make his Royal appointment this summer.

### Al Kazeem Roger Charlton

Easy to back on his Newbury introduction and considered still a bit weak by his trainer, the Dubawi colt produced a promising display until tiring on the easy ground in the closing stages. It was a different story when he returned to the Berkshire track a fortnight later as he put some well-touted rivals to the sword. Always travelling well, he produced a telling burst of speed at the distance and soon had the race in safe keeping, defeating Thimaar with a yawning gap back to third. This imposing individual should make his mark in the top middle-distance contests.

### Call To Reason Jeremy Noseda

Call To Reason is a lightly raced four-year-old from whom there should be plenty of improvement to come. Runner-up on her only juvenile outing, she was sidelined with a chipped hock until returning at Newmarket nine months later when she landed the odds in fine style. She did not enjoy the run of the race when a disappointing fourth in her first handicap at Goodwood in September and was beaten only a head and a neck when third in a tougher Newmarket race in October. A daughter of Pivotal, she likes ease in the ground and a decent handicap at around a mile could come her way when conditions are favourable.

### High Constable Roger Charlton

This four-year-old son of Shamardal is owned by the Queen and has had only three starts in his life. A beaten favourite on his juvenile debut at Wolverhampton, he then landed the odds with the minimum of fuss at the same track as a three-year-old and the form has worked out pretty well. Switched to turf, he was a promising runner-up behind Meezaan and was being primed for a crack at the Britannia but unfortunately suffered a stress of a foreleg and his campaign was ended abruptly. He has a favourable handicap mark and if things go to plan the Royal Hunt Cup could be on his agenda.

### Ladies Are Forever Geoff Oldroyd

This is the apple of her trainer's eye and no wonder. A six-length winner on her Beverley bow in May, she was then beaten a couple of necks in the Queen Mary but was the one to take out of the race as being a May foal she was almost 15 weeks younger than the winner. The Ascot dash took just under a minute, no mean feat and, after being sidelined with injury, she returned to plunder Redcar's valuable Totepool Trophy in October. Favoured by the weights, she won smoothly. How she fares on her planned return in the Nell Gwyn at Newmarket's Craven meeting will will determine whether she goes for one of the Guineas or reverts to sprinting.

### Sirius Prospect Dean Ivory

From the final crop of Gone West, Sirius Prospect made an eye-catching debut over seven furlongs at Newbury in September when beating all but Mantoba in a decent maiden. Three weeks later at Doncaster he again ran a race brimming with promise taking minor honours behind Bridgefield and earning his top speed figure. He deservedly got off the mark on the Polytrack at Kempton in November and should be effective at between a mile and a mile and a quarter on good to firm ground. He has matured over the winter and can leave his official rating of just 80 well behind.

### Specific Gravity Henry Cecil

Specific Gravity took a keen hold and ran green on his Yarmouth introduction in September but still finished a respectable fourth behind Seelo. The Warren Place colt showed he had benefited from the experience when romping home decisively at Nottingham three weeks later and the stablemate he beat there has since gone one better to give the form a boost. Related to several winners, he took command at the half-way stage at Nottingham and won in a decent time with plenty left in the locker. He holds an Epsom Derby entry.

### State Opera Mark Johnston

With all due respect to Hamilton not many juvenile newcomers merit a Topspeed rating in the high 80s but when one does clock-watchers invariably sit up and take notice. Towering over his rivals in the paddock, the Shamardal colt was never headed on his September debut and once he changed gear in the straight his rivals were left floundering. Made joint-favourite for a valuable Newmarket sales race the following month, he again made the running but he hung left and folded tamely two from home. Although he finished nearer last than first behind Fury, State Opera looks the sort to make a smart middle-distance three-year-old.

### Taqleed John Gosden

Taqleed was progressive last season and gave every reason to believe there will be even more to come from this talented four-year-old. He cut no ice on his only juvenile outing but returned at Nottingham last August to record a resounding wide-margin success. He made no mistake in a decent Newmarket handicap a fortnight later, earning a personal best on this timepiece. Largely on the strength of that performance and despite his relative inexperience, he went off second favourite for the Cambridgeshire and was far from disgraced, finishing sixth beaten just over three lengths. Considering that was only his fourth career start, connections can be optimistic for the future.

### Vita Nova Henry Cecil

An unbeaten daughter of Galileo, Vita Nova's official handicap mark of just 87 may seriously underestimate her talents if the clock is an accurate barometer. The Warren Place-trained filly was a decisive winner of a Kempton maiden on her introduction in June and at Salisbury seven weeks later she followed up with a bit left in the locker despite not liking the deteriorating ground. She earned the best time figures on the card and, while both her wins were over a mile and a half, she may stay further. ■

# Guide to the Flat 2011

## TOPSPEED'S TOP TWO-YEAR-OLDS OF 2010

KEY: Horse name, Best Topspeed figure [Finishing position when earning figure]
(Details of race where figure was earned)

Abjer (FR) 102[1] (1m, Asco, Sft, Oct 9)
Aciano (IRE) 87[1] (1m, Kemw, SD, Sep 20)
Ahlaain (USA) 91[5] (7f, Newm, Sft, Sep 30)
Al Madina (IRE) 92[2] (1m, Donc, Gd, Sep 10)
Amwell Pinot 88[3] (1m 3y, Yarm, GS, Aug 24)
Aneedah (IRE) 91[4] (7f, Newm, Gd, Oct 2)
Approve (IRE) 103[1] (6f, York, Gd, Aug 18)
Arctic Feeling (IRE) 92[6] (5f, Asco, GS, Oct 9)
Ardour (IRE) 91[2] (7f, Newm, Gd, Sep 17)
Attracted To You (IRE) 88[1] (6f 8y, Newb, GS, Aug 14)
Audacious 88[4] (1m, Donc, Gd, Sep 9)
Avonmore Star 94[2] (6f, Wind, GF, Aug 9)
Azrael 88[1] (7f, Newm, Gd, Sep 17)
Ballista (IRE) 90[1] (5f, Hayd, GS, May 29)
Ballybacka Lady (IRE) 87[2] (7f, Curr, GF, Aug 21)
Banimpire (IRE) 89[1] (7f, Curr, GF, Aug 21)
Bathwick Bear (IRE) 89[3] (6f, Ripo, GS, Aug 14)
Bible Belt (IRE) 103[3] (7f, Curr, Sft, Sep 26)
Big Issue (IRE) 93[3] (7f, Asco, GS, Oct 9)
Black Moth (IRE) 90[2] (5f, Linw, SD, Aug 6)
Blessed Biata (USA) 88[6] (7f, Newm, Sft, Oct 2)
Bridle Belle 88[4] (1m, Newm, Sft, Sep 30)
Buthelezi (USA) 94[1] (1m, Donc, Gd, Sep 11)
Byronic (IRE) 92[2] (7f, Donc, GS, Sep 8)
Cai Shen (IRE) 91[1] (1m, Sali, GF, Sep 2)
Capaill Liath (IRE) 89[1] (7f, Asco, GS, Sep 26)
Cape Dollar (IRE) 103[1] (7f, Newm, GS, Oct 16)
Cape To Rio (IRE) 93[5] (5f, Asco, GS, Oct 9)
Casamento (IRE) 121[1] (1m, Donc, Gd, Oct 23)
Casper's Touch (USA) 93[3] (7f, Asco, GF, Jun 19)
Catalyze 90[3] (7f, Donc, GS, Sep 8)
Chilworth Lad 92[2] (6f, Ripo, GS, Aug 14)
Choose Wisely (IRE) 101[3] (5f, Good, Gd, Jul 27)
Chrysanthemum (IRE) 104[1] (7f, Curr, Sft, Sep 26)
Clondinnery (IRE) 95[1] (6f, Cork, GF, Jun 13)
Cochabamba (IRE) 101[2] (7f, Newm, GS, Oct 16)
Cocktail Charlie 94[2] (5f, Muss, GF, Jun 5)
Coeus 87[1] (6f, Linw, SD, Jun 3)
Crown Prosecutor (IRE) 101[3] (6f 8y, Newb, GF, Sep 18)
Crying Lightening (IRE) 90[6] (6f, Asco, GF, Jun 18)
Darajaat (USA) 97[3] (5f, Asco, GS, Oct 9)
Date With Destiny (IRE) 89[5] (7f, Newm, GS, Oct 16)
Deep South 89[1] (7f, Kemw, SD, Jun 23)
Diamond Penny (IRE) 87[1] (7f, Newj, GS, Aug 13)
Dingle View (IRE) 87[1] (5f, Hayd, GS, Aug 7)
Dinkum Diamond (IRE) 95[4] (5f, Asco, GS, Oct 9)
Dordogne (IRE) 90[3] (1m, Newm, Gd, Oct 15)
Dr Green (IRE) 88[3] (6f 110y, Asco, GF, Jul 9)
Drawing Board 88[2] (6f, Pont, GF, Jun 28)
Dream Ahead (USA) 112[1] (6f, Newm, Sft, Oct 1)
Dubawi Gold 104[1] (7f, Asco, GS, Sep 25)
Dunboyne Express (IRE) 106[5] (1m, Donc, Gd, Oct 23)
Dux Scholar 102[2] (7f, Newb, GS, Oct 23)
Earl Of Leitrim (IRE) 89[1] (6f, Donc, Gd, Oct 23)
Easy Ticket (IRE) 99[1] (6f, Hayd, GF, Sep 4)
Ecliptic (USA) 87[1] (7f 16y, Sand, Gd, Jun 11)
Electric Waves (IRE) 105[1] (5f, Asco, GS, Oct 9)
Elzaam (AUS) 105[2] (6f, Asco, Gd, Jun 15)
Emerald Ring (IRE) 88[2] (6f, Naas, GF, Jun 7)
Emma's Gift (IRE) 94[5] (6f, Asco, GF, Jun 18)
Emperor Hadrian (IRE) 89[4] (6f, Curr, Yld, Aug 8)
Excel Bolt 94[1] (7f, Muss, GF, Jun 5)
Excelebration (IRE) 90[1] (6f, Newj, GF, Jul 23)
Excello 89[3] (5f, Asco, Gd, Jun 15)
Face The Problem (IRE) 87[1] (5f, York, GF, Jul 24)

Fifth Commandment (IRE) 89[1] (5f 216y, Wolw, SD, Nov 25)
Fight The Chance (IRE) 87[4] (6f, Wind, GF, Aug 9)
Forjatt (IRE) 87[1] (6f 15y, Nott, GF, Aug 10)
Formosina (IRE) 106[2] (6f 8y, Newb, GF, Sep 18)
Frankel 124[1] (7f, Newm, GS, Oct 16)
Fury 101[1] (7f, Newm, Sft, Oct 2)
Galtymore Lad 103[2] (6f, York, Gd, Aug 19)
Genius Beast (USA) 90[3] (1m, Donc, Gd, Sep 9)
Gentleman Duke (IRE) 87[1] (6f 110y, Slig, Sft, Sep 29)
Glor Na Mara (IRE) 111[3] (7f, Newm, GS, Oct 16)
Gold Pearl (USA) 87[1] (6f, Wind, GF, Aug 9)
Havant 104[1] (7f, Newm, GS, Oct 1)
Hooray 115[1] (6f, Newm, GS, Oct 1)
I Love Me 100[3] (7f, Newm, GS, Oct 16)
Imperialistic Diva (IRE) 87[5] (6f, York, Gd, Aug 19)
Indigo Way 91[2] (1m, Newm, Sft, Sep 30)
Jackaroo (IRE) 88[3] (1m 100y, Kill, GF, Aug 17)
Jerrazzi (IRE) 88[2] (6f, Wind, Sft, Aug 28)
Juliet Capulet (IRE) 88[1] (7f, Leop, GF, Sep 4)
Karam Albaari (IRE) 99[6] (1m, Donc, Gd, Oct 23)
Khawlah (IRE) 89[3] (7f, Newm, GS, Oct 1)
Khor Sheed 90[1] (6f, Newm, Gd, Sep 17)
King Torus (IRE) 88[4] (7f, Asco, GF, Jun 19)
Kissable (IRE) 98[3] (7f, Curr, GF, Aug 29)
Klammer 103[1] (7f, Newb, GS, Oct 23)
Krypton Factor 96[1] (6f, Epso, Gd, Sep 8)
Ladie's Choice (IRE) 101[2] (5f, Curr, GF, Aug 21)
Ladies Are Forever 104[3] (5f, Asco, GF, Jun 16)
Ladyanne (IRE) 87[4] (7f, Newm, GS, Oct 1)
Laughing Lashes (USA) 103[1] (7f, Curr, Yld, Aug 8)
Leiba Leiba 90[6] (5f, Good, Gd, Jul 27)
Libranno 102[1] (6f, Good, Gd, Jul 30)
Lightening Thief (IRE) 97[4] (5f, Curr, GF, Aug 21)
Lily Again 87[5] (7f, Newm, Sep 10)
Look At Me (IRE) 94[2] (7f, Newm, GS, Oct 1)
Lord Of The Stars (USA) 89[7] (5f, Good, Gd, Jul 27)
Loving Spirit 95[2] (1m, Newm, Gd, Oct 15)
Madany (IRE) 88[3] (6f, York, Gd, Aug 17)
Madawi 87[4] (7f, Newb, GS, Oct 23)
Magic Casement 100[1] (7f 2y, Ches, GS, Sep 10)
Majestic Myles (IRE) 91[2] (6f, Good, Gd, Jul 31)
Makeynn 87[1] (1m, Souw, SD, Nov 5)
Man Of The Match (IRE) 88[3] (6f, Hayd, GF, Sep 4)
Mantoba 102[1] (1m, Newm, Gd, Oct 15)
Mappin Time (IRE) 88[4] (5f 34y, Newb, Gd, Jul 17)
Maqaasid 107[1] (5f, Asco, GF, Jun 16)
Margot Did (IRE) 104[2] (6f, York, Gd, Aug 19)
Mariachi Man 93[2] (1m, Donc, Gd, Oct 22)
Marine Commando 96[1] (5f, Asco, Gd, Jun 15)
Masaya 95[1] (7f, Newm, Sft, Oct 2)
Master Of Hounds (USA) 113[3] (1m, Donc, Gd, Oct 23)
Mayson 94[1] (6f, Ripo, GS, Aug 14)
Measuring Time 89[4] (7f, Newm, Sft, Oct 2)
Memen (IRE) 90[1] (7f, Newj, GF, Jul 9)
Memory (IRE) 104[1] (6f, Asco, GF, Jun 18)
Meow (IRE) 105[2] (5f, Asco, GF, Jun 16)
Miss Clairton 87[1] (7f 32y, Wolw, SD, Aug 9)
Misty For Me (IRE) 102[1] (7f, Curr, GF, Aug 29)
Moment Of Weakness (IRE) 90[1] (5f, Dunw, SD, May 8)
Moonlit Garden (IRE) 98[3] (5f, Curr, GF, Aug 21)
Morache Music 90[1] (6f, Wind, Sft, Aug 28)
Moriarty (IRE) 90[1] (7f, Newj, GF, Aug 20)
Move In Time 100[2] (5f, Asco, GS, Oct 9)
Musharakaat (IRE) 89[3] (1m, Donc, Gd, Sep 10)
Nabah 91[4] (7f, Newm, GS, Oct 16)
Nathaniel (IRE) 94[2] (1m, Donc, Gd, Sep 9)
Native Khan (FR) 111[4] (1m, Donc, Gd, Oct 23)
Neebras (IRE) 97[2] (6f, Newj, GF, Jul 8)

# Topspeed ratings

## TOPSPEED'S TOP TWO-YEAR-OLDS OF 2010

New Planet (IRE) 96[1] (5f, York, Gd, Aug 18)
Pabusar 94[2] (5f, York, Gd, Aug 18)
Pathfork (USA) 92[1] (7f, Curr, GF, Aug 21)
Pausanias 97[2] (1m, Asco, Sft, Oct 9)
Penny's Pearl (IRE) 89[1] (5f 161y, Bath, Gd, Aug 21)
Peter Martins (USA) 90[1] (7f, Newj, GF, Jul 30)
Petronius Maximus (IRE) 95[2] (5f, Asco, Gd, Jun 15)
Phoebs 88[1] (5f 10y, Wind, Sft, Oct 4)
Picture Editor 95[1] (1m, Donc, Gd, Sep 9)
Pisco Sour (USA) 95[2] (7f, Newm, Sft, Oct 2)
Poplin 91[3] (1m, Newm, Sft, Sep 30)
Premier Clarets (IRE) 89[5] (6f, York, Gd, Aug 18)
Primo Lady 92[1] (5f, York, GF, May 14)
Princess Severus (IRE) 88[5] (7f, Good, Sft, Aug 28)
Puddle Duck 88[1] (6f, York, Gd, Aug 17)
Purple Glow (IRE) 91[2] (5f, Curr, GF, May 22)
Queen Of Spain (IRE) 89[7] (6f, Asco, GF, Jun 18)
Questioning (IRE) 87[5] (7f, Newm, Sft, Oct 2)
Quiet Oasis (IRE) 99[4] (7f, Curr, Sft, Sep 26)
Radharcnafarraige (IRE) 100[1] (6f, Naas, Gd, Jun 7)
Ragsah (IRE) 89[4] (6f, Newm, GS, Oct 1)
Reckless Reward (IRE) 89[2] (5f, Asco, GF, Jun 17)
Remotelinx (IRE) 87[7] (5f 34y, Newb, Gd, Jul 17)
Rerouted (USA) 96[1] (7f, Newm, Sft, Sep 30)
Rimth 97[2] (6f, Newm, GS, Oct 1)
Roayh (USA) 98[3] (6f, Asco, Gd, Jun 15)
Roderic O'connor (IRE) 118[2] (7f, Newm, GS, Oct 16)
Royal Exchange 94[3] (7f, Newm, Sft, Sep 30)
Saamidd 88[1] (7f, Donc, Gd, Sep 11)
Samuel Morse (IRE) 95[1] (5f, Curr, GF, May 22)
Seville (GER) 119[2] (1m, Donc, Gd, Oct 23)
Sheer Courage (IRE) 88[1] (5f 218y, Leic, GF, May 24)
Signs In The Sand 94[1] (6f, Kemw, SD, Oct 6)
Silvertrees (IRE) 91[2] (7f, York, Gd, Aug 17)

Sir Reginald 90[3] (6f, York, Gd, Aug 18)
Slim Shadey 88[1] (6f 110y, Asco, GF, Jul 9)
Sonning Rose (IRE) 90[2] (7f, Asco, GF, Jun 19)
State Opera 88[1] (1m 65y, Hami, GS, Sep 19)
Stone Of Folca 102[2] (5f, Good, Gd, Jul 27)
Strong Suit (USA) 109[3] (7f, Curr, Yld, Aug 8)
Suntan (IRE) 95[2] (7f, Galw, GF, Aug 30)
Surrey Star (IRE) 96[2] (7f, Newm, Sft, Sep 30)
Sweet Cecily (IRE) 96[2] (5f 34y, Newb, Gd, Aug 13)
Tale Untold (USA) 94[2] (7f, Newm, Sft, Oct 2)
Talley Close 90[1] (7f, Catt, Sft, Oct 5)
Tazahum (USA) 94[2] (7f, Asco, GS, Oct 9)
Temple Meads 110[1] (6f 8y, Newb, GF, Sep 18)
The Paddyman (IRE) 99[4] (6f 8y, Newb, GF, Sep 18)
The Thrill Is Gone 93[3] (5f 34y, Newb, Gd, Aug 13)
Theyskens' Theory (USA) 98[1] (7f, Good, Sft, Aug 28)
Timothy T 88[3] (7f, York, Gd, Aug 17)
Tiz My Time (USA) 96[3] (6f, Asco, GF, Jun 18)
Together (IRE) 99[2] (1m, Asco, GS, Sep 25)
Toolain (IRE) 98[7] (1m, Donc, Gd, Oct 23)
Treasure Beach 92[2] (1m, List, Yld, Sep 13)
Unex El Greco 89[2] (7f, Newb, Sft, Oct 7)
Vanguard Dream 98[1] (7f, Newb, Sft, Oct 7)
Waiter's Dream 110[4] (7f, Newm, GS, Oct 16)
What About You (IRE) 88[1] (5f 216y, Wolw, SD, Nov 26)
Whisper Louise (IRE) 92[1] (7f, Donc, GS, Sep 8)
White Moonstone (USA) 107[1] (1m, Donc, Gd, Sep 10)
Wild Wind (GER) 103[2] (7f, Curr, Sft, Sep 26)
Wootton Bassett 105[1] (6f, York, Gd, Aug 19)
Zaidan (USA) 104[1] (7f, Asco, GF, Jun 19)
Zebedee 103[1] (5f, Good, Gd, Jul 27)
Zoffany (IRE) 112[1] (6f, Curr, Yld, Aug 8)
Zoowraa 90[1] (7f, Redc, GS, Oct 2)

## TOPSPEED'S TOP THREE-YEAR-OLDS AND OLDER HORSES OF 2010

KEY: Horse name, Best Topspeed figure *Finishing position when earning figure* (Details of race where figure was earned)

Aajel (USA) 110[2] (2m, Asco, Gd, Apr 28)
Aattash (IRE) 105[1] (1m 1f 207y, Beve, Gd, Aug 28)
Across The Rhine (USA) 107[3] (1m, Curr, Sft, Sep 12)
Acrostic 112[2] (1m, York, Gd, Aug 19)
Address Unknown 106[2] (1m 2f, Leop, GF, May 9)
Admission 103[3] (1m 2f 6y, Newb, Gd, Apr 16)
Advanced 107[2] (6f, Newj, GS, Aug 28)
Aeroplane 107[3] (1m, Linw, SD, Jan 23)
Afsare 112[1] (1m 2f, Asco, GF, Jul 7)
Age Of Aquarius (IRE) 122[2] (2m 4f, Asco, GF, Jun 17)
Age Of Reason (UAE) 108[3] (1m 4f, Kemw, SD, Nov 3)
Air Chief Marshal (IRE) 112[1] (7f, Curr, Yld, Jul 17)
Akdarena 113[3] (1m 2f, Curr, GF, Jun 26)
Akmal 112[7] (2m 88y, York, Gd, Aug 18)
Al Khaleej (IRE) 108[1] (7f, Newj, GS, Aug 7)
Al Muheer (IRE) 106[4] (7f, Linw, SD, Apr 30)
Al Zir (USA) 111[4] (1m 1f, Newm, Gd, Oct 15)
Alainmaar (FR) 116[1] (1m 2f 18y, Epso, Gd, Apr 21)
Albaqaa 106[3] (1m 2f, Redc, GF, May 31)
Aldovrandi (IRE) 106[3] (1m 14y, Sand, GF, May 27)
Alexandros 117[2] (1m 114y, Epso, Gd, Jun 4)
Allybar (IRE) 112[3] (1m 2f 88y, York, GF, Jul 24)
Almiqdaad 108[2] (1m 1f 170y, Ripo, Gd, Apr 15)
Alrasm (IRE) 107[2] (1m 141y, Wolw, SD, Sep 16)
Alsace Lorraine (IRE) 107[4] (1m, Asco, GF, Jun 16)
Alverta (AUS) 119[3] (6f, Newj, GF, Jul 9)
Ameer (IRE) 106[2] (1m 2f, Newm, Gd, Apr 14)

Amico Fritz (GER) 114[5] (6f, Asco, GF, Jun 19)
Angel's Pursuit (IRE) 113[1] (7f, Kemw, SD, Dec 4)
Anhar (USA) 103[1] (1m 3f 200y, Hayd, GF, Jul 3)
Anna Salai (USA) 110[2] (1m, Curr, GF, May 23)
Antara (GER) 117[3] (1m 1f 192y, Good, Gd, Jul 31)
Antinori (IRE) 104[5] (1m 2f 18y, Epso, Gd, Jun 4)
Arabian Gleam 103[6] (7f, Curr, Yld, Jul 17)
Arctic Cosmos (USA) 122[1] (1m 6f 132y, Donc, Gd, Sep 11)
Arganil (USA) 113[1] (5f, Linw, SD, Mar 20)
Arthur's Edge 104[1] (5f, Souw, SD, Mar 18)
Ashram (IRE) 113[2] (7f, Donc, Gd, Oct 23)
Ask Jack (USA) 103[1] (1m 100y, Cork, Gd, Oct 16)
Aspectoflove (IRE) 111[1] (1m, Asco, GS, Sep 25)
Astrophysical Jet 114[1] (5f, Curr, Gd, Aug 29)
At First Sight (IRE) 117[2] (1m 4f 10y, Epso, GF, Jun 5)
Atlantic Story (USA) 113[2] (7f, Linw, SD, Jan 9)
Atlantis Star 108[1] (1m 141y, Wolw, SD, Sep 16)
Audacity Of Hope 104[6] (1m, Asco, GF, Jun 17)
Australia Day (IRE) 103[2] (1m 2f 7y, Sand, Gd, Jul 2)
Autumn Blades (IRE) 104[2] (7f, Linw, SD, Nov 20)
Aviate 111[1] (1m 2f 88y, York, Gd, May 12)
Await The Dawn (USA) 114[1] (1m 2f, Leop, Gd, Sep 4)
Awsaal 103[1] (1m 3f 200y, Hayd, GF, May 22)
Awzaan 114[3] (7f, Newb, Gd, Sep 17)
Axiom 110[1] (7f, Good, Sft, Aug 28)
Azmeel 111[1] (1m 2f 75y, Ches, GS, May 7)
Bagamoyo 105[2] (6f, Newj, GF, Jul 7)
Bajan Tryst (USA) 105[2] (5f 140y, Donc, Gd, Sep 11)
Balcarce Nov (ARG) 109[2] (1m 75y, Nott, GF, Jun 2)
Balducci 105[3] (1m, Newm, GS, Oct 30)

## TOPSPEED'S TOP THREE-YEAR-OLDS AND OLDER HORSES OF 2010

Balkan Knight 104$^6$ (2m 78y, Sand, GF, May 27)
Balthazaar's Gift (IRE) 118$^1$ (7f, Donc, Gd, Sep 11)
Banna Boirche (IRE) 103$^1$ (1m, Dunw, SD, Dec 8)
Bannaby (FR) 103$^4$ (2m 4f, Asco, GF, Jun 17)
Barney Mcgrew (IRE) 110$^1$ (6f, Newc, GF, Jun 26)
Barring Decree (IRE) 104$^3$ (1m, Curr, GF, Jun 27)
Barshiba (IRE) 112$^1$ (1m 3f 200y, Hayd, GF, Jul 3)
Bated Breath 111$^1$ (6f, Hayd, GF, Jul 3)
Bauer (IRE) 110$^4$ (1m 3f 5y, Newb, Gd, Sep 17)
Bay Willow (IRE) 107$^4$ (1m 4f, Asco, GS, Sep 26)
Beacon Lodge (IRE) 108$^5$ (1m 14y, Sand, Gd, Apr 24)
Beauchamp Viceroy 110$^2$ (7f, Kemw, SD, Nov 17)
Beauchamp Xerxes 106$^2$ (1m, Newm, GF, Oct 30)
Beethoven (IRE) 118$^4$ (1m, Asco, GS, Sep 25)
Bergo (GER) 109$^2$ (1m 6f, Good, Sft, Aug 28)
Bethrah (IRE) 110$^1$ (1m, Curr, GF, May 23)
Bewitched (IRE) 112$^1$ (6f, Asco, GS, Oct 9)
Beyond Desire 103$^2$ (6f, Leop, Gd, Jun 10)
Big Audio (IRE) 103$^6$ (1m 14y, Sand, GF, May 27)
Black Spirit (USA) 108$^4$ (1m 2f 60y, Donc, Gd, Sep 8)
Blizzard Blues (USA) 104$^4$ (1m 4f, Donc, Gd, Sep 11)
Blue Angel (IRE) 105$^2$ (7f, Asco, GS, Sep 25)
Blue Jack 113$^3$ (5f, Newm, GF, May 1)
Blue Maiden 110$^2$ (1m, Asco, GF, Jun 16)
Bob Le Beau (IRE) 103$^1$ (1m 2f 150y, Dunw, SD, Oct 1)
Bobbyscot (IRE) 104$^2$ (1m 2f, Curr, GF, May 23)
Border Patrol 106$^7$ (1m 14y, Sand, Gd, Apr 24)
Borderlescott 116$^3$ (5f, Asco, Gd, Jun 15)
Bould Mover 111$^5$ (5f, Asco, Gd, Jun 15)
Bounty Box 107$^1$ (6f, Pont, Gd, Aug 15)
Bridge Of Gold (USA) 110$^3$ (1m 6f, York, Gd, Aug 18)
Bronze Cannon (USA) 105$^3$ (1m 14y, Sand, Gd, Sep 15)
Brushing 105$^1$ (1m 4f, York, Gd, Aug 19)
Buachaill Dona (IRE) 106$^1$ (7f, Newc, GF, Apr 26)
Bullet Train 113$^5$ (1m 3f 135y, Wind, Sft, Aug 28)
Bushman 115$^2$ (1m 2f 88y, York, GF, Jul 24)
Buxted (IRE) 108$^1$ (1m 4f, Kemw, SD, Mar 17)
Buzzword 109$^3$ (1m 4f, Asco, GF, Jun 18)
Byword 125$^3$ (1m 2f 88y, York, Gd, Aug 17)
Calatrava Cape (IRE) 106$^2$ (1m 4f, Newm, GS, Oct 29)
Campanologist (USA) 117$^3$ (1m 3f 5y, Newb, Gd, Sep 17)
Canford Cliffs (IRE) 130$^1$ (1m, Asco, Gd, Jun 15)
Cape Blanco (IRE) 127$^1$ (1m 2f, Leop, Gd, Sep 4)
Capital Attraction (USA) 106$^3$ (1m, Kemw, SD, Aug 23)
Capponi (IRE) 111$^1$ (1m, Donc, Gd, Sep 11)
Captain Dunne (IRE) 108$^5$ (5f 89y, York, Gd, Aug 17)
Carioca (IRE) 107$^2$ (1m, York, GF, May 14)
Carnaby Street (IRE) 105$^1$ (7f, Newm, Sft, Oct 2)
Carraiglawn (IRE) 112$^6$ (1m 4f, Curr, GF, Jun 27)
Castles In The Air 109$^1$ (7f, Asco, Gd, Jul 24)
Cat Junior (USA) 116$^2$ (7f, Newm, GS, Oct 16)
Caucus 106$^3$ (1m 6f, Good, Sft, Aug 28)
Cavalryman 119$^5$ (1m 4f 10y, Epso, Gd, Jun 4)
Cesare 110$^1$ (1m, Donc, GF, Jul 15)
Chabal (IRE) 114$^1$ (1m 2f 7y, Sand, Gd, Apr 23)
Chachamaidee (IRE) 106$^2$ (1m, Asco, Gd, Jul 23)
Chapter And Verse (IRE) 106$^4$ (1m, Kemw, SD, Nov 27)
Cheveton 104$^1$ (5f, Hayd, Sft, Sep 25)
Chiberta King 104$^1$ (1m 6f, Newm, GF, May 15)
Chinese White (IRE) 116$^1$ (1m 2f, Curr, GF, Jun 26)
Chock A Block (IRE) 109$^4$ (1m 5f 89y, Ches, GS, Aug 21)
Choose Me (IRE) 106$^3$ (1m 2f, Curr, Sft, Sep 12)
Circumvent 113$^3$ (1m 2f, Ayr, Gd, Sep 18)
Citrus Star (USA) 107$^1$ (7f, Good, GF, Jul 29)
City Style (USA) 106$^4$ (7f, Good, Sft, Aug 28)
Cityscape 124$^1$ (1m, Newm, GS, Oct 1)
Claremont (IRE) 113$^1$ (1m 5f 61y, Newb, GF, May 15)
Class Is Class (IRE) 116$^1$ (1m 1f 192y, Good, Gd, May 31)

Classic Punch (IRE) 109$^3$ (1m 4f, Kemw, SD, Sep 4)
Clearwater Bay (IRE) 109$^1$ (1m 4f, List, Sft, Sep 15)
Cloudy Start 106$^3$ (1m, Linw, SD, Apr 30)
Clowance 111$^1$ (1m 4f 5y, Newb, GS, Oct 23)
Coin Of The Realm (IRE) 104$^4$ (1m 4f 10y, Epso, GF, Jun 5)
Colepeper 104$^2$ (1m, Ayr, Gd, Sep 18)
Colonel Mak 106$^1$ (6f, Ayr, Gd, Sep 18)
Confront 107$^6$ (1m 14y, Sand, Gd, Apr 24)
Contredanse (IRE) 111$^5$ (1m 1f 192y, Good, GF, Jul 31)
Corporal Maddox 105$^2$ (6f, Asco, Gd, Apr 28)
Corsica (IRE) 119$^3$ (1m 6f 132y, Donc, Gd, Sep 11)
Critical Moment (USA) 110$^1$ (1m, Good, GF, Jul 31)
Croisultan (IRE) 108$^2$ (6f, Curr, Sft, Sep 12)
Crowded House 107$^4$ (1m 2f 7y, Sand, Gd, Apr 24)
Crown Choice 104$^1$ (7f, Kemw, SD, Apr 21)
Crystal Capella 120$^1$ (1m 4f, Newm, GS, Oct 16)
Cumulus Nimbus 104$^4$ (1m 2f, Linw, SD, Nov 20)
Dafeef 110$^1$ (6f, Newj, Sft, Aug 14)
Dalghar (FR) 117$^2$ (6f, Asco, GS, Sep 26)
Damien (IRE) 107$^2$ (6f, Thir, GF, Apr 17)
Dancing David (IRE) 108$^2$ (1m 2f 75y, Ches, GS, May 7)
Dandino 116$^2$ (1m 4f, Good, GF, Jul 27)
Dandy Boy (ITY) 109$^2$ (1m, Leop, GF, Aug 12)
Dangerous Midge (USA) 121$^1$ (1m 3f 5y, Newb, Gd, Sep 17)
Dansili Dancer 113$^1$ (1m 4f, Kemw, SD, Nov 3)
Dar Re Mi 104$^4$ (1m 2f 7y, Sand, GF, Jul 3)
Darley Sun (IRE) 107$^3$ (2m 78y, Sand, GF, May 27)
Daryakana (FR) 109$^4$ (1m 4f, Asco, Gd, Jul 24)
Debussy (IRE) 121$^3$ (1m 2f, Newm, GS, Oct 16)
December Draw (IRE) 105$^3$ (1m 2f, Kemw, SD, Mar 27)
Definightly 113$^1$ (6f, Good, Sft, Sep 11)
Delegator 116$^1$ (7f, Newb, Gd, Sep 17)
Desert Myth (USA) 110$^2$ (1m, Good, GF, Jul 31)
Dever Dream 110$^1$ (7f, Donc, Gd, Sep 9)
Devoted To You (IRE) 104$^2$ (1m, Curr, Sft, Mar 21)
Dick Turpin (IRE) 120$^2$ (1m, Asco, Gd, Jun 15)
Dirar (IRE) 111$^1$ (1m 6f, York, Gd, Aug 18)
Distant Memories (IRE) 116$^1$ (1m 2f 7y, Wind, Sft, Aug 28)
Distinctive 104$^3$ (6f, Leop, Gd, Jun 10)
Don Carlos (GER) 104$^1$ (1m 2f, Nava, Yld, Oct 6)
Doncaster Rover (USA) 114$^2$ (7f 30y, Hayd, GS, May 29)
Dream Eater (IRE) 119$^3$ (1m, Asco, Gd, Jun 15)
Dream Lodge (IRE) 108$^3$ (1m 208y, York, Gd, Jun 12)
Dreamspeed (IRE) 108$^3$ (1m 4f 5y, Newb, GS, Oct 23)
Drunken Sailor (IRE) 117$^2$ (1m 6f, York, GF, Jul 10)
Dubai Dynamo 106$^1$ (7f, Newm, GF, May 28)
Dubawi Phantom 105$^2$ (1m 3f 106y, Ling, GF, May 8)
Duff (IRE) 116$^4$ (7f, Donc, Gd, Sep 11)
Duncan 123$^2$ (1m 4f, Asco, Gd, Jun 19)
Dunelight (IRE) 110$^1$ (7f 32y, Wolw, SD, Mar 13)
Dyna Waltz 105$^1$ (1m 3f 106y, Ling, GF, May 8)
Eastern Aria (UAE) 114$^1$ (1m 6f 132y, Donc, Gd, Sep 9)
Edge Closer 106$^5$ (6f, Wind, GF, Jun 26)
Eleanora Duse (IRE) 115$^3$ (1m 4f, York, Gd, Aug 19)
Electrolyser (IRE) 115$^2$ (2m, Good, GF, Jul 29)
Elliptical (USA) 104$^2$ (1m 2f 6y, Newb, GF, Sep 18)
Elnawin 109$^2$ (6f, Sali, GF, Jun 13)
Elusive Pimpernel (USA) 116$^1$ (1m, Newm, GF, Apr 15)
Emperor Claudius (USA) 108$^1$ (1m, Curr, GF, Jun 27)
Emulous 108$^1$ (7f 100y, Tipp, Sft, Oct 3)
Enact 104$^2$ (6f, Newm, GS, May 2)
Equiano (FR) 124$^2$ (6f, Newj, GF, Jul 9)
Evens And Odds (IRE) 110$^1$ (6f, Good, Gd, Jul 31)
Extraterrestrial 105$^4$ (1m 141y, Wolw, SD, Mar 13)
Fair Trade 113$^4$ (1m, Sali, GF, Aug 12)
Fallen Idol 107$^1$ (1m 14y, Sand, GF, May 27)
Fame And Glory 125$^1$ (1m 4f 10y, Epso, Gd, Jun 4)
Famous Name 121$^1$ (1m 1f, Leop, Yld, Jul 22)

# Topspeed ratings

## TOPSPEED'S TOP THREE-YEAR-OLDS AND OLDER HORSES OF 2010

Fanunalter 113 $^8$ (1m, Sali, GF, Aug 12)
Fareer 112 $^1$ (1m, York, GF, May 13)
Fathsta (IRE) 107 $^1$ (6f, York, Sft, Oct 9)
Fencing Master 114 $^7$ (1m, Newm, GF, May 1)
Ferdoos 107 $^2$ (1m 4f, Asco, GS, Sep 24)
Fictional Account (IRE) 106 $^1$ (2m, Asco, GS, Sep 26)
Field Day (IRE) 109 $^1$ (1m, Asco, Gd, Jul 23)
Field Of Dream 109 $^1$ (7f, Newm, Gd, May 29)
Fiery Lad (IRE) 114 $^1$ (1m 2f 18y, Epso, Gd, Jun 4)
Fighter Boy (IRE) 106 $^2$ (1m 1f, Newm, Gd, Apr 14)
Film Score (USA) 105 $^4$ (1m 2f, Asco, GF, Jun 17)
Final Drive (IRE) 105 $^1$ (1m 1f 103y, Wolw, SS, Dec 29)
Finjaan 105 $^5$ (7f, Newb, Gd, Sep 17)
First City 106 $^1$ (1m, Newb, Gd, Jul 17)
Fitz Flyer (IRE) 104 $^3$ (5f, Souw, SS, Jan 1)
Flambeau 104 $^2$ (6f, Newj, GF, Jul 17)
Fleeting Spirit (IRE) 115 $^5$ (6f, Newj, GF, Jul 9)
Flipando (IRE) 106 $^1$ (5f 216y, Wolw, SD, Feb 12)
Flora Trevelyan 105 $^3$ (1m 14y, Sand, GF, Aug 21)
Flying Cloud (IRE) 113 $^2$ (1m 2f, Curr, GF, Jun 26)
Flying Cross (IRE) 113 $^3$ (1m 6f, Curr, Sft, Sep 11)
Forgotten Voice (IRE) 114 $^7$ (1m, Asco, GF, Jun 16)
Forte Dei Marmi 116 $^1$ (1m 2f 6y, Newb, GF, Sep 18)
Fox Hunt (IRE) 107 $^2$ (1m 2f 75y, Ches, GS, Sep 25)
Fravashi (AUS) 115 $^3$ (7f, York, GF, Aug 20)
Free Agent 112 $^2$ (2m, Asco, GS, Sep 26)
Free Judgement (USA) 117 $^2$ (1m, Curr, GF, May 22)
Fuisse (FR ) 115 $^7$ (1m 2f, Newm, GS, Oct 16)
Gallagher 104 $^6$ (7f, Asco, Gd, Jul 24)
Gallic Star (IRE) 104 $^2$ (1m 1f 198y, Sali, Gd, Aug 11)
Gene Autry (USA) 106 $^2$ (6f, Asco, Gd, Aug 7)
Genki (IRE) 114 $^3$ (6f, Hayd, GF, Sep 4)
Georgebernardshaw (IRE) 105 $^5$ (7f 30y, Hayd, GS, May 29)
Gertrude Bell 104 $^1$ (1m 4f 10y, Epso, Gd, Jun 4)
Gile Na Greine (IRE) 113 $^2$ (1m, Asco, GF, Jun 18)
Gilt Edge Girl 109 $^1$ (6f, Leop, Gd, Jun 10)
Gitano Hernando 120 $^4$ (1m 2f, Newm, GS, Oct 16)
Glamorous Spirit (IRE) 105 $^2$ (5f, Linw, SD, Mar 20)
Glass Harmonium (IRE) 116 $^6$ (1m 2f, Newm, GS, Oct 16)
Gold Bubbles (USA) 106 $^2$ (1m 2f 88y, York, Gd, May 12)
Golden Desert (IRE) 107 $^2$ (7f, Newm, Gd, Oct 15)
Golden Destiny (IRE) 108 $^2$ (5f 34y, Newb, GF, Sep 18)
Golden Stream (IRE) 109 $^2$ (7f, Ling, GF, May 8)
Golden Sword 111 $^4$ (1m 5f 61y, Newb, GS, Aug 14)
Goldikova (IRE) 125 $^1$ (1m, Asco, Gd, Jun 15)
Gramercy (IRE) 105 $^1$ (6f, Asco, Gd, Aug 7)
Green Moon (IRE) 108 $^1$ (1m 2f, Newm, GF, May 29)
Greyfriarschorista 107 $^3$ (1m, Asco, GF, Jun 17)
Group Therapy 112 $^2$ (5f 6y, Sand, GF, Jul 3)
Habaayib 108 $^2$ (7f, Newb, Gd, Apr 17)
Halicarnassus (IRE) 109 $^4$ (1m 2f 110y, Curr, GF, May 23)
Hamish Mcgonagall 112 $^1$ (5f 89y, York, Gd, Aug 17)
Harbinger 135 $^1$ (1m 4f, Asco, Gd, Jul 24)
Harris Tweed 117 $^1$ (1m 4f 66y, Ches, Sft, Sep 11)
Harrison George (IRE) 114 $^1$ (7f 30y, Hayd, GS, Jul 17)
Hearts Of Fire 119 $^3$ (1m, Asco, Gd, Jun 15)
Heliodor (USA) 110 $^3$ (1m 4f, Newm, GS, May 2)
Hen Night (IRE) 107 $^4$ (1m, Leop, Gd, Sep 4)
Hibaayeb 109 $^1$ (1m 4f, Asco, GF, Jun 17)
High Heeled (IRE) 117 $^3$ (1m 4f 10y, Epso, Gd, Jun 4)
High Standing (USA) 114 $^1$ (5f, Hayd, Gd, May 29)
High Twelve (IRE) 106 $^1$ (1m 141y, Wolw, SD, Sep 23)
Hillview Boy (IRE) 104 $^4$ (1m 2f 88y, York, GF, Jul 10)
Himalya (IRE) 117 $^3$ (7f, Donc, Gd, Sep 11)
Hitchens (IRE) 110 $^3$ (6f, Ayr, Gd, Sep 16)
Holberg (UAE) 117 $^1$ (1m 4f, Good, GF, Jun 4)
Hoof It 106 $^1$ (5f, Donc, Gd, Oct 23)
Hot Prospect 116 $^1$ (1m 2f 95y, Hayd, Sft, Aug 7)

Hujaylea (IRE) 104 $^1$ (7f, Curr, Sft, Sep 26)
Huntdown (USA) 109 $^4$ (7f, Newb, Gd, Sep 17)
Icon Dream (IRE) 105 $^2$ (1m 4f 66y, Ches, GS, May 6)
Illustrious Blue 117 $^1$ (2m, Good, GF, Jul 29)
Imposing 111 $^2$ (1m 4f, Asco, GF, Jun 19)
Imprimis Tagula (IRE) 104 $^2$ (6f, Souw, SD, Jan 26)
Indian Days 113 $^1$ (1m 1f 192y, Good, GF, Jul 27)
Inler (IRE) 110 $^1$ (7f, Donc, Gd, Oct 23)
Invincible Ash (IRE) 105 $^1$ (5f, Tipp, Gd, Aug 6)
Invisible Man 111 $^2$ (1m, Good, GF, Jul 30)
Inxile (IRE) 111 $^1$ (6f, Donc, Sft, Mar 27)
Iver Bridge Lad 111 $^4$ (7f, Donc, GS, Nov 6)
Jaconet (USA) 111 $^1$ (6f, Linw, SD, Feb 27)
Jacqueline Quest (IRE) 111 $^1$ (1m, Newm, GS, May 2)
Jakkalberry (IRE) 106 $^6$ (1m 2f 88y, York, Gd, Aug 17)
Jan Vermeer (IRE) 119 $^3$ (1m 4f, Curr, GF, Jun 27)
Jedi 105 $^4$ (1m 4f 5y, Newb, GS, Oct 23)
Jet Away 111 $^2$ (1m 2f 18y, Epso, Gd, Aug 30)
Jimmy Styles 109 $^4$ (6f, Sali, GF, Jun 13)
Johannes (IRE) 105 $^1$ (5f, York, GF, May 13)
Jonny Mudball 111 $^1$ (6f, Newc, GF, Jun 26)
Joshua Tree (IRE) 114 $^5$ (1m 6f 132y, Donc, Gd, Sep 11)
Joy And Fun (NZ ) 105 (6f, Asco, GF, Jun 19)
Judge 'n Jury 104 $^8$ (5f, Curr, Gd, Aug 29)
Jukebox Jury (IRE) 120 $^1$ (1m 4f, Newm, GF, May 1)
Kakatosi 107 $^1$ (7f, Kemw, SD, Aug 16)
Kaldoun Kingdom (IRE) 111 $^2$ (6f, York, GF, Jul 24)
Kaptain Kirkup (IRE) 107 $^1$ (7f, York, Gd, May 12)
Kargali (IRE) 109 $^3$ (7f, Dunw, SD, Feb 26)
Keredari (IRE) 107 $^2$ (7f 100y, Tipp, Sft, Oct 3)
King Jock (USA) 107 $^2$ (1m, Leop, GF, May 9)
King Of Dixie (USA) 112 $^1$ (1m, Asco, Gd, Apr 28)
King Of Wands 114 $^3$ (2m 88y, York, Gd, Aug 18)
Kingdom Of Fife 114 $^3$ (1m 2f, Asco, GF, Jun 18)
Kings Destiny 111 $^1$ (1m 2f, Linw, SD, Apr 30)
Kings Gambit (SAF) 116 $^2$ (1m 2f 88y, York, GS, Oct 8)
Kingsfort (USA) 111 $^1$ (1m, Newm, GS, Oct 30)
Kingsgate Native (IRE) 121 $^1$ (5f, Hayd, GF, May 22)
Kinsale King (USA) 119 $^3$ (6f, Asco, GF, Jun 19)
Kirklees (IRE) 113 $^4$ (1m 2f, Ayr, Gd, Sep 18)
Kitty Kiernan 104 $^1$ (7f, Naas, GF, Jun 7)
Knot In Wood (IRE) 112 $^4$ (6f, Asco, GF, Jun 19)
La De Two (IRE) 113 $^1$ (1m 4f, York, GF, Jul 9)
Laaheb 118 $^1$ (1m 4f, Asco, GS, Sep 26)
Laddies Poker Two (IRE) 114 $^1$ (6f, Asco, GF, Jun 19)
Lady Darshaan (IRE) 104 $^6$ (1m, Curr, GF, May 23)
Lady Jane Digby 108 $^3$ (1m 3f 200y, Hayd, GF, Jul 3)
Lady Lupus (IRE) 104 $^3$ (1m 4f, Curr, Yld, Jul 18)
Lady Of The Desert (USA) 121 $^1$ (6f, Asco, GS, Sep 26)
Latin Love (IRE) 108 $^1$ (1m 1f, Curr, Yld, Jul 18)
Les Fazzani (IRE) 114 $^1$ (1m 3f 200y, Hayd, GS, May 29)
Light From Mars 105 $^5$ (7f, Kemw, SD, Apr 3)
Lillie Langtry (IRE) 117 $^1$ (1m, Leop, Gd, Sep 4)
Lolly For Dolly (IRE) 104 $^1$ (7f, Curr, Yld, May 3)
Long Lashes (USA) 106 $^2$ (1m 14y, Sand, GF, Aug 21)
Look Busy (IRE) 106 $^1$ (5f, Beve, GF, May 29)
Lord Shanakill (USA) 117 $^1$ (7f, Good, GF, Jul 27)
Lord Zenith 108 $^7$ (1m 2f, Asco, GF, Jun 17)
Lost In The Moment (IRE) 104 $^1$ (1m 2f 6y, Newb, GS, Oct 23)
Love Delta (USA) 105 $^1$ (5f, Souw, SS, Dec 7)
Lovelace 114 $^1$ (7f 30y, Hayd, GF, May 8)
Lowdown (IRE) 106 $^1$ (6f 5y, Hami, GS, Jul 16)
Lui Rei (ITY) 107 $^2$ (6f, Donc, Gd, Jul 31)
Luisant 114 $^1$ (6f, Curr, Sft, Oct 10)
Lush Lashes 104 $^4$ (1m 2f, Curr, Sft, Sep 12)
Mabait 116 $^1$ (1m 4y, Pont, GF, Jul 25)
Mahadee (IRE) 111 $^1$ (7f, Linw, SD, Feb 27)
Main Aim 116 $^3$ (7f, Newm, GS, Oct 16)

## TOPSPEED'S TOP THREE-YEAR-OLDS AND OLDER HORSES OF 2010

Majestic Concorde (IRE) 104[4] (2m 2f 147y, Ches, Gd, May 5)
Makfi 123[1] (1m, Newm, GF, May 1)
Malcheek (IRE) 106[1] (7f, Souw, SD, Dec 12)
Man Of Iron (USA) 106[4] (1m 4f, Kemw, SD, Nov 3)
Manifest 121[1] (1m 6f, York, GF, May 14)
Manighar (FR ) 115[2] (1m 4f, Good, GF, Jun 4)
Marchand D'or (FR ) 110 (6f, Asco, GF, Jun 19)
Marching (AUS) 111[2] (7f, York, GF, May 22)
Markab 121[1] (6f, Hayd, GF, Sep 4)
Martyr 109[1] (1m 6f, Good, GF, Jul 27)
Masamah (IRE) 107[1] (5f, Asco, GF, Jul 25)
Mass Rally (IRE) 104[2] (7f, Asco, GS, Sep 24)
Masta Plasta (IRE) 109[2] (5f, Beve, GF, May 29)
Mastery 113[1] (1m 4f, Kemw, SD, Nov 3)
Mata Keranjang (USA) 104[3] (7f, Newm, Gd, Apr 14)
Matsunosuke 110[1] (5f 20y, Wolw, SD, Jan 17)
Mawatheeq (USA) 109 (1m 2f, Asco, GF, Jun 16)
Meezaan (IRE) 104[2] (7f, Donc, GF, May 1)
Meeznah (USA) 115[2] (1m 4f 10y, Epso, Gd, Jun 4)
Merchant Of Dubai 107[2] (1m 5f, Nava, Gd, Apr 25)
Mia's Boy 113[2] (7f 30y, Hayd, GF, May 8)
Midas Touch 121[2] (1m 4f, Curr, GF, Jun 27)
Midday 124[1] (1m 4f, York, Gd, Aug 19)
Mikhail Glinka (IRE) 107[1] (2m, Asco, GF, Jun 18)
Mirror Lake 113[2] (1m 1f 192y, Good, GS, Sep 11)
Misheer 104[4] (7f, Newb, Gd, Apr 17)
Miss Gorica (IRE) 106[2] (6f, Cork, Yld, Apr 30)
Miss Jean Brodie (USA) 105[2] (1m 4f, Curr, Yld, Jul 18)
Mister Hughie (IRE) 108[1] (5f, Beve, Gd, Aug 28)
Mister Manannan (IRE) 106[3] (6f, Hayd, GS, May 29)
Modeyra 110[1] (1m 2f, Newm, Gd, Oct 15)
Monitor Closely (IRE) 110[5] (1m 3f 5y, Newb, Gd, Sep 17)
Monsieur Joe (IRE) 104[1] (5f, York, Gd, Aug 19)
Montaff 106[5] (2m 78y, Sand, GF, May 27)
Monterosso 117[4] (1m 4f, Curr, GF, Jun 27)
Moon Indigo 105[8] (2m 88y, York, Gd, Aug 18)
Moorhouse Lad 105[8] (5f, Good, Gd, Jul 29)
Mosqueras Romance 107[2] (7f, Donc, Gd, Sep 9)
Motrice 112[3] (2m 2f, Donc, Gd, Sep 10)
Mount Helicon 104[2] (2m, Galw, Yld, Jul 26)
Mudaaraah 105[3] (1m 1f 198y, Sali, Gd, Aug 11)
Mullionmileanhour (IRE) 114[2] (6f, Newm, GF, Apr 15)
Munsef 112[3] (1m 5f 89y, Ches, GS, May 7)
Music Show (IRE) 119[1] (1m, Newj, GF, Jul 7)
Myplacelater 112[2] (1m 4f, Newm, GS, Oct 16)
Mystery Star (IRE) 104[3] (1m 4f, York, GF, May 14)
Nanton (USA) 111[5] (1m 2f 88y, York, GF, Jul 24)
Nationalism 108[1] (1m 1f, Good, Sft, Sep 11)
Navajo Chief 108[1] (7f, Donc, Gd, Sep 8)
Nazreef 106[1] (1m, Souw, SD, Dec 14)
Nicconi (AUS) 116[4] (5f, Asco, Gd, Jun 15)
Nideeb 110[2] (1m 4f, Kemw, SD, Nov 27)
Noble Storm (USA) 109[1] (5f, Souw, SD, Nov 5)
Noble's Promise (USA) 115[5] (1m, Asco, Gd, Jun 15)
Noll Wallop (IRE) 111[1] (1m, Leop, Sft, Mar 28)
Nouriya 105[1] (1m 2f 88y, York, Gd, Jul 23)
Noverre To Go (IRE) 106[1] (6f, Newm, Gd, May 30)
Oasis Dancer 108[1] (7f, Newb, Gd, Jul 17)
Opinion Poll (IRE) 116[1] (2m 88y, York, Gd, Aug 18)
Ordnance Row 107[2] (1m 67y, Wind, GF, May 10)
Ottoman Empire (FR ) 108[1] (1m 2f, Kemw, SD, Nov 2)
Ouqba 121[2] (1m, Newb, GF, May 15)
Pachattack (USA) 108[1] (1m 4f 5y, Newb, GF, Aug 1)
Paco Boy (IRE) 127[2] (1m, Asco, Gd, Jun 15)
Palace Moon 114[2] (7f, Newj, GF, Jul 9)
Palavicini (USA) 111[3] (1m 1f, Newm, GF, Apr 15)
Pallodio (IRE) 110[3] (1m 2f, Linw, SD, Mar 20)
Parisian Pyramid (IRE) 104[2] (6f, Ripo, Gd, Aug 21)

Peligroso (FR ) 107[1] (1m 3f 183y, Leic, Hvy, Oct 25)
Penitent 116[1] (1m 14y, Sand, Gd, Sep 15)
Petara Bay (IRE) 111[3] (1m 5f 61y, Newb, GF, May 15)
Philario (IRE) 104[2] (7f, Leop, Sft, Mar 28)
Piccadilly Filly (IRE) 107[3] (5f, York, GF, Aug 20)
Pink Symphony 108[2] (1m 1f 192y, Good, GF, Sep 22)
Pipedreamer 111[4] (1m, Newb, GF, May 15)
Piscean (USA) 104[1] (5f 216y, Wolw, SD, Nov 25)
Poet 118[3] (1m 1f 192y, Good, GS, Sep 11)
Poet's Place (USA) 109[1] (6f, Hayd, GS, Aug 7)
Poet's Voice 123[1] (1m, Asco, GS, Sep 25)
Pollen (IRE) 105[1] (1m, Curr, Sft, Mar 21)
Polly's Mark (IRE) 110[2] (1m 6f, Good, GF, Jul 29)
Pompeyano (IRE) 111[5] (1m 5f 61y, Newb, GS, Aug 14)
Premio Loco (USA) 122[3] (1m, Good, GF, Jul 28)
Pressing (IRE) 120[2] (1m 14y, Sand, Gd, Apr 24)
Presvis 110[9] (1m 2f, Asco, GF, Jun 16)
Prime Defender 116[1] (6f, York, Gd, May 12)
Prime Exhibit 106[1] (7f 32y, Wolw, SF, Jul 12)
Prince Siegfried (FR ) 114[1] (1m 2f 18y, Epso, Gd, Aug 30)
Principal Role (USA) 104[1] (1m 2f 6y, Newb, GF, May 14)
Prizefighting (USA) 105[5] (1m 2f 60y, Donc, Gd, Sep 8)
Profound Beauty (IRE) 116[2] (1m 6f, Curr, GF, Jun 26)
Prohibit 112[1] (5f, Donc, Gd, Sep 8)
Prompter 109[6] (1m 4f, Donc, GS, Nov 6)
Prospect Wells (FR ) 107[1] (1m 4f 8y, Pont, GF, Jun 20)
Psychic Ability (USA) 104[1] (1m 2f 50y, Nott, GF, Oct 14)
Puff (IRE) 109[1] (7f, Newb, Gd, Apr 17)
Pure Champion (IRE) 114[8] (1m, Asco, Gd, Jun 15)
Purple Moon (IRE) 116[3] (2m 4f, Asco, GF, Jun 17)
Pyrrha 111[1] (7f, Ling, GF, May 8)
Quadrille 111[1] (1m, Newm, GF, May 13)
Quest For Success (IRE) 104[3] (5f, Newm, Sft, Sep 30)
Quick Wit 111[1] (7f, Linw, SD, Oct 28)
Rain Delayed (IRE) 110[2] (5f, Naas, GF, Jun 7)
Rainbow Peak (IRE) 117[2] (1m 208y, York, GF, Aug 20)
Rainfall (IRE) 116[1] (7f, Asco, GS, Sep 25)
Rajik (IRE) 111[4] (1m 6f, Curr, Sft, Sep 11)
Rakaan (IRE) 106[2] (7f, Good, GF, Jul 29)
Ransom Note 112[1] (1m, York, Gd, Aug 19)
Rasmy 108[3] (1m 2f 75y, Ches, GS, May 7)
Rayeni (IRE) 106[4] (7f, Curr, Yld, Jul 17)
Rebel Soldier (IRE) 116[1] (1m 4f, Good, GF, Jul 27)
Recharge (IRE) 111[2] (1m 2f 110y, Curr, GF, May 23)
Record Breaker (IRE) 104[5] (1m 4f, Linw, SD, Apr 10)
Red Badge (IRE) 118[1] (1m 1f 192y, Good, GS, Sep 11)
Red Cadeaux 105[2] (2m 2f, Newm, Gd, Sep 18)
Red Jazz (USA) 122[3] (1m, Asco, GS, Sep 25)
Redford (IRE) 117[1] (7f, Asco, GS, Sep 25)
Redwood 117[1] (1m 4f, Good, GF, Jul 30)
Regal Parade 117[1] (6f 8y, Newb, Gd, Jul 17)
Reggane 108[2] (1m 114y, Epso, GF, Jun 5)
Remember When (IRE) 112[3] (1m 4f 10y, Epso, Gd, Jun 4)
Reverence 108[2] (5f, Curr, GF, Jun 27)
Rewilding 124[1] (1m 4f, York, Gd, Aug 17)
Riggins (IRE) 111[2] (1m, Asco, GF, Jun 16)
Rileyskeepingfaith 108[2] (6f, Hayd, GF, Jul 3)
Rio De La Plata (USA) 118[1] (1m 208y, York, GF, Aug 20)
Rip Van Winkle (IRE) 129[2] (1m, Good, GF, Jul 28)
Rite Of Passage 122[1] (2m 4f, Asco, GF, Jun 17)
Rock And Roll Kid (IRE) 106[6] (1m, Curr, GF, Jun 27)
Rock Jock (IRE) 107[3] (7f, Asco, GF, Jun 16)
Rodrigo De Torres 107[1] (7f, Donc, GF, May 1)
Rosanara (FR ) 104[7] (1m 1f 192y, Good, GF, Jul 31)
Rose Blossom 109[2] (5f, Donc, Gd, Sep 8)
Roses For The Lady (IRE) 109[3] (1m 6f, Curr, GF, Jun 26)
Rosika 106[2] (1m 6f, York, GF, Aug 18)
Rowe Park 106[1] (5f, Asco, GF, Jul 10)

# Topspeed ratings

## TOPSPEED'S TOP THREE-YEAR-OLDS AND OLDER HORSES OF 2010

Royal Destination (IRE) 109[1] (1m 2f 60y, Donc, Gd, Sep 9)
Rumoush (USA) 112[2] (1m 6f 132y, Donc, Gd, Sep 9)
Run For The Hills 104[3] (6f, Newm, Gd, May 30)
Sabotage (UAE) 111[2] (1m 5f 61y, Newb, GF, May 15)
Safari Sunup (IRE) 106[2] (1m 2f, Kemw, SD, Mar 27)
Sahara Kingdom (IRE) 107[2] (1m, Souw, SD, Oct 5)
Sahpresa (USA) 119[1] (1m, Newm, Sft, Oct 2)
Sajjhaa 113[2] (1m, Asco, GS, Sep 25)
Salden Licht 108[5] (1m 4f, Donc, GS, Nov 6)
Salute Him (IRE) 109[4] (1m 6f, York, Gd, Aug 18)
Samuel 116[1] (2m 2f, Donc, Gd, Sep 10)
Sans Frontieres (IRE) 123[1] (1m 5f 61y, Newb, GS, Aug 14)
Santo Padre (IRE) 109[3] (5f, Curr, Gd, Aug 29)
Saphira's Fire (IRE) 106[5] (1m 4f, Newm, GS, Oct 16)
Saptapadi (IRE) 114[3] (1m 5f 61y, Newb, GS, Aug 14)
Sariska 119[2] (1m 4f 10y, Epso, Gd, Jun 4)
Sayif (IRE) 105[9] (6f, York, Gd, May 12)
Sea Lord (IRE) 116[1] (1m, Good, GF, Jul 30)
Secrecy 116[2] (1m 30y, Hayd, Gd, Sep 4)
Secret Asset (IRE) 106[4] (1m, Linw, SD, Dec 28)
Secret Witness 105[3] (6f, Asco, GS, Oct 9)
Senate 108[1] (1m 4f, Donc, Gd, Sep 11)
Sent From Heaven (IRE) 109[4] (1m, Newm, GS, May 2)
Sentry Duty (FR ) 106[6] (2m 2f, Newm, GS, Oct 16)
Serious Attitude (IRE) 107 (6f, Asco, Gd, Jun 19)
Set The Trend 104[1] (1m, Asco, Gd, Aug 7)
Seta 111[1] (1m 14y, Sand, GF, Aug 21)
Shakespearean (IRE) 118[1] (7f, Newb, GS, Aug 14)
Shalanaya (IRE) 110[8] (1m 2f, Asco, GF, Jun 16)
Shamwari Lodge (IRE) 113[1] (1m, Good, Gd, May 1)
She's Our Mark 110[3] (1m 4f, Newm, GS, Oct 16)
Shimmering Moment (USA) 105[1] (1m 2f 150y, Dunw, SD, Nov 6)
Shimmering Surf (IRE) 106[2] (1m 4f 5y, Newb, GF, Aug 1)
Ship's Biscuit 106[5] (1m 6f 132y, Donc, Gd, Sep 9)
Showcasing 111[2] (6f, York, Gd, May 12)
Side Glance 112[2] (7f, Asco, GS, Sep 25)
Signor Peltro 108[4] (6f, Wind, GF, Jun 26)
Sir Gerry (USA) 115[2] (7f, Newb, Gd, Sep 17)
Sirocco Breeze 110[3] (7f, York, GF, May 22)
Sirvino 105[4] (1m 4y, Pont, GF, Jul 25)
Six Of Hearts 104[1] (7f, Leop, GF, May 30)
Siyouni (FR ) 117[4] (1m, Asco, Gd, Jun 15)
Skysurfers 116[2] (7f, York, GF, Aug 20)
Snaefell (IRE) 113[1] (6f, Curr, Yld, Aug 8)
Snoqualmie Girl (IRE) 104[3] (1m 4f, Asco, GS, Sep 24)
Snow Fairy (IRE) 120[1] (1m 4f, Curr, Yld, Jul 18)
Society Rock (IRE) 117[2] (6f, Asco, GF, Jun 19)
Sole Power 119[1] (5f, York, GF, Aug 20)
South Easter (IRE) 109[6] (1m 4f 10y, Epso, Gd, Jun 4)
Spacious 117[2] (1m, Leop, Gd, Sep 4)
Spanish Moon (USA) 112[4] (1m 4f, Newj, GF, Jul 8)
Special Duty 111[2] (1m, Newm, GS, May 2)
Spin Cycle (IRE) 114[4] (5f, Hayd, GF, May 22)
Spirit Of Sharjah (IRE) 111[1] (7f, Kemw, SD, Dec 15)
Spruce (USA) 106[2] (1m 4f, Donc, GS, Mar 28)
Sri Putra 118[2] (1m 4f, Good, GF, Jul 30)
St Moritz (IRE) 106[1] (7f, Newj, GF, Jul 9)
St Nicholas Abbey (IRE) 115[6] (1m, Newm, GF, May 1)
Stacelita (FR ) 119[2] (1m 1f 192y, Good, GF, Jul 31)
Starspangledbanner (AUS) 125[1] (6f, Newj, GF, Jul 9)
Status Symbol (IRE) 105[3] (1m 4f, Kemw, SD, Nov 27)
Steele Tango (USA) 113[2] (1m 1f, Newb, Gd, Oct 15)
Stimulation (IRE) 117[4] (1m 2f, Asco, GF, Jun 16)
Stoic (IRE) 111[2] (1m, Donc, Gd, Sep 11)
Storm Ultralight (ARG) 112[1] (1m, Linw, SD, Apr 30)
Stotsfold 121[1] (1m 2f 7y, Sand, Gd, Jul 2)
Strawberrydaiquiri 117[1] (1m, Asco, GF, Jun 16)
Striking Spirit 105[2] (6f, Asco, GF, Jun 19)
Suits Me 111[2] (1m 2f, Linw, SD, Mar 20)
Summit Surge (IRE) 117[1] (1m 2f 88y, York, GF, Jul 24)
Suruor (IRE) 106[3] (7f, Good, Sft, Aug 28)
Sweet Lightning 106[2] (1m 2f 60y, Donc, Gd, Sep 9)
Swift Gift 105[2] (7f, Donc, Gd, Aug 14)
Swilly Ferry (USA) 108[1] (6f, Newm, Gd, May 29)
Swiss Diva 108[2] (6f, Naas, Yld, Jul 21)
Tactic 119[1] (1m 6f, Curr, GF, Jun 26)
Tajneed (IRE) 111[1] (6f, Ripo, Gd, Aug 21)
Tamaathul 110[2] (7f 122y, Ches, GS, Aug 21)
Tangerine Trees 108[1] (5f, Newm, Sft, Sep 30)
Tartan Gigha (IRE) 108[1] (1m 114y, Epso, Gd, Jun 4)
Tastahil (IRE) 115[1] (2m, Newm, GF, Oct 16)
Tax Free (IRE) 110[2] (5f, Curr, Gd, Aug 29)
Tazeez (USA) 120[3] (1m 2f, Asco, GF, Jun 16)
Ted Spread 106[1] (1m 4f 66y, Ches, GS, May 6)
The Betchworth Kid 104[2] (1m 4f, Donc, GS, Nov 6)
The Cheka (IRE) 113[3] (1m 14y, Sand, Gd, Apr 24)
The Rectifier (USA) 108[1] (1m 67y, Wind, GF, Jun 26)
Thebes 104[1] (7f, Linw, SD, Apr 30)
Theology 111[7] (1m 6f 132y, Donc, Gd, Sep 11)
Tiddliwinks 107[1] (5f 216y, Wolw, SD, Mar 13)
Tiger Reigns 108[1] (1m, Ayr, Gd, Sep 18)
Timepiece 113[1] (1m, Asco, GF, Jun 16)
Times Up 109[1] (1m 4f, Donc, GS, Nov 6)
Total Command 104[3] (2m, Asco, Gd, Jun 18)
Total Gallery (IRE) 113[6] (5f, Newm, GF, May 1)
Traffic Guard (USA) 114[1] (1m 2f, Newj, Sft, Aug 14)
Tranquil Tiger 116[2] (1m 1f, Newm, GF, Apr 15)
Treadwell (IRE) 105[1] (7f, Asco, GF, Jun 18)
Treasure Lands 104[1] (1m 2f, Newm, GF, May 1)
Triple Aspect (IRE) 114[1] (5f 6y, Sand, GF, Jul 3)
Tropical Paradise (IRE) 111[1] (7f, Good, GS, Aug 29)
Tropical Treat 108[2] (6f, York, GF, Jul 9)
Twice Over 127[2] (1m 2f 88y, York, Gd, Aug 17)
Varenar (FR ) 116[6] (6f, Newj, GF, Jul 9)
Verdant 109[1] (1m 4f, Good, GF, Jul 28)
Vertigineux (FR ) 118[2] (1m, Asco, GF, Jul 10)
Vesuve (IRE) 116[1] (1m 2f, Ayr, Gd, Sep 18)
Victoire De Lyphar (IRE) 112[2] (6f, Ayr, Gd, Sep 18)
Victor Delight (IRE) 112[3] (1m 2f 88y, York, GF, May 13)
Virginia Hall 107[1] (1m 14y, Sand, GF, Jul 3)
Viscount Nelson (USA) 117[3] (1m 2f 7y, Sand, GF, Jul 3)
Vision D'etat (FR ) 123[2] (1m 2f, Newm, GS, Oct 16)
Vitznau (IRE) 105[2] (1m, Good, Gd, May 22)
Viva Vettori 105[5] (1m, Kemw, SD, Aug 23)
Vulcanite (IRE) 105[1] (1m 4f, Asco, Sft, Oct 9)
Wade Giles (IRE) 111[1] (1m, Naas, Yld, Jul 21)
Waffle (IRE) 104[5] (5f, Donc, Gd, Oct 23)
Wajir (FR ) 105[3] (1m 6f, York, GF, May 14)
War Artist (AUS) 113[6] (6f, Asco, GF, Jun 19)
Waseet 116[1] (1m 2f 88y, York, GS, Oct 8)
What A Charm (IRE) 105[1] (2m, Leop, Sft, Oct 31)
Whispering Gallery 115[2] (1m 4f, Asco, GS, Sep 26)
Wi Dud 109[1] (5f 13y, Nott, Sft, Apr 7)
Wiener Walzer (GER) 117[5] (1m 2f, Asco, GF, Jun 16)
Wigmore Hall (IRE) 118[5] (1m 2f, Newm, GS, Oct 16)
Willing Foe (USA) 105[1] (1m 4f, Newm, Gd, Oct 15)
Workforce 129[1] (1m 4f 10y, Epso, GF, Jun 5)
Xtension (IRE) 117[4] (1m, Newm, GF, May 1)
Yaa Wayl (IRE) 115[1] (7f, York, GF, Aug 20)
Yahrab (IRE) 106[5] (1m 2f, Linw, SD, Mar 20)
Yamal (IRE) 104[3] (1m, Donc, GF, Jul 15)
Yes Mr President (IRE) 111[2] (1m 4f 17y, Hami, Gd, May 14)
You'll Be Mine (USA) 105[6] (1m 4f, Newm, GS, Oct 16)
Youmzain (IRE) 119[4] (1m 4f 10y, Epso, Gd, Jun 4)
Zacinto 118[4] (1m, Asco, Gd, Jun 15)

Guide to the Flat 2011

# No knocking Frankel in his quest for Classic year

**Simon Turner, Racing Post Ratings specialist, with ten who can improve this season on what they have already achieved**

### Hot Spice John Dunlop

An opening handicap mark in the mid-60s looks to underestimate Hot Spice. John Dunlop's son of Kodiac had the minimum three runs for a mark last year, completing his handicap education in just over a month. The third of those runs came at Leicester when catching the eye in a pretty good maiden. The bare form of that effort leaves him on a workable rating and, with the likelihood of much better to come, he should not be hard to place.

### Rien Ne Vas Plus Sir Michael Stoute

This filly is open to stacks of improvement. Not seen until late October, she looked in need of the experience but showed plenty of ability in a fair maiden at Newmarket, going on nicely close home under a considerate ride. Her dam's stock tend to need time with only two of her other eight foals managing win or placed form as a two-year-old. One of that pair was Derby winner North Light and the other was Group 3 winner Cover Up. Such achievements may be well beyond this daughter of Oasis Dream but she should be well up to winning races.

### Frankel Henry Cecil

There is simply no knocking Frankel's form. An opening maiden win earned a Racing Post Rating of 95 and was followed by a 13-length St Leger conditions race romp from subsequent Prix Marcel Boussac third Rainbow Springs and the 90-rated Diamond Geezah. Another annihilation followed as Frankel ran right away from subsequent Listed winner Klammer in the Royal Lodge, before capping a perfect first season with success in the Dewhurst. A reproduction of last year's Dewhurst RPR of 127 would have been sufficient for Frankel to win the past ten renewals of the 2,000 Guineas and he has the scope to light up the 2011 Flat season.

### History Note John Oxx

Few maiden winners created a better impression than History Note last year, John Oxx's filly showing a pleasing attitude and abundance of natural ability when scoring at the Curragh in October. Travelling with real purpose entering the business end of the race, she did what was required despite giving the distinct impression the experience was needed. The form of her win is solid and, with the likelihood of plenty better to come, it would be no surprise to see the daughter of Azamour make an impression in some good races in her three-year-old campaign.

### Tiddliwinks Kevin Ryan

Those with good memories may recall that last year's Ayr Silver Cup favourite Tiddliwinks endured a nightmare passage, finishing on the bridle after getting no run when it mattered. A talented performer who placed in the Stewards' Cup last year, this five-time Polytrack winner gives the impression he has yet to reach his potential on turf. Good enough to get in all the big sprints this year, it would be no surprise to see him bag one.

### Bajan Tryst Kevin Ryan

Having improved year to year since being in training, Bajan Tryst can now be safely considered a quality sprint handicapper. He made significant strides last year after winning off a mark of 83 in January, eventually ending up rated 100, with solid efforts like his second in the Portland Handicap at Doncaster highlighting his ability. By a sire who was a late bloomer, there is likely to be more to come from Bajan Tryst and he appeals as the type to do even better this year.

### Invent Sir Mark Prescott

Being by top sire Dansili out of a decent broodmare, Invent can be reasonably expected to better last year's two-year-old form. It's particularly interesting that this gelding was his dam's first juvenile runner – her previous three runners did not make the track until three. Despite the relatively early start, Invent made quite an impression on his debut at Wolverhampton in late September when not knocked about in a fair maiden. A further three quick runs in just over a month to secure a handicap rating were never likely to show Invent in a favourable light and much better is expected this year.

### Irish Heartbeat Richard Fahey

Richard Fahey enjoyed another fine year in 2010 and has any number of capable handicappers in his ranks including Irish Heartbeat. Winner of the William Hill Spring Mile last year, he showed his best form with juice underfoot and is highly likely to win races again this year when conditions are in his favour. He certainly started the year on a decent mark.

### Kepler's Law Sir Mark Prescott

Four runs in just 21 days qualified Kepler's Law for a rating and he shaped with some promise en route to completing his quick-fire handicap education, notably when not looking entirely comfortable on Brighton's undulations on his fourth and final start. From a family that tend to improve with age, it would be a big surprise if this half-brother Irish Derby sixth Bashkirov doesn't show significant improvement and win races this year.

### Majestic Bright Luca Cumani

It's highly unlikely we've seen the best of this 150,000gns daughter of Pivotal, who broke her maiden in a weak contest at Kempton last November. The bare form of her three runs is only modest but she has left the distinct impression there is plenty more to come. Her three siblings have achieved RPR highs of 87, 99 and 105 and, while that sort of level might be fanciful, she's potentially well treated off an opening mark in the mid-60s and could hardly be in better hands. ∎

**Irish Heartbeat**

# Guide to the Flat 2011

## RACING POST RATINGS TOP TWO-YEAR-OLDS OF 2010

KEY: Horse name, Best RPR figure [Finishing position when earning figure]
(Details of race where figure was earned)

Abjer (FR) 104[1] (1m, Asco, Sft, Oct 9)
Ahlaain (USA) 97[5] (7f, Newm, Sft, Sep 30)
Al Aasifh (IRE) 104[1] (6f 8y, Newb, Gd, Jul 16)
Al Madina (IRE) 95[2] (1m, Donc, Gd, Sep 10)
Alaskan Spirit (IRE) 95[6] (6f 110y, Donc, Gd, Sep 9)
Alben Star (IRE) 95[1] (6f, Ayr, Gd, Sep 17)
Aldaway (IRE) 100[1] (7f 100y, Tipp, Gd, Aug 6)
Alexander Pope (IRE) 96[1] (1m, Dunw, SD, Dec 8)
Anadolu (IRE) 95[1] (5f, Tipp, Gd, Jul 11)
Aneedah (IRE) 94[4] (7f, Newm, Sft, Oct 2)
Approve (IRE) 112[1] (6f, York, Gd, Aug 18)
Arctic Feeling (IRE) 99[1] (5f, Ayr, Gd, Sep 17)
Auld Burns 94[6] (7f, Newm, Gd, Sep 18)
Ballista (IRE) 94[3] (6f, Redc, GS, Oct 2)
Barefoot Lady (IRE) 97[3] (6f, Ayr, Gd, Sep 18)
Bathwick Bear (IRE) 99[1] (6f, Ripo, Gd, Aug 30)
Belle Bayardo (IRE) 94[3] (6f, Donc, Gd, Sep 8)
Bible Belt (IRE) 103[3] (7f, Curr, Sft, Sep 26)
Big Issue (IRE) 102[1] (6f 212y, Sali, Sft, Sep 29)
Black Moth (IRE) 103[4] (5f, Donc, Gd, Sep 10)
Blue Bunting (USA) 99[1] (1m, Newm, GS, Oct 30)
Brevity (USA) 101[1] (6f, Sali, Gd, Sep 2)
Buthelezi (USA) 94[1] (1m, Donc, Gd, Sep 11)
Cape Dollar (IRE) 104[1] (7f, Newm, GS, Oct 16)
Cape To Rio (IRE) 103[2] (6f 8y, Newb, Gd, Jul 16)
Carlton House (USA) 95[1] (1m, Newb, GS, Oct 23)
Casamento (IRE) 121[1] (1m, Donc, Gd, Oct 23)
Casper's Touch (USA) 95[3] (7f, Asco, GF, Jun 19)
Casual Glimpse 98[1] (6f, Newj, GF, Jul 8)
Chilworth Lad 101[4] (6f, Curr, Gf, Jun 27)
Choose Wisely (IRE) 101[3] (5f, Good, Gd, Jul 27)
Chrysanthemum (IRE) 104[1] (7f, Curr, Sft, Sep 26)
Clondinnery (IRE) 104[3] (6f, Curr, GF, Jun 27)
Cochabamba (IRE) 103[2] (7f, Newm, Gd, Oct 16)
Cocktail Charlie 97[2] (5f, Muss, GF, Jun 5)
Codemaster 95[2] (6f, Redc, GS, Oct 2)
Crown Prosecutor (IRE) 107[3] (6f 8y, Newb, GF, Sep 18)
Crying Lightening (IRE) 102[2] (7f, Newj, GS, Aug 7)
Darajaat (USA) 97[3] (5f, Asco, GS, Oct 9)
Dingle View (IRE) 106[1] (6f, Curr, Gd, Aug 29)
Dinkum Diamond (IRE) 107[2] (5f, Donc, Gd, Sep 10)
Drawing Board 101[2] (6f, Ayr, Gd, Sep 17)
Dream Ahead (USA) 125[1] (6f, Newm, Sft, Oct 1)
Dubai Prince (IRE) 111[1] (7f, Leop, GF, Oct 25)
Dubawi Gold 104[1] (7f, Asco, GS, Oct 9)
Dunboyne Express (IRE) 112[1] (6f 63y, Curr, Yld, Jul 18)
Dux Scholar 105[2] (7f, Newb, GS, Oct 23)
Earl Of Leitrim (IRE) 102[1] (6f, Donc, Gd, Oct 23)
Easy Ticket (IRE) 97[3] (6f 8y, Newb, GF, Sep 18)
Ecliptic (USA) 104[2] (7f, Newj, GF, Jul 9)
Elas Diamond 97[2] (1m, Newm, Gd, Sep 30)
Electric Waves (IRE) 105[1] (5f, Asco, GS, Oct 9)
Elzaam (AUS) 111[2] (6f, Asco, Gd, Jun 15)
Emma's Gift (IRE) 96[4] (6f, Newj, Gd, Jul 31)
Emperor Hadrian (IRE) 98[4] (6f, Curr, Gd, Aug 29)
Eskimo (IRE) 99[4] (1m, Asco, GS, Sep 25)
Eucharist (IRE) 98[1] (6f 110y, Donc, Gd, Sep 9)
Excel Bolt 101[3] (5f, Asco, GF, Jun 17)
Excello 95[3] (5f, Asco, Gd, Jun 15)
Face The Problem (IRE) 105[1] (5f, Thir, GF, Jul 31)
Factum (USA) 95[4] (1m, Curr, Sft, Sep 26)
Forjatt (IRE) 100[1] (6f 15y, Nott, GF, Aug 10)
Formosina (IRE) 112[2] (6f 8y, Newb, GF, Sep 18)
Frankel 127[1] (7f, Newm, GS, Oct 16)
Fury 101[1] (7f, Newm, Sft, Oct 2)

Galtymore Lad 106[2] (6f, York, Gd, Aug 19)
Garde Cotiere (USA) 94[1] (1m, Linw, SD, Oct 13)
Gatamalata (IRE) 96[2] (6f, Curr, Gd, Jun 25)
Glor Na Mara (IRE) 113[3] (7f, Newm, GS, Oct 16)
Havant 103[1] (7f, Newm, GS, Oct 1)
High Award (IRE) 98[1] (6f, Epso, GF, Jun 5)
High Ruler (USA) 104[4] (7f, Curr, GF, Aug 21)
Highly Composed 95[4] (7f, Leop, Gd, Jul 15)
Hooray 117[1] (6f, Newm, GS, Oct 1)
I Love Me 102[3] (7f, Newm, GS, Oct 16)
Imperialistic Diva (IRE) 99[4] (7f, Newm, Sft, Oct 2)
Indigo Way 100[1] (1m 2f, Newm, GS, Oct 30)
Invincible Ridge (IRE) 95[1] (6f 8y, Newb, GF, Sep 18)
Irish Field (IRE) 95[4] (6f, Newm, Sft, Oct 1)
Jackaroo (IRE) 96[3] (1m 100y, Kill, GF, Aug 17)
Janood (IRE) 100[1] (7f, Newb, GS, Aug 14)
Jolie Jioconde (IRE) 94[3] (7f, Leop, Yld, Jul 22)
Julius Geezer (IRE) 94[3] (5f, York, Gd, Aug 18)
Karam Albaari (IRE) 106[4] (7f, Donc, Gd, Sep 11)
Katla (IRE) 106[1] (6f, York, Sft, Oct 9)
Keratiya (FR) 97[6] (5f, Donc, Gd, Sep 10)
Khor Sheed 102[1] (6f, Newm, Gd, Sep 17)
King Torus (IRE) 114[1] (7f, Good, GF, Jul 28)
Kissable (IRE) 110[3] (7f, Curr, GF, Aug 29)
Klammer 105[1] (7f, Newb, GS, Oct 23)
Krypton Factor 100[3] (6f, Redc, GS, Oct 2)
Ladie's Choice (IRE) 101[2] (5f, Curr, GF, Aug 21)
Ladies Are Forever 105[3] (5f, Asco, GF, Jun 16)
Laughing Lashes (USA) 111[2] (7f, Curr, GF, Aug 29)
Leiba Leiba 94[1] (5f 16y, Ches, GF, Jun 26)
Libranno 111[1] (6f, Good, Gd, Jul 30)
Lightening Thief (IRE) 97[4] (5f, Curr, GF, Aug 21)
Lily Again 98[1] (7f 16y, Sand, GF, Jul 22)
Longhunter 101[1] (6f, Curr, Sft, Sep 11)
Look At Me (IRE) 95[2] (7f, Newm, GS, Oct 1)
Loving Spirit 97[2] (1m, Newm, Gd, Oct 15)
Magic Casement 102[1] (7f 2y, Ches, GS, Sep 10)
Majestic Dubawi 101[1] (6f, Ayr, Gd, Sep 18)
Majestic Myles (IRE) 95[2] (6f, Good, Gd, Jul 31)
Major Art 94[3] (7f, Good, Gd, Jul 28)
Makeynn 95[1] (1m, Souw, SD, Nov 5)
Mantoba 102[1] (1m, Newm, Gd, Oct 15)
Maqaasid 107[1] (5f, Asco, GF, Jun 16)
Margot Did (IRE) 108[2] (6f, York, Gd, Aug 19)
Marine Commando 101[1] (5f, Asco, Gd, Jun 15)
Masaya 96[1] (7f, Newm, Sft, Oct 2)
Master Of Hounds (USA) 115[3] (1m, Donc, Gd, Oct 23)
Mawaakef (IRE) 101[2] (1m, Curr, Sft, Sep 26)
Mayson 98[2] (6f, Ripo, Gd, Aug 30)
Measuring Time 103[2] (1m 2f, Newm, Gd, Sep 30)
Memory (IRE) 111[1] (6f, Newj, GF, Jul 7)
Meow (IRE) 106[2] (5f, Asco, GF, Jun 16)
Misty For Me (IRE) 114[1] (7f, Curr, GF, Aug 29)
Moonlit Garden (IRE) 98[3] (5f, Curr, GF, Aug 21)
Morache Music 94[1] (6f, Newm, GS, Oct 29)
Mortitia 95[4] (6f, Ayr, Gd, Sep 18)
Move In Time 100[2] (5f, Asco, GS, Oct 9)
Nabah 95[4] (7f, Newm, GS, Oct 16)
Native Khan (FR) 113[4] (1m, Donc, Gd, Oct 23)
Neebras (IRE) 107[2] (6f, Newj, GF, Jul 8)
New Planet (IRE) 104[3] (5f, Donc, Gd, Sep 10)
Night Carnation 96[2] (6f, Donc, Gd, Oct 23)
Obligation (FR) 95[2] (1m 1f, Leop, Sft, Oct 31)
Ocean Bay 97[5] (7f, Newj, GF, Jul 9)
Oor Jock (IRE) 96[7] (6f, Curr, Gd, Aug 29)
Pabusar 103[2] (5f, York, Gd, Aug 18)
Park Avenue (IRE) 95[3] (7f, Leop, GF, Oct 25)
Pathfork (USA) 119[1] (7f, Curr, Sft, Sep 11)

racingpost.com

# Racing Post Ratings

## RACING POST RATINGS TOP TWO-YEAR-OLDS OF 2010

Pausanias 100[2] (1m, Asco, Sft, Oct 9)
Perfect Tribute 98[3] (6f, Asco, Gd, Jul 24)
Peter Martins (USA) 98[1] (7f, Newj, GF, Jul 30)
Petronius Maximus (IRE) 100[2] (5f, Asco, Gd, Jun 15)
Picture Editor 97[3] (1m 2f, Newm, GS, Oct 30)
Pirateer (IRE) 96[1] (1m, Gowr, Yld, Sep 25)
Pisco Sour (USA) 97[2] (7f, Newm, Sft, Oct 2)
Premier Clarets (IRE) 98[5] (6f, York, Gd, Aug 18)
Purple Glow (IRE) 95[2] (5f, Curr, GF, May 22)
Question Times 96[2] (6f, Newm, GS, Oct 29)
Quiet Oasis (IRE) 100[4] (7f, Curr, Sft, Sep 26)
Radharcnafarraige (IRE) 99[4] (6f, Newj, GF, Jul 7)
Ragsah (IRE) 98[2] (6f, Ayr, Gd, Sep 18)
Reckless Reward (IRE) 103[2] (5f, Asco, GF, Jun 17)
Rerouted (USA) 102[1] (7f, Newm, Sft, Sep 30)
Retainer (IRE) 95[1] (5f, Newm, Gd, Apr 14)
Rimth 103[2] (6f, Newm, GS, Oct 1)
Roayh (USA) 103[3] (6f, Asco, Gd, Jun 15)
Robin Hood (IRE) 95[3] (1m, Curr, Sft, Sep 26)
Roderic O'connor (IRE) 120[2] (7f, Newm, GS, Oct 16)
Royal Exchange 101[3] (7f, Newm, Sft, Sep 30)
Rudolf Valentino 100[5] (7f, Curr, GF, Aug 21)
Saamidd 114[1] (7f, Donc, Gd, Sep 11)
Samuel Morse (IRE) 105[4] (7f, Curr, Sft, Sep 11)
Seeharn (IRE) 99[1] (6f, Curr, Gd, Jun 25)
Serena's Pride 95[6] (6f, Newj, GF, Jul 7)
Seville (GER) 119[2] (1m, Donc, Gd, Oct 23)
Sheer Courage (IRE) 96[1] (5f 218y, Leic, GF, May 24)
Signs In The Sand 97[1] (6f, Kemw, SD, Oct 6)
Silvertrees (IRE) 95[2] (7f, York, Gd, Aug 17)
Singapore Lilly (IRE) 99[1] (1m 30y, Hayd, Gd, Sep 4)
Sir Reginald 100[5] (6f 110y, Donc, Gd, Sep 9)
Slim Shadey 96[4] (6f 110y, Donc, Gd, Sep 9)
Soraaya (IRE) 106[1] (6f, Asco, Gd, Jul 24)
Stentorian (IRE) 96[2] (7f, Leop, GF, Jul 1)
Stone Of Folca 102[2] (5f, Good, Gd, Jul 27)
Strong Suit (USA) 114[1] (6f, Asco, Gd, Jun 15)
Suntan (IRE) 95[2] (7f, Galw, GF, Aug 30)
Surrey Star (IRE) 102[2] (7f, Newm, Sft, Sep 30)
Sweet Cecily (IRE) 97[1] (6f, Newm, GS, Oct 29)
Sydney Harbour (IRE) 97[2] (6f, Naas, Gd, Oct 17)
Tale Untold (USA) 96[2] (7f, Newm, Sft, Oct 2)
Tazahum (USA) 95[2] (7f, Asco, GS, Oct 9)
Temple Meads 114[1] (6f 8y, Newb, GF, Sep 18)
The Long Game 95[4] (6f, Good, Gd, Jul 30)
The Paddyman (IRE) 106[4] (6f 8y, Newb, GF, Sep 18)
The Thrill Is Gone 98[5] (5f, Donc, Gd, Sep 10)
Theyskens' Theory (USA) 109[3] (1m, Asco, GS, Sep 25)
Titus Mills (IRE) 104[1] (7f, Good, Gd, Sep 7)
Tiz My Time (USA) 97[3] (6f, Asco, GF, Jun 17)
Tiz The Shot (IRE) 97[1] (1m 1f, Leop, Sft, Oct 31)
Together (IRE) 111[2] (1m, Asco, GS, Sep 25)
Toolain (IRE) 103[7] (1m, Donc, Gd, Oct 23)
Trade Storm 96[6] (6f, York, Gd, Aug 18)
Treasure Beach 103[3] (1m, Asco, GS, Sep 25)
Treasury Devil (USA) 96[1] (7f 16y, Sand, Gd, Sep 15)
Vanguard Dream 98[1] (7f, Newb, Sft, Oct 7)
Waiter's Dream 112[4] (7f, Newm, GS, Oct 16)
Warning Flag (USA) 100[2] (7f, Leop, GF, Oct 25)
Whisper Louise (IRE) 97[3] (1m, Newm, GS, Oct 30)
White Moonstone (USA) 112[1] (1m, Asco, GS, Sep 25)
Wild Wind (GER) 104[2] (7f, Curr, Sft, Sep 26)
Wootton Bassett 109[1] (6f 110y, Donc, Gd, Sep 9)
Zaidan (USA) 104[1] (7f, Asco, GF, Jun 19)
Zebedee 108[1] (5f, Donc, Gd, Sep 10)
Zoffany (IRE) 115[1] (6f, Curr, Yld, Aug 8)
Zoowraa 102[1] (7f, Newb, GS, Oct 23)

## RPR TOP THREE-YEAR-OLDS AND OLDER HORSES OF 2010

KEY: Horse name, Best RPR figure [Finishing position when earning figure]
(Details of race where figure was earned)

Aaim To Prosper (IRE) 94[3] (2m 4f, Asco, Gd, Jun 15)
Aattash (IRE) 103[1] (1m 1f 207y, Beve, Gd, Aug 28)
Able Master (IRE) 97[7] (6f, Newm, GF, Apr 15)
Academy Blues (USA) 93[2] (7f 122y, Ches, GS, May 7)
Across The Rhine (USA) 94[1] (1m, Leop, GF, May 9)
Acrostic 111[2] (1m, York, Gd, Aug 19)
Address Unknown 102[2] (1m 2f, Leop, GF, May 9)
Admiral Barry (IRE) 99[1] (1m 6f, Curr, Sft, Sep 11)
Admission 98[2] (1m 3f 16y, Hami, Gd, May 14)
Advanced 95[3] (6f, Thir, GF, Apr 17)
Afsare 104[1] (1m 2f, Asco, GF, Jun 17)
Age Of Aquarius (IRE) 119[2] (2m 4f, Asco, GF, Jun 17)
Air Chief Marshal (IRE) 94[1] (7f, Curr, Yld, Jul 17)
Ajaan 101[5] (1m 6f, York, Gd, Aug 18)
Akdarena 113[3] (1m 2f, Curr, GF, Jun 26)
Al Farahidi (USA) 95[2] (1m 30y, Hayd, Gd, May 22)
Al Khaleej (IRE) 94[1] (7f, Newj, GS, Aug 7)
Al Zir (USA) 103[6] (1m 4f 10y, Epso, GF, Jun 5)
Aladdins Cave 93[1] (1m 4f, Gowr, Gd, Aug 11)
Alainmaar (FR) 110[1] (1m 2f 18y, Epso, Gd, Apr 21)
Albaqaa 94[8] (1m 1f, Newm, GF, May 1)
Alexandros 97[2] (1m 114y, Epso, Gd, Jun 4)
Almiqdaad 96[4] (1m 3f 200y, Hayd, Gd, Jul 3)
Alrasm (IRE) 107[1] (1m 4f 66y, Ches, Gd, May 5)
Alsace Lorraine (IRE) 99[1] (1m, Asco, GF, May 8)
Alverta (AUS) 102[3] (6f, Newj, GF, Jul 9)
Always Be True (IRE) 95[1] (7f, Gowr, Gd, May 2)
Amico Fritz (GER) 94[5] (6f, Asco, GF, Jun 19)
Amour Propre 99[8] (5f, Asco, Gd, Jun 15)
Angel's Pursuit (IRE) 112[1] (7f, Kemw, SD, Dec 4)
Anna Salai (USA) 101[2] (1m, Curr, GF, May 23)
Antinori (IRE) 101[5] (1m 2f 18y, Epso, Gd, Jun 4)
Arcano (IRE) 93[3] (7f, Newb, Gd, Apr 17)
Arctic Cosmos (USA) 121[1] (1m 6f 132y, Donc, Gd, Sep 11)
Arganil (USA) 103[1] (5f, Linw, SD, Mar 20)
Arlequin 96[1] (1m 2f 88y, York, GF, May 12)
Ashbrittle 97[1] (1m 6f 132y, Donc, Gd, Oct 22)
Ashram (IRE) 98[2] (7f, Donc, Gd, Oct 23)
Astrophysical Jet 114[1] (5f, Curr, Gd, Aug 29)
At First Sight (IRE) 114[2] (1m 4f 10y, Epso, GF, Jun 5)
Audacity Of Hope 104[6] (1m, Asco, GF, Jun 17)
Australia Day (IRE) 93[2] (1m 2f 7y, Sand, Gd, Jul 2)
Autumn Blades (IRE) 102[1] (7f 122y, Ches, Ches, GF, May 5)
Averroes (IRE) 97[2] (1m 4f 66y, Ches, Gd, May 5)
Aviate 96[5] (1m, Newm, Sft, Oct 2)
Await The Dawn (USA) 105[1] (1m 2f, Leop, Gd, Sep 4)
Awsaal 98[1] (1m 3f 200y, Hayd, GF, May 22)
Awzaan 97[3] (7f, Newb, Gd, Sep 17)
Axiom 104[1] (7f, Good, Sft, Aug 28)
Azmeel 97[1] (1m 2f 75y, Ches, GS, May 7)
Bagamoyo 100[2] (6f, Newj, GF, Jul 7)
Baglioni (IRE) 97[1] (7f, Leop, Sft, Mar 28)
Baila Me (GER) 96[1] (1m 5f, Linw, SD, Oct 28)
Bajan Tryst (USA) 96[2] (5f, Good, Gd, Jul 29)
Balcarce Nov (ARG) 101[7] (1m, York, Gd, Aug 19)
Balducci 96[1] (1m 30y, Hayd, GF, May 22)
Balthazaar's Gift (IRE) 104[1] (7f, Donc, Gd, Sep 11)

# Guide to the Flat 2011

## RPR TOP THREE-YEAR-OLDS AND OLDER HORSES OF 2010

Bannaby (FR) 100[4] (2m 4f, Asco, GF, Jun 17)
Barack (IRE) 99[3] (7f, Curr, Sft, Sep 26)
Barney Mcgrew (IRE) 99[5] (6f, Newm, GF, Apr 15)
Barring Decree (IRE) 100[3] (1m, Curr, GF, Jun 27)
Barshiba (IRE) 101[4] (1m 3f 200y, Hayd, GS, May 29)
Bay Willow (IRE) 107[1] (1m 4f, Asco, GF, Jul 25)
Bea Remembered 93[5] (1m, Curr, GF, Jun 27)
Beachfire 100[1] (1m 1f 192y, Good, GF, Jul 29)
Beauchamp Viceroy 94[7] (1m 2f, Linw, SD, Mar 20)
Becausewecan (USA) 94[5] (1m 3f, Kemw, SD, Mar 27)
Becqu Adoree (FR) 100[4] (1m 4f 5y, Newb, GF, Aug 1)
Beethoven (IRE) 116[4] (1m, Asco, GS, Sep 25)
Below Zero (IRE) 95[1] (7f 2y, Ches, GF, Jun 26)
Benandonner (USA) 96[1] (1m, Linw, SD, Jul 14)
Benbaun (IRE) 100 (5f, Curr, Gd, Aug 29)
Bencoolen (IRE) 96[3] (1m, Ripo, GS, May 25)
Berling (IRE) 94[1] (1m 3f 5y, Newb, GF, May 14)
Bethrah (IRE) 102[1] (1m, Curr, GF, May 23)
Bewitched (IRE) 100[1] (6f, Hayd, GS, May 29)
Black Snowflake (USA) 93[3] (1m 30y, Hayd, GF, May 22)
Blissful Moment (USA) 95[1] (1m 4f 16y, Beve, Gd, Sep 15)
Blizzard Blues (USA) 100[6] (1m 4f 5y, Newb, Gd, Apr 17)
Blue Jack 98[3] (5f, Newm, GF, May 1)
Blue Maiden 105[2] (7f, Newm, Gd, Apr 14)
Borderlescott 116[3] (5f, Hayd, GF, May 22)
Bould Mover 110[5] (5f, Asco, Gd, Jun 15)
Bounty Box 104[1] (6f, Pont, Gd, Aug 15)
Bowdler's Magic 95[5] (1m 4f, Asco, Gd, Aug 7)
Brae Hill (IRE) 95[4] (7f 122y, Ches, GS, May 7)
Breakheart (IRE) 97[2] (1m 2f, Asco, Gd, Jul 23)
Bridge Of Gold (USA) 109[3] (1m 6f, York, Gd, Aug 18)
Bright Horizon 100[1] (2m, Curr, Sft, Sep 26)
Brushing 97[8] (1m 6f 132y, Donc, Gd, Sep 9)
Buachaill Dona (IRE) 96[4] (6f, Thir, GF, Apr 17)
Bushman 102[7] (1m, Asco, GS, Sep 25)
Buxted (IRE) 101[5] (1m 4f 5y, Newb, Gd, Apr 17)
Buzzword 99[3] (1m 4f, Asco, GF, Jun 18)
Byword 94[3] (1m 2f 88y, York, Gd, Aug 17)
Calatrava Cape (IRE) 94[1] (1m 4f, Newm, Gd, Sep 18)
Camerooney 96[1] (7f, Newc, GF, Jun 26)
Canford Cliffs (IRE) 124[1] (1m, Asco, Gd, Jun 15)
Cansili Star 95[1] (7f, Epso, Gd, Jun 4)
Cape Blanco (IRE) 119[1] (1m 2f, Leop, Gd, Sep 4)
Capponi (IRE) 102[1] (1m, York, GF, Jul 10)
Captain Dunne (IRE) 95[5] (5f 89y, York, Gd, Aug 17)
Captain Ramius (IRE) 94[1] (7f 50y, Ayr, Gd, Sep 18)
Carioca (IRE) 107[2] (1m, York, GF, May 14)
Carnaby Street (IRE) 94[4] (7f, Good, GS, Sep 11)
Carraiglawn (IRE) 105[6] (1m 4f, Curr, GF, Jun 27)
Castles In The Air 96 (7f, Asco, GF, Jun 18)
Cat Junior (USA) 96[2] (7f, Newm, GS, Oct 16)
Cavalryman 111[5] (1m 4f 10y, Epso, Gd, Jun 4)
Celtic Sultan (IRE) 94[3] (7f 50y, Ayr, Gd, Sep 18)
Chachamaidee (IRE) 106[1] (1m, York, GF, May 14)
Charlie Cool 98[3] (1m, York, GF, Jul 10)
Cheveton 104[1] (5f, Hayd, Sft, Sep 25)
Chiberta King 102[1] (1m 6f, Newm, GF, May 15)
Chinese White (IRE) 115[1] (1m 2f, Curr, GF, Jun 26)
Chock A Block (IRE) 96[4] (1m 5f 89y, Ches, GS, Aug 21)
Choose Me (IRE) 96[2] (1m 2f, Curr, GF, Jun 4)
Chorus Of Angels 94[2] (7f, Gowr, Gd, May 2)
Circumvent 100[3] (1m 2f, Ayr, Gd, Sep 18)
Citrus Star (USA) 102[4] (7f, Epso, Gd, Jun 4)
City Style (USA) 102[4] (7f, Good, Sft, Aug 28)
Cityscape 117[1] (1m, Newm, GS, Oct 1)
Claremont (IRE) 109[3] (1m 4f 5y, Newb, Gd, Apr 17)
Class Is Class (IRE) 103[4] (1m 2f 7y, Wind, Sft, Aug 28)
Classic Colori (IRE) 98[1] (7f, Linw, SD, Mar 20)

Classic Punch (IRE) 103[1] (1m 2f, Newj, GF, Jul 24)
Clearwater Bay (IRE) 104[1] (1m 4f, List, Sft, Sep 15)
Clowance 109[1] (1m 4f 5y, Newb, GS, Oct 23)
Coin Of The Realm (IRE) 94[1] (1m 4f 10y, Epso, Gd, Apr 21)
Colepeper 99[3] (7f, Donc, Gd, Sep 8)
Comedy Act 93[2] (1m 6f 132y, Donc, Gd, Oct 22)
Confront 102[5] (1m 208y, York, GF, Aug 20)
Contract Caterer (IRE) 97[3] (1m 4f, Good, GF, Jul 28)
Cool Strike (UAE) 97[2] (1m 5f 22y, Bath, Fm, Apr 25)
Copperbeech (IRE) 94[4] (1m 5f, Linw, SD, Oct 28)
Corporal Maddox 105[2] (6f, Asco, Gd, Apr 28)
Corsica (IRE) 116[3] (1m 6f 132y, Donc, Gd, Sep 11)
Crackentorp 96[2] (1m 4f, York, GF, May 14)
Credit Swap 93[1] (1m 3y, Yarm, Sft, Sep 15)
Crimea (IRE) 93[3] (5f, Good, Gd, Jul 29)
Critical Moment (USA) 110[1] (1m, Good, GF, Jul 31)
Croisultan (IRE) 104[1] (6f, Fair, Sft, Jul 10)
Crowded House 93[4] (1m 2f 7y, Sand, Gd, Apr 24)
Crown Choice 94[1] (7f, Kemw, SD, Apr 21)
Cumulus Nimbus 96[4] (1m 1f 192y, Good, GF, Jul 29)
Dalghar (FR) 105[5] (1m, Asco, Gd, Jun 15)
Dalradian (IRE) 97[1] (1m 2f, Linw, SD, Feb 13)
Damien (IRE) 100[2] (6f, York, Sft, Oct 9)
Damika (IRE) 99[1] (6f, Ripo, GS, Aug 14)
Dancing Dancila (IRE) 103[2] (1m, Newm, GF, Apr 15)
Dandino 113[2] (1m 4f, Good, GF, Jul 27)
Dandy Boy (ITY) 102[1] (7f, Asco, Gd, May 8)
Dangerous Midge (USA) 108[8] (1m 6f, York, Gd, Aug 18)
Dansili Dancer 113[1] (1m 3f, Kemw, SD, Mar 27)
Dar Re Mi 94[4] (1m 2f 7y, Sand, Gd, Jul 3)
Darley Sun (IRE) 101 (1m 6f, York, Gd, Aug 18)
Daryakana (FR) 103[4] (1m 4f, Asco, Gd, Jul 24)
Day Of The Eagle (IRE) 96[1] (7f, Donc, GF, Jun 5)
Dayia (IRE) 95[4] (2m 4f, Asco, Gd, Jun 15)
Debussy (IRE) 117[1] (1m 2f 75y, Ches, GS, May 6)
Definightly 108[2] (6f, Curr, Sft, Oct 10)
Deirdre 99[3] (1m 1f 192y, Good, Gd, May 19)
Delegator 99[1] (7f, Newb, Gd, Sep 17)
Demolition 94[4] (1m 208y, York, Gd, Jun 12)
Desert Creek (IRE) 94[2] (7f, Good, Sft, Aug 28)
Desert Myth (USA) 109[2] (1m, Good, GF, Jul 31)
Desert Sea (IRE) 96[6] (1m 6f, York, Gd, Aug 18)
Dever Dream 96[2] (6f, Pont, Gd, Aug 15)
Dhaamer (IRE) 93[1] (1m 2f 7y, Sand, Gd, Sep 10)
Dick Turpin (IRE) 121[2] (1m, Asco, Gd, Jun 15)
Dirar (IRE) 110[1] (1m 6f, York, Gd, Aug 18)
Distant Memories (IRE) 113[1] (1m 208y, York, Gd, Jun 12)
Distinctive 93[6] (7f, Newm, Gd, Apr 14)
Docofthebay (IRE) 95[1] (7f 50y, Ayr, Gd, Sep 18)
Doncaster Rover (USA) 105[3] (6f, Newm, GF, Apr 15)
Dorback 94[3] (5f 6y, Sand, Gd, Apr 23)
Dream Eater (IRE) 116[3] (1m, Asco, GF, Jul 10)
Dream Lodge (IRE) 108[3] (1m 208y, York, Gd, Jun 12)
Dreamspeed (IRE) 105[3] (1m 4f 5y, Newb, GS, Oct 23)
Dubawi Phantom 100[4] (1m, Newm, GF, Apr 15)
Duchess Dora (IRE) 99[1] (5f 6y, Sand, Gd, Apr 23)
Duff (IRE) 102[4] (7f, Donc, Gd, Sep 11)
Duncan 110[2] (1m 4f, Asco, GF, Jun 19)
Dunelight (IRE) 102[1] (7f 32y, Wolw, SD, Mar 13)
Dunn'o (IRE) 97[2] (1m, Good, GS, Aug 29)
Eastern Aria (UAE) 111[1] (1m 6f 132y, Donc, Gd, Sep 9)
Electrolyser (IRE) 97[1] (2m, Good, GF, Jul 29)
Elna Bright 95[4] (7f, Kemw, SD, Dec 4)
Elnawin 94[3] (6f, Hayd, GF, May 8)
Elusive Pimpernel (USA) 112[1] (1m, Newm, GF, Apr 15)
Elyaadi 100[2] (2m 4f, Asco, Gd, Jun 15)
Emirates Dream (USA) 100[1] (1m, Good, GS, Aug 29)
Emperor Claudius (USA) 107[1] (1m, Curr, GF, Jun 27)

# Racing Post Ratings

## RPR TOP THREE-YEAR-OLDS AND OLDER HORSES OF 2010

Emulous 105 [1] (1m, Naas, Gd, Oct 17)
Enact 95 [2] (6f, Newm, GS, May 2)
Equiano (FR) 122 [1] (5f, Asco, Gd, Jun 15)
Esoterica (IRE) 95 [3] (7f, Newc, GF, Jun 26)
Eton Rifles 94 [2] (7f, York, GS, Oct 8)
Evens And Odds (IRE) 103 [4] (6f, Newm, GF, Apr 15)
Everymanforhimself (IRE) 95 [9] (7f, Asco, GF, Jun 18)
Fair Trade 108 [4] (1m, Sali, GF, Aug 12)
Fame And Glory 119 [1] (1m 4f 10y, Epso, Gd, Jun 4)
Famous (IRE) 94 [2] (7f, Curr, Yld, May 3)
Famous Name 106 [6] (1m 2f, Leop, Gd, Sep 4)
Fanunalter 104 [8] (1m, Sali, GF, Aug 12)
Fareer 101 [1] (1m, York, GF, May 13)
Fathom Five (IRE) 102 [1] (5f, Epso, GF, Apr 21)
Fathsta (IRE) 107 [1] (6f, York, Sft, Oct 9)
Favourite Girl (IRE) 99 [1] (5f, Ayr, Sft, Jul 19)
Fencing Master 108 [4] (1m 4f, Good, GF, Jul 27)
Field Of Dream 106 [3] (1m, Good, GF, Jul 31)
Fiery Lad (IRE) 110 [1] (1m 2f 18y, Epso, Gd, Jun 4)
Fighter Boy (IRE) 101 [2] (1m 1f, Newm, Gd, Apr 14)
Film Score (USA) 97 [4] (1m 2f, Asco, GF, Jun 17)
First City 98 [2] (1m, Asco, GF, May 8)
Fitz Flyer (IRE) 100 [3] (5f, Souw, SS, Jan 1)
Five Star Junior (USA) 99 [1] (5f, Ayr, GF, May 26)
Fleeting Spirit (IRE) 99 [5] (6f, Newj, GF, Jul 9)
Flipando (IRE) 94 [8] (7f, Asco, Gd, May 8)
Flora Trevelyan 94 [1] (1m 14y, Sand, GF, May 27)
Flying Cloud (IRE) 113 [2] (1m 2f, Curr, GF, Jun 26)
Fol Hollow (IRE) 102 [4] (5f, Epso, GF, Apr 21)
Forgotten Voice (IRE) 105 [7] (1m, Asco, GF, Jun 16)
Forte Dei Marmi 101 [1] (1m 2f 7y, Sand, GF, Aug 21)
Fratellino 101 [2] (5f 6y, Sand, Gd, Apr 23)
Free Judgement (USA) 110 [2] (1m, Curr, GF, May 22)
Freeforaday (USA) 101 [5] (1m, Good, GF, Jul 31)
Full Toss 98 [6] (1m 2f, Linw, SD, Feb 13)
Gala Evening 101 [2] (1m 6f, Newm, GF, May 15)
Gallagher 95 [6] (7f, Good, GS, Sep 11)
Gallic Star (IRE) 98 [5] (1m 4f 5y, Newb, GF, Aug 1)
Gene Autry (USA) 106 [2] (6f, Asco, Gd, Aug 7)
Genki (IRE) 99 [3] (6f, Hayd, GF, Sep 4)
Gertrude Bell 101 [5] (1m 4f 10y, Epso, Gd, Jun 4)
Ghimaar 95 [4] (2m 4f, Asco, Gd, Jun 15)
Giants Play (USA) 95 [3] (1m 5f, Linw, SD, Oct 28)
Gile Na Greine (IRE) 104 [2] (1m, Asco, GF, Jun 18)
Gilt Edge Girl 98 [3] (6f, York, GF, Jul 9)
Ginger Jack 97 [1] (1m, Muss, GF, Jul 13)
Gitano Hernando 112 [1] (1m 2f, Linw, SD, Feb 27)
Glamorous Spirit (IRE) 95 [2] (5f, Linw, SD, Mar 20)
Glass Harmonium (IRE) 115 [3] (1m 2f 7y, Sand, GF, May 27)
Gold Bubbles (USA) 102 [2] (1m, Curr, GF, Jun 27)
Golden Desert (IRE) 97 [9] (7f, Asco, Gd, May 8)
Golden Destiny (IRE) 94 [2] (5f 34y, Newb, GF, Sep 18)
Golden Stream (IRE) 97 [6] (6f, Newm, GF, Apr 15)
Golden Sword 107 [4] (1m 5f 61y, Newb, GS, Aug 14)
Goldikova (IRE) 117 [1] (1m, Asco, Gd, Jun 15)
Gramercy (IRE) 105 [1] (6f, Asco, Gd, Aug 7)
Green Moon (IRE) 96 [1] (1m 2f 6y, Newb, GF, May 15)
Green Park (IRE) 94 [1] (6f, Warw, Hvy, Oct 4)
Greyfriarschorista 107 [3] (5f, Curr, Gd, Aug 29)
Greylami (IRE) 98 [1] (1m 2f, Asco, GF, Jul 10)
Gunner Lindley (IRE) 99 [1] (1m, York, Sft, Oct 9)
Habaayib 95 [2] (7f, Newb, Gd, Apr 17)
Hafawa (IRE) 94 [5] (7f, Newm, Gd, Apr 14)
Hajoum (IRE) 101 [1] (7f, Dunw, SD, Oct 3)
Hamish Mcgonagall 108 [4] (7f, Curr, Gd, Aug 29)
Hanoverian Baron 96 [1] (1m 2f, Asco, Gd, Jul 23)
Harbinger 128 [1] (1m 4f, Asco, Gd, Jul 24)
Harris Tweed 113 [1] (1m 4f 66y, Ches, Sft, Sep 11)
Harrison George (IRE) 106 [1] (1m 4y, Pont, Gd, Apr 13)
Hawkeyethenoo (IRE) 96 [2] (5f, Epso, GF, Jun 5)
Hearts Of Fire 119 [3] (1m, Asco, Gd, Jun 15)
Hen Night (IRE) 99 [1] (1m, Cork, Gd, Aug 1)
Hevelius 94 [7] (1m 6f, Good, GF, Jun 18)
High Heeled (IRE) 112 [3] (1m 4f 10y, Epso, Gd, Jun 4)
High Standing (USA) 100 [2] (6f 8y, Newb, Gd, Jul 17)
Hillview Boy (IRE) 98 [9] (1m 6f, York, Gd, Aug 18)
Himalya (IRE) 111 [2] (7f, Asco, GF, Jun 18)
Hitchens (IRE) 97 [3] (6f, Ayr, Gd, Sep 18)
Holberg (UAE) 94 [1] (1m 4f, Good, GF, Jun 4)
Hoof It 101 [2] (5f, Hayd, Sft, Sep 25)
Horatio Carter 94 [2] (7f, Newc, GF, Jun 26)
Horseradish 94 [1] (7f, Donc, GS, Nov 6)
Hot Prospect 107 [2] (1m 2f 7y, Wind, Sft, Aug 28)
Hotham 95 [1] (6f, York, GF, Jul 10)
Hujaylea (IRE) 106 [1] (7f, Curr, Sft, Sep 26)
Icon Dream (IRE) 100 [2] (1m 4f, List, Sft, Sep 15)
Illustrious Blue 108 [2] (2m 78y, Sand, GF, Jul 3)
Imperial Guest 97 [3] (7f, Asco, GF, Jun 18)
Imposing 100 [2] (1m 4f, Asco, GF, Jun 19)
Indian Days 103 [1] (1m 1f 192y, Good, GF, Jul 27)
Inler (IRE) 94 [1] (7f, Donc, Gd, Oct 23)
Invincible Ash (IRE) 105 [1] (6f 63y, Curr, GF, Jun 27)
Invincible Soul (IRE) 103 [1] (1m 1f 192y, Good, GF, Jul 29)
Invisible Man 100 [2] (1m, Good, Gd, Jul 30)
Inxile (IRE) 99 [4] (5f, Linw, SD, Mar 20)
Irish Heartbeat (IRE) 95 [3] (6f, York, Sft, Oct 9)
Iver Bridge Lad 103 [4] (7f, Donc, GS, Nov 6)
Jack My Boy (IRE) 94 [1] (6f, Newm, GF, May 1)
Jaconet (USA) 94 [3] (5f, Linw, SD, Mar 20)
Jacqueline Quest (IRE) 99 [3] (1m, Asco, GF, Jun 18)
Jan Vermeer (IRE) 114 [3] (1m 4f, Curr, GF, Jun 27)
Jedi 100 [4] (1m 4f 5y, Newb, GS, Oct 23)
Jembatt (IRE) 99 [1] (7f, Naas, Gd, Jun 7)
Joe Packet 96 [1] (5f 6y, Sand, Gd, Sep 11)
Jonny Mudball 105 [1] (6f, Newc, GF, Jun 26)
Joshua Tree (IRE) 110 [3] (1m 4f, York, Gd, Aug 17)
Judge 'n Jury 104 [8] (5f, Curr, Gd, Aug 29)
Jukebox Jury (IRE) 95 [7] (1m 4f 10y, Epso, Gd, Jun 4)
Junior 96 [1] (2m 4f, Asco, Gd, Jun 15)
Just Lille (IRE) 98 [1] (1m 4f 17y, Hami, GF, Jun 9)
Kaldoun Kingdom (IRE) 101 [2] (6f, York, GF, Jul 24)
Kansai Spirit (IRE) 94 [1] (1m 5f 61y, Newb, Gd, Aug 13)
Kay Gee Be (IRE) 99 [1] (1m, Asco, GF, Jul 9)
Keredari (IRE) 98 [6] (1m, Curr, GF, May 22)
King Jock (USA) 101 [1] (7f, Naas, Gd, Apr 17)
King Of Dixie (USA) 105 [1] (5f, Asco, Gd, Apr 28)
King Of Wands 104 [1] (2m 78y, Sand, GF, Jul 3)
King Olav (UAE) 97 [2] (1m 3f, Kemw, SD, Mar 27)
Kingdom Of Fife 111 [3] (7f, Asco, GF, Jun 18)
Kings Destiny 104 [7] (1m 2f 18y, Epso, Gd, Jun 4)
Kings Gambit (SAF) 116 [3] (1m 208y, York, GF, Aug 20)
Kingsgate Native (IRE) 120 [1] (5f, Hayd, GF, May 22)
Kinsale King (USA) 99 [3] (6f, Asco, GF, Jun 19)
Kirklees (IRE) 99 [4] (1m 2f, Ayr, Gd, Sep 18)
Kitty Kiernan 96 [1] (7f, Naas, GF, Jun 7)
Kiwi Bay 95 [1] (1m, Redc, Gd, Jun 8)
Knight Eagle (IRE) 96 [5] (2m, Curr, Sft, Sep 26)
Knot In Wood (IRE) 102 [4] (6f, Curr, GF, Jun 19)
La De Two (IRE) 96 [5] (1m 4f 5y, Newb, GS, Oct 23)
Laaheb 112 [2] (1m 5f 61y, Newb, GS, Aug 14)
Laddies Poker Two (IRE) 103 [1] (6f, Asco, GF, Jun 19)
Lady Artemisia (IRE) 97 [6] (1m 4f 5y, Newb, GF, Aug 1)
Lady Jane Digby 97 [6] (1m 2f 7y, Sand, GF, May 22)
Lady Lupus (IRE) 98 [3] (1m 4f, Curr, Yld, Jul 18)
Lady Of The Desert (USA) 101 [1] (6f, Asco, GS, Sep 26)
Latin Love (IRE) 101 [1] (1m 1f, Curr, Yld, Jul 18)

## RPR TOP THREE-YEAR-OLDS AND OLDER HORSES OF 2010

Les Fazzani (IRE) 111[1] (1m 3f 200y, Hayd, GS, May 29)
Lethal Glaze (IRE) 96[2] (1m 5f 61y, Newb, Gd, Aug 13)
Light From Mars 99[5] (1m, York, Gd, Aug 19)
Lillie Langtry (IRE) 107[1] (1m, Asco, GF, Jun 18)
Lolly For Dolly (IRE) 99[1] (7f, Curr, Yld, May 3)
London Stripe (IRE) 95[2] (1m 4f, Asco, GF, Jun 17)
Long Lashes (USA) 97[4] (1m, Good, GF, Jul 31)
Look Busy (IRE) 94[6] (5f, Hayd, GF, May 22)
Lord Zenith 99[7] (1m 2f, Asco, GF, Jun 17)
Lovelace 99[3] (7f 32y, Wolw, SD, Mar 13)
Lowdown (IRE) 97[1] (6f 5y, Hami, GS, Jul 16)
Luisant 113[1] (6f, Curr, Sft, Oct 10)
Luscivious 99[1] (5f, Souw, SD, Aug 3)
Lutine Bell 96[3] (7f, Kemw, SD, Dec 4)
Mabait 110[2] (7f, Asco, Gd, May 8)
Mafeking (UAE) 95[1] (1m, Linw, SD, Dec 7)
Mahadee (IRE) 100[2] (7f, Donc, GF, Jul 2)
Main Aim 108[2] (1m, Good, Sft, Aug 28)
Makfi 121[1] (1m, Newm, GF, May 1)
Manifest 112[2] (1m 4f 5y, Newb, Gd, Apr 17)
Manighar (FR) 97[5] (2m 78y, Sand, GF, Jul 3)
Marajaa (IRE) 97[3] (7f, Asco, Gd, May 8)
Marie De Medici (USA) 97[3] (1m 1f 192y, Good, GS, Aug 29)
Markab 116[2] (5f, Asco, Gd, Jun 15)
Martyr 99[1] (1m 6f, Good, GF, Jul 27)
Masamah (IRE) 94[1] (6f 18y, Ches, GS, Aug 1)
Masta Plasta (IRE) 104[5] (5f, Epso, GF, Jun 5)
Mataaleb 98[2] (1m 4f, Good, GF, Jul 28)
Maybe Grace (IRE) 94[2] (1m, Cork, Gd, Aug 1)
Medicean Man 100[1] (6f, Asco, Gd, May 8)
Meezaan (IRE) 101[2] (7f, Donc, GF, May 1)
Meeznah (USA) 112[2] (1m 4f 10y, Epso, Gd, Jun 4)
Merchant Of Dubai 103[1] (1m 4f, Donc, GS, Mar 28)
Mia's Boy 101[2] (7f 32y, Wolw, SD, Mar 13)
Midas Touch 117[2] (1m 6f 132y, Donc, Gd, Sep 11)
Midday 107[2] (1m 4f 88y, York, GF, May 13)
Mirror Lake 99[1] (1m 1f 192y, Good, GS, Aug 29)
Miss Gorica (IRE) 99[9] (5f, Curr, Gd, Aug 29)
Miss Jean Brodie (USA) 100[2] (1m 4f, Curr, Yld, Jul 18)
Mister Angry (IRE) 94[1] (1m 4f, Asco, Gd, Aug 7)
Mister Green (FR ) 96[3] (1m 2f, Linw, SD, Feb 27)
Mister Manannan (IRE) 98[3] (6f, Hayd, GS, May 29)
Mon Cadeaux 100[3] (6f, Asco, Gd, Apr 28)
Monterosso 112[4] (1m 4f, Curr, GF, Jun 27)
Moorhouse Lad 104[7] (5f, Curr, Gd, Aug 29)
Motrice 103[3] (1m 6f, Good, GF, Jul 29)
Mujaazef 94[2] (1m, Leop, Gd, Jun 17)
Mujood 94[1] (1m, Good, Sft, Sep 12)
Mull Of Killough (IRE) 95[5] (1m 114y, Epso, Gd, Jun 4)
Mullionmileanhour (IRE) 111[2] (6f, Newm, GF, Apr 15)
Music Show (IRE) 109[1] (7f, Newm, Gd, Apr 14)
Myplacelater 98[1] (1m 1f 218y, Leic, Gd, Jul 15)
Mystery Star (IRE) 102[3] (1m 4f, York, GF, May 14)
Nafura 94[4] (1m 4f, Newm, Gd, Sep 18)
Nanton (USA) 101 (1m 6f, York, Gd, Aug 18)
Navajo Chief 103[1] (7f, Donc, Gd, Sep 8)
Nicconi (AUS) 113[4] (5f, Asco, Gd, Jun 15)
Nideeb 101[1] (1m 2f, Linw, SD, Nov 20)
Noble Storm (USA) 100[1] (5f, Souw, SD, Nov 5)
Noble's Promise (USA) 115[5] (1m, Asco, Gd, Jun 15)
Noll Wallop (IRE) 102[1] (1m, Leop, Sft, Mar 28)
Nosedive 95[5] (7f, Epso, Gd, Jun 4)
Noverre To Go (IRE) 97[3] (6f, Asco, Gd, May 8)
Oasis Dancer 101[1] (1m, Newm, GF, May 1)
Off Chance 96[2] (1m, Ripo, GS, May 25)
Once More Dubai (USA) 96[5] (1m 2f 7y, Sand, Gd, Jul 2)
Opinion Poll (IRE) 105[3] (2m 78y, Sand, GF, Jul 3)
Opus Maximus (IRE) 94[1] (7f 2y, Ches, GF, Jun 25)

Oratory (IRE) 99[2] (1m 208y, York, Gd, Jun 12)
Osteopathic Remedy (IRE) 97[3] (1m, York, Sft, Oct 9)
Ouqba 109[4] (1m, Asco, GF, Jul 10)
Our Jonathan 94[6] (6f, Asco, Gd, Apr 28)
Pachattack (USA) 108[1] (1m 4f 5y, Newb, GF, Aug 1)
Paco Boy (IRE) 119[2] (1m, Asco, Gd, Jun 15)
Palace Moon 100[3] (6f, Asco, GF, Jun 19)
Palavicini (USA) 108[3] (1m 1f, Newm, GF, Apr 15)
Pallodio (IRE) 102[3] (1m 2f, Linw, SD, Mar 20)
Paquerettza (FR) 94[1] (1m 2f 75y, Ches, GF, May 22)
Paraphernalia (IRE) 95[3] (1m, Naas, Gd, Oct 17)
Partner (IRE) 94[1] (5f, Tipp, Gd, Aug 6)
Pavershooz 95[2] (5f, Ayr, Sft, Jul 19)
Peligroso (FR ) 99[7] (1m 2f 7y, Sand, GF, May 27)
Penitent 108[1] (1m, Donc, Sft, Mar 27)
Philario (IRE) 104[2] (7f, Leop, Sft, Mar 28)
Pintura 95[2] (1m, York, Sft, Oct 9)
Pipette 100[2] (1m 1f 192y, Good, Gd, May 19)
Piscean (USA) 94[1] (5f, Kemw, SD, Oct 21)
Pleasant Day (IRE) 95 (1m, Asco, GF, Jun 17)
Poet 111[2] (1m 4f 5y, Newb, GS, Oct 23)
Poet's Place (USA) 94[1] (6f, Hayd, GS, Aug 7)
Poet's Voice 123[1] (1m, Asco, GS, Sep 25)
Polly's Mark (IRE) 108[2] (1m 3f 200y, Hayd, GS, May 29)
Pompeyano (IRE) 107[5] (1m 5f 61y, Newb, GS, Aug 14)
Porgy 94[8] (1m 3f, Kemw, SD, Mar 27)
Premio Loco (USA) 120[1] (1m, Asco, GF, Jul 10)
Pressing (IRE) 110[7] (1m, Sali, GF, Aug 12)
Prime Defender 104[1] (6f, York, Gd, May 12)
Prime Exhibit 95[2] (1m, Donc, Sft, Mar 27)
Prince Siegfried (FR ) 113[2] (1m 2f 7y, Sand, Gd, Jul 2)
Principal Role (USA) 98[3] (7f, Newm, Gd, Apr 14)
Private Story (USA) 94[2] (1m 3f 200y, Hayd, GF, May 22)
Profound Beauty (IRE) 98[2] (1m 6f, Curr, GF, Jun 26)
Prohibit 99[1] (5f, Asco, GF, Aug 7)
Prompter 98[2] (1m 4f, Asco, GS, Sep 26)
Proponent (IRE) 102[3] (1m, York, Gd, Aug 19)
Psychic Ability (USA) 98[2] (1m 2f, Newj, GS, Aug 7)
Puff (IRE) 95[1] (7f, Newb, Gd, Apr 17)
Pure Champion (IRE) 105[8] (1m, Asco, Gd, Jun 15)
Purple Moon (IRE) 113[3] (2m 4f, Asco, GF, Jun 17)
Quadrille 100[2] (1m 2f, Asco, GF, Jun 17)
Quest For Success (IRE) 99[5] (6f, Ripo, GS, Aug 14)
R Woody 98[1] (6f, Good, GS, Oct 10)
Rain Delayed (IRE) 102[4] (6f, Fair, Sft, Jul 10)
Rainbow Peak (IRE) 117[2] (1m 208y, York, GF, Aug 20)
Rainfall (IRE) 105[1] (7f, Asco, GF, Jun 16)
Rajik (IRE) 94[8] (2m 4f, Asco, Gd, Jun 15)
Ransom Note 111[1] (1m, York, Gd, Aug 19)
Raptor (GER) 94[5] (1m 2f, Linw, SD, Feb 13)
Rashaad (USA) 96[9] (1m 4f, Asco, GF, Jun 17)
Rasmy 96[3] (1m 2f 75y, Ches, GS, May 7)
Rebel Duke (IRE) 100[1] (5f, Souw, SS, Jan 1)
Rebel Soldier (IRE) 113[1] (1m 4f, Good, GF, Jul 27)
Record Breaker (IRE) 96[5] (1m 4f, Linw, SD, Apr 10)
Red Badge (IRE) 104[1] (1m 2f 6y, Newb, Gd, Jul 17)
Red Jade 94[1] (1m 2f 60y, Donc, Sft, Mar 27)
Red Jazz (USA) 121[3] (1m, Asco, GS, Sep 25)
Red Somerset (USA) 94[2] (1m, Kemw, SD, Aug 16)
Redford (IRE) 101[1] (6f, Ayr, Gd, Sep 18)
Redwood 104[2] (1m 2f 7y, Sand, Gd, Apr 24)
Regal Parade (IRE) 101[6] (6f 8y, Newb, Gd, Jul 17)
Reignier 95[4] (6f, Asco, Gd, Apr 28)
Remember When (IRE) 109[3] (1m 4f 10y, Epso, Gd, Jun 4)
Resurge (IRE) 98[1] (1m 1f, Epso, Sft, Oct 2)
Reve De Nuit (USA) 95[1] (1m 2f, Newj, GF, Jun 26)
Revered 94[2] (1m 2f 7y, Sand, GF, Jul 3)
Reverence 94[2] (5f, Curr, GF, Jun 27)

## RPR TOP THREE-YEAR-OLDS AND OLDER HORSES OF 2010

Rewilding 120[1] (1m 4f, York, Gd, Aug 17)
Riggins (IRE) 101[2] (1m, Asco, GF, Jun 16)
Right Step 94[2] (1m 1f 192y, Good, Gf, Jul 29)
Rigidity 97[2] (1m 2f 88y, York, GF, May 12)
Rileyskeepingfaith 103[4] (6f, Ripo, GS, Aug 14)
Rio De La Plata (USA) 118[1] (1m 208y, York, GF, Aug 20)
Rip Van Winkle (IRE) 122[2] (1m, Asco, GS, Sep 25)
Rite Of Passage 119[1] (2m 4f, Asco, GF, Jun 17)
Rock Jock (IRE) 102[2] (6f, Fair, Sft, Jul 10)
Rodrigo De Torres 104[2] (7f, Donc, GF, May 1)
Rose Blossom 103[1] (6f, York, GF, Jul 9)
Roses For The Lady (IRE) 100[6] (1m 6f 132y, Donc, Gd, Sep 9)
Rosika 105[2] (1m 6f, York, Gd, Aug 18)
Rowe Park 96[1] (5f, Asco, GF, Jul 10)
Roxy Flyer (IRE) 96[2] (1m 4f, Newm, Gd, Sep 18)
Royal Destination (IRE) 99[5] (1m 208y, York, Gd, Jun 12)
Rumoush (USA) 109[2] (1m 6f 132y, Donc, Gd, Sep 9)
Safina 95[4] (7f, Newm, Gd, Apr 14)
Sahpresa (USA) 105[1] (1m, Newm, Sft, Oct 2)
Salden Licht 95[5] (1m 4f, Donc, GS, Nov 6)
Salute Him (IRE) 108[4] (1m 6f, York, Gd, Aug 18)
Samuel 103[1] (2m 2f, Donc, Gd, Sep 10)
Sand Skier 95[3] (1m 2f, Asco, Gd, Jul 23)
Sandor 100[3] (1m 4f, Asco, GF, Jul 25)
Sans Frontieres (IRE) 119[1] (1m 5f 61y, Newb, GS, Aug 14)
Santo Padre (IRE) 109[3] (5f, Curr, Gd, Aug 29)
Saphira's Fire (IRE) 104[3] (1m 4f 5y, Newb, GF, Aug 1)
Saptapadi (IRE) 110[3] (1m 5f 61y, Newb, GS, Aug 14)
Sariska 114[2] (1m 4f 10y, Epso, Gd, Jun 4)
Sayif (IRE) 94[9] (6f, York, Gd, May 12)
Sea Lord (IRE) 110[1] (1m, Sali, GF, Aug 12)
Secrecy 109[3] (1m, Sali, GF, Aug 12)
Secret Asset (IRE) 98[4] (6f, Asco, Gd, May 8)
Seek The Fair Land 96[2] (7f, Kemw, SD, Dec 4)
Sentry Duty (FR) 97[3] (1m 6f, Good, GF, Jul 27)
Set The Trend 97[2] (1m 114y, Epso, Gd, Jun 4)
Shamali 96[6] (1m 1f, Newm, GF, May 1)
She's Our Mark 100[3] (1m 1f, Curr, Yld, Jul 18)
Sherman Mccoy 95[1] (1m 5f 22y, Bath, Fm, Apr 25)
Shimmering Surf (IRE) 104[2] (1m 4f 5y, Newb, GF, Aug 1)
Shintoh (USA) 98[1] (1m, Nava, GF, May 16)
Ship's Biscuit 104[5] (1m 6f 132y, Donc, Gd, Sep 9)
Showcasing 99[2] (6f, York, Gd, May 12)
Signor Peltro 101[3] (6f, Ripo, GS, Aug 14)
Silaah 94[2] (6f, Souw, SS, Dec 18)
Singeur (IRE) 96[7] (6f, Newm, GF, May 1)
Sir Gerry (USA) 98[2] (7f, Newb, Gd, Sep 17)
Sirvino 102[2] (1m 2f 6y, Pont, GF, Sep 23)
Six Of Hearts 99[4] (7f, Naas, Gd, Apr 17)
Siyouni (FR) 117[4] (1m, Asco, Gd, Jun 15)
Snaefell (IRE) 107[1] (6f, Curr, Yld, Aug 8)
Snow Fairy (IRE) 113[1] (1m 4f, Curr, Yld, Jul 18)
Society Rock (IRE) 105[1] (6f, Asco, Gd, Apr 28)
Sohraab 94[1] (5f 6y, Sand, GF, Aug 21)
Sole Power 97[1] (5f, Dunw, SD, Apr 3)
Something (IRE) 96[1] (6f, Epso, GF, Jul 1)
Sopranist 101[7] (1m 6f, York, Gd, Aug 18)
South Easter (IRE) 107[3] (1m 2f 75y, Ches, GF, May 6)
Spacious 105[2] (1m, Newj, GF, Jul 7)
Spanish Duke (IRE) 102[1] (1m 2f, Newj, GS, Aug 7)
Sparkling Smile (IRE) 96[1] (1m 4f, Linw, SD, Sep 3)
Special Duty 96[2] (1m, Newm, GS, May 2)
Spin Cycle 113[4] (5f, Hayd, GF, May 22)
Spirit Of Sharjah (IRE) 96[1] (7f, Linw, SD, Nov 20)
Spruce (USA) 102[2] (1m 4f, Donc, SD, Mar 28)
Sri Putra 112[1] (1m 1f, Newm, GF, Apr 15)
St Nicholas Abbey (IRE) 109[6] (1m, Newm, GF, May 1)
Stargaze (IRE) 98[3] (7f, Linw, SD, Mar 20)
Starspangledbanner (AUS) 108[1] (6f, Newj, GF, Jul 9)
Start Right 100[1] (1m, Good, GF, Jul 27)
Steele Tango (USA) 105[4] (1m 1f, Newm, GF, Apr 15)
Stoic (IRE) 103[6] (1m, York, Gd, Aug 19)
Stotsfold 120[1] (1m 2f 7y, Sand, Gd, Jul 2)
Strawberrydaiquiri 101[2] (1m, Newm, Sft, Oct 2)
Striking Spirit 98[2] (5f, Muss, GF, Apr 30)
Suited And Booted (IRE) 96[1] (7f, Newj, GF, Jun 19)
Suits Me 102[2] (1m 2f, Linw, SD, Mar 20)
Summit Surge (IRE) 105[2] (1m 2f, Linw, SD, Nov 20)
Sunraider (IRE) 97[1] (6f, Hayd, GS, Jun 9)
Suruor (IRE) 104[3] (7f 122y, Ches, GS, May 7)
Sweet Sonnet (USA) 97[3] (1m, York, GF, May 14)
Swift Gift 101[6] (7f, York, Gd, Jun 18)
Swilly Ferry (USA) 94[6] (6f, Newm, GF, May 1)
Tactic 105[1] (1m 6f, York, GF, May 22)
Tajneed (IRE) 98[2] (6f, Ripo, GS, Aug 14)
Taqleed (IRE) 97[1] (1m 2f, Newj, GS, Aug 28)
Tartan Gigha (IRE) 104[1] (1m 114y, Epso, Gd, Jun 4)
Tastahil (IRE) 101[2] (2m 2f, Donc, Gd, Sep 10)
Tax Free (IRE) 110[2] (5f, Curr, Gd, Aug 29)
Tazeez (USA) 116[2] (1m 2f 7y, Sand, GF, May 27)
Ted Spread 98[4] (1m 4f, York, Gd, Aug 17)
Tepmokea (IRE) 95[1] (1m 4f, York, Sft, Oct 9)
The Confessor 97[1] (7f, Souw, SD, Aug 9)
Thebes 97[2] (5f 216y, Wolw, SD, Mar 13)
Theology 103[7] (1m 6f 132y, Donc, Gd, Sep 11)
Thin Red Line (IRE) 96[3] (1m 2f 18y, Epso, Gd, Jun 4)
Three Moons (IRE) 99[5] (1m 2f, Asco, GF, Jun 18)
Tiddliwinks 103[1] (5f 216y, Wolw, SD, Mar 13)
Timepiece 97[1] (1m, Asco, GF, Jun 16)
Times Up 100[4] (1m 4f, Asco, GF, Jul 25)
Togiak (IRE) 96[2] (1m 2f 18y, Epso, Sft, Oct 2)
Total Gallery (IRE) 107[5] (5f, Hayd, GF, May 22)
Traffic Guard (USA) 107[3] (1m 2f 7y, Sand, Gd, Jul 2)
Tranquil Tiger 113[2] (1m 1f, Newm, GF, Apr 15)
Treadwell (IRE) 105[1] (7f, Asco, GF, Jun 18)
Triple Aspect (IRE) 111[5] (5f, Curr, Gd, Aug 29)
Troas (IRE) 97[4] (1m 4f, Gowr, Gd, Aug 11)
Tropical Treat 103[2] (6f, York, GF, Jul 9)
Twice Over 109[3] (1m 2f, Leop, Gd, Sep 4)
Vainglory (USA) 95[3] (1m 114y, Epso, Gd, Jun 4)
Varenar (FR) 100[6] (6f, Newj, GF, Jul 9)
Verdant 109[1] (1m 4f, Good, GF, Jul 28)
Vertigineux (FR) 117[2] (1m, Asco, GF, Jul 10)
Very Good Day (FR) 94[7] (1m 4f, Good, GF, Jul 27)
Vesuve (IRE) 114[4] (1m 208y, York, GF, Aug 20)
Victoire De Lyphar (IRE) 103[2] (6f, Good, Gd, Jul 30)
Victor Delight (IRE) 109[3] (1m 2f 88y, York, GF, May 13)
Viscount Nelson (USA) 107[3] (1m 2f 7y, Sand, GF, Jul 3)
Vitznau (IRE) 96[6] (1m 114y, Epso, Gd, Jun 4)
Viva Vettori 97[1] (1m, Kemw, SD, Feb 14)
Wade Giles (IRE) 110[1] (1m, Naas, Yld, Jul 21)
Warling (IRE) 98[7] (1m 6f 132y, Donc, Gd, Sep 9)
Webbow (IRE) 94[4] (1m, York, GF, Jul 10)
What A Charm (IRE) 96[2] (2m, Curr, Sft, Sep 26)
Wi Dud 97[1] (5f 13y, Nott, Sft, Apr 7)
Wigmore Hall (IRE) 100[3] (1m 2f, Asco, GF, Jun 17)
Wildcat Wizard (USA) 97[3] (6f, Good, Gd, Jul 30)
Willing Foe (USA) 95[1] (1m 2f 60y, Donc, Gd, Sep 10)
Woolfall Treasure 97[1] (1m 6f, Good, GF, Jun 18)
Workforce 128[1] (1m 4f 10y, Epso, GF, Jun 5)
Xtension (IRE) 112[4] (1m, Newm, GF, May 1)
Yahrab (IRE) 98[5] (1m 2f, Linw, SD, Mar 20)
Youmzain (IRE) 113[4] (1m 4f 10y, Epso, Gd, Jun 4)
Zacinto 110[4] (1m, Asco, Gd, Jun 15)
Zero Money (IRE) 96[2] (7f 50y, Ayr, Gd, Sep 18)

… Guide to the Flat 2011 — Pricewise Logic

# Golden rule to remember – it's not about the draw

**Tom Segal, Racing Post Pricewise expert, explains picking winners can be more straightforward than many think**

SKINNING cats is not a process with which I'm especially familiar but I'm reliably informed there is more than one way to do said deed. Similarly, there are loads of different methods that work when it comes to predicting which racehorse can run the fastest and no one way is better than any other.

It's all about finding a punting style that suits your individual temperament and then sticking with that through thick and thin.

Personally, my success has always come in the big-field handicaps and betting ante-post. As a result I have virtually no bets in any other type of race and spend most of my time targeting the races that suit my temperament best, such as the valuable handicaps, especially on straight tracks, where trouble in running is less likely than round a bend.

Five years ago there is no doubt the draw played a big part in trying to find the winners of these races. Such were the biases at certain tracks, half the field or more couldn't win before the race even started due to the draw. However, that has all changed in recent years and yet the market has been extremely slow to react.

For example, one of my favourite races of the Flat season is the Stewards' Cup at Goodwood. When the draw is made the trainers almost unanimously choose a high or low stall, yet the past six winners have all been drawn in the middle of the track and last year eight of the first nine home were drawn between stalls ten and 19. The same has been the case recently in the Ayr Gold Cup as well. For example, two years ago the last horse out of the hat, Jimmy Styles, won the race from the middle stall. In other words, there is value to be had going against the grain.

I'm also a huge believer in trying to keep finding winners simple. There are so many punters who spend hours more than I would on a certain race but over-confuse the issue and end up not being able to see the wood for the trees. Ground, draws, trainer form; they all play a part for sure, but not to the extent than many would have us believe. By far the biggest factor in finding the winner of any race is uncovering which horse can run the fastest. That sounds simple but if you look at any pre-race analysis of a big handicap all the trainers and pundits want to talk about are those small factors, rather than concentrating on which is the best horse (as we do in the Racing Post Guide to the Flat every year.)

The modern way of handicapping is to not drop horses in the weights very quickly, if at all, and that has given punters a huge chance in the type of races I like. The older exposed horses are the ones who get to run in the Lincoln or the Ayr Gold Cup, while only a few progressive younger horses have shown enough to earn a rating high enough to get into such races.

A good example would be Richard Fahey's Utmost Respect in the 2007 Ayr Silver Cup. This horse went on to win no less than four Group races and he hacked up at 11-4 after

**Laddies Poker Two**

being 8-1 in the morning. In reality his 'real' price was nearer evens. Quite simply he was miles better than his opposition and was getting weight from most of them. He'd have had to fall over to get beaten and yet was available at a huge price on the day of race. Similarly, Pipedreamer would have had to be hampered 20 times not to have won the 2007 Cambridgeshire and Laddies Poker Two had pounds in hand in last year's Wokingham.

Bets like these are far from uncommon. Let's not forget last year's Lincoln winner Penitent either, and in essence that is why I love big-field handicaps. Quite simply punters are getting big prices about horses with miles more ability than the horses they are competing against. Punting nirvana in my book.

As you can see, it is the shape of the race that is the essence of any success I may have had punting. So, as a result, I'm certainly not one for concentrating on the major meetings. The newly relaid tracks at Ascot and York have led to some strange results in the past few years. Who can forget Sole Power winning the Nunthorpe at 100-1 in August? The increase in watering means no one really knows how the ground is going to ride until after the first race of the day. My tipping and punting doesn't allow me to wait that long. Consequently, I don't get bogged down in ground conditions, which is a hugely overplayed factor in my book.

Here's my own ten to follow of races in which the punter may have an edge:

**1. Stewards' Cup (Goodwood)**
**2. Cambridgeshire (Newmarket)**
**3. Ayr Silver and Gold Cups (Ayr)**
**4. Lincoln (Doncaster)**
**5. Bunbury Cup (Newmarket)**
**6. Northumberland Plate (Newcastle)**
**7. Wokingham (Royal Ascot)**
**8. Royal Hunt Cup (Royal Ascot)**
**9. Cesarewitch (Newmarket)**
**10. Ebor (York)** ■

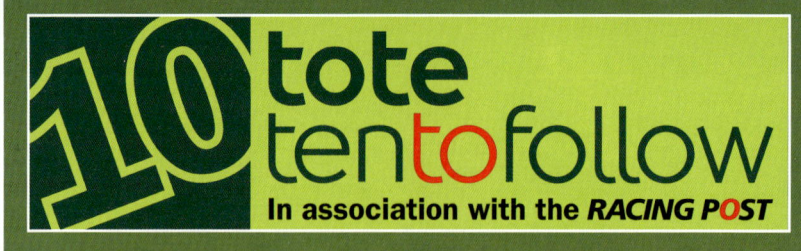

# 10 tote tentofollow
**In association with the RACING POST**

# WIN BIG

## IN THE BIGGEST AND MOST SUCCESSFUL HORSERACING COMPETITION

**BIG-MONEY DIVIDENDS FOR THE TEN HIGHEST SCORING OVERALL ENTRIES – PLUS MONTHLY AND ROYAL ASCOT MEETING PRIZES AND NEW OCTOBER PRIZE**

▶▶ Add two free horses during the bonus window

**MAKE YOUR SELECTIONS NOW FROM THE LIST OF 250 HORSES STARTING ON PAGE 113**

BET RESPONSIBLY AND HAVE FUN: WWW.GAMBLEAWARE.CO.UK

### How to play Ten to Follow

## HOW TO ENTER

From the list of 250 horses starting on page 113, select ten to follow in Flat races during the competition – Saturday April 30 to Saturday October 15, 2011 inclusive.

▶▶**Postal entries cost £12 or €15**
▶▶**OR ENTER ONLINE AND SAVE**
▶▶**Online entries cost only £10. You may enter as many lists as you wish**

**online** ttf.totesport.com Online entries will be accepted up to 12.00 noon Saturday, April 30. We recommend that you place your entry before the closing date to avoid the inevitable late rush which can result in online processing delays and possible disappointment. Entries are not accepted by telephone.

**post** PO Box 116, Wigan, WN3 4WW
Postal entries must be received by 12.00 noon Thursday, April 28. The earlier closing date for postal entries is due to there being no postal deliveries or collections on Friday, April 29, which this year is a UK public holiday.

If you place an entry from outside the UK, it is your responsibility to ensure that you comply with any laws applicable to online gambling in the country from where the entry is placed. Totesport does not accept responsibility for any action resulting from use of its online betting operation from jurisdictions where betting may be illegal. It is also your responsibility to ensure that your credit card or debit card issuer allows their card to be used for gambling purposes. Totesport does not accept responsibility for any action taken by a card issuer for use of a card to obtain gambling services.

## BONUS HORSES

During the bonus horse window you can add TWO FREE selections to your original list and then the highest scoring 10 horses from your 12 selections will count*. The bonus horse window opens from Sunday, July 10 until 6pm Friday, July 15.

*Points scored by Bonus selections qualify for points from Saturday, July 23 (Ascot King George Day)*

**ONLINE ENTRANTS** Add your bonus selections online at **ttf.totesport.com**

**POSTAL ENTRANTS** Will be sent a form to add their additional selections which must be returned to arrive by no later than 6pm on Friday, July 15. Postal entrants cannot add bonus selections online.

## MINI-LEAGUES

Online entrants can set up their own private mini-league for friends, families or a pub or club, where in addition to entering the tote Ten to Follow competition, you will also be able to view your own online leaderboard listing the scores of all entries in your mini-league.

To set-up a mini-league you need to appoint a member of your group as the organiser, who when placing their online entry will need to register a name for the mini-league.

After completing an entry and registering the mini-league name, the organiser will be issued with a unique PIN which will enable access to the mini-league. Other members of the mini-league will need to input this PIN to join the mini-league at the time of making each online entry. Please note that you cannot join a mini-league after your entry has been placed.

---

The leaderboard will be published in the Racing Post each Tuesday & Friday of the competition and also at
**ttf.totesport.com**

## SCORING AND PRIZE-MONEY

Selections winning Flat races under the Rules of Racing (excluding NH Flat races) in Great Britain and Ireland or Group races in France, Germany or Italy and Grade One stakes races in North America during the period of the competition will be awarded points as follows:

- **25 points** Group 1/Grade 1 race
- **20 points** Group 2 race
- **15 points** Group 3 race
- **12 points** Listed race
- **10 points** Other race

In the event of a dead-heat, points will be divided by the number of horses dead-heating with fractions rounded down. No points for a walkover. The official result on the day will be used for the calculation of points with any subsequent disqualifications disregarded.

- Ascot Gold Cup (Royal Ascot, June 16)
- Coronation Stakes (Royal Ascot, June 17)
- Golden Jubilee Stakes (Royal Ascot, June 18)
- Irish Derby (Curragh, June 26)
- Eclipse Stakes (Sandown Park, July 2)
- July Cup (Newmarket, July 9)
- King George VI & Queen Elizabeth Stakes (Ascot, July 23)
- Sussex Stakes (Goodwood, July 27)
- International Stakes (York, August 17)
- Nunthorpe Stakes (York, August 19)
- Irish Champion Stakes (Leopardstown, September 3)
- St Leger Stakes (Doncaster, September 10)
- Prix de l'Arc de Triomphe (Longchamp, October 2)
- Champion Stakes (Ascot, October 15)
- Queen Elizabeth II Stakes (Ascot, October 15)

Any of the above races rescheduled to take place outside the dates of the competition will not count.

## BONUS POINTS

Bonus points according to the official Tote win dividend odds, including a £1 unit stake, will be awarded as follows to winning selections:

- £4 to £7............................**4 points**
- Over £7 up to £11.............**7 points**
- Over £11 up to £16........**11 points**
- Over £16 up to £22........**16 points**
- Over £22 up to £29........**22 points**
- Over £29 up to £37........**29 points**
- Over £37.......................**37 points**

In the event of no Tote win dividend being declared, the starting price will determine any bonus points. Should neither a Tote win dividend nor a starting price be returned, bonus points will not apply.

## BONUS RACES

An additional **25 points** will also be awarded to the winner and **12 points** to the runner-up in each of these races:

- 2,000 Guineas (Newmarket, April 30)
- 1,000 Guineas (Newmarket, May 1)
- Oaks (Epsom Downs, June 3)
- Derby (Epsom Downs, June 4)
- Queen Anne Stakes (Royal Ascot, June 14)
- St James's Palace Stakes (Royal Ascot, June 14)
- Prince of Wales's Stakes (Royal Ascot, June 15)

## PRIZE-MONEY

The Ten to Follow competition is operated as a pool by the Tote. Entry forms are available from totesport and Racing Post publications and online at ttf.totesport.com. All stake money will be aggregated and paid out in dividends after a 30% deduction to cover administration/expenses etc. An amount of £70,000 will be allocated for the monthly and Royal Ascot dividends with the balance divided as follows to the overall winners:

- WINNER ...................70%
- 2nd ...........................10%
- 3rd .............................5%
- 4th ............................4.5%
- 5th .............................3%
- 6th ............................2.5%
- 7th .............................2%
- 8th ............................1.5%
- 9th .............................1%
- 10th ..........................0.5%

Seven dividends of £10,000 each, will be paid for scoring most points during –

1) April 30-May 31
2) Royal Ascot (June 14-18)
3) June
4) July
5) August
6) September
7) October (1-15 inc)

In the event of a tie for any places, the dividends for the places concerned will be shared.

# How to play Ten to Follow

## THE RULES

- ▶▶You must be aged 18 or over to enter and may be required to provide proof of age before receiving payment of any winnings.
- ▶▶Entries are accepted subject to independent age verification checks and by placing an entry you authorise the Tote to undertake any such age verification as may be required to confirm that you are aged 18 or over. If age cannot be verified the entry will be void.
- ▶▶The competition is operated by the Horserace Totalisator Board (referred to as "the tote" ) whose Head Office is: Douglas House, Tote Park, Chapel Lane, Wigan, WN3 4HS.
- ▶▶Selections cannot be changed or cancelled after an entry has been placed.
- ▶▶Members of staff (or their immediate families) of the Tote or the Racing Post are not eligible to enter.
- ▶▶The names of winners/leaders will be published in the Racing Post and at ttf.totesport.com. Any disagreement with the published list must be made in writing and received within five days of the publication date at: Tote Ten to Follow, PO Box 116, Wigan WN3 4WW OR by e-mail at: totetentofollow@totesport.com. Claims received after the five-day period or telephone enquiries will not be considered.
- ▶▶The Tote reserves the right to refuse to accept or disqualify any entries which, in its sole opinion, do not comply with any of the information stated herein. In all cases the decision of the Tote is final.
- ▶▶Once accepted, entries are non-refundable.
- ▶▶Totesport betting rules apply to any point not covered above.

## POSTAL ENTRIES

Write the reference numbers – not the horse names – clearly on the entry form using a ballpoint pen. Only horses contained in the list are eligible and must be entered by their reference numbers. Postal entries cannot be viewed online.

Should a selection be duplicated, points will only be awarded once with the duplication disregarded. Where a selection number is illegible, capable of dual interpretation or is not contained in the prescribed list, the selection will be void and the remaining selections count. Entries containing less than ten selections count for the number of selections made. Where more than ten selections are stated in one line, the first ten selections count with the remainder disregarded.

You can enter as many lists as you wish, each entry must be made on an official entry form although photocopy entry forms are accepted for multiple entries.

Each entry form must contain the Name, Address, Date of Birth and Telephone number of the entrant. Entries in the name of a syndicate must also contain the name and address etc of the organiser.

Completed entry forms must be accompanied by cheque/postal order payable to: Totesport for the amount staked in Sterling or Euro. Payment is not accepted in other currencies. Cash should only be sent by guaranteed delivery. Where the remittance is insufficient to cover the number of entries required, the amount received will be allocated to entries in the order of processing with any remaining entries void.

Neither the Tote, nor the publishers of the Racing Post accept any responsibility for non-receipt of entries. Proof of posting will not be taken as proof of delivery.

---

**If you require help with your entry, call the Tote Ten to Follow Helpline on:**

# 0800 666 160

Guide to the Flat **2011**

# ENTRY FORM

EACH SELECTION REQUIRES A FOUR-DIGIT NUMBER. NUMBERS ARE LISTED FROM PAGE 113 ONWARDS

| EXAMPLE | | | | |
|---|---|---|---|---|
| 1 | 1 | 0 | 8 | 9 |
| 2 | 1 | 2 | 2 | 4 |

**ENTRY ONE**
1
2
3
4
5
6
7
8
9
10

**ENTRY TWO**
1
2
3
4
5
6
7
8
9
10

**ENTRY THREE**
1
2
3
4
5
6
7
8
9
10

**ENTRY FOUR**
1
2
3
4
5
6
7
8
9
10

**ENTRY FIVE**
1
2
3
4
5
6
7
8
9
10

**ENTRY SIX**
1
2
3
4
5
6
7
8
9
10

**ENTRY SEVEN**
1
2
3
4
5
6
7
8
9
10

**ENTRY EIGHT**
1
2
3
4
5
6
7
8
9
10

Title_____ Surname_____ Forename (s)_____
Syndicate Name (max 20 characters)_____
Address_____
Post Code_____ Phone _____
I am 18 or over – tick box ❏   Date of Birth_____ DD / MM / YYYY
Number of Entries (each entry costs £12 or €15)_____ I enclose Cheque/Postal Order payable to: Totesport – Value: £_____ or €_____

Post completed entry form together with your remittance to: Tote Ten to Follow, PO Box 116, WIGAN WN3 4WW to arrive by no later than 12.00 noon on Thursday, April 28

By entering this competition you agree to the tote notifying you of future Ten to Follow competitions and also forwarding reminders for the Bonus Horse Window. You can opt out at any time by letting us know in writing.

You must be aged 18 or over to enter and may be required to provide proof of age before receiving payment of any winnings

Tick this box if you do NOT want to be informed of other totesport betting offers: ❏

BET RESPONSIBLY AND HAVE FUN: WWW.GAMBLEAWARE.CO.UK

How to play **Ten to Follow**

# BORN TO PUNT
## MY BETTING YEAR
# STEVE PALMER

**ONLY £13.99**

*Signed copies*

The hilarious account of a year in the life of celebrated sports betting journalist Steve Palmer. These stories involve the hideous misfortune and sometime joy which befalls the many millions of punters who regularly bet each week

"Steve Palmer's a legend. I remember trying to prepare for a game one Sunday and couldn't stop laughing at his column"

**Michael Owen**

## ORDER NOW
### RACINGPOST.com/shop
**ORDERLINE 01933 304858** *Quote ref: PUNT11*

# How to read the profiles of the 250 horses in this year's Ten to Follow competition

The number to put on your entry form

Age, colour, sex, sire, dam, dam's sire

Trainer

Career form figures to February 25, 2011

**1079 Frankel**
3 b c Galileo - Kind (Danehill)
Henry Cecil                                K Abdulla
**PLACINGS: 1111-**                        **RPR 127+**

| Starts | 1st | 2nd | 3rd | 4th | Win & Pl |
|--------|-----|-----|-----|-----|----------|
| 4      | 4   | -   | -   | -   | £266,474 |

| 10/10 | NmkR | 7f Cls1 Gp1 2yo gd-sft | £180,074 |
| 9/10  | Asct | 1m Cls1 Gp2 2yo gd-sft | £70,963 |
| 9/10  | Donc | 7f Cls2 2yo good | £10,904 |
| 8/10  | NmkJ | 1m Cls4 Mdn 2yo soft | £4,533 |

Ante-post favourite for 2,000 Guineas and Derby following sensational juvenile campaign, winning Royal Lodge Stakes by 10l and easily adding Dewhurst Stakes at Newmarket; trainer unsure whether he will stay 1m4f.

Owner

Current Racing Post Rating

Career wins

Profile of the horse, including significant going and distance information and, where appropriate, its prospects for the coming season

## Contenders Ten to Follow

### 1000 Abjer (Fr) *(pictured)*
*3 b c Singspiel - Fine And Mellow (Lando)*
Clive Brittain                    Mohammed Al Shafar
**PLACINGS: 54110-0**                    **RPR 104**

| Starts | 1st | 2nd | 3rd | 4th | Win & Pl |
|---|---|---|---|---|---|
| 6 | 2 | - | - | 1 | £25,686 |
| | 10/10 | Asct | 1m Cls1 Gp3 2yo soft | | £22,708 |
| | 9/10 | Rdcr | 1m1f Cls5 Mdn 2yo good | | £2,979 |

Surprise 33-1 winner of Group 3 at Ascot on penultimate start, relishing tough test of stamina to outstay Dux Scholar having also won Redcar maiden over 1m1f; never competitive behind Roderic O'Connor at Saint-Cloud next time.

### 1001 Afsare
*4 b c Dubawi - Jumaireyah (Fairy King)*
Luca Cumani         Sheikh Mohammed Obaid Al Maktoum
**PLACINGS: 2111-**                    **RPR 112+**

| Starts | 1st | 2nd | 3rd | 4th | Win & Pl |
|---|---|---|---|---|---|
| 4 | 3 | 1 | - | - | £54,150 |
| | 6/10 | Asct | 1m2f Cls1 List 3yo gd-fm | | £28,385 |
| | 6/10 | Donc | 2m1/2f Cls2 3yo gd-fm | | £19,428 |
| | 5/10 | NmkR | 1m Cls4 Mdn 3yo gd-fm | | £5,181 |

Unraced as a juvenile but progressed quickly enough last year to win at Royal Ascot, landing strong Listed race under a penalty, only to miss rest of season following a setback; strong galloper who seems sure to be suited by step up to 1m4f.

### 1002 Akdarena
*4 b f Hernando - Akdariya (Shirley Heights)*
Jim Bolger (Ir)                    Miss K Rausing
**PLACINGS: 43133/4115365-**                    **RPR 113**

| | | | | | 7,298 |
|---|---|---|---|---|---|
| | 5/10 | Naas | 1m2f Gp3 good | | £46,018 |
| | 4/10 | Navn | 1m2f List 3yo good | | £35,951 |
| | 8/09 | Gway | 1m1/2f Mdn 2yo heavy | | £11,740 |

Bold front-running filly who won twice over 1m2f last season and produced her best effort at that trip when close third in Group 1 Pretty Polly Stakes at the Curragh; doesn't quite seem to stay 1m4f and well beaten over 1m on final start.

### 1003 Al Zir (USA) *(pictured)*
*4 b c Medaglia D'Oro - Bayou Plans (Bayou Hebert)*
Saeed Bin Suroor                    Godolphin
**PLACINGS: 113/9634-**                    **RPR 111+**

| Starts | 1st | 2nd | 3rd | 4th | Win & Pl |
|---|---|---|---|---|---|
| 7 | 2 | - | 2 | 1 | £61,364 |
| | 9/09 | Donc | 7f Cls2 2yo gd-fm | | £10,904 |
| | 8/09 | NmkJ | 7f Cls4 Mdn 2yo gd-sft | | £5,181 |

Slightly disappointing last season having been touted as Classic contender during smart juvenile campaign; still showed useful form on all four runs and not beaten far behind Tazeez on final start; was due to return at Meydan this spring.

### 1004 Alainmaar (Fr)
*5 b g Johar - Lady Elgar (Sadler's Wells)*
Roger Varian                    Hamdan Al Maktoum
**PLACINGS: 211/11-**                    **RPR 116+**

| Starts | 1st | 2nd | 3rd | 4th | Win & Pl |
|---|---|---|---|---|---|
| 5 | 4 | 1 | - | - | £60,858 |
| | 5/10 | Ling | 1m2f Cls2 gd-fm | | £12,462 |
| 102 | 4/10 | Epsm | 1m2f Cls2 76-102 Hcap good | | £31,155 |
| 97 | 10/09 | NmkR | 1m2f Cls5 83-97 3yo Hcap gd-fm | | £12,462 |
| | 9/09 | Pont | 1m2f Cls5 Mdn gd-fm | | £3,238 |

Remains lightly raced having missed second half of last season with fracture of off-fore pastern; had taken winning run to four in conditions race at Lingfield having run away with big handicap at Epsom; looks ready for Group races.

### 1005 Alexandros
*6 ch h Kingmambo - Arlette (King Of Kings)*
Saeed Bin Suroor                    Godolphin
**PLACINGS: 13/11372817/1202358-**                    **RPR 117+**

| Starts | 1st | 2nd | 3rd | 4th | Win & Pl |
|---|---|---|---|---|---|
| 28 | 8 | 6 | 5 | 1 | £788,711 |
| | 2/10 | Meyd | 1m1f Gp3 gd-fm | | £74,074 |
| | 11/09 | Nott | 1m1/2f Cls2 soft | | £15,578 |
| 112 | 2/09 | Ndas | 1m1f 98-113 Hcap gd-fm | | £62,500 |
| 108 | 1/09 | Ndas | 1m 95-109 Hcap good | | £50,000 |
| | 10/08 | Bath | 1m Cls3 good | | £7,570 |
| | 7/07 | Deau | 6f Gp3 2yo soft | | £27,027 |
| | 7/07 | Lonc | 7f List 2yo gd-sft | | £17,568 |
| | 6/07 | StCl | 7f 2yo gd-sft | | £9,459 |

Happiest when dominating modest opposition and has fine record up to Group 3 level but has struggled in higher grade (twice beaten favourite); well below best even in lesser company on final two starts and has plenty to prove.

## 1006 Allied Powers (Ire)
*6 b h Invincible Spirit - Always Friendly (High Line)*
Michael Bell                               David Fish & Edward Ware
**PLACINGS: 3210/7102327/011557-**               **RPR 115**

| Starts | 1st | 2nd | 3rd | 4th | Win & Pl |
|---|---|---|---|---|---|
| 25 | 7 | 3 | 4 | 1 | £206,323 |
| 6/10 | Chan | 1m4f Gp2 soft ................................................. £65,575 |
| 5/10 | Lonc | 1m4f Gp3 good ................................................ £35,398 |
| 97 5/09 | Haml | 1m4f Cls1 List 87-101 Hcap good .................... £23,843 |
| 92 9/08 | Ayr | 1m2f Cls2 78-92 Hcap heavy ........................... £12,952 |
| 82 5/08 | Newb | 1m3f Cls4 71-82 3yo Hcap good ........................ £5,505 |
| 77 5/08 | Ches | 1m4½f Cls3 77-90 3yo Hcap good .................. £10,038 |
| 68 4/08 | Pont | 1m4f Cls5 60-74 3yo Hcap heavy ...................... £3,238 |

Struggled in Britain following handicap win at Hamilton in 2009 but flourished when sent abroad last season, winning pair of Group races over 1m4f in France; suited by stiff test of stamina and easy ground; should stay further.

## 1007 Antara (Ger)
*5 b m Platini - Auenpracht (General Assembly)*
Saeed Bin Suroor                                              Godolphin
**PLACINGS: 11/333111/133202-**                     **RPR 117**

| Starts | 1st | 2nd | 3rd | 4th | Win & Pl |
|---|---|---|---|---|---|
| 14 | 6 | 2 | 5 | - | £278,240 |
| 6/10 | Epsm | 1m¼f Cls1 Gp3 gd-fm ....................................... £36,901 |
| 10/09 | Hopp | 1m2f Gp3 good ................................................ £31,068 |
| 9/09 | Hanv | 1m List good ................................................... £11,650 |
| 8/09 | Muni | 1m 3yo good .................................................... £24,272 |
| 11/08 | Muni | 1m 2yo soft ...................................................... £18,382 |
| 10/08 | Hopp | 1m 2yo soft ........................................................ £2,205 |

Bought by Godolphin last season having won last three starts in Germany and kept up winning run for new yard in Group 3 at Epsom; ran several other good races, including when head second to Stacelita in Group 1 at Deauville.

## 1008 Arctic Cosmos (USA)
*4 b c North Light - Fifth Avenue Doll (Marquetry)*
John Gosden                            Rachel Hood & Robin Geffen
**PLACINGS: 44/131231-**                            **RPR 122**

| Starts | 1st | 2nd | 3rd | 4th | Win & Pl |
|---|---|---|---|---|---|
| 8 | 3 | 1 | 2 | 2 | £333,280 |
| 9/10 | Donc | 1m6½f Cls1 Gp1 3yo good ............................. £283,850 |
| 78 6/10 | Kemp | 1m4f Cls4 68-81 3yo Hcap stand ........................ £4,204 |
| 4/10 | Wolv | 1m1½f Cls6 Auct Mdn 3yo stand ........................ £1,774 |

Progressed through handicap ranks last season to be placed twice at Pattern level (despite not handling track at Goodwood) before relishing step up to 1m6f when winning strongly run St Leger at Doncaster; promises to stay further.

## 1009 Ashram (Ire)
*5 ch g Indian Haven - Tara's Girl (Fayruz)*
Saeed Bin Suroor                                              Godolphin
**PLACINGS: 16/02329115/64162-50**               **RPR 113**

| Starts | 1st | 2nd | 3rd | 4th | Win & Pl |
|---|---|---|---|---|---|
| 19 | 5 | 4 | 1 | 1 | £113,104 |
| 8/10 | Wwck | 7f Cls3 gd-sft .................................................... £6,476 |
| 9/09 | Newb | 7f Cls1 List gd-fm ........................................... £22,708 |
| 8/09 | Kemp | 1m Cls3 stand .................................................. £8,599 |
| 10/08 | NmkR | 7f Cls2 2yo gd-fm .......................................... £34,062 |
| 8/08 | NmkJ | 7f Cls4 Auct Mdn 2yo good .............................. £4,533 |

Yet to add to sole Group 3 victory gained as a two-year-old but continued to run well in decent conditions event last season, winning at Warwick and finishing good second to Inler at Doncaster; returned to action at Meydan this spring.

## 1010 Astrophysical Jet
*4 b f Dubawi - Common Knowledge (Rainbow Quest)*
Ed McMahon                                                       Ladas
**PLACINGS: 135/7261311-**                           **RPR 114**

| Starts | 1st | 2nd | 3rd | 4th | Win & Pl |
|---|---|---|---|---|---|
| 10 | 4 | 1 | 2 | - | £112,483 |
| 9/10 | Newb | 5f Cls1 Gp3 gd-fm ......................................... £34,062 |
| 8/10 | Curr | 5f Gp3 good ................................................... £36,239 |
| 93 7/10 | NmkJ | 5f Cls5 79-93 gd-fm ......................................... £9,714 |
| 8/09 | Nott | 6f Cls5 Mdn 2yo good ...................................... £3,400 |

Blossomed in second half of last season, running away with Newmarket handicap off 93 and following up promising third behind Borderlescott at Goodwood with pair of Group 3 wins; may be a Group 1 contender over 5f.

## 1011 Aviate
*4 b f Dansili - Emplane (Irish River)*
Henry Cecil                                                    K Abdulla
**PLACINGS: 1/116554-**                              **RPR 111+**

| Starts | 1st | 2nd | 3rd | 4th | Win & Pl |
|---|---|---|---|---|---|
| 7 | 3 | - | - | 1 | £63,551 |
| 5/10 | York | 1m2½f Cls1 Gp3 3yo good ............................. £36,901 |
| 4/10 | Asct | 1m Cls3 3yo good ............................................ £6,543 |
| 11/09 | Kemp | 1m Cls5 Mdn 2yo stand .................................... £3,238 |

Sent off Oaks favourite following Musidora win but failed to stay when sixth at Epsom; disappointing behind Eleanora Duse back at 1m2f next time but showed more promise on final two starts; may benefit from being dropped in grade.

Contenders **Ten to Follow**

## 1012 Await The Dawn (USA)
*4 b c Giant's Causeway - Valentine Band (Dixieland Band)*

Aidan O'Brien (Ir)  M Tabor & Mrs John Magnier

**PLACINGS: 17/11-**  **RPR 114+**

| Starts | 1st | 2nd | 3rd | 4th | Win & Pl |
|---|---|---|---|---|---|
| 4 | 3 | - | - | - | £54,987 |
| 9/10 | Leop | 1m2f Gp3 good | | | £34,513 |
| 8/10 | Cork | 1m2f gd-fm | | | £10,075 |
| 7/09 | Naas | 1m Mdn 2yo soft | | | £10,399 |

Still very inexperienced having raced only four times but hinted at big things to come with stunning nine-length win in Group 3 at Leopardstown; ruled out of Champion Stakes after that but sure to be given his chance at Group 1 level.

## 1013 Awzaan
*4 br c Alhaarth - Nufoos (Zafonic)*

Mark Johnston  Hamdan Al Maktoum

**PLACINGS: 1111/0339-**  **RPR 114**

| Starts | 1st | 2nd | 3rd | 4th | Win & Pl |
|---|---|---|---|---|---|
| 8 | 4 | - | 2 | - | £174,447 |
| 10/09 | NmkR | 6f Cls1 Gp1 2yo gd-fm | | | £104,116 |
| 9/09 | Newb | 6f Cls1 Gp2 2yo gd-fm | | | £45,416 |
| 7/09 | NmkJ | 6f Cls2 2yo good | | | £12,952 |
| 6/09 | Haml | 6f Cls5 Mdn 2yo good | | | £3,886 |

Won Middle Park Stakes as a juvenile but clearly not ready for 2,000 Guineas on return last season; proved he had trained on following lengthy break, most notably when third to Delegator in Listed race; failed to act on good to soft on final run.

## 1014 Azmeel
*4 b c Azamour - Best Side (King's Best)*

John Gosden  M Al-Qatami & K M Al-Mudhaf

**PLACINGS: 110/1109-00**  **RPR 111+**

| Starts | 1st | 2nd | 3rd | 4th | Win & Pl |
|---|---|---|---|---|---|
| 9 | 4 | - | - | - | £99,026 |
| 5/10 | Ches | 1m2½f Cls1 Gp3 3yo gd-sft | | | £39,739 |
| 4/10 | Sand | 1m2f Cls1 Gp3 3yo good | | | £37,076 |
| 8/09 | Newb | 7f Cls1 List 2yo gd-fm | | | £17,031 |
| 7/09 | Sand | 7f Cls4 Mdn 2yo good | | | £5,181 |

Made bright start to last season when winning pair of Derby trials but disappointed at Epsom and put away after another poor effort at Maisons-Laffitte next time; back in action at Meydan this spring; useful prospect on pick of his form.

## 1015 Balthazaar's Gift (Ire) *(pictured)*
*8 b h Xaar - Thats Your Opinion (Last Tycoon)*

Clive Cox  H E Sheikh Sultan Bin Khalifa Al Nahyan

**PLACINGS: 74/9310322175/78510-**  **RPR 118**

| Starts | 1st | 2nd | 3rd | 4th | Win & Pl |
|---|---|---|---|---|---|
| 49 | 8 | 6 | 5 | 5 | £566,169 |
| 9/10 | Donc | 7f Cls1 Gp2 good | | | £90,832 |
| 8/09 | Newb | 7f Cls1 Gp2 gd-fm | | | £56,770 |
| 110 2/09 | Ndas | 6½f 97-110 Hcap gd-fm | | | £50,000 |
| 6/08 | Wind | 6f Cls1 List gd-sft | | | £14,760 |
| 7/07 | Asct | 6f Cls1 Gp3 gd-sft | | | £19,873 |
| 11/05 | MsnL | 6f Gp2 2yo gd-sft | | | £76,829 |
| 10/05 | York | 6f Cls1 List 2yo gd-sft | | | £15,000 |
| 7/05 | Wind | 5f Cls4 Mdn 2yo good | | | £4,823 |

Group 2 winner at 7f in each of last two seasons, producing smart efforts both times, though largely below that level in between; finds 6f too short but well beaten on only start at 1m; best on quick ground.

## 1016 Bated Breath

*4 b c Dansili - Tantina (Distant View)*
Roger Charlton                                    K Abdulla
**PLACINGS: 11134-**                           **RPR 111+**

| Starts | 1st | 2nd | 3rd | 4th | Win & Pl |
|---|---|---|---|---|---|
| 5 | 3 | - | 1 | 1 | £30,689 |
| 95 | 7/10 | Hayd | 6f Cls2 83-95 3yo Hcap gd-fm | | £12,952 |
| 90 | 6/10 | Pont | 6f Cls3 71-90 3yo Hcap gd-fm | | £9,714 |
| | 4/10 | Pont | 6f Cls5 Mdn good | | £3,238 |

Unraced as a juvenile but quickly made up into good sprinter last season, nearly defying mark of 105 when bidding for third successive handicap; fourth in Listed contest at Newmarket having nearly been scratched with foot problem; worth another chance.

## 1017 Behkabad (Fr)

*4 b c Cape Cross - Behkara (Kris)*
Jean-Claude Rouget (Fr)                         H H Aga Khan
**PLACINGS: 111/3141143-**                     **RPR 125+**

| Starts | 1st | 2nd | 3rd | 4th | Win & Pl |
|---|---|---|---|---|---|
| 10 | 6 | - | 2 | 2 | £935,062 |
| | 9/10 | Lonc | 1m4f Gp2 3yo soft | | £65,575 |
| | 7/10 | Lonc | 1m4f Gp1 3yo v soft | | £303,398 |
| | 5/10 | Chan | 1m1f Gp3 3yo good | | £35,398 |
| | 9/09 | Lonc | 1m Gp3 2yo good | | £38,835 |
| | 8/09 | Deau | 7½f 2yo good | | £16,505 |
| | 7/09 | Buch | 6f 2yo good | | £6,490 |

Blossomed as he stepped up in trip last season, winning Grand Prix de Paris and Prix Niel to earn Arc favouritism; unlucky in running when fourth on the big day and third in Breeders' Cup Turf when among few not on Lasix.

## 1018 Bethrah (Ire)

*4 br f Marju - Reve D'Iman (Highest Honor)*
Dermot Weld                              Hamdan Al Maktoum
**PLACINGS: 0/1115-**                          **RPR 110+**

| Starts | 1st | 2nd | 3rd | 4th | Win & Pl |
|---|---|---|---|---|---|
| 5 | 3 | - | - | - | £211,836 |
| | 5/10 | Curr | 1m Gp1 3yo gd-fm | | £166,814 |
| | 5/10 | Leop | 1m Gp3 3yo gd-fm | | £37,389 |
| | 4/10 | Limk | 7f Mdn 3yo yield | | £7,633 |

Started last season on a roll but has been restricted to just one run since completing hat-trick in Irish 1,000 Guineas; form of that Classic is mixed and she was only fifth next time in Matron Stakes behind Lillie Langtry but is better than that if managing to stay injury-free.

## 1019 Bewitched (Ire)

*4 gr f Dansili - Abbatiale (Kaldoun)*
Charles O'Brien (Ir)      Mrs J Magnier & Mrs J O'Brien
**PLACINGS: 767317/11361311-**                 **RPR 112+**

| Starts | 1st | 2nd | 3rd | 4th | Win & Pl |
|---|---|---|---|---|---|
| 14 | 6 | - | 3 | - | £158,867 |
| | 10/10 | Asct | 6f Cls1 Gp3 gd-sft | | £34,062 |
| | 9/10 | Curr | 6f Gp3 soft | | £34,513 |
| | 7/10 | Naas | 6f List yield | | £35,951 |
| | 5/10 | Hayd | 6f Cls1 List 3yo gd-sft | | £22,708 |
| 85 | 6/10 | Naas | 6f 74-94 3yo Hcap good | | £12,367 |
| 71 | 10/09 | Dund | 5f 71-88 2yo Hcap stand | | £9,057 |

Won five races at 6f last season, the last three against her elders including twice at Group 3 level; particularly impressive when winning fiercely contested sprint at Ascot on final start; could be top-class.

## 1020 Bible Belt (Ire)

*3 br f Big Bad Bob - Shine Silently (Bering)*
Jessica Harrington (Ir)                     Anamoine Limited
**PLACINGS: 413-**                              **RPR 103**

| Starts | 1st | 2nd | 3rd | 4th | Win & Pl |
|---|---|---|---|---|---|
| 3 | 1 | - | 1 | 1 | £12,101 |
| | 9/10 | Rosc | 7f Mdn 2yo sft-hvy | | £7,022 |

Progressed from debut when 5l winner of Roscommon maiden and took step up to Pattern level in her stride when close third behind Chrysanthemum at the Curragh, just collared close home; looks useful.

## 1021 Biondetti (USA)

*3 b c Bernardini - Lyphard's Delta (Lyphard)*
Mahmood Al Zarooni                                Godolphin
**PLACINGS: 1114-**                             **RPR 105**

| Starts | 1st | 2nd | 3rd | 4th | Win & Pl |
|---|---|---|---|---|---|
| 4 | 3 | - | - | 1 | £203,580 |
| | 10/10 | Siro | 1m Gp1 2yo soft | | £119,469 |
| | 9/10 | Kemp | 7f Cls3 2yo stand | | £5,505 |
| | 8/10 | NmkJ | 7f Cls4 Mdn 2yo good | | £4,533 |

Won weak Group 1 in Italy last season to take unbeaten record to three but badly drawn and only fourth in Breeders' Cup Juvenile on dirt; looks potentially top-class.

## 1022 Blu Constellation (Ity)

*3 b c Orpen - Stella Celtica (Celtic Swing)*
Vittorio Caruso (It)                               Incolinx
**PLACINGS: 1111-**                            **RPR 119+**

| Starts | 1st | 2nd | 3rd | 4th | Win & Pl |
|---|---|---|---|---|---|
| 4 | 4 | - | - | - | £153,053 |
| | 11/10 | MsnL | 6f Gp2 2yo v soft | | £95,841 |
| | 10/10 | Siro | 6f 2yo good | | £15,044 |
| | 6/10 | Siro | 6f Gp3 2yo v soft | | £35,398 |
| | 5/10 | Siro | 6f 2yo good | | £6,770 |

Leading Italian juvenile last year; finished

unbeaten in four starts, culminating in Group 2 at Maisons-Laffitte when thrashing a good field including Approve by 6l; will be kept to sprint distances with Royal Ascot possibly on the agenda.

## 1023 Blue Bunting (USA)

*3 gr f Dynaformer - Miarixa (Linamix)*

Mahmood Al Zarooni                                    Godolphin
**PLACINGS: 211-**                                    **RPR 99+**

| Starts | 1st | 2nd | 3rd | 4th | Win & Pl |
|---|---|---|---|---|---|
| 3 | 2 | 1 | - | - | £18,779 |
| | 10/10 | NmkR | 1m Cls1 List 2yo gd-sft | | £14,193 |
| | 8/10 | Donc | 1m Cls5 Mdn 2yo good | | £3,238 |

Relished step up to 1m when winning final two starts, including decent Listed contest at Newmarket from Elas Diamond; seems sure to stay 1m4f and has ability to develop into Oaks candidate; was due to return at Meydan before that.

## 1024 Borderlescott

*9 b g Compton Place - Jeewan (Touching Wood)*

Robin Bastiman          James Edgar & William Donaldson
**PLACINGS: 31/32514160/2333168-**              **RPR 116**

| Starts | 1st | 2nd | 3rd | 4th | Win & Pl |
|---|---|---|---|---|---|
| 52 | 13 | 15 | 8 | 3 | £743,078 |
| | 7/10 | Gdwd | 5f Cls1 Gp2 good | | £56,770 |
| | 8/09 | York | 5f Cls1 Gp1 gd-fm | | £136,248 |
| | 7/09 | Ches | 5f Cls1 List gd-fm | | £22,708 |
| | 10/08 | Dund | 5f List stand | | £23,934 |
| | 8/08 | NmkJ | 5f Cls1 Gp1 good | | £93,671 |
| | 5/08 | Muss | 5f Cls2 gd-sft | | £12,462 |
| 102 | 8/06 | Gdwd | 6f Cls2 91-107 Hcap gd-fm | | £62,320 |
| 97 | 5/06 | York | 6f Cls2 86-100 Hcap soft | | £12,954 |
| 92 | 10/05 | York | 6f Cls2 88-100 Hcap soft | | £19,500 |
| 78 | 8/05 | Ripn | 6f Cls4 61-78 3yo Hcap gd-fm | | £6,856 |
| 74 | 8/05 | Rdcr | 6f Cls4 65-83 3yo Hcap gd-fm | | £5,931 |
| 68 | 6/05 | Hayd | 6f Cls4 61-81 Hcap gd-fm | | £7,396 |
| 64 | 7/04 | Haml | 6f Cls4 64-87 2yo Hcap gd-fm | | £5,187 |

Veteran sprinter who relishes big fields, landing back-to-back Nunthorpes in 2008 and 2009 having run well in major handicaps for several years; not quite at that level last season despite narrow Group 2 win at Goodwood.

## 1025 Brevity (USA)

*3 b f Street Cry - Cut Short (Diesis)*

Brian Meehan                                    Mrs Lucinda Freedman
**PLACINGS: 411-**                                    **RPR 101**

| Starts | 1st | 2nd | 3rd | 4th | Win & Pl |
|---|---|---|---|---|---|
| 3 | 2 | - | - | 1 | £22,008 |
| | 9/10 | Sals | 6f Cls1 List 2yo gd-fm | | £17,031 |
| | 8/10 | Ffos | 6f Cls4 2yo good | | £4,015 |

Yet to run above Listed level having missed potential late-season targets but won arguably strongest fillies' race of that type when getting better of Rimth and Margot Did at Salisbury; expected to improve but unclear what will be her best trip.

## 1026 Broox (Ire)

*3 b c Xaar - Miss Brooks (Bishop Of Cashel)*

Eoghan O'Neill (Fr)          G Lucas & Mme H Marsh
**PLACINGS: 2112419-**                          **RPR 111+**

| Starts | 1st | 2nd | 3rd | 4th | Win & Pl |
|---|---|---|---|---|---|
| 7 | 3 | 2 | | 1 | £108,305 |
| | 9/10 | MsnL | 5f/½f Gp3 2yo gd-sft | | £35,398 |
| | 6/10 | Chan | 6f 2yo good | | £15,044 |
| | 5/10 | Chan | 5½f 2yo good | | £10,619 |

Given busy campaign last season, doing best when easily landing Group 3 at Maisons-Laffitte; had twice run well at a higher level before that, finishing second in Prix Robert Papin and fourth behind Dream Ahead in Prix Morny.

## 1027 Bullet Train

*4 b c Sadler's Wells - Kind (Danehill)*

Henry Cecil                                              K Abdulla
**PLACINGS: 1/210655-**                          **RPR 113**

| Starts | 1st | 2nd | 3rd | 4th | Win & Pl |
|---|---|---|---|---|---|
| 7 | 2 | 1 | - | - | £46,702 |
| | 5/10 | Ling | 1m3½f Cls1 Gp3 3yo gd-fm | | £36,901 |
| | 10/09 | Yarm | 1m Cls5 Mdn 2yo good | | £3,469 |

Bitterly disappointing following fine win in Lingfield Derby Trial; ran poorly when well fancied for Derby and King Edward VII Stakes before faring little better when dropped to 1m2f on final start; potentially high-class but plenty to prove.

## 1028 Bushman

*7 gr g Maria's Mon - Housa Dancer (Fabulous Dancer)*

David Simcock                                    Khalifa Dasmal
**PLACINGS: 27/76751293/11297-50**              **RPR 115**

| Starts | 1st | 2nd | 3rd | 4th | Win & Pl |
|---|---|---|---|---|---|
| 20 | 5 | 3 | 2 | - | £132,277 |
| | 6/10 | Epsm | 1m½f Cls1 Gp3 good | | £36,901 |
| | 5/10 | Wind | 1m½f Cls1 List gd-fm | | £22,708 |
| | 8/09 | NmkJ | 1m Cls2 good | | £12,462 |
| 92 | 5/08 | Sand | 1m Cls3 80-94 Hcap soft | | £9,347 |
| | 4/08 | Wind | 1m2f Cls5 Mdn good | | £3,730 |

Not up to Group 1 level on final two starts last season but had done well in slightly lower grade prior to that, winning Group 3 at Epsom before just edged out in York Stakes when upped to 1m2f; returned at Meydan this spring.

## 1029 Buzzword

*4 b c Pivotal - Bustling (Danehill)*

Mahmood Al Zarooni　　　　　　　　　　　Godolphin

**PLACINGS: 21221355/048313-8　　　RPR 111**

| Starts | 1st | 2nd | 3rd | 4th | Win & Pl |
|---|---|---|---|---|---|
| 15 | 3 | 3 | 3 | 1 | £476,172 |
| 7/10 | Hamb | 1m4f Gp1 3yo good | | | £265,487 |
| 9/09 | Lonc | 7f Gp3 2yo gd-sft | | | £38,835 |
| 7/09 | Wind | 6f Cls5 Mdn 2yo good | | | £2,730 |

Consistent middle-distance performer who gained Group 1 breakthough in last season's German Derby; otherwise fell short at top level and only third in Group 2 in Turkey next time; returned to action at Meydan this spring.

## 1030 Byword

*5 ch h Peintre Celebre - Binche (Woodman)*

Andre Fabre (Fr)　　　　　　　　　　　K Abdulla

**PLACINGS: 1144/112134-　　　　　RPR 126**

| Starts | 1st | 2nd | 3rd | 4th | Win & Pl |
|---|---|---|---|---|---|
| 10 | 5 | 1 | 1 | 3 | £537,173 |
| 6/10 | Asct | 1m2f Cls1 Gp1 gd-fm | | | £255,465 |
| 5/10 | StCl | 1m Gp2 gd-sft | | | £65,575 |
| 4/10 | MsnL | 1m1f List v soft | | | £23,009 |
| 7/09 | Comp | 1m2f List 3yo gd-sft | | | £26,699 |
| 6/09 | MsnL | 1m 3yo good | | | £16,505 |

Developed into high-class colt at 1m2f last season, though was slightly lucky to land Prince of Wales's Stakes at Royal Ascot (got first run on fast-finishing Twice Over, who reversed form next time at York); modest fourth on only try at 1m4f.

## 1031 Campanologist (USA)

*6 b h Kingmambo - Ring Of Music (Sadler's Wells)*

Saeed Bin Suroor　　　　　　　　　　　Godolphin

**PLACINGS: 2/82821329/19431130-　　RPR 118**

| Starts | 1st | 2nd | 3rd | 4th | Win & Pl |
|---|---|---|---|---|---|
| 26 | 9 | 4 | 3 | 3 | £653,598 |
| 8/10 | Colo | 1m4f Gp1 soft | | | £88,496 |
| 7/10 | Hamb | 1m4f Gp1 good | | | £79,646 |
| 3/10 | Meyd | 1m4½f Gp2 gd-fm | | | £92,593 |
| 8/09 | Wind | 1m2f Cls Gp3 gd-fm | | | £39,739 |
| 6/08 | Asct | 1m4f Cls2 3yo firm | | | £134,318 |
| 4/08 | NmkR | 1m1f Cls1 List 3yo good | | | £17,031 |
| 3/08 | Kemp | 1m1f Cls2 3yo stand | | | £16,193 |
| 9/07 | Hayd | 1m Cls2 2yo gd-fm | | | £12,954 |
| 8/07 | Sand | 7f Cls4 Mdn 2yo good | | | £4,534 |

Consistent middle-distance performer who was campaigned almost exclusively abroad last season and gained Group 1 win in Germany; Group 2 winner in Britain in 2008 but has largely come up short in domestic races since.

## 1032 Canford Cliffs (Ire)

*4 b c Tagula - Mrs Marsh (Marju)*

Richard Hannon　　　Heffer Syndicate, Mrs Roy & Mrs Instance

**PLACINGS: 113/23111-　　　　　RPR 130+**

| Starts | 1st | 2nd | 3rd | 4th | Win & Pl |
|---|---|---|---|---|---|
| 8 | 5 | 1 | 2 | - | £645,951 |
| 7/10 | Gdwd | 1m Cls1 Gp1 gd-fm | | | £179,677 |
| 6/10 | Asct | 1m Cls1 Gp1 3yo good | | | £141,925 |
| 5/10 | Curr | 1m Gp1 3yo gd-fm | | | £166,814 |
| 6/09 | Asct | 6f Cls1 Gp2 2yo good | | | £56,770 |
| 5/09 | Newb | 6f Cls4 Mdn 2yo good | | | £4,857 |

Crack miler, who put a fair third in the 2,000 Guineas (ridden as if stamina was in question) behind him with wins in St James's Palace Stakes and Sussex Stakes; should be hard to beat and may even stay 1m2f.

## 1033 Cape Blanco (Ire)

*4 ch c Galileo - Laurel Delight (Presidium)*

Aidan O'Brien (Ir)　　　D Smith, Mrs J Magnier, M Tabor

**PLACINGS: 111/101210-　　　　　RPR 127**

| Starts | 1st | 2nd | 3rd | 4th | Win & Pl |
|---|---|---|---|---|---|
| 9 | 6 | 1 | - | - | £1,443,707 |
| 9/10 | Leop | 1m2f Gp1 good | | | £384,513 |
| 6/10 | Curr | 1m4f Gp1 3yo gd-fm | | | £641,593 |
| 5/10 | York | 1m2½f Cls1 Gp2 3yo gd-fm | | | £85,155 |
| 8/09 | Fair | 7f Gp2 2yo soft | | | £66,990 |
| 7/09 | Leop | 7f Gp3 2yo yld-sft | | | £39,186 |
| 6/09 | Fair | 7f 2yo good | | | £11,069 |

Won Irish Derby last year but produced best form over 1m2f, landing Dante Stakes and Irish Champion Stakes in brilliant fashion, and should have plenty more Group 1 targets this season; was due to return in Dubai World Cup.

## 1034 Cape Dollar (Ire)

*3 b f Cape Cross - Green Dollar (Kingmambo)*

Sir Michael Stoute　　　　　　　　　　Saeed Suhail

**PLACINGS: 3131-　　　　　　　RPR 104**

| Starts | 1st | 2nd | 3rd | 4th | Win & Pl |
|---|---|---|---|---|---|
| 4 | 2 | - | 2 | - | £66,381 |
| 10/10 | NmkR | 7f Cls1 Gp2 2yo gd-sft | | | £56,770 |
| 6/10 | Newb | 7f Cls4 Mdn 2yo good | | | £4,533 |

Won strong maiden at Newbury before coming up short in third to Theyskens' Theory on first try at Pattern level but looked much more the finished article when winning Rockfel Stakes; likely to improve again on fast ground and should stay 1m.

## Contenders Ten to Follow

### 1035 Carlton House (USA)
*3 b c Street Cry - Talented (Bustino)*

Sir Michael Stoute — The Queen
**PLACINGS: 21-** — **RPR 95+**

| Starts | 1st | 2nd | 3rd | 4th | Win & Pl |
|---|---|---|---|---|---|
| 2 | 1 | 1 | - | - | £5,558 |
| | 10/10 | Newb | 1m Cls4 Mdn 2yo gd-sft | | £4,209 |

Brilliant nine-length winner of Newbury maiden on second start (runner-up won easily next time), clearly learning plenty from debut second; likely to stay at least 1m4f on pedigree and has already been backed to win the Derby.

### 1036 Casamento (Ire) *(pictured)*
*3 ch c Shamardal - Wedding Gift (Always Fair)*

Mahmood Al Zarooni — Sheikh Mohammed
**PLACINGS: 1211-** — **RPR 121**

| Starts | 1st | 2nd | 3rd | 4th | Win & Pl |
|---|---|---|---|---|---|
| 4 | 3 | 1 | - | - | £240,183 |
| | 10/10 | Donc | 1m Cls1 Gp1 2yo good | | £140,790 |
| | 9/10 | Curr | 1m Gp2 2yo yld-sft | | £57,522 |
| | 8/10 | Tipp | 7½f Mdn 2yo gd-fm | | £8,243 |

Switched to Mahmood Al Zarooni having done well for Mick Halford last season in colours of Sheikh Mohammed, winning Racing Post Trophy at Doncaster on final start; likely to be a leading contender for the Derby at Epsom.

### 1037 Casual Conquest (Ire)
*6 b g Hernando - Lady Luck (Kris)*

Dermot Weld (Ir) — Moyglare Stud Farm
**PLACINGS: 1/132/21317/**

| Starts | 1st | 2nd | 3rd | 4th | Win & Pl |
|---|---|---|---|---|---|
| 9 | 4 | 2 | 2 | - | £695,786 |
| | 8/09 | Curr | 1m2f Gp2 sft-hvy | | £68,107 |
| | 5/09 | Curr | 1m2½f Gp1 heavy | | £168,204 |
| | 5/08 | Leop | 1m2f Gp2 3yo good | | £59,743 |
| | 9/07 | Leop | 7f Mdn 2yo gd-fm | | £8,797 |

Missed last season with injury but was third in 2008 Derby and won Group 1 Tattersalls Gold Cup next year; back in training and aimed at Tattersalls repeat.

### 1038 Cavalryman
*5 b h Halling - Silversword (Highest Honor)*

Saeed Bin Suroor — Godolphin
**PLACINGS: 41/421113/75504383-** — **RPR 120**

| Starts | 1st | 2nd | 3rd | 4th | Win & Pl |
|---|---|---|---|---|---|
| 16 | 4 | 1 | 3 | 3 | £1,107,447 |
| | 9/09 | Lonc | 1m4f Gp2 3yo good | | £71,942 |
| | 7/09 | Lonc | 1m4f Gp1 3yo gd-sft | | £332,854 |
| | 6/09 | StCl | 1m2f List 3yo gd-sft | | £26,699 |
| | 10/08 | StCl | 1m 2yo gd-sft | | £10,662 |

Won Grand Prix de Paris and third in Arc for Andre Fabre in 2009 but struggled to find same form for Godolphin last term, doing best when fourth in Juddmonte International; may benefit from drop in class.

## 1039 Chabal (Ire)
*4 b c Galileo - Vagary (Zafonic)*

Saeed Bin Suroor   Godolphin
**PLACINGS: 120/1d42-**   **RPR 114**

| Starts | 1st | 2nd | 3rd | 4th | Win & Pl |
|---|---|---|---|---|---|
| 6 | 1 | 2 | | 1 | £68,621 |
| | 9/09 | Leop | 7f Mdn 2yo gd-yld | | £11,740 |

Talented on his day as he showed when easily winning Sandown Classic Trial on return last year (later disqualified for failed drugs test); well held by Wigmore Hall at Newmarket on final start.

## 1040 Chrysanthemum (Ire)
*3 b f Danehill Dancer - Well Spoken (Sadler's Wells)*

David Wachman (Ir)   Michael Tabor
**PLACINGS: 11-**   **RPR 104+**

| Starts | 1st | 2nd | 3rd | 4th | Win & Pl |
|---|---|---|---|---|---|
| 2 | 2 | - | - | - | £71,327 |
| | 9/10 | Curr | 7f Gp3 2yo yld-gd | | £34,513 |
| | 9/10 | Curr | 1m List 2yo soft | | £36,814 |

Unbeaten in two starts last season, winning when pitched straight into Listed company on debut and following up with game victory in triple photo in Group 3; exciting.

## 1041 Circumvent
*4 ch g Tobougg - Seren Devious (Dr Devious)*

Paul Cole   The Fairy Story Partnership
**PLACINGS: 12112/3518530-**   **RPR 113**

| Starts | 1st | 2nd | 3rd | 4th | Win & Pl |
|---|---|---|---|---|---|
| 12 | 4 | 2 | 2 | | £140,026 |
| 103 | 7/10 | NmkJ | 1m2f Cls2 81-103 3yo Hcap gd-fm | | £49,848 |
| | 10/09 | StCl | 1m Gp3 2yo v soft | | £38,835 |
| | 9/09 | Leic | 7f Cls4 2yo gd-fm | | £5,181 |
| | 8/09 | Sthl | 6f Cls4 Auct Mdn 2yo stand | | £4,640 |

Inconsistent last season but showed plenty of ability when 40-1 winner of competitive Newmarket handicap off 103; ran to similar level when third in Listed race at Ayr but struggled in better company in between.

## 1042 Cirrus Des Aigles (Fr)
*5 b g Even Top - Taille De Guepe (Septieme Ciel)*

Corine Barande-Barbe (Fr)   J-C Dupouy & X Niel
**PLACINGS: 11223312115/4311297-**   **RPR 120**

| Starts | 1st | 2nd | 3rd | 4th | Win & Pl |
|---|---|---|---|---|---|
| 25 | 7 | 9 | 4 | 2 | £433,341 |
| | 10/10 | Lonc | 1m2f Gp2 v soft | | £65,575 |
| | 9/10 | Lonc | 1m2f List good | | £23,009 |
| | 10/09 | Lonc | 1m4f Gp2 gd-sft | | £71,942 |
| | 9/09 | Lonc | 1m2f Gp3 3yo good | | £38,835 |
| | 8/09 | Le L | 1m2f List 3yo gd-sft | | £26,699 |
| | 5/09 | Lonc | 1m2½f 3yo soft | | £27,760 |
| | 5/09 | Lonc | 1m2f 3yo good | | £14,078 |

Consistent performer at Pattern and Listed level for past two seasons and produced career-best effort with clear-cut win in Group 2 Prix Dollar before just losing out at same level next time; seems equally effective at 1m2f and 1m4f.

## 1043 Cityscape
*5 ch h Selkirk - Tantina (Distant View)*

Roger Charlton   K Abdulla
**PLACINGS: 212/20/4211-**   **RPR 124**

| Starts | 1st | 2nd | 3rd | 4th | Win & Pl |
|---|---|---|---|---|---|
| 9 | 3 | 4 | - | 1 | £116,061 |
| | 10/10 | NmkR | 1m Cls1 Gp3 gd-sft | | £34,062 |
| | 9/10 | Hayd | 1m Cls1 List good | | £22,708 |
| | 9/08 | Sals | 1m Cls4 2yo good | | £4,695 |

Suffered several injury problems since promising juvenile campaign in 2008 but returned from latest setback last autumn better than ever, most notably when romping to seven-length win in Group 3 at Newmarket; could be a leading Group 1 miler.

## 1044 Claremont (Ire)
*5 b h Sadler's Wells - Mezzo Soprano (Darshaan)*

Mahmood Al Zarooni   Godolphin
**PLACINGS: 3/132144/463310-051**   **RPR 113**

| Starts | 1st | 2nd | 3rd | 4th | Win & Pl |
|---|---|---|---|---|---|
| 16 | 4 | 1 | 4 | 3 | £218,526 |
| | 2/11 | Meyd | 1m6f List good | | £67,308 |
| | 5/10 | Newb | 1m5½f Cls1 List gd-fm | | £22,708 |
| | 6/09 | Chan | 1m4f Gp3 3yo good | | £38,835 |
| | 4/09 | Lonc | 1m3f 3yo good | | £16,505 |

Moved to Godolphin from Andre Fabre at start of last season; won only once for new connections in Listed event at Newbury but ran well at higher level, most notably when third behind Harbinger in Group 3 John Porter Stakes.

## 1045 Class Is Class (Ire)
*5 b g Montjeu - Hector's Girl (Hector Protector)*

Sir Michael Stoute   R Ahamad & P Scott
**PLACINGS: 92/13240/70124-**   **RPR 116**

| Starts | 1st | 2nd | 3rd | 4th | Win & Pl |
|---|---|---|---|---|---|
| 12 | 1 | 3 | 1 | 2 | £59,869 |
| | 5/10 | Gdwd | 1m2f Cls1 List good | | £22,708 |
| | 5/09 | Yarm | 1m Cls5 Mdn good | | £2,526 |

Has struggled to live up to lofty home reputation and was beaten when favourite for fifth successive race on return last season; again hinted at vast potential with 14-1 win over Laaheb in Listed race at Goodwood; hard to predict.

## Contenders Ten to Follow

### 1046 Cochabamba (Ire)
3 ch f Hurricane Run - Bolivia (Distant View)
Roger Teal                           The Rat Racers
**PLACINGS: 12262-**                       **RPR 103**

| Starts | 1st | 2nd | 3rd | 4th | Win & Pl |
|---|---|---|---|---|---|
| 5 | - | 1 | 3 | - | £38,095 |
| | 7/10 | Ling | 6f Cls6 Mdn Auct 2yo stand | | £2,047 |

Ran several good races in defeat last season, finishing second three times in decent company, most notably when half a length behind Cape Dollar in Rockfel Stakes; looked equally effective on soft and good to firm and seems sure to pay her way.

### 1047 Crown Prosecutor (Ire)
3 b c Exceed And Excel - Miss Brief (Brief Truce)
Brian Meehan                      Sangster Families
**PLACINGS: 11623-**                       **RPR 107**

| Starts | 1st | 2nd | 3rd | 4th | Win & Pl |
|---|---|---|---|---|---|
| 5 | 2 | 1 | 1 | - | £53,547 |
| | 6/10 | Sals | 6f Cls2 Auct 2yo gd-fm | | £8,100 |
| | 5/10 | Gdwd | 6f Cls5 Mdn Auct 2yo good | | £3,238 |

Earned big reputation when winning first two starts and sent off 6-4 to win Vintage Stakes at Goodwood only to get badly hampered and finished distressed; did better back at 6f subsequently when second in Gimcrack and third in Mill Reef Stakes.

### 1048 Crystal Capella
6 b m Cape Cross - Crystal Star (Mark Of Esteem)
Sir Michael Stoute       Sir Evelyn De Rothschild
**PLACINGS: 2/211111/152/10-**             **RPR 120**

| Starts | 1st | 2nd | 3rd | 4th | Win & Pl |
|---|---|---|---|---|---|
| 12 | 7 | 3 | - | - | £242,175 |
| | 10/10 | NmkR | 1m4f Cls1 Gp2 gd-sft | | £51,093 |
| | 5/09 | York | 1m2¹/₂f Cls1 Gp3 good | | £36,901 |
| | 10/08 | NmkR | 1m4f Cls1 Gp2 good | | £60,829 |
| | 9/08 | Asct | 1m4f Cls1 List good | | £24,979 |
| 93 | 8/08 | Gdwd | 1m2f Cls1 List 86-100 Hcap soft | | £24,979 |
| 80 | 7/08 | York | 1m2¹/₂f Cls3 71-89 Hcap gd-fm | | £9,714 |
| | 5/08 | Newc | 1m2f Cls5 Mdn gd-fm | | £3,562 |

Well established among top middle-distance fillies in Britain despite injury problems, winning Pride Stakes at Newmarket for second time last season having finished second in same race on previous start in 2009; best with cut in ground.

### 1049 Dalghar (Fr)
5 gr h Anabaa - Daltawa (Miswaki)
Alain De Royer-Dupre (Fr)             H H Aga Khan
**PLACINGS: 8312/11/2153223-**             **RPR 119**

| Starts | 1st | 2nd | 3rd | 4th | Win & Pl |
|---|---|---|---|---|---|
| 13 | 4 | 4 | 3 | - | £200,393 |
| | 6/10 | Lonc | 7f Gp3 good | | £35,398 |
| | 12/09 | Deau | 7¹/₂f List stand | | £25,243 |
| | 10/09 | Lonc | 1m 3yo gd-sft | | £16,505 |
| | 10/08 | MsnL | 7f 2yo soft | | £8,088 |

Couldn't quite live up to rich promise last season when beaten favourite on each of last four starts; twice won over 1m in 2009 but steadily dropped down in trip since and good second to Lady Of The Desert over 6f on penultimate start.

### 1050 Dandino
4 br c Dansili - Generous Diana (Generous)
James Given                         Elite Racing Club
**PLACINGS: 72/1111280-**                  **RPR 116**

| Starts | 1st | 2nd | 3rd | 4th | Win & Pl |
|---|---|---|---|---|---|
| 9 | 4 | 2 | - | - | £85,379 |
| 91 | 6/10 | Asct | 1m4f Cls2 78-99 3yo Hcap gd-fm | | £31,155 |
| 82 | 6/10 | Epsm | 1m2f Cls2 79-93 3yo Hcap gd-fm | | £31,155 |
| 77 | 4/10 | Donc | 1m2¹/₂f Cls4 73-82 3yo Hcap good | | £4,777 |
| | 4/10 | Rdcr | 1m1f Cls5 Mdn soft | | £2,072 |

Made stunning progress last season, winning maiden and three successive handicaps before running smart Rebel Soldier to a head in Group 3 Gordon Stakes; twice disappointing at top level but maybe more to come; prefers fast ground.

### 1051 Dangerous Midge (USA)
5 b h Lion Heart - Adored Slew (Seattle Slew)
Brian Meehan                            Iraj Parvizi
**PLACINGS: 0131/1661811-**                **RPR 121**

| Starts | 1st | 2nd | 3rd | 4th | Win & Pl |
|---|---|---|---|---|---|
| 11 | 6 | 1 | 1 | - | £1,109,760 |
| | 11/10 | Chur | 1m4f Gd1 firm | | £1,000,000 |
| | 9/10 | Newb | 1m3f Cls1 Gp3 good | | £32,359 |
| 96 | 7/10 | Hayd | 1m4f Cls2 88-110 Hcap gd-fm | | £56,079 |
| 88 | 4/10 | Donc | 1m2¹/₂f Cls3 77-90 Hcap gd-fm | | £6,543 |
| | 9/09 | Donc | 1m2¹/₂f Cls3 gd-fm | | £9,347 |
| | 6/09 | Sals | 1m2f Cls5 Mdn good | | £3,886 |

Inconsistent but showed fine form in all four wins last year, landing Old Newton Cup by 8l and running away with Group 3 at Newbury before breakthrough triumph in Breeders' Cup Turf; was due to return at Meydan this spring; needs fast ground.

### 1052 Date With Destiny (Ire)
3 b f George Washington - Flawlessly (Rainbow Quest)
Richard Hannon                                    Mrs J Wood
**PLACINGS: 165-**                                **RPR 93**

| Starts | 1st | 2nd | 3rd | 4th | Win & Pl |
|---|---|---|---|---|---|
| 3 | 1 | - | - | - | £7,763 |
| | 7/10 | Newb | 7f Cls4 Mdn 2yo gd-fm | | £4,533 |

Only progeny of ill-fated George Washington and sure to be highly tried as a result; made striking debut at Newbury and both subsequent disappointments came in much softer conditions; may well bounce back on quicker surface.

### 1053 Debussy (Ire)
5 b h Diesis - Opera Comique (Singspiel)
Mahmood Al Zarooni            H R H Princess Haya Of Jordan
**PLACINGS: 4/1138015d/90174135-**                **RPR 122**

| Starts | 1st | 2nd | 3rd | 4th | Win & Pl |
|---|---|---|---|---|---|
| 16 | 5 | - | 2 | 2 | £743,851 |
| | 8/10 | Arlt | 1m2f Gd1 good | | £359,259 |
| | 5/10 | Ches | 1m2½f Cls1 Gp3 gd-sft | | £36,901 |
| | 7/09 | MsnL | 1m2f Gp2 3yo gd-sft | | £221,359 |
| | 4/09 | Epsm | 1m2f Cls2 3yo good | | £12,462 |
| | 3/09 | Ling | 1m2f Cls4 Mdn 3yo stand | | £4,857 |

Progressive last season at 1m2f when trained by John Gosden, winning Arlington Million before running another fine race when third to Twice Over in Champion Stakes; appeared not to stay 1m4f on first attempt at trip in Breeders' Cup Turf.

### 1054 Delegator *(pictured, 6)*
5 b h Dansili - Indian Love Bird (Efisio)
Saeed Bin Suroor                                  Godolphin
**PLACINGS: 215/12821d35/148-**                   **RPR 116+**

| Starts | 1st | 2nd | 3rd | 4th | Win & Pl |
|---|---|---|---|---|---|
| 13 | 3 | 3 | 1 | 1 | £290,618 |
| | 9/10 | Newb | 7f Cls1 List good | | £19,870 |
| | 4/09 | NmkR | 1m Cls1 Gp3 3yo gd-fm | | £36,901 |
| | 8/08 | NmkJ | 7f Cls4 Mdn 2yo good | | £5,181 |

Dual Group 1 runner-up as a three-year-old but hasn't shown similar form since move to Godolphin; won Listed race at Newbury on return last year but didn't enjoy good to soft ground when fourth next time.

### 1055 Dick Turpin (Ire)
4 b c Arakan - Merrily (Sharrood)
Richard Hannon                                    John Manley
**PLACINGS: 111156/1222153-**                     **RPR 124+**

| Starts | 1st | 2nd | 3rd | 4th | Win & Pl |
|---|---|---|---|---|---|
| 13 | 6 | 3 | 1 | - | £722,776 |
| | 7/10 | Chan | 1m Gp1 3yo gd-sft | | £202,265 |
| | 4/10 | Newb | 7f Cls1 Gp3 3yo good | | £36,901 |
| | 8/09 | Fair | 6f 2yo soft | | £142,718 |
| | 7/09 | Gdwd | 6f Cls1 Gp2 2yo good | | £45,416 |
| | 7/09 | Sals | 6f Cls5 Auct 2yo good | | £3,886 |
| | 6/09 | Wind | 6f Cls5 Auct Mdn 2yo gd-sft | | £2,730 |

Tough and consistent Group 1 miler last season who gained deserved win at top level in Prix Jean Prat following second-place finishes in 2,000 Guineas and St James's Palace Stakes; disappointing on only start at 1m2f.

## Contenders Ten to Follow

### 1056 Dinkum Diamond (Ire)
3 b c Aussie Rules - Moving Diamonds (Lomitas)
Henry Candy                              Eight Star Syndicate
**PLACINGS: 116724-**                          **RPR 107**

| Starts | 1st | 2nd | 3rd | 4th | Win & Pl |
|---|---|---|---|---|---|
| 6 | 2 | 1 | - | 1 | £39,792 |
| | 5/10 | Sand | 5f Cls1 List 2yo gd-fm | | £15,328 |
| | 5/10 | Sals | 5f Cls4 Mdn 2yo gd-fm | | £3,886 |

Among top spring juveniles last season, doing best when close second to retired Zebedee in Flying Childers Stakes; fair seventh against his elders in Nunthorpe and did best of those drawn high when fourth in Cornwallis Stakes.

### 1057 Distant Memories (Ire)
5 b g Falbrav - Amathia (Darshaan)
Tom Tate                                    Mrs Fitri Hay
**PLACINGS: 61/27112/212313-**                  **RPR 116**

| Starts | 1st | 2nd | 3rd | 4th | Win & Pl |
|---|---|---|---|---|---|
| 13 | 5 | 4 | 2 | - | £114,899 |
| | 8/10 | Wind | 1m2f Cls1 Gp3 soft | | £36,901 |
| 104 | 6/10 | York | 1m1f Cls2 87-105 Hcap good | | £17,485 |
| 90 | 9/09 | Ripn | 1m2f Cls3 71-90 Hcap gd-sft | | £8,723 |
| 83 | 7/09 | Ripn | 1m2f Cls4 71-83 Hcap soft | | £6,939 |
| | 11/08 | Ayr | 7f Cls5 Mdn 2yo heavy | | £3,886 |

Progressed out of handicaps last season to win Group 3 at Windsor on penultimate start, showing fine battling qualities, before fine third to Cirrus Des Aigles in Prix Dollar; seems reliant on soft ground (never tried on quicker to good).

### 1058 Doncaster Rover (USA)
5 b h War Chant - Rebridled Dreams (Unbridled's Song)
David Brown         P Holling I Raeburn S Halsall S Bolland
**PLACINGS: /021317/3423461773-7**              **RPR 114**

| Starts | 1st | 2nd | 3rd | 4th | Win & Pl |
|---|---|---|---|---|---|
| 21 | 4 | 3 | 4 | 2 | £134,883 |
| | 8/10 | NmkJ | 6f Cls1 List gd-sft | | £21,005 |
| | 8/09 | Ches | 6f Cls1 List good | | £22,708 |
| | 7/09 | Hayd | 6f Cls2 gd-fm | | £15,578 |
| | 5/08 | Ches | 5f Cls2 2yo good | | £13,085 |

Useful performer over 6f and 7f, twice finishing placed in Group 3 races last season and taking advantage of rare drop in class to win Listed contest at Newmarket (second victory at that level during his career); acts on any going.

### 1059 Dream Ahead (USA)
3 b c Diktat - Land Of Dreams (Cadeaux Genereux)
David Simcock                              Khalifa Dasmal
**PLACINGS: 1115-**                           **RPR 125+**

| Starts | 1st | 2nd | 3rd | 4th | Win & Pl |
|---|---|---|---|---|---|
| 4 | 3 | - | - | - | £295,123 |
| | 10/10 | NmkR | 6f Cls1 Gp1 2yo soft | | £106,046 |
| | 8/10 | Deau | 6f Gp1 2yo good | | £176,982 |
| | 7/10 | Nott | 6f Cls5 Mdn 2yo gd-sft | | £3,562 |

Sensational nine-length winner of Middle Park Stakes last season on soft ground, having also run away with Prix Morny on good; disappointing fifth in Dewhurst after that; being trained for 2,000 Guineas but could return to sprinting

## 1060 Dream Eater (Ire) *(pictured)*
6 gr h Night Shift - Kapria (Simon Du Desert)

Andrew Balding                J C Smith

**PLACINGS: 295444128/333562018-        RPR 119**

| Starts | 1st | 2nd | 3rd | 4th | Win & Pl |
|---|---|---|---|---|---|
| 29 | 3 | 5 | 7 | 4 | £609,504 |
| | 11/10 | Kemp | 7f Cls3 stand | | £6,282 |
| | 8/09 | York | 7f Cls1 List gd-fm | | £16,334 |
| | 9/07 | Donc | 6½f Cls2 2yo gd-fm | | £191,533 |

Smart miler who ran succession of good races last season, though needed to drop well down in grade to claim only win on all-weather at Kempton; fine third at Royal Ascot in Queen Anne Stakes and second in Group 2 in Turkey.

## 1061 Dubai Prince (Ire)
3 b c Shamardal - Desert Frolic (Persian Bold)

Mahmood Al Zarooni           Sheikh Mohammed

**PLACINGS: 11-                          RPR 111+**

| Starts | 1st | 2nd | 3rd | 4th | Win & Pl |
|---|---|---|---|---|---|
| 2 | 2 | - | - | - | £35,445 |
| | 10/10 | Leop | 7f Gp3 2yo gd-fm | | £28,761 |
| | 9/10 | Gowr | 1m Mdn 2yo yield | | £6,584 |

Looked good in quiet campaign for Dermot Weld last season before being switched to Mahmood Al Zarooni; showed fine turn of foot to land Group 3 over 7f on final start; expected to improve over middle distances.

## 1062 Duff (Ire)
8 b g Spinning World - Shining Prospect (Lycius)

Edward Lynam (Ir)              Kilboy Estate

**PLACINGS: /28188110/425026483-        RPR 116**

| Starts | 1st | 2nd | 3rd | 4th | Win & Pl |
|---|---|---|---|---|---|
| 36 | 8 | 6 | 4 | 5 | £371,543 |
| | 10/09 | Tipp | 7½f Gp3 gd-fm | | £45,437 |
| | 9/09 | Donc | 7f Cls1 Gp2 gd-fm | | £90,832 |
| | 6/09 | Leop | 7f Gp3 good | | £41,019 |
| | 12/08 | Kemp | 7f Cls1 List stand | | £22,708 |
| | 11/08 | Ling | 6f Cls1 List stand | | £22,708 |
| | 8/08 | Cork | 1m List gd-yld | | £23,934 |
| | 8/07 | York | 7f Cls1 List good | | £20,745 |
| | 5/05 | Gowr | 7f Mdn 2yo gd-fm | | £8,331 |

Couldn't get his head in front last term, twice finishing second in Group 3 races and close fourth to Balthazaar's Gift in Group 2 at Doncaster; has won over 6f but needs further now and may be best at 1m.

## 1063 Dunboyne Express (Ire)
3 b c Shamardal - Love Excelling (Polish Precedent)

Kevin Prendergast (Ir)           J Connaughton

**PLACINGS: 115-                         RPR 112+**

| Starts | 1st | 2nd | 3rd | 4th | Win & Pl |
|---|---|---|---|---|---|
| 3 | 2 | - | - | - | £48,994 |
| | 7/10 | Curr | 6½f Gp3 2yo yield | | £31,637 |
| | 6/10 | Leop | 7f Mdn 2yo good | | £10,686 |

Eight-length winner of Anglesey Stakes at the Curragh on second start but failed to build on that run when fifth in Racing Post

## Contenders Ten to Follow

Trophy, failing to stay having pulled hard; bred for middle distances.

### 1064 Duncan
*6 b g Dalakhani - Dolores (Danehill)*

John Gosden — Normandie Stud Ltd

**PLACINGS: 22167/11493/22410-**     **RPR 123**

| Starts | 1st | 2nd | 3rd | 4th | Win & Pl |
|---|---|---|---|---|---|
| 15 | 4 | 4 | 1 | 2 | £185,568 |
| | 9/10 | Lonc | 1m4f Gp2 soft | | £65,575 |
| | 5/09 | Asct | 1m4f Cls1 List gd-fm | | £22,708 |
| 99 | 4/09 | Epsm | 1m2f Cls2 86-102 Hcap good | | £31,155 |
| | 9/08 | Pont | 1m2f Cls5 Mdn gd-sft | | £3,886 |

Hard to win with but benefited from fine front-running ride to land Prix Foy and underlined talent when second to Harbinger in Hardwicke Stakes.

### 1065 Dux Scholar
*3 b c Oasis Dream - Alumni (Selkirk)*

Sir Michael Stoute — Juddmonte Farms Inc

**PLACINGS: 42132-**     **RPR 105**

| Starts | 1st | 2nd | 3rd | 4th | Win & Pl |
|---|---|---|---|---|---|
| 5 | 1 | 2 | 1 | 1 | £17,607 |
| | 9/10 | Bath | 1m Cls5 Mdn 2yo good | | £3,238 |

Looked likely middle-distance prospect when winning Bath maiden over 1m but failed to see out that trip when upped in class in Group 3 at Ascot, but shaped with promise in third; showed similar form when second in Horris Hill Stakes over 7f.

### 1066 Elas Diamond
*3 gb f Danehill Dancer - Ela Athena (Ezzoud)*

Jeremy Noseda — Newsells Park Stud

**PLACINGS: 212-**     **RPR 97+**

| Starts | 1st | 2nd | 3rd | 4th | Win & Pl |
|---|---|---|---|---|---|
| 3 | 1 | 2 | - | - | £9,870 |
| | 10/10 | Nott | 1m½f Cls5 Mdn 2yo good | | £3,238 |

Won Nottingham maiden by 12l to go off favourite for Listed contest at Newmarket; just outstayed in second having quickened into lead; sure to stay 1m2f.

### 1067 Eleanora Duse (Ire)
*4 b f Azamour - Drama Class (Caerleon)*

Sir Michael Stoute — Ballymacoll Stud

**PLACINGS: 691/231310-**     **RPR 115**

| Starts | 1st | 2nd | 3rd | 4th | Win & Pl |
|---|---|---|---|---|---|
| 9 | 3 | 1 | 2 | - | £126,094 |
| | 9/10 | Curr | 1m2f Gp2 soft | | £57,522 |
| | 6/10 | Newb | 1m2f Cls1 List 3yo gd-fm | | £22,708 |
| | 11/09 | Kemp | 1m Cls5 Mdn 2yo stand | | £3,238 |

Progressed throughout last season until poor run on final start; produced best effort when third behind world-class pair Midday and Snow Fairy in Yorkshire Oaks and won Group 3 next time despite preferring 1m4f and better ground.

### 1068 Electrolyser (Ire)
*6 gr h Daylami - Iviza (Sadler's Wells)*

Clive Cox — Mr And Mrs P Hargreaves

**PLACINGS: 21210/4510/3240-**     **RPR 115**

| Starts | 1st | 2nd | 3rd | 4th | Win & Pl |
|---|---|---|---|---|---|
| 13 | 3 | 3 | 1 | 2 | £82,885 |
| | 9/09 | Asct | 2m Cls1 List gd-fm | | £22,708 |
| 88 | 10/08 | Leic | 1m4f Cls2 80-92 3yo Hcap soft | | £11,216 |
| | 2/08 | Ling | 1m2f Cls5 Mdn 3yo stand | | £2,332 |

Had become disappointing prior to tremendous second at 33-1 in Goodwood Cup last summer and ran similarly well at York next time; dropped out tamely when stepped up to 2m2f in Doncaster Cup but had looked ready for longer trip.

### 1069 Elusive Pimpernel (USA)
*4 b/br c Elusive Quality - Cara Fantasy (Sadler's Wells)*

John Dunlop — Windflower Overseas Holdings Inc

**PLACINGS: 112/15-**     **RPR 116+**

| Starts | 1st | 2nd | 3rd | 4th | Win & Pl |
|---|---|---|---|---|---|
| 5 | 3 | 1 | - | - | £130,044 |
| | 4/10 | NmkR | 1m Cls1 Gp3 3yo gd-fm | | £36,901 |
| | 8/09 | York | 7f Cls1 Gp3 2yo gd-fm | | £29,630 |
| | 7/09 | NmkJ | 7f Cls2 Mdn 2yo good | | £9,714 |

Ran only twice last season before suffering a setback but looked to have developed into top-class performer when routing opposition in Craven Stakes on return; only fifth in 2,000 Guineas next time, looking in need of 1m2f at least.

### 1070 Elzaam (Aus)
*3 b c Redoute's Choice - Mambo In Freeport (Kingmambo)*

Roger Varian — Hamdan Al Maktoum

**PLACINGS: 1233-**     **RPR 111+**

| Starts | 1st | 2nd | 3rd | 4th | Win & Pl |
|---|---|---|---|---|---|
| 4 | 1 | 1 | 2 | - | £40,221 |
| | 5/10 | York | 6f Cls3 Mdn 2yo gd-fm | | £7,124 |

Suffering fron an infection when well beaten third at 4-7 in July Stakes on penultimate start and showed fair level of form otherwise; just pipped by Strong Suit in Coventry Stakes and close third in Horris Hill despite wanting good ground.

## 1071 Emerald Commander (Ire)
4 b c Pivotal - Brigitta (Sadler's Wells)
Saeed Bin Suroor                       Godolphin
**PLACINGS: 41212/31713-        RPR 116**

| Starts | 1st | 2nd | 3rd | 4th | Win & Pl |
|---|---|---|---|---|---|
| 10 | 4 | 2 | 2 | 1 | £187,252 |
| 8/10 | Badn | 1m Gp2 soft | | | £35,398 |
| 7/10 | Lonc | 1m1f Gp3 3yo soft | | | £35,398 |
| 9/09 | Hayd | 1m Cls1 List 2yo soft | | | £19,870 |
| 7/09 | Newb | 7f Cls4 Mdn 2yo soft | | | £6,476 |

Given international campaign last season after being bought by Godolphin, winning Group races at Baden-Baden and Chantilly, though found wanting in stronger company; has marked preference for soft ground.

## 1072 Espirita (Fr)
3 b f Iffraaj - Belle Esprit (Warning)
Elie Lellouche (Fr)                   Bruno Mettoudi
**PLACINGS: 211-        RPR 108+**

| Starts | 1st | 2nd | 3rd | 4th | Win & Pl |
|---|---|---|---|---|---|
| 3 | 2 | 1 | - | - | £54,690 |
| 10/10 | Deau | 1m Gp3 2yo soft | | | £35,398 |
| 8/10 | Deau | 7¹/₂f 2yo gd-sft | | | £15,044 |

Just beaten on debut over 6f but improved for step up to 1m, particularly when winning Deauville Group 3; seems sure to stay further and could be leading Classic contender.

## 1073 Exemplify
3 b f Dansili - Quest To Peak (Distant View)
Criquette Head-Maarek (Fr)                   K Abdulla
**PLACINGS: 15-        RPR 88**

| Starts | 1st | 2nd | 3rd | 4th | Win & Pl |
|---|---|---|---|---|---|
| 2 | 1 | - | - | - | £12,123 |
| 8/10 | Deau | 1m 2yo good | | | £10,619 |

Lived up to home reputation when winning on debut at Deauville and then earmarked as trainer's Cheveley Park filly only to flop on soft ground next time; remains a leading prospect on quicker going.

## 1074 Face The Problem (Ire)
3 b c Johannesburg - Foofaraw (Cherokee Run)
Barry Hills      Sir A Ferguson, Cavendish Inv ltd & J Hanson
**PLACINGS: 411188-        RPR 105+**

| Starts | 1st | 2nd | 3rd | 4th | Win & Pl |
|---|---|---|---|---|---|
| 6 | 3 | - | - | 1 | £16,771 |
| 89 | 7/10 | Thsk | 5f Cls3 65-89 2yo Hcap gd-fm | | £6,929 |
| 82 | 7/10 | York | 5f Cls3 66-85 2yo Hcap gd-fm | | £6,800 |
| | 7/10 | Wind | 6f Cls5 Mdn 2yo gd-fm | | £2,730 |

Won Thirsk nursery by 6l off 89 and badly drawn when beaten favourite in Listed race at York next time; seemed to have few excuses when eighth in Flying Childers Stakes but may be capable of better.

## 1075 Fame And Glory
5 b h Montjeu - Gryada (Shirley Heights)
Aidan O'Brien (Ir)      D Smith, Mrs J Magnier & M Tabor
**PLACINGS: 11/1121266/311115-        RPR 125+**

| Starts | 1st | 2nd | 3rd | 4th | Win & Pl |
|---|---|---|---|---|---|
| 15 | 9 | 2 | 1 | - | £1,956,015 |
| 8/10 | Curr | 1m2f Gp2 good | | | £53,097 |
| 6/10 | Epsm | 1m4f Cls1 Gp1 good | | | £127,733 |
| 5/10 | Curr | 1m2¹/₂f Gp1 gd-fm | | | £123,451 |
| 5/10 | Curr | 1m2f Gp3 good | | | £43,142 |
| 6/09 | Curr | 1m4f Gp1 3yo gd-yld | | | £818,447 |
| 5/09 | Leop | 1m2f Gp2 3yo good | | | £75,728 |
| 4/09 | Leop | 1m2f Gp3 3yo gd-yld | | | £41,083 |
| 11/08 | StCl | 1m2f Gp1 2yo heavy | | | £105,037 |
| 10/08 | Navn | 1m Mdn 2yo heavy | | | £6,097 |

Top-class performer at 1m2f and 1m4f who has won Group 1 races in each of last three seasons; best on a galloping track, as when easily landing Tattersalls Gold Cup and Coronation Cup last season, but has twice been slightly below best in the Arc.

## 1076 Famous Name
6 b h Dansili - Fame At Last (Quest For Fame)
Dermot Weld (Ir)                   K Abdulla
**PLACINGS: 2231/2211123/111671-        RPR 121**

| Starts | 1st | 2nd | 3rd | 4th | Win & Pl |
|---|---|---|---|---|---|
| 21 | 10 | 6 | 2 | - | £768,439 |
| 10/10 | Leop | 1m2f List gd-fm | | | £24,447 |
| 7/10 | Leop | 1m1f Gp3 yield | | | £34,513 |
| 5/10 | Leop | 1m Gp3 gd-fm | | | £34,513 |
| 4/10 | Leop | 1m List gd-fm | | | £24,447 |
| 8/09 | Curr | 1m Gp3 sft-hvy | | | £39,126 |
| 7/09 | Curr | 1m1f Gp3 soft | | | £44,175 |
| 6/09 | Curr | 1m List gd-yld | | | £39,502 |
| 10/08 | Leop | 1m2f List yld-sft | | | £23,934 |
| 4/08 | Leop | 1m Gp3 3yo yield | | | £33,507 |
| 7/07 | Naas | 6f Mdn 2yo soft | | | £7,937 |

Falls short at Group 1 level (has finished second three times but well beaten on both attempts last year); prolific in lower grade, however, and won four times last season, including pair of Group 3 contests; was due to return at Meydan this spring.

## 1077 Flying Cross (Ire)
4 b c Sadler's Wells - Ramruma (Diesis)
John Gosden                   R J H Geffen
**PLACINGS: 41/139-        RPR 113**

| Starts | 1st | 2nd | 3rd | 4th | Win & Pl |
|---|---|---|---|---|---|
| 5 | 2 | - | 1 | 1 | £40,382 |
| 8/10 | Tipp | 1m4f gd-fm | | | £10,075 |
| 10/09 | Navn | 1m Mdn 2yo yield | | | £10,399 |

Trained for most of last season by Aidan

O'Brien when winning soft conditions race on return and finishing good third in Irish St Leger behind Sans Frontieres; immediately stepped up to 2m by new connections but ran poorly at Longchamp.

## 1078 Forte Dei Marmi
*5 b g Selkirk - Frangy (Sadler's Wells)*

Luca Cumani                                       Fittocks Stud
**PLACINGS: 974/17/141011-**              **RPR 116+**

| Starts | 1st | 2nd | 3rd | 4th | Win & Pl |
|---|---|---|---|---|---|
| 11 | 5 | - | - | 2 | £127,301 |
| 102 | 9/10 | Newb | 1m2f Cls5 85-103 Hcap gd-fm | | £62,310 |
| 98 | 8/10 | Sand | 1m2f Cls5 77-102 Hcap gd-fm | | £31,155 |
| 92 | 5/10 | Rdcr | 1m2f Cls5 79-99 Hcap gd-fm | | £22,666 |
| 81 | 4/10 | Newb | 1m2f Cls4 72-85 Hcap gd-fm | | £5,181 |
| 73 | 5/09 | Gdwd | 1m1f Cls4 72-83 3yo Hcap good | | £4,673 |

One of last season's most successful handicappers, winning four times, all on good to firm, and finishing off by defying mark of 102 in hugely impressive fashion at Newbury with first two well clear; looks surefire Pattern performer.

## 1079 Frankel
*3 b c Galileo - Kind (Danehill)*

Henry Cecil                                       K Abdulla
**PLACINGS: 1111-**                           **RPR 127+**

| Starts | 1st | 2nd | 3rd | 4th | Win & Pl |
|---|---|---|---|---|---|
| 4 | 4 | - | - | - | £266,474 |
| | 10/10 | NmkR | 7f Cls1 Gp2 2yo gd-sft | | £180,074 |
| | 9/10 | Asct | 1m Cls1 Gp2 2yo gd-sft | | £70,963 |
| | 9/10 | Donc | 7f Cls2 2yo good | | £10,904 |
| | 8/10 | NmkJ | 1m Cls4 Mdn 2yo soft | | £4,533 |

Ante-post favourite for 2,000 Guineas and Derby following sensational juvenile campaign, winning Royal Lodge Stakes by 10l and easily adding Dewhurst Stakes at Newmarket; trainer unsure whether he will stay 1m4f.

## 1080 French Navy
*3 b c Shamardal - First Fleet (Woodman)*

Mahmood Al Zarooni                       Godolphin Snc
**PLACINGS: 1115-**                          **RPR 108**

| Starts | 1st | 2nd | 3rd | 4th | Win & Pl |
|---|---|---|---|---|---|
| 4 | 3 | - | - | - | £67,389 |
| | 9/10 | Lonc | 1m Gp3 2yo gd-sft | | £35,398 |
| | 8/10 | Deau | 1m 2yo gd-sft | | £15,044 |
| | 8/10 | Deau | 1m 2yo good | | £10,619 |

Impressive winner of first three starts, twice beating Salto before landing Group 3 at Longchamp; hugely disappointing favourite in Group 1 at Saint-Cloud after that, struggling on heavy ground, but may well bounce back after move from Andre Fabre to Godolphin.

## 1081 Fury
*3 gb c Invincible Spirit - Courting (Pursuit Of Love)*

William Haggas                            Cheveley Park Stud
**PLACINGS: 11-**                            **RPR 101+**

| Starts | 1st | 2nd | 3rd | 4th | Win & Pl |
|---|---|---|---|---|---|
| 2 | 2 | - | - | - | £283,431 |
| | 10/10 | NmkR | 7f Cls2 2yo soft | | £278,898 |
| | 9/10 | Newb | 7f Cls4 Mdn 2yo gd-fm | | £4,533 |

Unbeaten in two starts, stepping up on debut success to land big payday with fine win in Tattersalls Millions at Newmarket; already looks well up to Group level on that form and could be one for Jersey Stakes if 2,000 Guineas comes too soon.

## 1082 Gile Na Greine (Ire)
*4 b f Galileo - Scribonia (Danehill)*

Jim Bolger (Ir)          Mrs J S Bolger & John Corcoran
**PLACINGS: 15/2302606-**                **RPR 113**

| Starts | 1st | 2nd | 3rd | 4th | Win & Pl |
|---|---|---|---|---|---|
| 9 | 1 | 2 | 1 | - | £133,011 |
| | 8/09 | Curr | 7f 2yo sft-hvy | | £20,225 |

Inconsistent but talented filly at her best, demontrated by her close third in 1,000 Guineas and when second to Lillie Langtry in Coronation Stakes; went badly off the boil subsequently, including when well-beaten favourite dropping down to Listed level.

## 1083 Gitano Hernando
*5 ch h Hernando - Gino's Spirits (Perugino)*

Marco Botti           Team Valor International & Gary Barber
**PLACINGS: 621/1211/1614-5**           **RPR 120+**

| Starts | 1st | 2nd | 3rd | 4th | Win & Pl |
|---|---|---|---|---|---|
| 12 | 6 | 2 | - | 1 | £355,277 |
| | 10/10 | Dund | 1m2½f Gp3 stand | | £34,513 |
| | 2/10 | Ling | 1m2f Cls1 List stand | | £22,708 |
| | 10/09 | SnAt | 1m1f Gd1 fast | | £114,583 |
| | 9/09 | Wolv | 1m½f Cls3 stand | | £7,570 |
| 84 | 3/09 | Donc | 1m2½f Cls3 74-85 3yo Hcap good | | £7,771 |
| | 11/08 | Wolv | 1m1½f Cls5 Mdn 2yo stand | | £3,886 |

Has pursued globetrotting campaign since surprise Grade 1 win in America in 2009 but just came up short last season, finishing sixth in Dubai World Cup and fourth in Champion Stakes; was due for another World Cup bid this spring.

### 1084 Glass Harmonium (Ire)
5 gr h Verglas - Spring Symphony (Darshaan)
Sir Michael Stoute      Rupert Legh, Rohan Aujard Et Al
**PLACINGS: 71/56142/13660-**        **RPR 116**

| Starts | 1st | 2nd | 3rd | 4th | Win & Pl |
|---|---|---|---|---|---|
| 12 | 3 | 1 | 1 | 1 | £106,496 |
| 4/10 | Sand | 1m2f Cls1 Gp3 good | | | £36,901 |
| 6/09 | Asct | 1m2f Cls1 List 3yo gd-fm | | | £28,385 |
| 9/08 | Yarm | 7f Cls4 Mdn 2yo good | | | £4,731 |

Won Group 3 at Sandown on return last season but disappointing subsequently; reportedly found ground too quick next twice and raced too keenly when sixth in Champion Stakes; may need 1m4f and worth another chance.

### 1085 Glor Na Mara (Ire)
3 b c Leroidesanimaux - Sister Angelina (Saint Ballado)
Jim Bolger (Ir)                    Mrs J S Bolger
**PLACINGS: 422253-**        **RPR 113**

| Starts | 1st | 2nd | 3rd | 4th | Win & Pl |
|---|---|---|---|---|---|
| 6 | - | 3 | 1 | 1 | £99,693 |

Remarkably failed to win last season despite showing consistently high level of form, missing best chance when odds-on second at the Curragh in a Listed race; produced best effort when third to Frankel in the Dewhurst.

### 1086 Goldikova (Ire) *(pictured)*
6 b m Anabaa - Born Gold (Blushing Groom)
Freddie Head (Fr)            Wertheimer & Frere
**PLACINGS: 31111/711131/111211-**        **RPR 125+**

| Starts | 1st | 2nd | 3rd | 4th | Win & Pl |
|---|---|---|---|---|---|
| 21 | 15 | 3 | 2 | - | £3,735,878 |
| 11/10 | Chur | 1m Gd1 firm | | | £666,667 |
| 10/10 | Lonc | 7f Gp1 v soft | | | £126,416 |
| 8/10 | Deau | 1m Gp1 gd-sft | | | £151,699 |
| 6/10 | Asct | 1m Cls1 Gp1 good | | | £141,925 |
| 5/10 | Lonc | 1m1f Gp1 good | | | £126,416 |
| 11/09 | SnAt | 1m Gd1 firm | | | £750,000 |
| 8/09 | Deau | 1m Gp1 good | | | £332,854 |
| 8/09 | Deau | 1m Gp1 soft | | | £138,689 |
| 7/09 | NmkJ | 1m Cls1 Gp1 good | | | £113,540 |
| 10/08 | SnAt | 1m Gd1 firm | | | £577,990 |
| 9/08 | Lonc | 1m Gp1 gd-sft | | | £168,059 |
| 8/08 | Deau | 1m Gp1 gd-sft | | | £105,037 |
| 7/08 | MsnL | 1m Gp3 3yo gd-sft | | | £29,412 |
| 10/07 | Chan | 1m 2yo gd-sft | | | £11,486 |
| 9/07 | Chan | 1m 2yo good | | | £7,095 |

Sensational miler who has won 12 Group 1 races, including last three Breeders' Cup Miles and both starts in Britain, most notably last season's Queen Anne Stakes; acts on any going and sure to be hard to beat wherever she runs.

## Contenders Ten to Follow

### 1087 Handassa
3 br f *Dubawi - Starstone (Diktat)*
Kevin Prendergast (Ir)  Hamdan Al Maktoum
**PLACINGS: 1-**  **RPR 89+**

| Starts | 1st | 2nd | 3rd | 4th | Win & Pl |
|---|---|---|---|---|---|
| 1 | 1 | - | - | - | £10,685 |
| | 10/10 | Curr | 7f Mdn Auct 2yo yield | | £10,686 |

Made big impression on only start at the Curragh, drawing well clear of an admittedly modest field of maidens to justify strong market support; looked to need the run and big improvement likely; subsequently backed for 1,000 Guineas.

### 1088 Harris Tweed
4 b g *Hernando - Frog (Akarad)*
William Haggas  B Haggas
**PLACINGS: 75/1212711-**  **RPR 117**

| Starts | 1st | 2nd | 3rd | 4th | Win & Pl |
|---|---|---|---|---|---|
| 9 | 4 | 2 | - | - | £110,167 |
| | 9/10 | NmkR | 1m6f Cls1 List 3yo soft | | £19,870 |
| | 9/10 | Ches | 1m4½f Cls1 List soft | | £21,926 |
| 86 | 6/10 | Muss | 1m4½f Cls2 81-104 3yo Hcap gd-fm | | £49,848 |
| | 4/10 | Ripn | 1m2f Cls5 Mdn 3yo gd-fm | | £2,914 |

Progressive stayer last season who bounced back from Great Voltigeur flop to win final two races in impressively, appreciating step up to 1m6f last time; could be a Cup horse.

### 1089 Harrison George (Ire)
6 b g *Danetime - Dry Lightning (Shareef Dancer)*
Richard Fahey  P D Smith Holdings Ltd
**PLACINGS: 09253615/9118136010-**  **RPR 114**

| Starts | 1st | 2nd | 3rd | 4th | Win & Pl |
|---|---|---|---|---|---|
| 34 | 8 | 7 | 4 | 4 | £109,700 |
| | 10/10 | Rdcr | 7f Cls1 List gd-sft | | £19,870 |
| | 7/10 | Hayd | 7f Cls3 gd-sft | | £8,095 |
| | 5/10 | York | 7f Cls3 gd-fm | | £8,095 |
| 95 | 4/10 | Pont | 1m Cls3 81-95 Hcap good | | £6,854 |
| 90 | 9/09 | Ayr | 7f Cls3 83-93 Hcap good | | £11,091 |
| 83 | 7/08 | York | 7f Cls4 69-85 Hcap heavy | | £6,800 |
| 79 | 6/08 | York | 6f Cls4 60-79 Hcap good | | £7,124 |
| | 5/08 | Donc | 6f Cls5 Auct Mdn 3-4yo gd-fm | | £3,238 |

Left handicapping ranks following stunning 7l win at Pontefract in April and confirmed progress with two more victories; equally effective at 7f and 1m; best on easy ground.

### 1090 Havant
3 b f *Halling - Louella (El Gran Senor)*
Sir Michael Stoute  Mr & Mrs James Wigan
**PLACINGS: 11-**  **RPR 103+**

| Starts | 1st | 2nd | 3rd | 4th | Win & Pl |
|---|---|---|---|---|---|
| 2 | 2 | - | - | - | £26,917 |
| | 10/10 | NmkR | 7f Cls1 Gp2 2yo gd-sft | | £22,708 |
| | 8/10 | NmkJ | 7f Cls4 Mdn 2yo soft | | £4,209 |

Twice won well over 7f at Newmarket, particularly when five-length winner of Group 3; looks leading contender for 1,000 Guineas on that evidence, with pedigree suggesting she may also be an Oaks filly, but untried on ground better than good to soft.

### 1091 Head Space (Ire)
3 b c *Invincible Spirit - Danzelline (Danzero)*
Jim Bolger  Mrs J S Bolger & John Corcoran
**PLACINGS: 1-**  **RPR 90+**

| Starts | 1st | 2nd | 3rd | 4th | Win & Pl |
|---|---|---|---|---|---|
| 1 | 1 | - | - | - | £9,464 |
| | 4/10 | Naas | 5f Mdn 2yo good | | £9,465 |

Looked a leading candidate for Royal Ascot following impressive debut win at Naas in April from several subsequent useful performers but met with a setback and missed rest of season; remains a top prospect and potential 2,000 Guineas contender.

### 1092 Helleborine
3 b f *Observatory - New Orchid (Quest For Fame)*
Criquette Head-Maarek (Fr)  K Abdulla
**PLACINGS: 1112-**  **RPR 112+**

| Starts | 1st | 2nd | 3rd | 4th | Win & Pl |
|---|---|---|---|---|---|
| 4 | 3 | 1 | - | - | £131,044 |
| | 9/10 | Lonc | 1m Gp3 2yo soft | | £35,398 |
| | 7/10 | Deau | 7f List 2yo good | | £24,336 |
| | 6/10 | MsnL | 6f 2yo good | | £10,619 |

Barely extended to win first three starts, including Group 3 at Longchamp by 5l, before being outfought by more battle-hardened Misty For Me in Prix Marcel Boussac; looks capable of better and trainer has fine record with fillies.

### 1093 Hibaayeb
4 b f *Singspiel - Lady Zonda (Lion Cavern)*
Saeed Bin Suroor  Godolphin Racing Llc
**PLACINGS: 3221/03107718-**  **RPR 109**

| Starts | 1st | 2nd | 3rd | 4th | Win & Pl |
|---|---|---|---|---|---|
| 12 | 3 | 2 | 2 | - | £331,840 |
| | 10/10 | Holl | 1m2f Gd1 firm | | £92,593 |
| | 6/10 | Asct | 1m4f Cls1 Gp2 3yo gd-fm | | £70,963 |
| | 9/09 | Asct | 1m Cls1 Gp1 2yo good | | £123,759 |

Won Fillies' Mile in 2009 for Clive Brittain before move to Godolphin; in and out last season (all at sea on three runs on ground softer than good) but showed true colours with impressive Ribblesdale victory and Grade 1 win in America.

racingpost.com

## 1094 High Heeled (Ire)

5 b m High Chaparral - Uncharted Haven (Turtle Island)

John Gosden      G Strawbridge & J Wigan

**PLACINGS: 616/14331541/372828-**      **RPR 117**

| Starts | 1st | 2nd | 3rd | 4th | Win & Pl |
|---|---|---|---|---|---|
| 18 | 4 | 3 | 3 | 2 | £213,664 |
| | 10/09 Newb | 1m4f Cls1 Gp3 soft | | | £36,901 |
| | 7/09 York | 1m2½f Cls1 List good | | | £22,708 |
| | 4/09 Newb | 1m2f Cls3 3yo gd-sft | | | £7,477 |
| | 9/08 Kemp | 1m Cls4 Mdn 2yo stand | | | £3,562 |

Bought for 600,000gns last winter and made fine start for new connections when third in Coronation Cup; bitterly disappointing after when beaten four times in France and eighth in Group 2 at Newmarket on final start.

## 1095 High Standing (USA)

6 b g High Yield - Nena Maka (Selkirk)

William Haggas      Tony Bloom

**PLACINGS: 1/122/111134/102356-**      **RPR 114+**

| Starts | 1st | 2nd | 3rd | 4th | Win & Pl |
|---|---|---|---|---|---|
| 21 | 8 | 3 | 2 | 1 | £233,717 |
| | 5/10 Hayd | 5f Cls1 List good | | | £22,708 |
| | 7/09 Newb | 6f Cls1 Gp3 soft | | | £36,901 |
| 96 | 6/09 Asct | 6f Cls2 94-108 Hcap gd-fm | | | £62,310 |
| 91 | 5/09 Gdwd | 6f Cls2 85-98 Hcap good | | | £11,216 |
| 85 | 5/09 Donc | 6f Cls3 77-90 Hcap good | | | £7,771 |
| 76 | 5/08 Leic | 7f Cls4 74-80 3yo Hcap gd-fm | | | £4,209 |
| 66 | 10/07 Wolv | 6f Cls6 50-66 2yo Hcap stand | | | £2,048 |
| 60 | 10/07 Kemp | 6f Cls6 55-71 2yo Hcap stand | | | £2,048 |

Expected to take sprinting scene by storm after runaway win in 2009 Wokingham but has just come up short at top level despite running several fine races, notably when third to Regal Parade in Prix Maurice de Gheest; best form at 6f.

## 1096 Holberg (UAE) *(pictured, nearest)*

5 b h Halling - Sweet Willa (Assert)

Saeed Bin Suroor      Godolphin

**PLACINGS: 64511/131/15216-**      **RPR 112aw**

| Starts | 1st | 2nd | 3rd | 4th | Win & Pl |
|---|---|---|---|---|---|
| 13 | 6 | 1 | 1 | 1 | £191,508 |
| | 9/10 Gdwd | 1m2f Cls1 List gd-fm | | | £19,870 |
| | 6/10 Gdwd | 1m4f Cls1 List good | | | £23,704 |
| | 6/09 Asct | 2m Cls1 Gp3 3yo gd-fm | | | £39,739 |
| 85 | 4/09 Leic | 1m4f Cls3 78-85 3yo Hcap gd-fm | | | £9,347 |
| 79 | 12/08 Kemp | 1m Cls4 59-79 2yo Hcap stand | | | £4,094 |
| | 11/08 Sthl | 7f Cls5 Auct Mdn 2yo stand | | | £3,562 |

Won Queen's Vase over 2m for Mark Johnston in 2009 but surprisingly campaigned over shorter by Godolphin last season prior to sixth in Melbourne Cup; won twice at Goodwood and looks obvious Goodwood Cup candidate.

## 1097 Hooray

3 b f Invincible Spirit - Hypnotize (Machiavellian)

Sir Mark Prescott      Cheveley Park Stud

**PLACINGS: 1836111-**      **RPR 117 RPR**

| Starts | 1st | 2nd | 3rd | 4th | Win & Pl |
|---|---|---|---|---|---|
| 7 | 4 | - | 1 | - | £189,399 |
| | 10/10 NmkR | 6f Cls1 Gp1 2yo gd-sft | | | £98,439 |
| | 9/10 Kemp | 6f Cls1 Gp3 2yo stand | | | £22,708 |
| | 8/10 York | 6f Cls1 Gp2 2yo good | | | £56,770 |
| | 6/10 Kemp | 6f Cls5 Mdn 2yo stand | | | £3,627 |

Took form to another level in final three runs last season when switched to front-running tactics; rounded off campaign with clear-cut win in Cheveley Park Stakes on good to soft ground despite trainer doubting her ability to handle conditions.

Contenders **Ten to Follow**

### 1098 Hot Prospect
*4 b c Motivator - Model Queen (Kingmambo)*

Roger Varian                                      A D Spence
**PLACINGS: 216/33951246-**            **RPR 116+**

| Starts | 1st | 2nd | 3rd | 4th | Win & Pl |
|---|---|---|---|---|---|
| 11 | 2 | 2 | 2 | 1 | £97,847 |
| 103 | 8/10 | Hayd | 1m2¹/₂f Cls2 80 103 Hcap soft | | £40,502 |
|  | 9/09 | Sand | 1m Cls4 Mdn 2yo gd-fm | | £5,181 |

Found wanting as a Derby horse when ninth at Epsom but rejuvenated by drop to 1m2f on favoured soft ground when winning handicap off 103 and finishing second in Group 3 at Windsor.

### 1099 Hung Parliament (Fr)
*3 b c Numerous - Sensational Mover (Theatrical)*

Tom Dascombe                          The Tipperary Partners
**PLACINGS: 4212-**                           **RPR 107**

| Starts | 1st | 2nd | 3rd | 4th | Win & Pl |
|---|---|---|---|---|---|
| 4 | 1 | 2 | - | 1 | £44,933 |
|  | 8/10 | Deau | 7f List 2yo v soft | | £24,336 |

Campaigned in France following last of four on debut at Newbury and landed 22-1 win in Listed company at Deauville, enjoying testing conditions; proved that was no fluke with good second to My Name Is Bond in Group 3 at Longchamp.

### 1100 I Love Me
*3 b f Cape Cross - Garanciere (Anabaa)*

Andrew Balding                                        N Botica
**PLACINGS: 153-**                             **RPR 102**

| Starts | 1st | 2nd | 3rd | 4th | Win & Pl |
|---|---|---|---|---|---|
| 3 | 1 | - | 1 | - | £129,908 |
|  | 9/10 | NmkR | 7f Cls2 2yo good | | £111,539 |

50-1 winner of valuable Newmarket sales race on her debut, overcoming greenness to point to rich potential; ran well from bad draw in similar event next time and travelled best for a long way when third in Rockfel Stakes; 1,000 Guineas candidate.

### 1101 Indian Days
*6 ch h Daylami - Cap Coz (Indian Ridge)*

James Given                                           D J Fish
**PLACINGS: 859648330/524671169-**       **RPR 115**

| Starts | 1st | 2nd | 3rd | 4th | Win & Pl |
|---|---|---|---|---|---|
| 34 | 5 | 3 | 4 | 3 | £315,094 |
|  | 9/10 | Veli | 1m4f Gp2 soft | | £159,292 |
| 102 | 7/10 | Gdwd | 1m2f Cls2 81-106 Hcap gd-fm | | £31,155 |
| 91 | 7/08 | Gdwd | 1m2f Cls2 88-106 3yo Hcap gd-fm | | £62,310 |
| 79 | 5/08 | Rdcr | 1m2f Cls4 69-84 3yo Hcap gd-fm | | £6,476 |
| 69 | 9/07 | Sand | 7f Cls4 69-90 2yo Hcap gd-fm | | £5,182 |

Went two years without a win prior to last summer but found improvement to win big handicap at Glorious Goodwood off mark of 102 and valuable Group 2 in Turkey; effective from 1m2f to 1m4f and acts on any going.

### 1102 Inler (Ire)
*4 br c Red Ransom - Wedding Gift (Always Fair)*

Brian Meehan                                 Sangster Family
**PLACINGS: 1/0561-**                          **RPR 110**

| Starts | 1st | 2nd | 3rd | 4th | Win & Pl |
|---|---|---|---|---|---|
| 5 | 2 | - | - | - | £16,723 |
|  | 10/10 | Donc | 7f Cls2 good | | £9,347 |
|  | 10/09 | NmkR | 6f Cls4 Mdn 2yo gd-fm | | £5,828 |

Once seen as a top 2,000 Guineas prospect by John Best but twice ran badly for him early last season and switched to Brian Meehan; did well on second start for new trainer at Doncaster, just getting home over 7f, and looks smart sprinting prospect.

### 1103 Jacqueline Quest (Ire)
*4 b f Rock Of Gibraltar - Coquette Rouge (Croco Rouge)*

Henry Cecil                                          N Martin
**PLACINGS: 217/71d35-**                   **RPR 111**

| Starts | 1st | 2nd | 3rd | 4th | Win & Pl |
|---|---|---|---|---|---|
| 7 | 1 | 2 | 1 | - | £123,668 |
|  | 9/09 | Ches | 7f Cls4 Mdn 2yo gd-fm | | £5,181 |

Demoted to second in last season's 1,000 Guineas having been first past the post at 66-1; proved that was no fluke when third in much stronger Coronation Stakes next time, though disappointing fifth when favourite in Group 3 on final start.

### 1104 Jan Vermeer (Ire)
*4 b c Montjeu - Shadow Song (Pennekamp)*

Aidan O'Brien (Ir)   M Tabor, D Smith & Mrs John Magnier
**PLACINGS: 411/1433-**                    **RPR 119**

| Starts | 1st | 2nd | 3rd | 4th | Win & Pl |
|---|---|---|---|---|---|
| 7 | 3 | - | 2 | 2 | £414,567 |
| | 5/10 | Curr | 1m2f Gp3 3yo gd-fm | | £31,637 |
| | 11/09 | StCl | 1m Gp1 2yo v soft | | £138,689 |
| | 9/09 | Gowr | 1m Mdn 2yo gd-fm | | £10,399 |

Failed to fulfil his juvenile promise last season when perhaps suffering from rushed Derby preparation, finishing no better than third in three attempts at top level; put away in July for four-year-old campaign and looks capable of better.

## 1105 Janood (Ire)

*3 b c Medicean - Alluring Park (Green Desert)*

Saeed Bin Suroor                    Godolphin

**PLACINGS: 1189-45**               **RPR 100+**

| Starts | 1st | 2nd | 3rd | 4th | Win & Pl |
|---|---|---|---|---|---|
| 6 | 2 | - | - | 1 | £27,406 |
| 8/10 | Newb | 7f Cls1 List 2yo gd-sft | | | £13,341 |
| 7/10 | NmkJ | 6f Cls4 Mdn 2yo gd-fm | | | £4,533 |

Impressed when winning Listed race on second start only to disappoint in better company on final two outings last year; connections blamed soft ground for his failures and retain plenty of faith; returned to action at Meydan this spring.

## 1106 Joanna (Ire)

*4 b f High Chaparral - Secrete Marina (Mujadil)*

Jean-Claude Rouget (Fr)         Hamdan Al Maktoum

**PLACINGS: 12113/131125-**         **RPR 116**

| Starts | 1st | 2nd | 3rd | 4th | Win & Pl |
|---|---|---|---|---|---|
| 11 | 6 | 2 | 2 | - | £358,315 |
| 7/10 | Lonc | 7f Gp3 soft | | | £35,398 |
| 6/10 | Chan | 1m Gp2 3yo soft | | | £65,575 |
| 4/10 | MsnL | 7f Gp3 3yo v soft | | | £35,398 |
| 8/09 | Deau | 7f Gp3 2yo good | | | £38,835 |
| 6/09 | Siro | 6f List 2yo good | | | £27,184 |
| 5/09 | Siro | 5f 2yo good | | | £8,252 |

Good third in French 1,000 Guineas last year before twice winning at slightly lower level but produced best effort when dropped to extended 6f to finish second to Regal Parade in Prix Maurice de Gheest; handles soft ground well.

## 1107 Joshua Tree (Ire) (pictured)

*4 b c Montjeu - Madeira Mist (Grand Lodge)*

Aidan O'Brien (Ir)           Khalifa Bin Hamad Al Attiyah

**PLACINGS: 121/3510-41**           **RPR 115**

| Starts | 1st | 2nd | 3rd | 4th | Win & Pl |
|---|---|---|---|---|---|
| 9 | 4 | 1 | 1 | 1 | £891,627 |
| 2/11 | Dohr | 1m4f good | | | £50,532 |
| 10/10 | Wood | 1m4f Gd1 good | | | £705,882 |
| 9/09 | Asct | 1m Cls1 Gp2 2yo good | | | £86,188 |
| 8/09 | Gowr | 7f Mdn 2yo soft | | | £10,499 |

Has changed ownership since last year but still ran for Aidan O'Brien at Meydan this spring; had missed much of 2010 but returned to win Grade 1 Canadian International following one-paced fifth in St Leger.

## 1108 Jukebox Jury (Ire)

*5 gr h Montjeu - Mare Aux Fees (Kenmare)*

Mark Johnston                    A D Spence

**PLACINGS: 14312/7614112/01794-**   **RPR 120**

| Starts | 1st | 2nd | 3rd | 4th | Win & Pl |
|---|---|---|---|---|---|
| 17 | 6 | 2 | 1 | 3 | £697,879 |
| 5/10 | NmkR | 1m4f Cls1 Gp2 gd-fm | | | £56,770 |
| 9/09 | Colo | 1m4f Gp1 good | | | £97,087 |
| 8/09 | Deau | 1m4½f Gp2 good | | | £110,680 |
| 8/09 | Hayd | 1m2½f Cls1 Gp3 good | | | £36,901 |
| 9/08 | Asct | 1m Cls1 Gp2 2yo good | | | £76,038 |
| 8/08 | Gdwd | 7f Cls2 Mdn 2yo good | | | £12,952 |

Five-time Pattern winner, including Group 1 in Germany by a nose in 2009, but proved slightly disappointing last season after landing Group 2 at Newmarket on second start; likely to be highly tried again in top middle-distance races.

## Contenders Ten to Follow

### 1109 Katla (Ire)
*3 b f Majestic Missile - Bratislava (Dr Fong)*

John Grogan (Ir)     J F Grogan
**PLACINGS: 3212513-**     **RPR 106**

| Starts | 1st | 2nd | 3rd | 4th | Win & Pl |
|---|---|---|---|---|---|
| 7 | 2 | 2 | 2 | - | £60,863 |
| 10/10 | York | 6f Cls1 List 2yo soft | | | £23,704 |
| 8/10 | Cork | 6f Mdn 2yo good | | | £9,465 |

Useful filly at 6f last season though perhaps flattered by 6l win in Listed event at York with main rivals below best; failed to stay 7f when fifth on only try at that trip.

### 1110 Keratiya (Fr)
*3 b f Iron Mask - Kerasha (Daylami)*

Jean-Claude Rouget (Fr)     H H Aga Khan
**PLACINGS: 12196-**     **RPR 105**

| Starts | 1st | 2nd | 3rd | 4th | Win & Pl |
|---|---|---|---|---|---|
| 6 | 2 | 1 | - | - | £50,018 |
| 7/10 | Chan | 5f Gp3 2yo gd-sft | | | £35,398 |
| 5/10 | Bord | 5f 2yo v soft | | | £7,522 |

Showed useful form to win Group 3 at Chantilly from subsequent Prix Robert Papin winner Irish Field; twice below par over 6f but beaten only 2l in sixth when reverting to 5f in Flying Childers.

### 1111 Khor Sheed
*3 ch f Dubawi - Princess Manila (Manila)*

Luca Cumani     Sheikh Mohammed Obaid Al Maktoum
**PLACINGS: 21310-**     **RPR 102**

| Starts | 1st | 2nd | 3rd | 4th | Win & Pl |
|---|---|---|---|---|---|
| 5 | 2 | 1 | 1 | - | £76,424 |
| 9/10 | NmkR | 6f Cls2 Auct 2yo good | | | £55,769 |
| 6/10 | NmkJ | 6f Cls1 List 2yo gd-fm | | | £15,328 |

Showed smart form when defying top weight to land to land strong sales race at Newmarket on penultimate start; twice disappointing on good to soft either side of that effort, including on only try at 7f, but should stay further back on quicker surface.

### 1112 King Of Wands
*5 b g Galileo - Maid To Treasure (Rainbow Quest)*

John Gosden     R J H Geffen
**PLACINGS: 843/12115/1413-**     **RPR 114**

| Starts | 1st | 2nd | 3rd | 4th | Win & Pl |
|---|---|---|---|---|---|
| 12 | 5 | 1 | 2 | 2 | £63,794 |
| 7/10 | Sand | 2m½f Cls1 List gd-fm | | | £21,005 |
| 4/10 | Ripn | 1m4f Cls3 gd-fm | | | £6,543 |
| 86 7/09 | Sand | 1m6f Cls3 81-90 3yo Hcap gd-fm | | | £7,771 |
| 83 6/09 | Sals | 1m6f Cls4 75-83 3yo Hcap gd-fm | | | £4,727 |
| 4/09 | Folk | 1m4f Cls5 Mdn good | | | £2,730 |

Useful stayer who won Listed race at Sandown on penultimate start on first attempt at 2m but just ran out of steam in final furlong having looked likely winner of Lonsdale Cup at York; last four wins all came on good to firm.

### 1113 King Torus (Ire)
*3 b c Oratorio - Dipterous (Mujadil)*

Richard Hannon     Sir Robert Ogden
**PLACINGS: 14117-**     **RPR 114+**

| Starts | 1st | 2nd | 3rd | 4th | Win & Pl |
|---|---|---|---|---|---|
| 5 | 3 | - | - | 1 | £92,373 |
| 7/10 | Gdwd | 7f Cls1 Gp2 2yo gd-fm | | | £45,416 |
| 7/10 | NmkJ | 7f Cls1 Gp2 2yo gd-fm | | | £39,739 |
| 5/10 | Leic | 6f Cls4 Mdn 2yo gd-fm | | | £4,533 |

Badly drawn when fourth at Royal Ascot and hit back to land Group 2 double at Newmarket and Goodwood (by 6l in Vintage Stakes), both on good to firm; ran no race on very soft ground at Longchamp on final start.

### 1114 Kingdom Of Fife
*6 b g Kingmambo - Fairy Godmother (Fairy King)*

Sir Michael Stoute     The Queen
**PLACINGS: 361133/21233/753566-**     **RPR 114**

| Starts | 1st | 2nd | 3rd | 4th | Win & Pl |
|---|---|---|---|---|---|
| 19 | 3 | 2 | 6 | - | £106,420 |
| 92 5/09 | Rdcr | 1m2f Cls2 88-102 3yo Hcap gd-fm | | | £32,380 |
| 76 8/08 | Sand | 1m2f Cls4 61-78 3yo Hcap good | | | £7,124 |
| 70 8/08 | Sand | 1m2f Cls4 70-79 3yo Hcap gd-sft | | | £6,476 |

Progressive middle-distance handicapper in 2009 who has just come up short at Pattern level since then; has twice shown best form at Ascot, including when third in Listed handicap off 110 behind Rainbow Peak last year.

### 1115 Kings Gambit (SAF)
*7 ch g Silvano - Lady Brompton (Al Mufti)*

Tom Tate     Mrs Fitri Hay
**PLACINGS: 1/54503645/14522322-**     **RPR 116**

| Starts | 1st | 2nd | 3rd | 4th | Win & Pl |
|---|---|---|---|---|---|
| 22 | 5 | 5 | 2 | 3 | £213,526 |
| 4/10 | Ripn | 1m2f Cls3 good | | | £6,567 |
| 5/08 | Turf | 1m4f Gd1 3yo soft | | | £45,956 |
| 4/08 | Turf | 1m1f Gd1 3yo good | | | £55,147 |
| 2/08 | Turf | 6f good | | | £3,676 |
| 1/08 | Vaal | 6f Mdn good | | | £3,217 |

Desperately unlucky to finish second four times last season, running into several progressive horses, most notably when pipped by Wigmore Hall in John Smith's Cup; looks capable of winning Group races at 1m2f; acts on any going.

## 1116 Kingsfort (USA)
4 br c War Chant - Princess Kris (Kris)
Saeed Bin Suroor                                    Godolphin
**PLACINGS: 11/51-35**                              **RPR 113**

| Starts | 1st | 2nd | 3rd | 4th | Win & Pl |
|---|---|---|---|---|---|
| 6 | 3 | - | 1 | - | £188,520 |
| 10/10 | NmkR | 1m Cls1 List gd-sft | | | £19,870 |
| 9/09 | Curr | 7f Gp1 2yo sft-hvy | | | £145,728 |
| 6/09 | Curr | 7f Mdn 2yo soft | | | £11,405 |

Group 1 winner in Ireland as a juvenile; missed most of last season but showed he had lost none of his ability when winning Listed race at Newmarket.

## 1117 Kingsgate Native (Ire)
6 b g Mujadil - Native Force (Indian Ridge)
Sir Michael Stoute                           Cheveley Park Stud
**PLACINGS: 12/0153/016/1649436-**                  **RPR 121**

| Starts | 1st | 2nd | 3rd | 4th | Win & Pl |
|---|---|---|---|---|---|
| 18 | 4 | 3 | 2 | 2 | £613,484 |
| 5/10 | Hayd | 5f Cls1 Gp2 gd-fm | | | £56,770 |
| 7/09 | Gdwd | 5f Cls1 Gp3 good | | | £39,739 |
| 6/08 | Asct | 6f Cls1 Gp1 good | | | £212,888 |
| 8/07 | York | 5f Cls1 Gp1 good | | | £136,158 |

Three-time Group 1 winner but has become frustrating since returning from stud duty; showed ability remains with fine win in Temple Stakes on return last season but largely disappointing subsequently.

## 1118 Kissable (Ire)
3 b f Danehill Dancer - Kitty O'Shea (Sadler's Wells)
Kevin Prendergast (Ir)                          Lady O'Reilly
**PLACINGS: 2133-**                                 **RPR 110**

| Starts | 1st | 2nd | 3rd | 4th | Win & Pl |
|---|---|---|---|---|---|
| 4 | 1 | 1 | 2 | - | £35,792 |
| 7/10 | Leop | 7f Mdn 2yo gd-fm | | | £10,486 |

Smart juvenile filly last season; unlucky in running when third to Together in July and did much better when staying-on third behind Misty For Me in Moyglare; seems sure to improve over middle distances and may appreciate easy ground.

## 1119 Kite Wood (Ire)
5 b h Galileo - Kite Mark (Mark Of Esteem)
Saeed Bin Suroor                                    Godolphin
**PLACINGS: 211/59112/1767-**                       **RPR 112**

| Starts | 1st | 2nd | 3rd | 4th | Win & Pl |
|---|---|---|---|---|---|
| 12 | 2 | 2 | - | - | £296,624 |
| 5/10 | Lonc | 1m7½f Gp2 good | | | £65,575 |
| 8/09 | Newb | 1m5½f Cls1 Gp3 gd-fm | | | £36,901 |
| 7/09 | NmkJ | 1m5f Cls1 Gp3 good | | | £36,901 |
| 10/08 | Asct | 1m Cls1 Gp3 gd-sft | | | £28,385 |
| 9/08 | Donc | 1m Cls4 Mdn 2yo soft | | | £6,152 |

Showed smart form in 2009 when second in St Leger and kicked off last season well with second Group 2 win in France over 2m; found ground too quick in Ascot Gold Cup next time and well below best on final two starts.

## 1120 Laaheb
5 b g Cape Cross - Maskunah (Sadler's Wells)
Roger Varian                              Hamdan Al Maktoum
**PLACINGS: 011211/321211-**                        **RPR 118**

| Starts | 1st | 2nd | 3rd | 4th | Win & Pl |
|---|---|---|---|---|---|
| 12 | 7 | 3 | 1 | - | £171,535 |
| | 9/10 | Asct | 1m4f Cls1 Gp3 gd-sft | | £36,901 |
| | 9/10 | Kemp | 1m4f Cls1 Gp3 stand | | £34,062 |
| | 6/10 | NmkJ | 1m4f Cls1 List gd-fm | | £22,708 |
| | 10/09 | NmkR | 1m2f Cls1 List good | | £22,708 |
| 94 | 9/09 | Pont | 1m2f Cls2 80-94 Hcap gd-fm | | £12,462 |
| 82 | 7/09 | NmkJ | 1m2f Cls3 76-95 3yo Hcap soft | | £9,347 |
| | 7/09 | Yarm | 1m2f Cls5 Mdn 3yo good | | £2,776 |

Never out of first three on last 11 starts, though confined to single-figure fields every time; won three out of four when stepped up to at least 1m4f, losing only to high-class Sans Frontieres; lightly raced and open to further progress.

## 1121 Laddies Poker Two (Ire)
6 gr m Choisir - Break Of Day (Favorite Trick)
Jeremy Noseda                    D Smith, Mrs J Magnier & M Tabor
**PLACINGS: 1316/1-**                              **RPR 114+**

| Starts | 1st | 2nd | 3rd | 4th | Win & Pl |
|---|---|---|---|---|---|
| 5 | 3 | - | 1 | - | £79,305 |
| 95 | 6/10 | Asct | 6f Cls2 94-108 Hcap good | | £62,310 |
| 91 | 9/08 | Asct | 6f Cls2 86-100 3yo Hcap good | | £12,462 |
| | 1/08 | Kemp | 7f Cls5 Auct Mdn 3yo stand | | £2,591 |

Has run only once in past two seasons but made it count when landing big gamble in Wokingham at Royal Ascot; suffered further injury soon after but still highly rated and will be aimed at Group 1 sprints this year.

## 1122 Ladies Are Forever
3 b f Monsieur Bond - Forever Bond (Danetime)
Geoffrey Oldroyd                                     R C Bond
**PLACINGS: 131-**                                  **RPR 105**

| Starts | 1st | 2nd | 3rd | 4th | Win & Pl |
|---|---|---|---|---|---|
| 3 | 2 | - | 1 | - | £143,581 |
| 10/10 | Rdcr | 6f Cls1 List 2yo gd-sft | | | £130,003 |
| 5/10 | Bevl | 5f Cls4 Auct Mdn 2yo gd-fm | | | £3,886 |

Good third in Queen Mary Stakes and returned from long break to win Two-Year-Old Trophy at Redcar, though strongly favoured by weights and didn't need to run anywhere near Royal Ascot form; should have much more to come this season.

## Contenders Ten to Follow

### 1123 Lady Of The Desert (USA)
4 ch f Rahy - Queen's Logic (Grand Lodge)
Brian Meehan                                    Jaber Abdullah
**PLACINGS: 16113/356212-**              **RPR 121**

| Starts | 1st | 2nd | 3rd | 4th | Win & Pl |
|---|---|---|---|---|---|
| 11 | 4 | 2 | 2 | - | £308,511 |
| 9/10 | Asct | 6f Cls1 Gp2 gd-sft | | | £61,397 |
| 8/09 | York | 6f Cls1 Gp2 2yo gd-fm | | | £56,770 |
| 7/09 | Asct | 6f Cls1 Gp3 2yo good | | | £31,224 |
| 5/09 | Leic | 5f Cls4 Mdn 2yo gd-fm | | | £4,857 |

Found wanting over 1m last season but found niche when dropped down in trip, winning Diadem Stakes and finishing second in Haydock Sprint Cup and Prix de l'Abbaye; could be leading contender for champion sprinter honours.

### 1124 Laughing Lashes (USA)
3 gr f Mr Greeley - Adventure (Unbridled's Song)
Jessica Harrington (Ir)                        Mcelroy Syndicate
**PLACINGS: 2212-**                       **RPR 111**

| Starts | 1st | 2nd | 3rd | 4th | Win & Pl |
|---|---|---|---|---|---|
| 4 | 1 | 3 | - | - | £108,061 |
| 8/10 | Curr | 7f Gp2 2yo yield | | | £57,522 |

Not far off best Irish juvenile fillies last season, beating Misty For Me in Debutante Stakes at the Curragh before that one reversed placings in Moyglare; only win came on yielding ground and may not quite produce best on faster.

### 1125 Libranno (pictured)
3 b c Librettist - Annabelle Ja (Singspiel)
Richard Hannon                                 Mcdowell Racing
**PLACINGS: 11165-**                      **RPR 111+**

| Starts | 1st | 2nd | 3rd | 4th | Win & Pl |
|---|---|---|---|---|---|
| 5 | 3 | - | - | - | £92,111 |
| 7/10 | Gdwd | 6f Cls1 Gp2 2yo good | | | £45,416 |
| 7/10 | NmkJ | 6f Cls1 Gp2 2yo gd-fm | | | £39,739 |
| 5/10 | NmkR | 6f Cls4 Mdn 2yo good | | | £5,181 |

Won first three starts, landing Group 2 double at Newmarket and Goodwood when making all both times; struggled after that, though, when down the field in Prix Morny and Mill Reef; may be best in small fields.

### 1126 Liliside (Fr)
4 b f American Post - Miller's Lily (Miller's Mate)
Francois Rohaut (Fr)                           Katsumi Yoshida
**PLACINGS: 9212/1111d518-**              **RPR 115**

| Starts | 1st | 2nd | 3rd | 4th | Win & Pl |
|---|---|---|---|---|---|
| 11 | 5 | 2 | - | - | £96,370 |
| 9/10 | Lonc | 1m List 3yo good | | | £24,336 |
| 4/10 | StCl | 1m List 3yo heavy | | | £24,336 |
| 2/10 | Cagn | 7¹/₂f List 3yo heavy | | | £24,336 |
| 2/10 | Cagn | 7¹/₂f 3yo Hcap v soft | | | £8,850 |
| 10/09 | Angl | 1m1f 2yo firm | | | £4,854 |

Denied finest hour when disqualified in French 1,000 Guineas last year when aiming for fourth successive win and largely disappointing after that despite Listed win at Longchamp; equally effective on all going.

## 1127 Lillie Langtry (Ire)
4 b/br f Danehill Dancer - Hoity Toity (Darshaan)
Aidan O'Brien (Ir)　　　　　　　　Michael Tabor
**PLACINGS: 2121318/5151-**　　　**RPR 117+**

| Starts | 1st | 2nd | 3rd | 4th | Win & Pl |
|---|---|---|---|---|---|
| 11 | 5 | 2 | 1 | - | £888,802 |
| 9/10 | Leop | 1m Gp1 good | | | £115,044 |
| 6/10 | Asct | 1m Cls1 Gp1 3yo gd-fm | | | £154,698 |
| 10/09 | NmkR | 7f Cls2 2yo gd-fm | | | £433,360 |
| 8/09 | Leop | 7f Gp2 2yo gd-yld | | | £72,573 |
| 6/09 | Naas | 6f Gp3 2yo gd-fm | | | £63,204 |

Bounced back from a knee fracture at the end of a long juvenile campaign to establish herself as the best three-year-old filly in Britain and Ireland over 1m last season with wins in Coronation Stakes and Matron Stakes; should stay further.

## 1128 Lily Of The Valley (Fr)
4 b f Galileo - Pennegale (Pennekamp)
Jean-Claude Rouget (Fr)　　　　　Bernard Barsi
**PLACINGS: 851/11111-**　　　**RPR 121**

| Starts | 1st | 2nd | 3rd | 4th | Win & Pl |
|---|---|---|---|---|---|
| 8 | 6 | - | - | - | £275,420 |
| 10/10 | Lonc | 1m2f Gp1 v soft | | | £151,699 |
| 8/10 | Deau | 1m2f Gp3 3yo good | | | £35,398 |
| 7/10 | Chan | 1m1f Gp3 3yo gd-sft | | | £35,398 |
| 5/10 | StCl | 1m List 3yo good | | | £24,336 |
| 4/10 | StCl | 1m 3yo gd-sft | | | £15,044 |
| 11/09 | Toul | 7f 2yo soft | | | £12,136 |

Brilliant French filly who never stopped improving last season, starting off at a relatively modest level and beating stablemate Stacelita in Group 1 Prix de l'Opera on final start; sees out 1m2f well and may well be aimed at the Arc this year.

## 1129 Mabait
5 b h Kyllachy - Czarna Roza (Polish Precedent)
Luca Cumani　　Sheikh Mohammed Obaid Al Maktoum
**PLACINGS: /1770111/1237135-060**　　**RPR 116+**

| Starts | 1st | 2nd | 3rd | 4th | Win & Pl |
|---|---|---|---|---|---|
| 23 | 7 | 1 | 3 | 2 | £131,923 |
| 7/10 | Pont | 1m Cls1 List gd-fm | | | £15,658 |
| 4/10 | Sand | 1m Cls2 86-100 Hcap good | | | £9,970 |
| 10/09 | Leic | 1m½f Cls3 76-96 Hcap gd-fm | | | £7,789 |
| 9/09 | Wolv | 7f Cls4 72-83 3yo Hcap stand | | | £5,046 |
| 9/09 | Wolv | 7f Cls4 69-80 Hcap stand | | | £5,046 |
| 6/09 | Ripn | 6f Cls4 70-84 3yo Hcap gd-fm | | | £5,181 |
| 9/08 | Hayd | 6f Cls4 54-77 2yo Hcap gd-fm | | | £6,475 |

Forced into Pattern company after flying start to last season, easily winning Sandown handicap before close second in Victoria Cup at Ascot; fared reasonably well, dead-heating in Listed race at Pontefract; returned to action at Meydan this spring.

## 1130 Maiguri (Ire)
3 ch c Panis - Zanada (Sinndar)
Christophe Baillet (Fr)　　　　　Ecurie Jarlan
**PLACINGS: 3111323-**　　　**RPR 114**

| Starts | 1st | 2nd | 3rd | 4th | Win & Pl |
|---|---|---|---|---|---|
| 7 | 3 | 1 | 3 | - | £147,949 |
| 7/10 | Lonc | 7f List 2yo v soft | | | £24,336 |
| 6/10 | Comp | 7f 2yo soft | | | £16,372 |
| 5/10 | Chan | 6f 2yo gd-sft | | | £15,044 |

Improved with every run last season until seeming to find 1m on heavy ground just beyond his stamina when well-beaten third to Roderic O'Connor at Saint-Cloud; had earlier dead-heated for second behind Wootton Bassett in Prix Jean-Luc Lagardere.

## 1131 Main Aim
6 b h Oasis Dream - Orford Ness (Selkirk)
Sir Michael Stoute　　　　　　　K Abdulla
**PLACINGS: 108/1142804/310423-**　　**RPR 116**

| Starts | 1st | 2nd | 3rd | 4th | Win & Pl |
|---|---|---|---|---|---|
| 20 | 6 | 2 | 3 | 3 | £270,699 |
| 5/10 | Hayd | 7f Cls1 Gp3 gd-sft | | | £36,901 |
| 5/09 | Hayd | 7f Cls1 Gp3 good | | | £39,739 |
| 5/09 | Newb | 7f Cls2 86-100 Hcap gd-sft | | | £12,462 |
| 9/08 | Donc | 6f Cls3 80-90 Hcap soft | | | £9,714 |
| 7/08 | Sand | 7f Cls3 76-94 3yo Hcap gd-fm | | | £9,347 |
| 6/08 | Sals | 7f Cls5 Mdn 3yo gd-fm | | | £3,400 |

Looked likely to prove high-class having finished second in 2009 July Cup and won Group 3 on second run last season but came up short afterwards; still ran several good races, most notably when third to Red Jazz in Group 2 at Newmarket.

## 1132 Manifest
5 b h Rainbow Quest - Modena (Roberto)
Henry Cecil　　　　　　　　　　K Abdulla
**PLACINGS: 213/210-**　　　**RPR 121+**

| Starts | 1st | 2nd | 3rd | 4th | Win & Pl |
|---|---|---|---|---|---|
| 6 | 2 | 2 | 1 | - | £105,845 |
| 5/10 | York | 1m6f Cls1 Gp2 gd-fm | | | £79,478 |
| 8/09 | NmkJ | 1m4f Cls4 Mdn good | | | £5,181 |

Late developer who only got started towards end of three-year-old season and stepped up hugely last year with brilliant eight-length win in Yorkshire Cup; patent non-stayer in Ascot Gold Cup but plenty more to come over slightly shorter.

## Contenders Ten to Follow

### 1133 Mantoba
*3 b c Noverre - Coming Home (Vettori)*
Brian Meehan                         J Paul Reddam
**PLACINGS: 4110-**                  **RPR 102**

| Starts | 1st | 2nd | 3rd | 4th | Win & Pl |
|---|---|---|---|---|---|
| 4 | 2 | - | - | 1 | £12,945 |
| 10/10 | NmkR | 1m Cls2 2yo good | | | £8,723 |
| 9/10 | Newb | 7f Cls4 Mdn 2yo good | | | £3,886 |

Disappointing in Breeders' Cup Juvenile Turf on final start but had looked progressive prior to that, doing particularly well to land easy win in decent conditions race at Newmarket; dam won at 1m6f so seems likely to relish middle distances.

### 1134 Maqaasid
*3 b f Green Desert - Eshaadeh (Storm Cat)*
John Gosden                          Hamdan Al Maktoum
**PLACINGS: 1143-**                  **RPR 107+**

| Starts | 1st | 2nd | 3rd | 4th | Win & Pl |
|---|---|---|---|---|---|
| 4 | 2 | - | 1 | 1 | £79,671 |
| 6/10 | Asct | 5f Cls1 Gp2 2yo gd-fm | | | £51,093 |
| 5/10 | Sand | 5f Cls4 Mdn 2yo good | | | £4,533 |

Impressive winner of Queen Mary Stakes at Royal Ascot but twice struggled on step up to 6f subsequently, fading into fourth in Lowther Stakes and well-beaten third behind Hooray in Cheveley Park; still likely to be aimed at 1,000 Guineas initially.

### 1135 Margot Did (Ire)
*3 b f Exceed And Excel - Special Dancer (Shareef Dancer)*
Michael Bell                         T Redman And P Philipps
**PLACINGS: 1122235-**               **RPR 108**

| Starts | 1st | 2nd | 3rd | 4th | Win & Pl |
|---|---|---|---|---|---|
| 7 | 2 | 3 | 1 | - | £60,505 |
| 6/10 | Yarm | 6f Cls5 2yo gd-fm | | | £3,532 |
| 5/10 | Newb | 6f Cls5 Mdn 2yo gd-fm | | | £3,886 |

Became frustrating last season having run Memory to a head in Albany Stakes at Royal Stakes, finishing second twice more at Pattern level and third at 11-10 in a Listed race at Salisbury; well below best on good to soft in Cheveley Park Stakes.

### 1136 Markab *(pictured, winning)*
*8 b g Green Desert - Hawafiz (Nashwan)*
Henry Candy                          Tight Lines Partnership
**PLACINGS: 400122/644105/11261-**   **RPR 121+**

| Starts | 1st | 2nd | 3rd | 4th | Win & Pl |
|---|---|---|---|---|---|
| 30 | 8 | 4 | 3 | 3 | £380,158 |
| 9/10 | Hayd | 6f Cls1 Gp1 gd-fm | | | £163,810 |
| 5/10 | Curr | 6f Gp3 gd-fm | | | £38,827 |
| 4/10 | Thsk | 6f Cls2 gd-fm | | | £11,216 |
| 100 | 8/09 | Ripn | 6f Cls2 94-107 Hcap gd-fm | | £37,386 |
| 90 | 11/08 | Ling | 7f Cls3 81-90 Hcap stand | | £9,714 |
| 86 | 4/08 | Newc | 7f Cls2 82-95 Hcap gd-sft | | £9,970 |
| 82 | 3/08 | Kemp | 7f Cls4 71-85 Hcap stand | | £4,210 |
| | 3/06 | MsnL | 1m 3yo heavy | | £6,552 |

Continued stunning improvement to become top-class sprinter last season, culminating in first Group 1 win in Haydock Sprint Cup having been fine

racingpost.com

second in King's Stand Stakes on first run at 5f; likely to win fair share again.

### 1137 Masaya *(pictured, winning)*
3 b f Dansili - Anbella (Common Grounds)
Clive Brittain                                Saeed Manana
**PLACINGS: 102431-**                        **RPR 96**

| Starts | 1st | 2nd | 3rd | 4th | Win & Pl |
|---|---|---|---|---|---|
| 6 | 2 | 1 | 1 | 1 | £186,850 |
| 10/10 | NmkR | 7f Cls2 2yo soft | | | £167,339 |
| 5/10 | Wind | 5f Cls5 Mdn 2yo good | | | £3,368 |

Benefited from Together's waywardness to run out tenacious winner of valuable sales race at Newmarket having previously looked just short of that level; trainer intent on training her for crack at 1,000 Guineas.

### 1138 Masked Marvel
3 b c Montjeu - Waldmark (Mark Of Esteem)
John Gosden                                  B E Nielsen
**PLACINGS: 16-**                            **RPR 83+**

| Starts | 1st | 2nd | 3rd | 4th | Win & Pl |
|---|---|---|---|---|---|
| 2 | 1 | - | - | - | £4,749 |
| 9/10 | Sand | 1m Cls4 Mdn 2yo good | | | £4,209 |

Major springer in Derby market following successful Sandown debut but had been green that day and may have found step up to Group 3 level at Ascot coming too soon next time; interesting for middle distances.

### 1139 Master Of Hounds (USA)
3 b c Kingmambo - Silk And Scarlet (Sadler's Wells)
Aidan O'Brien (Ir)                          Mrs John Magnier
**PLACINGS: 522136-**                        **RPR 115**

| Starts | 1st | 2nd | 3rd | 4th | Win & Pl |
|---|---|---|---|---|---|
| 6 | 1 | 2 | 1 | - | £40,191 |
| 7/10 | Tipp | 7½f Mdn 2yo good | | | £8,243 |

Won only one out of six starts last season but highly-rated by connections having been chosen mount of Johnny Murtagh over Seville when third in Racing Post Trophy; flopped again, though, when sixth at Breeders' Cup.

### 1140 Mastery
5 b h Sulamani - Moyesii (Diesis)
Saeed Bin Suroor                              Godolphin
**PLACINGS: 13/4133213/5311-**              **RPR 120 RPR**

| Starts | 1st | 2nd | 3rd | 4th | Win & Pl |
|---|---|---|---|---|---|
| 13 | 5 | 1 | 5 | 1 | £1,654,848 |
| 12/10 | ShTn | 1m4f Gp1 good | | | £634,845 |
| 11/10 | Kemp | 1m4f Cls1 List stand | | | £14,484 |
| 9/09 | Donc | 1m6½f Cls1 Gp1 3yo gd-fm | | | £306,586 |
| 5/09 | Capa | 1m3f Gp2 3yo gd-fm | | | £359,223 |
| 10/08 | Nott | 1m½f Cls5 Mdn 2yo soft | | | £2,914 |

Top-class middle-distance performer who won 2009 St Leger and has speed to be competitive over much shorter (finished fifth in last year's Dubai World Cup); added second Group 1 win in Hong Kong before planned spring campaign at Meydan.

## 1141 Meeznah (USA)
4 b f Dynaformer - String Quartet (Sadler's Wells)
David Lanigan                    Saif Ali & Saeed H Altayer
**PLACINGS: 33/12d4437-**                **RPR 115**

| Starts | 1st | 2nd | 3rd | 4th | Win & Pl |
|---|---|---|---|---|---|
| 8 | 1 | - | 3 | 2 | £45,216 |
| | 5/10 | NmkR | 1m4f Cls4 Mdn 3yo gd-fm | | £5,181 |

Ran a blinder to push Snow Fairy close in Oaks (later disqualified due to failed drugs test) but has since come up short.

## 1142 Memory (Ire)
3 b f Danehill Dancer - Nausicaa (Diesis)
Richard Hannon
                Highclere Thoroughbred Racing-Masquerade
**PLACINGS: 1116-**                        **RPR 111+**

| Starts | 1st | 2nd | 3rd | 4th | Win & Pl |
|---|---|---|---|---|---|
| 4 | 3 | - | - | - | £85,119 |
| | 7/10 | NmkJ | 6f Cls1 Gp2 2yo gd-fm | | £39,739 |
| | 6/10 | Asct | 6f Cls1 Gp3 2yo gd-fm | | £39,739 |
| | 5/10 | Gdwd | 6f Cls5 Mdn 2yo good | | £3,562 |

Created huge impression early last season, particularly in Cherry Hinton Stakes at Newmarket; blotted her copybook with poor effort at the Curragh and never right after, missing succession of targets, but still a leading contender for 1,000 Guineas.

## 1143 Mendip (USA)
4 br c Harlan's Holiday - Well Spring (Coronado's Quest)
Saeed Bin Suroor
                    Sheikh Hamdan Bin Mohammed Al Maktoum
**PLACINGS: 1/113-1**                    **RPR 117+aw**

| Starts | 1st | 2nd | 3rd | 4th | Win & Pl |
|---|---|---|---|---|---|
| 5 | 4 | - | - | 1 | £316,671 |
| | 1/11 | Meyd | 1m Gp3 stand | | £76,923 |
| | 3/10 | Meyd | 1m1¹/₂f List 3yo stand | | £92,593 |
| | 2/10 | Meyd | 7f 3yo stand | | £18,519 |
| | 9/09 | Kemp | 1m Cls4 Mdn 2yo stand | | £5,181 |

Missed nearly a year following third in last season's UAE Derby but made winning return at Meydan this spring; has already shown smart form and is potentially high-class from 1m to 1m2f; yet to run on turf.

## 1144 Meow (Ire)
3 b f Storm Cat - Airwave (Air Express)
David Wachman (Ir)
                    M Tabor, D Smith & Mrs John Magnier
**PLACINGS: 21210-**                        **RPR 106**

| Starts | 1st | 2nd | 3rd | 4th | Win & Pl |
|---|---|---|---|---|---|
| 5 | 2 | 2 | - | - | £53,841 |
| | 8/10 | Curr | 5f List 2yo gd-fm | | £24,447 |
| | 5/10 | Tipp | 5f Mdn 2yo gd-fm | | £6,412 |

Kept to 5f last season and looked pure speed, finishing second to Maqaasid in Queen Mary and just landing Listed event at the Curragh when hanging on all out at the line; became upset and lost her action when tailed off in Flying Childers Stakes.

## 1145 Midas Touch
4 b c Galileo - Approach (Darshaan)
Aidan O'Brien (Ir)
                    Mrs Magnier, M Tabor, D Smith & Denford Stud
**PLACINGS: 314/152220-**                    **RPR 121**

| Starts | 1st | 2nd | 3rd | 4th | Win & Pl |
|---|---|---|---|---|---|
| 9 | 2 | 3 | 1 | 1 | £466,879 |
| | 5/10 | Leop | 1m2f Gp2 3yo gd-fm | | £57,522 |
| | 10/09 | Curr | 7f Mdn 2yo soft | | £8,721 |

Showed consistently smart level of form last season after slightly disappointing fifth in Epsom Derby, finishing second three times in a row including in Irish Derby and St Leger; just too one-paced over 1m4f but should stay a lot further.

## 1146 Midday
5 b m Oasis Dream - Midsummer (Kingmambo)
Henry Cecil                        Juddmonte Farms Inc
**PLACINGS: 7314/2123131/21112-**            **RPR 124+**

| Starts | 1st | 2nd | 3rd | 4th | Win & Pl |
|---|---|---|---|---|---|
| 16 | 7 | 4 | 3 | 1 | £1,770,584 |
| | 9/10 | Lonc | 1m4f Gp1 soft | | £176,982 |
| | 8/10 | York | 1m4f Cls1 Gp1 good | | £175,987 |
| | 7/10 | Gdwd | 1m2f Cls1 Gp1 gd-fm | | £122,169 |
| | 11/09 | SnAt | 1m2f Gd1 firm | | £750,000 |
| | 8/09 | Gdwd | 1m2f Cls1 Gp1 soft | | £113,540 |
| | 5/09 | Ling | 1m3¹/₂f Cls1 List 3yo gd-fm | | £28,385 |
| | 9/08 | NmkR | 1m Cls4 Mdn 2yo gd-fm | | £6,476 |

Brilliant middle-distance filly who took Group 1 tally to five last season and came close to second successive victory at Breeders' Cup on final start; easily beat Snow Fairy in Yorkshire Oaks and equally effective at 1m2f; another great season anticipated.

## 1147 Mirror Lake
4 b f Dubai Destination - Reflections (Sadler's Wells)
Amanda Perrett                        K Abdulla
**PLACINGS: 5/21112-**                        **RPR 113**

| Starts | 1st | 2nd | 3rd | 4th | Win & Pl |
|---|---|---|---|---|---|
| 6 | 3 | 2 | - | - | £41,518 |
| 96 | 8/10 | Gdwd | 1m2f Cls1 List 83-100 Hcap gd-sft | | £19,870 |
| 88 | 8/10 | Gdwd | 1m2f Cls3 86-95 Hcap good | | £5,828 |
| | 6/10 | Kemp | 1m2f Cls5 Mdn stand | | £2,590 |

Went from strength to strength last year when winning three in a row, including two handicaps, to earn step up to Pattern level when second to Red Badge; regarded as better on faster ground and looks well up to winning Group races at 1m2f.

## 1148 Mister Manannan (Ire)
*4 b g Desert Style - Cover Girl (Common Grounds)*
David Nicholls                                Mrs Maureen Quayle
**PLACINGS: 3192231/17300-56            RPR 110**

| Starts | 1st | 2nd | 3rd | 4th | Win & Pl |
|---|---|---|---|---|---|
| 14 | 3 | 2 | 3 | - | £87,699 |
| 4/10 | Chan | 6f List 3yo good | | | £24,336 |
| 9/10 | Ayr | 5f Cls1 List 2yo good | | | £19,870 |
| 4/09 | Pont | 4f Mdn 2yo good | | | £5,181 |

Smart sprinting juvenile in 2009 but predictably struggled against older rivals last year; twice ran well against own age group, including winning Listed prize at Chantilly, to hint at revival; returned to action at Meydan this spring.

## 1149 Misty For Me (Ire)
*3 b f Galileo - Butterfly Cove (Storm Cat)*
Aidan O'Brien (Ir)         M Tabor, D Smith & Mrs John Magnier
**PLACINGS: 01211-                        RPR 114**

| Starts | 1st | 2nd | 3rd | 4th | Win & Pl |
|---|---|---|---|---|---|
| 5 | 3 | 1 | - | - | £299,818 |
| 10/10 | Lonc | 1m Gp1 2yo v soft | | | £151,699 |
| 8/10 | Curr | 7f Gp1 2yo gd-fm | | | £120,619 |
| 7/10 | Curr | 6f Mdn 2yo gd-yld | | | £10,686 |

Arguably Europe's leading juvenile filly of last season on strength of Group 1 double at the Curragh and Longchamp, showing great battling qualities to beat Laughing Lashes and Helleborine; tough sort who could go well in 1,000 Guineas and Oaks.

## 1150 Monterosso
*4 b c Dubawi - Porto Roca (Barathea)*
Mark Johnston                                            Godolphin
**PLACINGS: 5/2111211475-                 RPR 117**

| Starts | 1st | 2nd | 3rd | 4th | Win & Pl |
|---|---|---|---|---|---|
| 11 | 5 | 2 | 1 | - | £159,188 |
| 6/10 | Asct | 1m4f Cls1 Gp2 3yo gd-fm | | | £92,947 |
| 94 | 5/10 | NmkR | 1m2f Cls2 84-94 3yo Hcap good | | £11,657 |
| 83 | 4/10 | Ripn | 1m Cls3 76-95 3yo Hcap good | | £7,477 |
| 78 | 2/10 | Ling | 1m Cls4 70-78 3yo Hcap stand | | £4,209 |
| | 1/10 | Ling | 1m Cls5 Mdn 3yo stand | | £2,457 |

Easily forgiven disappointing efforts at end of last season having been on the go since making debut on all-weather in November 2009; had previously made rapid progress to win King Edward VII Stakes and finish good fourth in Irish Derby.

## 1151 Moonlight Cloud
*3 b f Invincible Spirit - Ventura (Spectrum)*
Freddie Head (Fr)                          George Strawbridge
**PLACINGS: 114-                           RPR 107+**

| Starts | 1st | 2nd | 3rd | 4th | Win & Pl |
|---|---|---|---|---|---|
| 3 | 2 | - | - | 1 | £43,349 |
| 9/10 | Lonc | 7f 2yo soft | | | £15,044 |
| 8/10 | Deau | 6½f 2yo stand | | | £10,619 |

Hailed by trainer as his best ever juvenile following stunning six-length romp in conditions event at Longchamp but disappointing fourth taking on colts in Prix Jean-Luc Lagardere; should stay 1m and remains fascinating Guineas contender.

## 1152 Morning Charm (USA)
*3 b f North Light - Vignette (Diesis)*
John Gosden                                George Strawbridge
**PLACINGS: 1-                             RPR 80+**

| Starts | 1st | 2nd | 3rd | 4th | Win & Pl |
|---|---|---|---|---|---|
| 1 | 1 | - | - | - | £4,533 |
| 8/10 | NmkJ | 7f Cls4 Mdn 2yo gd-sft | | | £4,533 |

Half-sister to St Leger winner Lucarno and won hot Newmarket maiden on her debut, running on strongly to win by a head; sure to relish a step up in trip and no surprise to see her progress into a leading Oaks candidate.

## 1153 Motrice
*4 gr f Motivator - Entente Cordiale (Affirmed)*
Sir Mark Prescott                              Miss K Rausing
**PLACINGS: 9070/52111332-                 RPR 112+**

| Starts | 1st | 2nd | 3rd | 4th | Win & Pl |
|---|---|---|---|---|---|
| 12 | 3 | 2 | 2 | - | £43,030 |
| 76 | 7/10 | York | 1m6f Cls3 76-85 3yo Hcap gd-fm | | £6,800 |
| 70 | 7/10 | Hayd | 1m6f Cls5 51-70 3yo Hcap gd-fm | | £2,590 |
| 59 | 6/10 | Yarm | 1m6f Cls5 52-70 3yo Hcap good | | £2,461 |

Typical improver for her trainer over staying trips last season, rising 49lb in the handicap; placed three times at Pattern level too and could improve again.

## 1154 Music Show (Ire)
*4 b f Noverre - Dreamboat (Mr Prospector)*
Mick Channon                                    Jaber Abdullah
**PLACINGS: 1101/16341234-                 RPR 119+**

| Starts | 1st | 2nd | 3rd | 4th | Win & Pl |
|---|---|---|---|---|---|
| 12 | 5 | 1 | 2 | 2 | £325,696 |
| 7/10 | NmkJ | 1m Cls1 Gp1 gd-fm | | | £105,025 |
| 4/10 | NmkR | 7f Cls1 Gp3 3yo good | | | £36,901 |
| 10/09 | NmkR | 7f Cls1 Gp2 2yo good | | | £45,416 |
| 8/09 | Bath | 5½f Cls4 2yo firm | | | £3,950 |
| 8/09 | Bath | 5½f Cls6 Mdn 2yo good | | | £2,202 |

Ran consistently well in top fillies' races

## Contenders Ten to Follow

over 1m last season, showing smart turn of foot to win Falmouth Stakes having been badly drawn in 1,000 Guineas and Coronation Stakes; connections hopeful of improvement stepping up to 1m2f.

### 1155 My Name Is Bond (Fr)
*3 b c Monsieur Bond - Lady Oriande (Makbul)*

Jean-Claude Rouget (Fr)      Daniel-Yves Treves
**PLACINGS: 312116-**      **RPR 111+**

| Starts | 1st | 2nd | 3rd | 4th | Win & Pl |
|---|---|---|---|---|---|
| 6 | 3 | 1 | 1 | - | £72,610 |
| 9/10 | Lonc | 7f Gp3 2yo good | | | £35,398 |
| 8/10 | Buch | 6f List 2yo soft | | | £24,336 |
| 6/10 | Buch | 6f 2yo gd-sft | | | £6,195 |

Looked a smart prospect when winning Group 3 at Longchamp on penultimate start; didn't seem to enjoy very soft ground when disappointing sixth in Prix Jean-Luc Lagardere and may well be worth another chance.

### 1156 Myplacelater
*4 ch f Where Or When - Star Welcome (Most Welcome)*

David Elsworth      A J Thompson
**PLACINGS: 612514710112-**      **RPR 112**

| Starts | 1st | 2nd | 3rd | 4th | Win & Pl |
|---|---|---|---|---|---|
| 12 | 5 | 2 | - | 1 | £76,467 |
| 10/10 | NmkR | 1m4f Cls1 List soft | | | £19,870 |
| 9/10 | Donc | 1m2½f Cls2 3-5yo good | | | £15,578 |
| 7/10 | Leic | 1m2f Cls3 3yo good | | | £6,119 |
| 4/10 | Newb | 1m2f Cls3 3yo good | | | £7,477 |
| 2/10 | Wolv | 1m⅟₂f Cls5 Mdn stand | | | £2,457 |

Remarkable success story last season, improving rapidly and winning at some big prices, most notably when pipping smart Wigmore Hall at 22-1; followed up in Listed event before fine second to Crystal Capella last time; needs good ground or softer.

### 1157 Native Khan (Fr)
*3 gr c Azamour - Viva Maria (Kendor)*

Ed Dunlop      V I Araci
**PLACINGS: 114-**      **RPR 113**

| Starts | 1st | 2nd | 3rd | 4th | Win & Pl |
|---|---|---|---|---|---|
| 3 | 2 | - | - | 1 | £44,320 |
| 8/10 | Sand | 7f Cls1 Gp3 2yo gd-fm | | | £21,289 |
| 7/10 | NmkL | 7f Cls2 Mdn 2yo gd-fm | | | £9,714 |

Impressive winner of albeit modest Solario Stakes at Sandown and did well to finish fourth when losing unbeaten record in Racing Post Trophy; should handle all ground conditions and likely to do better when stepped up to middle distances.

### 1158 New Planet (Ire)
*3 ch c Majestic Missile - Xena (Mull Of Kintyre)*

John Quinn      Ross Harmon
**PLACINGS: 113-**      **RPR 104**

| Starts | 1st | 2nd | 3rd | 4th | Win & Pl |
|---|---|---|---|---|---|
| 3 | 2 | - | 1 | - | £30,279 |
| 8/10 | York | 5f Cls1 List 2yo good | | | £17,778 |
| 7/10 | Pont | 5f Cls4 Mdn 2yo gd-fm | | | £3,886 |

Ran well in all three races last season over 5f, winning competitive Listed sprint at York and extending superiority over many of those rivals when third in Flying Childers Stakes; may well improve with experience; untested on ground softer than good.

### 1159 Opinion Poll (Ire)
*5 b h Halling - Ahead (Shirley Heights)*

Mahmood Al Zarooni      Godolphin
**PLACINGS: 01/3171/1313143-22**      **RPR 116+**

| Starts | 1st | 2nd | 3rd | 4th | Win & Pl |
|---|---|---|---|---|---|
| 15 | 6 | 2 | 4 | 1 | £272,225 |
| 8/10 | York | 2m⅟₂f Cls1 Gp2 good | | | £79,478 |
| 6/10 | Chan | 1m7f List gd-sft | | | £23,009 |
| 4/10 | Nott | 1m6f Cls1 List soft | | | £22,708 |
| 95 10/09 | Asct | 1m4f Cls2 89-102 Hcap gd-sft | | | £46,733 |
| 88 5/09 | Hayd | 1m4f Cls2 79-98 3yo Hcap heavy | | | £12,462 |
| 10/08 | Leic | 1m⅟₂f Cls4 Mdn 2yo good | | | £5,181 |

Smart stayer on easy ground who made debut for Godolphin at Meydan this spring having previously run for Michael Jarvis; gained biggest win in Lonsdale Cup at York before finding 2m2f too far at Doncaster.

### 1160 Overdose
*6 b h Starborough - Our Poppet (Warning)*

Jozef Roszival (Hun)      Miko Racing & Trading Kft
**PLACINGS: 11111/111111/1/117-**      **RPR 96**

| Starts | 1st | 2nd | 3rd | 4th | Win & Pl |
|---|---|---|---|---|---|
| 15 | 14 | - | - | - | £151,310 |
| 8/10 | KcPk | 5f good | | | £7,087 |
| 7/10 | Brat | 5f soft | | | £4,425 |
| 4/09 | KcPk | 5f good | | | £13,818 |
| 11/08 | Capa | 6f Gp3 heavy | | | £26,801 |
| 8/08 | Badn | 6f Gp2 good | | | £30,882 |
| 7/08 | Hamb | 6f Gp3 soft | | | £29,418 |
| 6/08 | Brat | 6f good | | | £9,290 |
| 5/08 | Badn | 6f List 3yo good | | | £11,029 |
| 4/08 | MagR | 5⅟₂f fast | | | £2,316 |
| 10/07 | MagR | 6⅟₂f 2yo good | | | £6,081 |
| 9/07 | KcPk | 7f good | | | £3,484 |
| 9/07 | Freu | 6f good | | | £5,068 |
| 7/07 | Brat | 6f good | | | £1,075 |
| 6/07 | KcPk | 5f good | | | £536 |

Record-breaking Hungarian sprinter who won first 14 races before becoming mulish entering stalls and finishing seventh in Germany last time; suffered minor setback but set to come to Britain for Temple Stakes in May before Royal Ascot bid.

racingpost.com      141

## 1161 Pathfork (USA)
*3 b c Distorted Humor - Visions Of Clarity (Sadler's Wells)*
Jessica Harrington (Ir)  Silverton Hill Partnership
**PLACINGS: 111-**  **RPR 119+**

| Starts | 1st | 2nd | 3rd | 4th | Win & Pl |
|---|---|---|---|---|---|
| 3 | 3 | - | - | - | £165,216 |
| 9/10 | Curr | 7f Gp1 2yo soft | | | £102,655 |
| 8/10 | Curr | 7f Gp2 2yo gd-fm | | | £53,097 |
| 7/10 | Curr | 7f Mdn 2yo yield | | | £9,465 |

Won Futurity Stakes on good to firm and National Stakes on soft ground (by a head from Casamento), but connections think he wants good; set to return in 2,000 Guineas.

## 1162 Patkai (Ire)
*6 ch g Indian Ridge - Olympienne (Sadler's Wells)*
Sir Michael Stoute  Ballymacoll Stud
**PLACINGS: 61/32114/122/**

| Starts | 1st | 2nd | 3rd | 4th | Win & Pl |
|---|---|---|---|---|---|
| 10 | 4 | 3 | 1 | 1 | £170,718 |
| 4/09 | Asct | 2m Cls1 Gp3 gd-fm | | | £36,901 |
| 6/08 | Asct | 2m Cls1 Gp3 3yo firm | | | £34,062 |
| 95 5/08 | Hayd | 1m4f Cls2 83-100 3yo Hcap gd-fm | | | £12,462 |
| 10/07 | Nott | 1m Cls5 Mdn 2yo gd-sft | | | £2,591 |

Not seen since second to Yeats in 2009 Ascot Gold Cup but had recovered from injury last autumn when denied a run by soft ground; had looked a top-class stayer before absence and may be a force again.

## 1163 Penitent
*5 b g Kyllachy - Pious (Bishop Of Cashel)*
William Haggas  Cheveley Park Stud
**PLACINGS: 21212/17125-**  **RPR 116+**

| Starts | 1st | 2nd | 3rd | 4th | Win & Pl |
|---|---|---|---|---|---|
| 10 | 4 | 4 | - | - | £129,558 |
| 9/10 | Sand | 1m Cls1 List good | | | £19,870 |
| 98 3/10 | Donc | 1m Cls2 91-106 Hcap soft | | | £77,888 |
| 86 9/09 | Kemp | 1m Cls3 85-91 3yo Hcap stand | | | £4,777 |
| 7/09 | NmkJ | 7f Cls4 Mdn 3yo good | | | £5,181 |

Clear-cut Lincoln winner last March and did enough to suggest he can cut it at Pattern level when landing Listed race at Sandown and beating all bar Cityscape in Group 3 at Newmarket; failed to stay 1m2f final start.

## 1164 Peter Martins (USA)
*3 ch c Johannesburg - Pretty Meadow (Meadowlake)*
Jeremy Noseda  The Honorable Earle I Mack
**PLACINGS: 1-**  **RPR 98+**

| Starts | 1st | 2nd | 3rd | 4th | Win & Pl |
|---|---|---|---|---|---|
| 1 | 1 | - | - | - | £6,476 |
| 7/10 | NmkJ | 7f Cls4 Mdn 2yo gd-fm | | | £6,476 |

Won well in novice company on debut at Newmarket, striding 5l clear of two previous winners with Dux Scholar fourth; missed autumn targets following setback but back in training early and aimed at Craven Stakes.

## 1165 Picture Editor
*3 b c Dansili - Shirley Valentine (Shirley Heights)*
Henry Cecil  K Abdulla
**PLACINGS: 113-**  **RPR 97**

| Starts | 1st | 2nd | 3rd | 4th | Win & Pl |
|---|---|---|---|---|---|
| 3 | 2 | - | 1 | - | £13,135 |
| 10/10 | Leic | 1m2f Cls3 2yo heavy | | | £5,236 |
| 9/10 | Donc | 1m Cls3 Mdn 2yo good | | | £6,800 |

Won first two starts in hugely impressive fashion before being turned over at 4-6 in Zetland Stakes; has won on heavy ground but only in modest company and latest run suggested he needs much quicker; remains big Derby hope.

## 1166 Planteur (Ire)
*4 b c Danehill Dancer - Plante Rare (Giant's Causeway)*
Elie Lellouche (Fr)  Ecurie Wildenstein
**PLACINGS: 121/1222dis5-**  **RPR 124**

| Starts | 1st | 2nd | 3rd | 4th | Win & Pl |
|---|---|---|---|---|---|
| 9 | 3 | 4 | - | - | £602,979 |
| 4/10 | Lonc | 1m2½f Gp2 3yo soft | | | £65,575 |
| 9/09 | StCl | 1m 2yo gd-sft | | | £16,505 |
| 8/09 | Deau | 1m 2yo soft | | | £11,650 |

Developed into high-class middle-distance performer despite failing to add to Group 2 win over Rewilding at Longchamp in April, twice finishing second to Behkabad; showed tendency to race freely and may need strong pace.

## 1167 Plumania
*5 b m Anabaa - Featherquest (Rainbow Quest)*
Andre Fabre (Fr)  Wertheimer & Frere
**PLACINGS: 414/253323/4411200-**  **RPR 116**

| Starts | 1st | 2nd | 3rd | 4th | Win & Pl |
|---|---|---|---|---|---|
| 16 | 3 | 3 | 3 | 4 | £576,772 |
| 6/10 | Lonc | 1m4f Gp1 gd-sft | | | £202,265 |
| 5/10 | StCl | 1m2½f Gp2 good | | | £65,575 |
| 9/08 | Lonc | 1m 2yo gd-sft | | | £12,500 |

Short of top class as a three-year-old but made Group 1 breakthrough at fifth attempt when just winning Grand Prix de Saint-Cloud and confirmed improvement when second to Midday next time; disliked firm ground at Breeders' Cup.

## Contenders Ten to Follow

### 1168 Poet's Voice
*4 b c Dubawi - Bright Tiara (Chief's Crown)*
Saeed Bin Suroor                               Godolphin
**PLACINGS: 31314/892119-**              **RPR 123+**

| Starts | 1st | 2nd | 3rd | 4th | Win & Pl |
|---|---|---|---|---|---|
| 11 | 4 | 1 | 2 | 1 | £301,680 |

| | | | |
|---|---|---|---|
| 9/10 | Asct | 1m Cls1 Gp1 gd-sft | £151,860 |
| 8/10 | Gdwd | 1m Cls1 Gp2 soft | £56,770 |
| 9/09 | Donc | 7f Cls1 Gp2 2yo gd-fm | £56,770 |
| 7/09 | NmkJ | 7f Cls4 2yo good | £6,476 |

Disappointing early last year but bounced back in second half of season, most notably when landing Queen Elizabeth II Stakes by a nose; never going well when last in Champion Stakes over 1m2f; was due to return at Meydan this spring.

### 1169 Pontenuovo (Fr)
*3 ch f Green Tune - Porlezza (Sicyos)*
Roger Charlton                           Mme Erika Hilger
**PLACINGS: 2135-**                              **RPR 109**

| Starts | 1st | 2nd | 3rd | 4th | Win & Pl |
|---|---|---|---|---|---|
| 4 | 1 | 1 | 1 | - | £78,588 |

| | | | |
|---|---|---|---|
| 8/10 | Deau | 6f Gp3 2yo gd-sft | £35,398 |

Smart filly who showed she could mix it with the colts for Yves de Nicolay with a fine third behind Dream Ahead in the Prix Morny; poor last of five when stepped up to 1m on heavy ground in Group 3 at Saint-Cloud on final start; bought since for big money.

### 1170 Premio Loco (USA)
*7 ch g Prized - Crazee Mental (Magic Ring)*
Chris Wall                                  Bernard Westley
**PLACINGS: 116/1121211/5711328-**      **RPR 122**

| Starts | 1st | 2nd | 3rd | 4th | Win & Pl |
|---|---|---|---|---|---|
| 23 | 11 | 3 | 1 | - | £374,825 |

| | | | |
|---|---|---|---|
| 7/10 | Asct | 1m Cls1 Gp2 gd-fm | £56,770 |
| 6/10 | NmkJ | 7f Cls1 Gp3 gd-fm | £36,901 |
| 9/09 | Colo | 1m Gp2 good | £38,835 |
| 9/09 | Badn | 1m Gp2 good | £38,835 |
| 5/09 | Gdwd | 1m Cls1 List good | £22,708 |
| 2/09 | Kemp | 1m Cls1 List stand | £22,708 |
| 1/09 | Ling | 1m Cls3 stand | £7,771 |
| 99 9/08 | Kemp | 1m Cls2 77-99 Hcap stand | £30,825 |
| 92 7/08 | Kemp | 1m Cls3 82-95 Hcap stand | £7,477 |
| 83 9/07 | Newb | 7f Cls4 75-85 3yo Hcap gd-fm | £4,858 |
| 4/07 | Ling | 1m Cls5 Auct Mdn 3yo stand | £2,915 |

Better than ever last season when surprise 25-1 winner in Group 3 at Newmarket and proved that was no fluke by following up at Ascot and finishing terrific third in Group 1 Sussex Stakes; well below best on good to soft on final start.

### 1171 Presvis
*7 b g Sakhee - Forest Fire (Never So Bold)*
Luca Cumani                         Leonidas Marinopoulos
**PLACINGS: 221/1121223/210559-1**      **RPR 122**

| Starts | 1st | 2nd | 3rd | 4th | Win & Pl |
|---|---|---|---|---|---|
| 21 | 7 | 6 | 2 | - | £2,341,076 |

| | | | | |
|---|---|---|---|---|
| | 1/11 | Meyd | 1m1f Gp2 good | £76,923 |
| | 3/10 | Meyd | 1m1f Gp2 gd-fm | £92,593 |
| | 4/09 | ShTn | 1m2f Gp1 yield | £718,133 |
| 112 | 2/09 | Ndas | 1m2f 101-116 Hcap gd-fm | £72,917 |
| 106 | 4/09 | Ndas | 1m2f 95-110 Hcap gd-fm | £50,000 |
| 92 | 9/08 | Newb | 1m2f Cls2 84-104 Hcap good | £62,310 |
| 72 | 7/08 | Sand | 1m2f Cls4 68-80 Hcap gd-fm | £5,828 |

Genuine Group 1 performer over middle distances; generally disappointing last year but given extended break following ninth place at Royal Ascot and looked better than ever when making winning return at Meydan this spring.

### 1172 Prime Defender
*7 ch h Bertolini - Arian Da (Superlative)*
Barry Hills                    S Falle, M Franklin & J Sumsion
**PLACINGS: 28550/0892411905400-**      **RPR 116**

| Starts | 1st | 2nd | 3rd | 4th | Win & Pl |
|---|---|---|---|---|---|
| 47 | 7 | 6 | 3 | 4 | £261,644 |

| | | | | |
|---|---|---|---|---|
| | 5/10 | York | 6f Cls1 Gp2 good | £56,770 |
| | 5/10 | Hayd | 6f Cls2 gd-fm | £12,462 |
| | 3/09 | Donc | 6f Cls1 List gd-fm | £22,708 |
| | 5/07 | Hayd | 6f Cls1 List 3yo gd-fm | £14,763 |
| 106 | 4/07 | NmkR | 7f Cls1 List 100-108 3yo Hcap gd-fm | £17,034 |
| | 11/06 | Wolv | 6f Cls3 2yo std-fst | £6,855 |
| | 7/06 | Sand | 5f Cls5 Mdn Auct 2yo gd-fm | £3,886 |

Not far off best sprinters for last four seasons, winning three times in Listed company and making most of fitness edge to land Group 2 Duke of York Stakes last year; also fine fourth in Nunthorpe Stakes; should knock on the door again.

### 1173 Prince Bishop (Ire)
*4 ch c Dubawi - North East Bay (Prospect Bay)*
Andre Fabre (Fr)                              Godolphin Snc
**PLACINGS: 2581111-**                           **RPR 118**

| Starts | 1st | 2nd | 3rd | 4th | Win & Pl |
|---|---|---|---|---|---|
| 7 | 4 | 1 | - | - | £126,194 |

| | | | |
|---|---|---|---|
| 10/10 | Lonc | 1m4f Gp2 gd-sft | £65,575 |
| 9/10 | Lonc | 1m2f Gp3 3yo gd-sft | £35,398 |
| 8/10 | Claf | 1m1f 3yo v soft | £10,619 |
| 7/10 | Vich | 1m2f 3yo heavy | £9,292 |

Unraced as a juvenile and took time to find his feet last year but finished on a roll by winning last four starts, culminating in strong Group 2 at Longchamp; may well progress again and likely to have top middle-distance races on agenda.

## 1174 Purple Moon (Ire)

*8 ch g Galileo - Vanishing Prairie (Alysheba)*

Luca Cumani                                     Craig Bennett
**PLACINGS: /41162/5292/43/7233-**              **RPR 116**

| Starts | 1st | 2nd | 3rd | 4th | Win & Pl |
|---|---|---|---|---|---|
| 21 | 3 | 5 | 4 | 3 | £1,173,194 |
| 101 | 8/07 | York | 1m6f Cls2 92-111 Hcap good | | £124,640 |
| | 8/07 | Gdwd | 1m4f Cls1 List gd-fm | | £17,034 |
| | 4/06 | Newb | 1m Cls5 Mdn 3yo good | | £4,858 |

Lightly raced since ending 2007 with second in Melbourne Cup; returned from year-long absence to prove close to top stayers last season, finishing placed in Cup races at York, Ascot and Goodwood.

## 1175 Rainbow Peak (Ire)

*5 b g Hernando - Celtic Fling (Lion Cavern)*

Saeed Bin Suroor                                P D Savill
**PLACINGS: 111/21221-**                        **RPR 118**

| Starts | 1st | 2nd | 3rd | 4th | Win & Pl |
|---|---|---|---|---|---|
| 8 | 5 | 3 | - | - | £214,211 |
| | 10/10 | Siro | 1m4f Gp1 v soft | | £119,469 |
| 107 | 6/10 | Asct | 1m2f Cls1 List 99-110 Hcap gd-fm | | £28,385 |
| 97 | 10/09 | Newb | 1m2f Cls2 85-97 Hcap soft | | £11,216 |
| | 9/09 | Asct | 1m2f Cls3 good | | £11,216 |
| | 5/09 | Kemp | 1m Cls4 Mdn 3yo stand | | £4,404 |

Unbeaten in three starts at three and continued to progress last year for Michael Jarvis, winning Group 1 in Italy on final start; future lies over 1m4f or further.

## 1176 Rainbow Springs

*3 b f Selkirk - Pearl Dance (Nureyev)*

John Gosden                                     George Strawbridge
**PLACINGS: 23-**                               **RPR 105**

| Starts | 1st | 2nd | 3rd | 4th | Win & Pl |
|---|---|---|---|---|---|
| 2 | - | 1 | 1 | - | £33,610 |

Highly tried in two starts last season; had no chance against Frankel on debut but did extremely well to finish third behind Misty For Me in Prix Marcel Boussac, staying on nicely; expected to be best over 1m2f and could be aimed at Prix de Diane.

## 1177 Rainfall (Ire)

*4 b f Oasis Dream - Molomo (Barathea)*

Mark Johnston       Sheikh Hamdan Bin Mohammed Al Maktoum
**PLACINGS: 12135813-**                         **RPR 116+**

| Starts | 1st | 2nd | 3rd | 4th | Win & Pl |
|---|---|---|---|---|---|
| 8 | 3 | 1 | 2 | - | £129,204 |
| | 9/10 | Asct | 7f Cls1 List gd-sft | | £22,708 |
| | 6/10 | Asct | 7f Cls1 Gp3 3yo gd-fm | | £45,416 |
| | 5/10 | Thsk | 7f Cls4 Mdn 3yo good | | £5,569 |

Quickly made mark last year when winning Jersey Stakes at Royal Ascot on third start; never quite as convincing when stepped up to 1m subsequently but still performed well and should get stronger.

## 1178 Red Badge (Ire)

*4 ch c Captain Rio - Red Fuschia (Polish Precedent)*

Richard Hannon                                  Michael Pescod
**PLACINGS: 232610/42011-**                     **RPR 118**

| Starts | 1st | 2nd | 3rd | 4th | Win & Pl |
|---|---|---|---|---|---|
| 11 | 3 | 3 | 1 | 1 | £88,554 |
| | 9/10 | Gdwd | 1m2f Cls1 Gp3 gd-sft | | £32,359 |
| | 7/10 | Newb | 1m2f Cls1 List good | | £21,005 |
| 84 | 8/09 | NmkJ | 7f Cls2 68-91 2yo Hcap gd-fm | | £12,952 |

Looked exposed in handicap company for much of last season before winning Listed race at Newbury at 28-1 and following up in Group 3 contest at Goodwood; easy ground looks key having raced largely on good to firm prior to that.

## 1179 Red Jazz (USA)

*4 b c Johannesburg - Now That's Jazz (Sword Dance)*

Barry Hills                                     R J Arculli
**PLACINGS: 1173/182228531-**                   **RPR 122**

| Starts | 1st | 2nd | 3rd | 4th | Win & Pl |
|---|---|---|---|---|---|
| 13 | 4 | 3 | 2 | - | £160,310 |
| | 10/10 | NmkR | 7f Cls1 Gp2 gd-sft | | £51,093 |
| 107 | 4/10 | NmkR | 7f Cls1 List 100-108 3yo Hcap good | | £22,708 |
| | 4/09 | Asct | 5f Cls2 2yo gd-fm | | £6,543 |
| | 4/09 | Wind | 5f Cls5 Mdn 2yo good | | £2,730 |

Struggled for much of last season, despite fine second in Jersey Stakes at Royal Ascot, but finished 40-1 third in Queen Elizabeth II Stakes and followed up by winning Challenge Stakes at Newmarket; seemingly best on good to soft ground.

## 1180 Redford (Ire)

*6 b g Bahri - Ida Lupino (Statoblest)*

David Nicholls                                  Dr Marwan Koukash
**PLACINGS: 4/436300/4920093110-**              **RPR 117+**

| Starts | 1st | 2nd | 3rd | 4th | Win & Pl |
|---|---|---|---|---|---|
| 24 | 5 | 1 | 3 | 4 | £252,175 |
| 103 | 9/10 | Asct | 7f Cls2 92-106 Hcap gd-sft | | £93,465 |
| 97 | 9/10 | Ayr | 6f Cls2 96-105 Hcap good | | £93,465 |
| 93 | 6/08 | Newc | 7f Cls2 82-99 Hcap soft | | £12,462 |
| 87 | 6/08 | Donc | 1m Cls2 82-93 3yo Hcap gd-sft | | £12,952 |
| | 10/07 | Newc | 1m Cls4 Mdn 2yo good | | £4,340 |

Long looked capable of landing a big handicap and atoned for several expensive failures when landing Ayr Gold Cup and Challenge Cup at Ascot (under 6lb penalty) in successive weeks; set to have sights raised to Listed level at least.

## 1181 Redwood

*5 b h High Chaparral - Arum Lily (Woodman)*
Barry Hills                                    K Abdulla
**PLACINGS: 1/19/275212132-**            **RPR 117**

| Starts | 1st | 2nd | 3rd | 4th | Win & Pl |
|---|---|---|---|---|---|
| 12 | 4 | 4 | 1 | - | £752,345 |
| 9/10 | Wood | 1m4f Gd1 firm | | | £229,412 |
| 7/10 | Gdwd | 1m4f Cls1 Gp3 gd-fm | | | £39,739 |
| 4/09 | NmkR | 1m1f Cls1 List 3yo gd-fm | | | £25,547 |
| 10/08 | NmkR | 1m Cls4 Mdn 2yo gd-fm | | | £6,476 |

Had promising three-year-old campaign cut short by injury but began to realise potential last season, particularly when stepped up to 1m4f; won Grade 1 in Canada before fine second to Mastery in Hong Kong; could improve again.

## 1182 Regal Parade *(pictured)*

*7 ch g Pivotal - Model Queen (Kingmambo)*
David Nicholls                          Dab Hand Racing
**PLACINGS: 014/62191321/001164-**       **RPR 121**

| Starts | 1st | 2nd | 3rd | 4th | Win & Pl |
|---|---|---|---|---|---|
| 35 | 10 | 5 | 2 | 4 | £594,078 |
| 8/10 | Deau | 6½f Gp1 gd-sft | | | £126,416 |
| 7/10 | Newb | 6f Cls1 Gp3 good | | | £34,062 |
| 9/09 | Hayd | 6f Cls1 Gp1 gd-sft | | | £163,810 |
| 7/09 | Ches | 7f Cls1 gd-fm | | | £22,708 |
| 5/09 | York | 7f Cls3 gd-fm | | | £8,095 |
| 99 | 9/08 | Ayr | 6f Cls2 92-108 Hcap heavy | | £93,465 |
| 92 | 6/08 | Asct | 7f Cls2 80-105 Hcap firm | | £37,486 |
| 86 | 5/07 | NmkR | 7f Cls2 79-93 3yo Hcap gd-fm | | £12,954 |
| 79 | 2/07 | Sthl | 7f Cls4 72-82 3yo Hcap stand | | £4,858 |
| | 1/07 | Wolv | 7f Cls5 Mdn 3yo std-slw | | £3,071 |

Top-class sprinter on easy ground, having won four out of last five starts at shorter than 7f on good or softer, including two Group 1 victories in 2009 Haydock Sprint Cup and last year's Prix Maurice de Gheest; needs 7f on quicker going.

## 1183 Remember When (Ire)

*4 ch f Danehill Dancer - Lagrion (Diesis)*
Aidan O'Brien (Ir)                   Mrs John Magnier
**PLACINGS: 2/34249-**                   **RPR 112**

| Starts | 1st | 2nd | 3rd | 4th | Win & Pl |
|---|---|---|---|---|---|
| 6 | - | 2 | 1 | 2 | £100,543 |

Lost her way in final two runs last season but had previously looked a high-class filly; good fourth in Irish 1,000 Guineas and proved equally effective at 1m4f when third past the post in Oaks at Epsom (later promoted to second).

## 1184 Rerouted (USA)

*3 ch c Stormy Atlantic - Rouwaki (Miswaki)*
Barry Hills                                    K Abdulla
**PLACINGS: 313414-**                    **RPR 105**

| Starts | 1st | 2nd | 3rd | 4th | Win & Pl |
|---|---|---|---|---|---|
| 6 | 2 | - | 2 | 2 | £48,156 |
| 9/10 | NmkR | 7f Cls3 Gp3 2yo soft | | | £28,385 |
| 5/10 | Hayd | 6f Cls5 Mdn 2yo gd-fm | | | £3,432 |

Took time to get going last season, twice losing in nurseries off modest marks after maiden win, but left that form behind when stepped up in class to win Group 3 at Newmarket and finish fourth behind Roderic O'Connor in Group 1 at Saint-Cloud.

## 1185 Rewilding
*4 b c Tiger Hill - Darara (Top Ville)*

Mahmood Al Zarooni                                   Godolphin
**PLACINGS: 21/21316-**                              **RPR 124+**

| Starts | 1st | 2nd | 3rd | 4th | Win & Pl |
|---|---|---|---|---|---|
| 7 | 3 | 2 | 1 | - | £305,261 |
| | 8/10 York | 1m4f Cls1 Gp2 3yo good | | | £82,964 |
| | 5/10 Gdwd | 1m3f Cls1 List 3yo good | | | £22,708 |
| | 11/09 MsnL | 1m 2yo heavy | | | £16,505 |

Did well following move to Godolphin early last season, with fast-finishing third in Epsom Derby and easy win in Great Voltigeur at York; failed to stay 1m6f when sixth in St Leger; was due to return at Meydan this spring.

## 1186 Rimth
*3 b f Oasis Dream - Dorelia (Efisio)*

Paul Cole                                           Denford Stud
**PLACINGS: 13272-**                                 **RPR 103**

| Starts | 1st | 2nd | 3rd | 4th | Win & Pl |
|---|---|---|---|---|---|
| 5 | 1 | 2 | 1 | - | £58,751 |
| | 5/10 Wind | 5f Cls4 Mdn 2yo gd-fm | | | £4,209 |

Showed consistent form in strong fillies' races last season, with only flop coming when unlucky in running at Ayr; beaten a nose by Brevity in strong Listed event at Salisbury and best of rest behind runaway winner Hooray in Cheveley Park Stakes.

## 1187 Rio De La Plata (USA) *(pictured)*
*6 ch h Rahy - Express Way (Ahmad)*

Saeed Bin Suroor                                     Godolphin
**PLACINGS: 14/273/025/01171211-**                   **RPR 119**

| Starts | 1st | 2nd | 3rd | 4th | Win & Pl |
|---|---|---|---|---|---|
| 20 | 8 | 4 | 2 | 1 | £758,925 |
| | 11/10 Capa | 1m2f Gp1 soft | | | £119,469 |
| | 10/10 Siro | 1m Gp1 soft | | | £119,469 |
| | 8/10 York | 1m1f Cls1 Gp3 gd-fm | | | £48,255 |
| | 7/10 Pont | 1m Cls1 List gd-fm | | | £15,658 |
| | 6/10 Nott | 1m¹/₂f Cls2 gd-fm | | | £9,970 |
| | 10/07 Lonc | 7f Gp1 2yo gd-sft | | | £135,128 |
| | 8/07 Gdwd | 7f Cls1 Gp2 2yo good | | | £39,746 |
| | 7/07 NmkJ | 7f Cls2 Mdn 2yo good | | | £9,716 |

Steadily rediscovered best form last season having missed much of previous two years with injury; beaten a head in slowly-run Prix du Moulin before making amends with Group 1 double in Italy.

## 1188 Rite Of Passage
*7 ch g Giant's Causeway - Dahlia's Krissy (Kris S)*

Dermot Weld (Ir)                                    Dr R Lambe
**PLACINGS: 11/1-**                                  **RPR 122**

| Starts | 1st | 2nd | 3rd | 4th | Win & Pl |
|---|---|---|---|---|---|
| 3 | 3 | - | - | - | £170,974 |
| 88 | 6/10 Asct | 2m4f Cls1 Gp1 gd-fm | | | £141,925 |
| | 11/09 Leop | 2m 73-97 Hcap heavy | | | £24,017 |
| | 9/09 Baln | 1m6f Mdn yld-sft | | | £5,032 |

Remarkably won Ascot Gold Cup last year on only third Flat start having previously run in novice hurdles, including when third at Cheltenham Festival; missed rest of season after a setback but being geared up for repeat bid at Ascot.

### 1189 Roderic O'Connor (Ire)

*3 b c Galileo - Secret Garden (Danehill)*

Aidan O'Brien (Ir)
               Mrs Magnier, M Tabor, D Smith & Sangster Family

**PLACINGS: 3121-**                                    **RPR 120+**

| Starts | 1st | 2nd | 3rd | 4th | Win & Pl |
|---|---|---|---|---|---|
| 4 | 2 | 1 | 1 | - | £207,668 |
| | 10/10 StCl | 1m Gp1 2yo heavy | | | £126,416 |
| | 6/10 Curr | 7f Mdn 2yo gd-fm | | | £11,907 |

Only horse to give Frankel a race in his final three outings last season when good second in Dewhurst Stakes; showed that was no fluke with impressive Group 1 win at Saint-Cloud, though he was worryingly wayward in straight.

### 1190 Royal Bench (Ire)

*4 b c Whipper - Hit The Sky (Cozzene)*

Robert Collet (Fr)                                         R C Strauss

**PLACINGS: 316/101512-**                       **RPR 117+**

| Starts | 1st | 2nd | 3rd | 4th | Win & Pl |
|---|---|---|---|---|---|
| 9 | 4 | 1 | 1 | - | £417,746 |
| | 10/10 Lonc | 1m Gp2 v soft | | | £65,575 |
| | 7/10 Deau | 1m List 3yo good | | | £24,336 |
| | 4/10 Lonc | 1m 3yo heavy | | | £15,044 |
| | 10/09 Lonc | 1m 2yo soft | | | £14,078 |

Looked out of his depth on first two tries at Group 1 level, both after good wins in lesser company, but did much better when fast-finishing second in Hong Kong in December and rated top class by connections; was due to return at Meydan this spring.

### 1191 Rumoush (USA)

*4 b f Rahy - Sarayir (Mr Prospector)*

Marcus Tregoning                                   Hamdan Al Maktoum

**PLACINGS: 1/173329-**                             **RPR 112**

| Starts | 1st | 2nd | 3rd | 4th | Win & Pl |
|---|---|---|---|---|---|
| 7 | 2 | 1 | 2 | - | £97,742 |
| | 4/10 NmkR | 1m1f Cls1 List 3yo good | | | £22,708 |
| | 11/09 Ling | 1m Cls5 Mdn 2yo stand | | | £3,412 |

Failed to add to Listed win at Newmarket in April but shaped with promise several times; ran well from bad draw when seventh in 1,000 Guineas but seemed suited by much longer trips when second in 1m6f Group 2 on penultimate start.

### 1192 Saamidd

*3 b c Street Cry - Aryaamm (Galileo)*

Saeed Bin Suroor                                            Godolphin

**PLACINGS: 116-**                                          **RPR 114+**

| Starts | 1st | 2nd | 3rd | 4th | Win & Pl |
|---|---|---|---|---|---|
| 3 | 2 | | - | | £76,525 |
| | 9/10 Donc | 7f Cls1 Gp2 2yo good | | | £67,386 |
| | 8/10 Newb | 7f Cls4 Mdn 2yo gd-fm | | | £4,857 |

Impressive when winning first two starts, including strong Champagne Stakes at Doncaster; ran appallingly in the Dewhurst, though, having also been reluctant to enter stalls, with connections blaming good to soft ground; being aimed at 2,000 Guineas.

### 1193 Sahpresa (USA)

*6 b m Sahm - Sorpresa (Pleasant Tap)*

Rod Collet (Fr)                                        Teruya Yoshida

**PLACINGS: 1314/124213/81143-**         **RPR 119+**

| Starts | 1st | 2nd | 3rd | 4th | Win & Pl |
|---|---|---|---|---|---|
| 15 | 6 | 2 | 3 | 3 | £779,824 |
| | 10/10 NmkR | 1m Cls1 Gp1 soft | | | £102,186 |
| | 9/10 Lonc | 7f Gp3 good | | | £35,398 |
| | 10/09 NmkR | 1m Cls1 Gp1 gd-fm | | | £113,540 |
| | 5/09 Lonc | 1m List good | | | £25,243 |
| | 9/08 StCl | 1m List 3yo good | | | £20,221 |
| | 7/08 MsnL | 1m 3yo gd-sft | | | £8,088 |

Top-class French miler who proved different class to best British fillies when winning Group 1 Sun Chariot Stakes at Newmarket for second successive year; just short in top international races since.

### 1194 Sajjhaa

*4 b f King's Best - Anaamil (Darshaan)*

Roger Varian                                     Sheikh Ahmed Al Maktoum

**PLACINGS: 104121-**                                  **RPR 113**

| Starts | 1st | 2nd | 3rd | 4th | Win & Pl |
|---|---|---|---|---|---|
| 6 | 3 | 1 | - | 1 | £69,261 |
| | 10/10 Siro | 1m Gp3 soft | | | £35,398 |
| | 8/10 Bath | 1m Cls1 List good | | | £19,870 |
| | 5/10 Sand | 1m2f Cls5 Mdn 3-4yo good | | | £3,238 |

Not ready for Epsom when sent off 8-1 for Oaks on second start but made her mark later, hacking up in Listed race at Bath and winning Group 3 in Italy having been beaten by a nose in between; more to come.

### 1195 Salto (Ire)

*3 b c Pivotal - Danzigaway (Danehill)*

Freddie Head (Fr)                                      Wertheimer & Frere

**PLACINGS: 2212-**                                       **RPR 117**

| Starts | 1st | 2nd | 3rd | 4th | Win & Pl |
|---|---|---|---|---|---|
| 4 | 1 | 3 | - | - | £75,884 |
| | 10/10 MsnL | 1m 2yo v soft | | | £15,044 |

Made quiet progress on first three starts

before proving himself among France's leading juveniles when only horse to run Roderic O'Connor close in 1m Group 1 at Saint-Cloud; well suited by soft ground and looks leading contender for French Classics.

### 1196 Samuel
*7 ch g Sakhee - Dolores (Danehill)*

John Gosden                                    Normandie Stud Ltd
**PLACINGS: 0/32329/312/421-**                 **RPR 116+**

| Starts | 1st | 2nd | 3rd | 4th | Win & Pl |
|---|---|---|---|---|---|
| 12 | 2 | 4 | 3 | 1 | £141,090 |
| | 9/10 | Donc | 2m2f Cls1 Gp2 good | | £56,770 |
| | 5/08 | York | 1m6f Cls1 List good | | £17,031 |

Missed two years with a tendon injury prior to return last season but quickly proved better than ever, finishing half-length second to Opinion Poll at York before appreciating longer trip in Doncaster Cup; should stay 2m4f.

### 1197 Sans Frontieres (Ire)
*5 ch h Galileo - Llia (Shirley Heights)*

Jeremy Noseda                                  Sir Robert Ogden
**PLACINGS: 1/23/664111-**                     **RPR 123**

| Starts | 1st | 2nd | 3rd | 4th | Win & Pl |
|---|---|---|---|---|---|
| 9 | 4 | 1 | 1 | 1 | £251,501 |
| | 9/10 | Curr | 1m6f Gp1 soft | | £123,363 |
| | 8/10 | Newb | 1m5½f Cls1 Gp3 gd-sft | | £32,359 |
| | 7/10 | NmkJ | 1m4f Cls1 Gp3 gd-fm | | £53,932 |
| | 9/08 | Ling | 7f Cls5 Mdn 2yo good | | £3,238 |

Went from strength to strength in second half of last season, completing hat-trick in Irish St Leger on soft ground; seems even better on quicker going having won good races at Pattern level before that; will be aimed at top 1m4f races.

### 1198 Sarafina (Fr)
*4 b f Refuse To Bend - Sanariya (Darshaan)*

Alain De Royer-Dupre (Fr)                       H H Aga Khan
**PLACINGS: 11133-**                            **RPR 124+**

| Starts | 1st | 2nd | 3rd | 4th | Win & Pl |
|---|---|---|---|---|---|
| 5 | 3 | - | 2 | - | £981,570 |
| | 6/10 | Chan | 1m2½f Gp1 3yo soft | | £404,531 |
| | 5/10 | Lonc | 1m2f Gp1 3yo good | | £126,416 |
| | 5/10 | Chan | 1m 3yo soft | | £10,619 |

Top-class French filly; won first three starts at 1m2f last season, including Prix de Diane in fine style, and looked equally good at 1m4f despite two defeats, particularly when third in Arc having been badly squeezed before straight.

### 1199 Sea Lord (Ire)
*4 b c Cape Cross - First Fleet (Woodman)*

Mahmood Al Zarooni
                Sheikh Hamdan Bin Mohammed Al Maktoum
**PLACINGS: 219020/511811115-869**              **RPR 116**

| Starts | 1st | 2nd | 3rd | 4th | Win & Pl |
|---|---|---|---|---|---|
| 18 | 7 | 2 | - | - | £239,711 |
| | 8/10 | Sals | 1m Cls1 Gp3 gd-fm | | £34,062 |
| 106 | 7/10 | Gdwd | 1m Cls2 91-106 Hcap gd-fm | | £93,465 |
| 101 | 7/10 | NmkJ | 1m Cls2 80-101 3yo Hcap gd-fm | | £24,924 |
| 95 | 6/10 | Curr | 1m 78-105 Hcap gd-fm | | £35,951 |
| 91 | 6/10 | Donc | 1m Cls2 77-91 3yo Hcap good | | £16,190 |
| 86 | 5/10 | Wolv | 1m1½f Cls3 77-88 3yo Hcap stand | | £7,570 |
| | 7/09 | Asct | 7f Cls3 Mdn 2yo good | | £7,771 |

Made first appearances for current yard at Meydan this spring having been switched from Mark Johnston after successful 2010; won six times in all last year, following five win in handicap company with success in Salisbury Group 3 before finishing close fifth in Irish Champion Stakes.

### 1200 Sea Moon
*3 b c Beat Hollow - Eva Luna (Alleged)*

Sir Michael Stoute                              K Abdulla
**PLACINGS: 21-**                               **RPR 82+**

| Starts | 1st | 2nd | 3rd | 4th | Win & Pl |
|---|---|---|---|---|---|
| 2 | 1 | 1 | - | - | £4,250 |
| | 10/10 | Yarm | 1m Cls5 Mdn 2yo heavy | | £2,902 |

Beaten a short head on debut at Leicester before making amends at 1-5 in workmanlike fashion in maiden at Yarmouth maiden; has smart pedigree (related to Workforce) and still seen as Derby hope, though yet to fully show potential on racecourse.

### 1201 Secrecy
*5 b g King's Best - Wink (Salse)*

Saeed Bin Suroor                                Godolphin
**PLACINGS: 12/331/331214-**                    **RPR 116**

| Starts | 1st | 2nd | 3rd | 4th | Win & Pl |
|---|---|---|---|---|---|
| 11 | 4 | 2 | 4 | 1 | £70,467 |
| | 10/10 | Sals | 7f Cls2 gd-sft | | £8,723 |
| | 8/10 | Kemp | 1m Cls3 stand | | £7,290 |
| 102 | 10/09 | NmkR | 1m Cls2 86-105 Hcap good | | £11,216 |
| | 9/08 | Donc | 7f Cls3 2yo soft | | £9,347 |

Useful and consistent miler who won twice in modest company last season and ran a stormer to be close second to Cityscape in Listed race at Haydock; given too much to do when beaten favourite in Group 3 on final start.

**RACINGPOST.com LIVE REPORTER – STRAIGHT FROM THE PADDOCK EVERY DAY**

## Contenders Ten to Follow

### 1202 Seta
*4 ch f Pivotal - Bombazine (Generous)*
Luca Cumani                              Miss Sarah J Leigh
**PLACINGS: 13/01118-**                           **RPR 111+**

| Starts | 1st | 2nd | 3rd | 4th | Win & Pl |
|---|---|---|---|---|---|
| 7 | 4 |  | 1 | - | £66,343 |
| 8/10 | Sand | 1m Cls1 List gd-fm | | | £19,870 |
| 6/10 | Wwck | 7f Cls1 List 3yo good | | | £22,708 |
| 5/10 | Leic | 7f Cls2 gd-fm | | | £9,970 |
| 8/09 | NmkJ | 7f Cls4 Mdn 2yo good | | | £5,181 |

Well beaten in 1,000 Guineas but had confidence restored with three wins in lower grade, battling well to gain second Listed victory at Sandown by a short head; seen as type to improve with age.

### 1203 Seville (Ger)
*3 b c Galileo - Silverskaya (Silver Hawk)*
Aidan O'Brien (Ire)   M Tabor, D Smith & Mrs John Magnier
**PLACINGS: 212-**                                **RPR 119**

| Starts | 1st | 2nd | 3rd | 4th | Win & Pl |
|---|---|---|---|---|---|
| 3 | 1 | 2 | - | - | £65,550 |
| 10/10 | Tipp | 7½f 2yo soft | | | £10,686 |

Made his debut last September and progressed rapidly to finish second in Racing Post Trophy on final start behind Casamento (pulled clear of third); still looked green that day and pedigree suggests he'll come into his own at 1m4f.

### 1204 Shakespearean (Ire)
*4 b c Shamardal - Paimpolaise (Priolo)*
Saeed Bin Suroor                                   Godolphin
**PLACINGS: 153116/165100-**                      **RPR 118**

| Starts | 1st | 2nd | 3rd | 4th | Win & Pl |
|---|---|---|---|---|---|
| 12 | 5 | - | 1 | - | £1,079,663 |
| 8/10 | Newb | 7f Cls1 Gp2 gd-sft | | | £51,093 |
| 6/10 | Epsm | 7f Cls1 List 3yo good | | | £22,708 |
| 9/09 | Curr | 1m 2yo good | | | £956,311 |
| 8/09 | Sand | 7f Cls1 Gp3 2yo good | | | £28,385 |
| 5/09 | Hayd | 6f Cls5 Mdn 2yo gd-sft | | | £3,886 |

High-class 7f performer when able to dominate small fields, producing best effort when winning Group 2 at Newbury in August; was due to return at Meydan.

### 1205 Shimraan (Fr)
*4 b c Rainbow Quest - Shemriyna (King Of Kings)*
Alain De Royer-Dupre (Fr)                        H H Aga Khan
**PLACINGS: 121453-**                             **RPR 119**

| Starts | 1st | 2nd | 3rd | 4th | Win & Pl |
|---|---|---|---|---|---|
| 6 | 2 | 1 | 1 | 1 | £255,044 |
| 7/10 | MsnL | 1m2f Gp2 3yo gd-sft | | | £201,770 |
| 5/10 | MsnL | 1m4f 3yo soft | | | £15,044 |

Unraced as a juvenile but made rapid strides last year, winning Group 2 at Maisons-Laffitte on third outing; best at 1m2f (given far too much to do when fifth in Prix Dollar on only other try at that trip) despite racing mainly over further.

### 1206 Simon De Montfort (Ire)
*4 b c King's Best - Noble Rose (Caerleon)*
Mahmood Al Zarooni                                 Godolphin
**PLACINGS: 118/11-1**                            **RPR 111+**

| Starts | 1st | 2nd | 3rd | 4th | Win & Pl |
|---|---|---|---|---|---|
| 6 | 5 | - | - | - | £134,043 |
| 1/11 | Meyd | 1m2f 100-109 Hcap good | | | £46,154 |
| 4/10 | Lonc | 1m2f Gp3 3yo good | | | £35,398 |
| 4/10 | StCl | 1m2f List 3yo heavy | | | £24,336 |
| 10/09 | Lonc | 1m1f 2yo good | | | £16,505 |
| 10/09 | Chan | 1m 2yo v soft | | | £11,650 |

Regarded as a Classic prospect by former trainer Andre Fabre after winning four out of five races in France, most notably in Group 3 at Longchamp; put away for 2011 after move to Godolphin and made winning debut for new connections at Meydan.

### 1207 Skysurfers
*5 b h E Dubai - Fortune (Night Shift)*
Saeed Bin Suroor                                   Godolphin
**PLACINGS: 1/1533220-1**                         **RPR 116**

| Starts | 1st | 2nd | 3rd | 4th | Win & Pl |
|---|---|---|---|---|---|
| 9 | 3 | 2 | 2 | - | £196,331 |
| 2/11 | Meyd | 1m List stand | | | £67,308 |
| 2/10 | Meyd | 1m stand | | | £40,741 |
| 10/09 | Sthl | 7f Cls6 Auct Mdn 3-5yo stand | | | £2,047 |

Had debut delayed until October 2009 and produced fine performance to win at Meydan on second start; made steady progress on turf last summer when beaten just half a length by Penitent and Yaa Wayl in Listed races; should win at that level.

### 1208 Snow Fairy (Ire)
*4 b f Intikhab - Woodland Dream (Charnwood Forest)*
Ed Dunlop                                    Anamoine Limited
**PLACINGS: 312439/1112411-**                     **RPR 120**

| Starts | 1st | 2nd | 3rd | 4th | Win & Pl |
|---|---|---|---|---|---|
| 13 | 6 | 2 | 2 | 2 | £2,090,457 |
| 12/10 | ShTn | 1m2f Gp1 good | | | £906,921 |
| 11/10 | Kyot | 1m3f Gd1 firm | | | £624,927 |
| 7/10 | Curr | 1m4f Gp1 3yo gd-yld | | | £218,142 |
| 6/10 | Epsm | 1m4f Cls1 Gp1 3yo good | | | £208,119 |
| 5/10 | Gdwd | 1m2f Cls1 List 3yo good | | | £23,704 |
| 7/09 | Ling | 6f Cls5 Mdn Auct 2yo stand | | | £2,388 |

Went from strength to strength last season,

landing Oaks double and dropping down in trip for stunning Group 1 win in Hong Kong Cup; given winter break prior to possible Dubai trip and should again figure highly in top fillies' races.

### 1209 So You Think (NZ)
5 b/br c High Chaparral - Triassic (Tights)
Aidan O'Brien (Ir)                    Dato Tan Chin Nam & Tunku Ahmad Yahaya

**PLACINGS: 121512/111113-**                **RPR 128**

| Starts | 1st | 2nd | 3rd | 4th | Win & Pl |
|---|---|---|---|---|---|
| 12 | 8 | 2 | 1 | - | £3,027,573 |
| | 10/10 | Flem | 1m2f Gp1 gd-sft | | £334,722 |
| | 10/10 | Moon | 1m2f Gp1 gd-sft | | £1,027,778 |
| | 10/10 | Caul | 1m2f Gp1 good | | £135,000 |
| | 9/10 | Caul | 1m1f Gp1 good | | £117,778 |
| | 8/10 | Caul | 7f Gp2 soft | | £67,222 |
| | 10/09 | Moon | 1m2f Gp1 good | | £898,058 |
| | 9/09 | Rose | 1m1f Gp3 3yo good | | £79,757 |
| | 5/09 | Rose | 7f Hcap gd-sft | | £8,519 |

Latest Australian superstar at Ballydoyle following Group 1 winners Haradasun and Starspangledbanner; signed off down under with honourable third in Melbourne Cup over 2m having won last year from 7f to 1m2f, showing remarkable versatility.

### 1210 Society Rock (Ire)
4 b c Rock Of Gibraltar - High Society (Key Of Luck)
James Fanshawe                                Simon Gibson

**PLACINGS: 5117/1227-**                **RPR 117**

| Starts | 1st | 2nd | 3rd | 4th | Win & Pl |
|---|---|---|---|---|---|
| 8 | 3 | 2 | - | - | £277,104 |
| | 4/10 | Asct | 6f Cls1 List 3yo good | | £22,708 |
| | 9/09 | NmkR | 6f Cls2 2yo good | | £135,425 |
| | 8/09 | Nott | 6f Cls5 Mdn 2yo good | | £3,724 |

Showed plenty of promise when winning three of first five starts and defied odds of 50-1 when taking big step up in class in Golden Jubilee Stakes to chase home Starspangledbanner; only seventh in July Cup next time but may still be one to follow.

### 1211 Sole Power
4 b g Kyllachy - Demerger (Distant View)
Edward Lynam (Ir)                            Mrs S Power

**PLACINGS: 323814/145651-**                **RPR 119**

| Starts | 1st | 2nd | 3rd | 4th | Win & Pl |
|---|---|---|---|---|---|
| 12 | 3 | 1 | - | 2 | £199,341 |
| | 8/10 | York | 5f Cls1 Gp1 gd-sft | | £136,248 |
| | 4/10 | Dund | 5f stand | | £10,075 |
| | 11/09 | Dund | 5f Mdn 2yo stand | | £9,057 |

Shock 100-1 winner of Nunthorpe Stakes last season but still seen as having plenty to prove with main rivals all below best that day; seems best over quick 5f and withdrawn from Prix de l'Abbaye due to soft ground.

### 1212 Soraaya (Ire)
3 b f Elnadim - Date Mate (Thorn Dance)
Mick Channon                    Sheikh Ahmed Al Maktoum

**PLACINGS: 1218-**                **RPR 106**

| Starts | 1st | 2nd | 3rd | 4th | Win & Pl |
|---|---|---|---|---|---|
| 4 | 2 | 1 | - | - | £42,305 |
| | 7/10 | Asct | 6f Cls1 Gp3 2yo good | | £22,708 |
| | 6/10 | Haml | 6f Cls4 Mdn 2yo gd-fm | | £4,533 |

From a family of top juveniles and duly blossomed early last season, winning Princess Margaret Stakes from Margot Did having been second to Memory in Cherry Hinton; something to prove after finishing disappointing eighth in Prix Morny last time.

### 1213 Sri Putra
5 b h Oasis Dream - Wendylina (In The Wings)
Roger Varian                    H R H Sultan Ahmad Shah

**PLACINGS: 1188/451157/1822280-**                **RPR 118**

| Starts | 1st | 2nd | 3rd | 4th | Win & Pl |
|---|---|---|---|---|---|
| 17 | 3 | 5 | - | 1 | £374,649 |
| | 4/10 | NmkR | 1m1f Cls1 Gp3 gd-fm | | £36,901 |
| | 8/09 | Deau | 1m2f Gp2 3yo good | | £71,942 |
| 105 | 7/09 | Asct | 1m Cls2 82-105 3yo Hcap good | | £28,040 |
| | 8/08 | Sand | 7f Cls1 Gp3 2yo good | | £28,385 |
| | 6/08 | Newb | 6f Cls4 Mdn 2yo good | | £5,828 |

Progressed into smart 1m2f performer early last season on good to firm before finding softer conditions against him later; won Group 3 at Newmarket on return and produced career-best when half-length second in Coral-Eclipse.

### 1214 St Nicholas Abbey (Ire)
4 b c Montjeu - Leaping Water (Sure Blade)
Aidan O'Brien (Ir)                            Derrick Smith

**PLACINGS: 111/6-**                **RPR 115+**

| Starts | 1st | 2nd | 3rd | 4th | Win & Pl |
|---|---|---|---|---|---|
| 4 | 3 | - | - | - | £203,253 |
| | 10/09 | Donc | 1m Cls1 Gp1 2yo gd-sft | | £113,540 |
| | 9/09 | Curr | 1m Gp2 2yo good | | £72,573 |
| | 8/09 | Curr | 1m Mdn 2yo sft-hvy | | £11,740 |

Brilliant Racing Post Trophy winner as a juvenile but only sixth when even-money favourite in 2,000 Guineas and kept on track since due to succession of setbacks; connections still hopeful he can return with step up in trip to 1m4f planned.

## 1215 Strong Suit (USA) *(pictured, far)*
3 ch c Rahy - Helwa (Silver Hawk)

Richard Hannon     Mrs J Wood

**PLACINGS: 1132-**     **RPR 114+**

| Starts | 1st | 2nd | 3rd | 4th | Win & Pl |
|---|---|---|---|---|---|
| 4 | 2 | 1 | 1 | - | £117,107 |
| | 6/10 Asct | 6f Cls1 Gp2 2yo good .................................£56,770 | | | |
| | 5/10 Newb | 6f Cls4 Mdn 2yo gd-fm ...............................£4,209 | | | |

Failed to progress as expected following win in Coventry Stakes, which didn't work out very well; had excuses on final two starts, racing too freely when third to Zoffany at the Curragh and unsuited by soft ground behind Dream Ahead at Newmarket.

## 1216 Summit Surge (Ire)
7 b g Noverre - Lady Peculiar (Sunshine Forever)

Luca Cumani     W Bellew

**PLACINGS: 1178/15051/46302152-**     **RPR 117**

| Starts | 1st | 2nd | 3rd | 4th | Win & Pl |
|---|---|---|---|---|---|
| 30 | 7 | 5 | 3 | 3 | £325,505 |
| | 7/10 York | 1m2½f Cls1 Gp2 gd-fm ..............................£56,770 | | | |
| | 5/09 Leop | 1m Gp3 good ............................................£41,019 | | | |
| 109 | 2/09 Ndas | 7½f 97-109 Hcap good ..............................£50,000 | | | |
| | 6/08 Leop | 7f Gp3 gd-fm ............................................£33,456 | | | |
| 104 | 5/08 Curr | 1m 81-105 Hcap firm .................................£25,131 | | | |
| 99 | 11/07 Dund | 7f 80-99 Hcap stand ..................................£11,656 | | | |
| | 7/06 Leop | 7f Mdn Auct 2yo good ................................£8,979 | | | |

Joined new yard from Ger Lyons in Ireland last winter and took form to new level when stepped up in trip towards end of season; won Group 2 York Stakes in good fashion and ran well twice more at 1m2f; best on quicker ground.

## 1217 Swiss Diva
5 b m Pivotal - Swiss Lake (Indian Ridge)

David Elsworth     Lordship Stud

**PLACINGS: 3221/313142/2721110-**     **RPR 114**

| Starts | 1st | 2nd | 3rd | 4th | Win & Pl |
|---|---|---|---|---|---|
| 18 | 6 | 5 | 3 | 1 | £201,999 |
| | 9/10 Lonc | 5f Gp3 soft ...............................................£35,398 | | | |
| | 8/10 Deau | 6f Gp3 soft ...............................................£35,398 | | | |
| | 8/10 Deau | 5f List gd-sft ............................................£23,009 | | | |
| 91 | 6/09 York | 6f Cls2 83-97 3yo Hcap good .....................£64,760 | | | |
| 85 | 5/09 Ling | 6f Cls3 77-90 3yo Hcap stand ......................£7,771 | | | |
| | 11/08 Ling | 6f Cls5 Mdn 2yo stand ................................£3,562 | | | |

Took progressive form up several notches when racing in France last season, relishing soft ground and front-running tactics; won three times in a row, last twice at Group 3 level, but broke badly and never competitive in Prix de l'Abbaye.

## 1218 Tactic
5 b g Sadler's Wells - Tanaghum (Darshaan)

John Dunlop     Hamdan Al Maktoum

**PLACINGS: 43/21442454/21196-**     **RPR 119**

| Starts | 1st | 2nd | 3rd | 4th | Win & Pl |
|---|---|---|---|---|---|
| 15 | 3 | 3 | 1 | 5 | £90,960 |
| | 6/10 Curr | 1m6f Gp3 gd-fm .......................................£34,513 |
| | 5/10 York | 1m6f Cls1 List gd-fm .................................£22,708 |
| | 5/09 Gdwd | 1m4f Cls5 Mdn gd-fm ..................................£3,238 |

Produced stunning performance when landing Listed race at York by 14l on second start last season and ran just as well to follow up in Curragh Cup; returned lame next time and may have found soft ground against him after.

## 1219 Tastahil (Ire)
7 ch g Singspiel - Luana (Shaadi)
Barry Hills                                      Hamdan Al Maktoum
**PLACINGS: 3283/131329/0286241-**               **RPR 115**

| Starts | 1st | 2nd | 3rd | 4th | Win & Pl |
|---|---|---|---|---|---|
| 23 | 4 | 6 | 4 | 1 | £172,726 |
| | 10/10 | NmkR | 2m Cls1 Gp3 gd-sft | | £32,359 |
| | 5/09 | Newb | 1m5½f Cls1 List soft | | £22,708 |
| | 3/09 | Donc | 1m4f Cls2 good | | £12,952 |
| | 9/06 | Kemp | 1m Cls4 Mdn 2yo stand | | £4,534 |

Established himself not far off Britain's leading stayers last season, taking advantage of soft Group 3 on final start at Newmarket having been second to Samuel in Doncaster Cup; needs cut in the ground to produce best.

## 1220 Tazeez (USA)
7 b/br g Silver Hawk - Soiree Russe (Nureyev)
John Gosden                                      Hamdan Al Maktoum
**PLACINGS: 731401/1956/2233311-**               **RPR 120**

| Starts | 1st | 2nd | 3rd | 4th | Win & Pl |
|---|---|---|---|---|---|
| 20 | 6 | 4 | 4 | 1 | £349,450 |
| | 10/10 | NmkR | 1m1f Cls1 Gp3 gd-sft | | £32,359 |
| | 9/10 | Newb | 1m1f Cls3 gd-fm | | £6,231 |
| | 4/09 | NmkR | 1m1f Cls1 Gp3 gd-fm | | £36,901 |
| 102 | 10/08 | NmkR | 1m1f Cls2 90-107 Hcap gd-fm | | £99,696 |
| 94 | 8/08 | NmkJ | 1m2f Cls2 83-97 Hcap gd-sft | | £12,952 |
| | 5/08 | Yarm | 1m Cls5 Mdn good | | £2,914 |

Put patchy run of form behind him to perform consistently well at Pattern level last season, gaining first Group 3 win since April 2009 on final start having twice been third in Group 1 races; was due to return at Meydan this spring.

## 1221 Temple Meads
3 ch c Avonbridge - Harryana (Efisio)
Ed McMahon                                       J C Fretwell
**PLACINGS: 11418-**                             **RPR 114**

| Starts | 1st | 2nd | 3rd | 4th | Win & Pl |
|---|---|---|---|---|---|
| 5 | 3 | - | - | 1 | £154,163 |
| | 9/10 | Newb | 6f Cls1 Gp2 2yo gd-fm | | £37,468 |
| | 7/10 | Newb | 5f Cls2 2yo good | | £98,480 |
| | 5/10 | NmkR | 5f Cls2 Mdn 2yo gd-sft | | £9,714 |

Landed two big prizes at Newbury last season, looking particularly good winning Mill Reef Stakes over 6f; had pulled too hard when fourth in Gimcrack on first try at that trip but forgiven disappointment when saddle slipped in Middle Park.

## 1222 The Paddyman (Ire)
3 b c Giant's Causeway - Winds Of Time (Danehill)
William Haggas                                   Mr & Mrs R Scott
**PLACINGS: 21244-**                             **RPR 106**

| Starts | 1st | 2nd | 3rd | 4th | Win & Pl |
|---|---|---|---|---|---|
| 5 | 1 | 2 | - | 2 | £28,393 |
| | 7/10 | Yarm | 6f Cls1 Mdn 2yo gd-fm | | £3,406 |

Won Yarmouth maiden by 8l but just came up short at Pattern level; looked set to win Group 3 at Newmarket on first attempt at 7f last time only to tire on soft ground; remains solid at his own level.

## 1223 Theology
4 b g Galileo - Biographie (Mtoto)
Jeremy Noseda   Highclere Thoroughbred Racing Touchstone
**PLACINGS: 30/41267-**                          **RPR 111**

| Starts | 1st | 2nd | 3rd | 4th | Win & Pl |
|---|---|---|---|---|---|
| 7 | 1 | 1 | 1 | 1 | £20,078 |
| | 5/10 | Gdwd | 1m4f Cls5 Mdn good | | £2,914 |

Produced terrific effort over 2m in Queen's Vase at Royal Ascot, losing out by a nose; found drop down to 1m4f against him next time and again looked short of pace when seventh in St Leger; should improve for much stiffer test of stamina.

## 1224 Theyskens' Theory (USA)
3 b f Bernardini - Heat Lightning (Summer Squall)
Brian Meehan                                     Andrew Rosen
**PLACINGS: 91136-**                             **RPR 109**

| Starts | 1st | 2nd | 3rd | 4th | Win & Pl |
|---|---|---|---|---|---|
| 5 | 2 | 1 | 1 | - | £50,719 |
| | 8/10 | Gdwd | 7f Cls1 Gp3 2yo soft | | £22,708 |
| | 7/10 | NmkJ | 7f Cls4 Mdn 2yo good | | £4,533 |

Bred for dirt but did best on soft turf last season, winning Prestige Stakes at Goodwood and finishing close third in Fillies' Mile at Ascot only to flop on dirt at Breeders' Cup; connections have promised another crack at Breeders' Cup this year.

## 1225 Timepiece
4 b f Zamindar - Clepsydra (Sadler's Wells)
Henry Cecil                                      K Abdulla
**PLACINGS: 211/428121-**                        **RPR 113**

| Starts | 1st | 2nd | 3rd | 4th | Win & Pl |
|---|---|---|---|---|---|
| 9 | 4 | 3 | - | 1 | £91,152 |
| | 10/10 | NmkR | 1m2f Cls1 List gd-sft | | £19,870 |
| 105 | 6/10 | Asct | 1m Cls1 List 93-107 3yo Hcap gd-fm | | £28,385 |
| | 10/09 | NmkR | 1m Cls1 List 2yo good | | £17,031 |
| | 10/09 | Ling | 1m Cls4 Mdn 2yo std-slw | | £3,886 |

Leading Oaks contender at start of last

## Contenders Ten to Follow

season but surprisingly lacked enough stamina, finishing eighth on big day; proved a smart filly dropping down in trip, though, winning over 1m at Royal Ascot and easily landing Listed race at Newmarket.

### 1226 Tin Horse (Ire)
*3 gr c Sakhee - Joyeuse Entree (Kendor)*

Dider Guillemin (Fr)　　　　　Marquesa De Moratalla
**PLACINGS: 11522-　　　　　　　　RPR 114**

| Starts | 1st | 2nd | 3rd | 4th | Win & Pl |
|---|---|---|---|---|---|
| 5 | 2 | 2 | - | - | £153,599 |
| 6/10 | MsnL | 5½f 2yo good | | | £15,044 |
| 5/10 | Chan | 5f 2yo good | | | £10,619 |

Put poor effort in Prix Robert Papin behind him when 33-1 second to Dream Ahead in Prix Morny and made bigger impression on first try at 7f in Prix Jean-Luc Lagardere, dead-heating for second.

### 1227 Titus Mills (Ire)
*3 ch c Dubawi - Anayid (A.P. Indy)*

Brian Meehan　　　　　　　　　Sangster Family
**PLACINGS: 110-　　　　　　　　RPR 104+**

| Starts | 1st | 2nd | 3rd | 4th | Win & Pl |
|---|---|---|---|---|---|
| 3 | 1 | - | - | - | £19,169 |
| 9/10 | Gdwd | 7f Cls1 List 2yo good | | | £13,341 |
| 7/10 | Asct | 7f Cls4 Mdn 2yo good | | | £5,828 |

Sent off the shortest-priced British candidate for Racing Post Trophy at 13-2 having won first two races but ran no sort of race, finishing distant last; plenty to prove but remains promising middle-distance type.

### 1228 Together (Ire)
*3 b f Galileo - Shadow Song (Pennekamp)*

Aidan O'Brien (Ir)　　D Smith, Mrs J Magnier & M Tabor
**PLACINGS: 31134235-　　　　　　RPR 111**

| Starts | 1st | 2nd | 3rd | 4th | Win & Pl |
|---|---|---|---|---|---|
| 8 | 2 | 2 | 3 | 1 | £150,315 |
| 7/10 | Leop | 7f Gp3 2yo good | | | £28,761 |
| 6/10 | Leop | 7f Mdn 2yo good | | | £10,686 |

Highly talented filly but looked far from straightforward last season, twice drifting badly left and throwing away victory in valuable sales race at Newmarket; Classic contender if problems have been sorted.

### 1229 Triple Aspect (Ire)
*5 b h Danetime - Wicken Wonder (Distant Relative)*

William Haggas　　　　　　　　　Tony Bloom
**PLACINGS: 111/21242/101U500-　　RPR 114+**

| Starts | 1st | 2nd | 3rd | 4th | Win & Pl |
|---|---|---|---|---|---|
| 15 | 6 | 3 | - | 1 | £159,002 |
| 7/10 | Sand | 5f Cls1 Gp3 gd gd | | | £34,062 |
| 5/10 | Wind | 6f Cls1 List gd-fm | | | £22,708 |
| 6/09 | Sand | 5f Cls1 List 3yo good | | | £22,708 |
| 9/08 | Chan | 5½f Gp3 2yo good | | | £29,412 |
| 8/08 | Bath | 5½f Cls4 2yo good | | | £4,857 |
| 7/08 | Sand | 5f Cls4 Mdn 2yo gd-fm | | | £5,181 |

Lost his way towards end of last season but has plenty of solid form behind him over 5f and 6f; seems particularly well suited to Sandown and gained third win at that track when landing second Group 3 triumph there in July.

### 1230 Twice Over
*6 b h Observatory - Double Crossed (Caerleon)*

Henry Cecil　　　　　　　　　　K Abdulla
**PLACINGS: 172/33471113/021231-　RPR 127**

| Starts | 1st | 2nd | 3rd | 4th | Win & Pl |
|---|---|---|---|---|---|
| 22 | 9 | 3 | 6 | 1 | £1,841,956 |
| 10/10 | NmkR | 1m2f Cls1 Gp1 gd-sft | | | £213,739 |
| 7/10 | Sand | 1m2f Cls1 Gp1 gd-fm | | | £283,850 |
| 10/09 | NmkR | 1m2f Cls1 Gp1 good | | | £213,739 |
| 9/09 | Gdwd | 1m2f Cls1 List good | | | £22,708 |
| 9/09 | Donc | 1m2½f Cls2 3-5yo good | | | £15,578 |
| 7/08 | MsnL | 1m Gp2 2yo good | | | £167,647 |
| 4/08 | NmkR | 1m Cls1 Gp3 2yo good | | | £28,385 |
| 11/07 | NmkR | 1m2f Cls2 2yo good | | | £9,348 |
| 10/07 | NmkR | 1m Cls3 Mdn 2yo good | | | £6,477 |

Top-class 1m2f specialist who has got better with age, only making Group 1 breakthrough at end of 2009 before landing Coral-Eclipse and completing stunning Champion Stakes double last season; was due to return at Meydan this spring.

### 1231 Utley (USA)
*3 b c Smart Strike - No Matter What (Nureyev)*

John Gosden　　　　　　　　　Augustin Stable
**PLACINGS: 5157-　　　　　　　　RPR 108**

| Starts | 1st | 2nd | 3rd | 4th | Win & Pl |
|---|---|---|---|---|---|
| 4 | 1 | - | - | - | £12,390 |
| 9/10 | Yarm | 7f Cls5 Mdn 2yo soft | | | £3,532 |

Given step up in class after just winning maiden at Yarmouth and came up short when fifth in Prix Jean-Luc Lagardere and seventh at Breeders' Cup; should do better over further.

**RACINGPOST.com GET READY FOR THE BIG MEETINGS WITH OUR FESTIVAL SITES**

## 1232 Varenar (Fr)

5 ch h Rock Of Gibraltar - Visor (Mr Prospector)
Alain De Royer-Dupre (Fr)                     H H Aga Khan
**PLACINGS: 331/7112421/4860-            RPR 116+**

| Starts | 1st | 2nd | 3rd | 4th | Win & Pl |
|---|---|---|---|---|---|
| 14 | 4 | 2 | 2 | 2 | £239,091 |
| 10/09 | Lonc | 7f Gp1 gd-sft | | | £138,689 |
| 5/09 | Comp | 1m gd-sft | | | £16,505 |
| 5/09 | StCl | 7¹/₂f 3yo good | | | £14,078 |
| 10/08 | Comp | 7f 2yo heavy | | | £10,662 |

Surprise winner of Prix de la Foret in 2009 and shaped well over 6f last term, finishing second on his side in Golden Jubilee and staying-on sixth in July Cup; disappointing favourite in Prix Maurice de Gheest.

## 1233 Vesuve (Ire)

5 b h Green Tune - Verveine (Lear Fan)
Saeed Bin Suroor                                Godolphin
**PLACINGS: 26/1137756/26821415-        RPR 116**

| Starts | 1st | 2nd | 3rd | 4th | Win & Pl |
|---|---|---|---|---|---|
| 18 | 4 | 3 | 2 | 1 | £116,635 |
| 9/10 | Ayr | 1m2f Cls1 List good | | | £28,385 |
| 7/10 | NmkJ | 1m Cls2 good | | | £9,970 |
| 4/09 | Lonc | 1m2f 3yo good | | | £16,505 |
| 3/09 | StCl | 1m2¹/₂f 3yo heavy | | | £11,650 |

Bought by Godolphin last winter having been previously trained by Elie Lellouche; disappointed at Meydan but did better during summer, most notably when beating Kings Gambit in Listed race at Ayr.

## 1234 Viscount Nelson (USA)

4 b c Giant's Causeway - Imagine (Sadler's Wells)
Aidan O'Brien (Ire)    Mrs John Magnier & Mrs David Nagle
**PLACINGS: 31128/20353-                     RPR 117**

| Starts | 1st | 2nd | 3rd | 4th | Win & Pl |
|---|---|---|---|---|---|
| 10 | 2 | 2 | 3 | - | £193,720 |
| 8/09 | Tipp | 7¹/₂f List 2yo soft | | | £33,182 |
| 7/09 | Leop | 1m Mdn 2yo yield | | | £11,740 |

Missed second half of last season but had improved steadily before that, particularly when stepped up to 1m2f to finish fifth in strong Prix du Jockey-Club and close third in Coral-Eclipse; may benefit from slight drop in grade.

## 1235 Waiter's Dream

3 b c Oasis Dream - Sarah Georgina (Persian Bold)
Brian Meehan                                     R P Foden
**PLACINGS: 621134-                            RPR 112**

| Starts | 1st | 2nd | 3rd | 4th | Win & Pl |
|---|---|---|---|---|---|
| 6 | 2 | 1 | 1 | 1 | £66,025 |
| 8/10 | York | 7f Cls1 Gp3 2yo good | | | £29,630 |
| 7/10 | Newb | 7f Cls4 Mdn 2yo good | | | £5,181 |

Took three runs to win his maiden before exploding on to scene with wide-margin win in Acomb Stakes at York; limitations looked to be exposed on final two starts, though, when well beaten by Saamidd and Frankel; still useful at slightly lower level.

## 1236 Waseet

4 ch g Selkirk - Najayeb (Silver Hawk)
John Dunlop                                Hamdan Al Maktoum
**PLACINGS: 312/5571-                          RPR 116**

| Starts | 1st | 2nd | 3rd | 4th | Win & Pl |
|---|---|---|---|---|---|
| 7 | 2 | 1 | 1 | - | £49,394 |
| 10/10 | York | 1m2¹/₂f Cls3 gd-sft | | | £7,771 |
| 8/09 | Sand | 1m Cls4 Mdn 2yo good | | | £5,181 |

Bitterly disappointing in three runs early last season but returned from lengthy layoff to show his true colours in decent conditions event at York on final start; may well have benefited from easier ground and should be able to progress.

## 1237 Whispering Gallery

5 b g Daylami - Echoes In Eternity (Spinning World)
Saeed Bin Suroor                                Godolphin
**PLACINGS: 1411/1427127-1                   RPR 115**

| Starts | 1st | 2nd | 3rd | 4th | Win & Pl |
|---|---|---|---|---|---|
| 12 | 6 | 2 | - | 2 | £205,998 |
| 1/11 | Meyd | 1m6f 95-113 Hcap good | | | £57,692 |
| 8/10 | Wind | 1m3¹/₂f Cls5 List soft | | | £19,870 |
| 1/10 | Meyd | 1m2f 102-110 Hcap stand | | | £64,815 |
| 8/09 | York | 1m4f Cls2 80-99 Hcap gd-fm | | | £19,428 |
| 8/09 | NmkJ | 1m2f Cls2 82-99 Hcap good | | | £12,952 |
| 6/09 | Haml | 1m1f Cls6 Auct Mdn 3-5yo good | | | £2,388 |

Unlucky not to win more than once in Britain last season having twice finished second behind Laaheb, including when beaten by a nose in Group 3 at Ascot; may be one for Cup races judging by winning return over 1m6f at Meydan.

## 1238 White Moonstone (USA) (pictured)

3 b f Dynaformer - Desert Gold (Seeking The Gold)
Saeed Bin Suroor                                Godolphin
**PLACINGS: 1111-                              RPR 112+**

| Starts | 1st | 2nd | 3rd | 4th | Win & Pl |
|---|---|---|---|---|---|
| 4 | 4 | - | - | - | £197,711 |
| 9/10 | Asct | 1m Cls1 Gp1 2yo gd-sft | | | £123,759 |
| 9/10 | Donc | 1m Cls1 Gp2 2yo good | | | £45,416 |
| 8/10 | NmkJ | 7f Cls1 Gp3 2yo good | | | £22,708 |
| 7/10 | Asct | 6f Cls4 Mdn 2yo good | | | £5,828 |

Unbeaten in four starts to raise hopes of a potential 1,000 Guineas/Oaks double; most impressive when 5l winner of May Hill Stakes and battled through unsuitably slower conditions to edge out Together in Fillies' Mile.

Contenders **Ten to Follow**

### 1239 Wiener Walzer (Ger)
*5 b h Dynaformer - Walzerkoenigin (Kingmambo)*

Andre Fabre (Fr)                                        Gestut Schlenderhan

**PLACINGS: 5/11114/35260-**                            **RPR 117**

| Starts | 1st | 2nd | 3rd | 4th | Win & Pl |
|---|---|---|---|---|---|
| 11 | 4 | 2 | 1 | 1 | £532,442 |
| 8/09 | Colo | 1m4f Gp1 good | | | £97,087 |
| 7/09 | Hamb | 1m4f Gp1 3yo good | | | £291,262 |
| 6/09 | Colo | 1m3f Gp2 3yo good | | | £58,252 |
| 4/09 | Brem | 1m2½f 3yo good | | | £2,913 |

Dual Group 1 winner in Germany in 2009 but struggled during ambitious campaign last year, doing best when fifth in Prince of Wales's Stakes behind Byword; since switched to Andre Fabre, following same path as superstars Manduro and Shirocco.

### 1240 Wigmore Hall (Ire)
*4 b g High Chaparral - Love And Laughter (Theatrical)*

Michael Bell                                                    M B Hawtin

**PLACINGS: 815/122311225-**                            **RPR 118**

| Starts | 1st | 2nd | 3rd | 4th | Win & Pl |
|---|---|---|---|---|---|
| 12 | 4 | 4 | 1 | - | £205,231 |
| | 8/10 | NmkJ | 1m2f Cls3 3yo good | | £8,723 |
| 101 | 7/10 | York | 1m2½f Cls2 90-105 Hcap gd-fm | | £97,140 |
| 88 | 4/10 | NmkR | 1m2f Cls3 78-88 3yo Hcap gd-fm | | £9,066 |
| | 9/09 | NmkR | 1m Cls4 Auct Mdn 2yo gd-fm | | £3,886 |

Progressive handicapper in first half of last season, winning John Smith's Cup at York off 101; did well when stepped up in class, finishing second in Grade 1 at Arlington and fair fifth in Champion Stakes; was due to return at Meydan this spring.

### 1241 Wild Wind (Ger)
*3 b f Danehill Dancer - Woman Secret (Sadler's Wells)*

Aidan O'Brien (Ir)   Mrs John Magnier, M Tabor & D Smith

**PLACINGS: 21528-**                                    **RPR 104**

| Starts | 1st | 2nd | 3rd | 4th | Win & Pl |
|---|---|---|---|---|---|
| 5 | 1 | 2 | - | - | £28,022 |
| 6/10 | Curr | 7f Mdn 2yo gd-fm | | | £11,296 |

Found wanting against vintage bunch of Irish juvenile fillies when fifth in Moyglare Stud Stakes but subsequently ran Chrysanthemum to a head at Group 3 level; sent off 5-1 for Cheveley Park Stakes but finished disappointing eighth.

### 1242 Wonder Of Wonders (USA)
*3 b f Kingmambo - All Too Beautiful (Sadler's Wells)*

Aidan O'Brien (Ir)                                              Michael Tabor

**PLACINGS: 2-**                                        **RPR 81+**

| Starts | 1st | 2nd | 3rd | 4th | Win & Pl |
|---|---|---|---|---|---|
| 1 | - | 1 | - | - | £2,477 |

Beautifully bred Coolmore filly who figures prominently in Oaks market despite finishing only second on debut at Leopardstown when very green; certain to prove much better than that bare form and fascinating middle-distance prospect.

## 1243 Wootton Bassett
3 b c Iffraaj - Balladonia (Primo Dominie)
Richard Fahey    Frank Brady & The Cosmic Cases
**PLACINGS: 11111-**    **RPR 120**

| Starts | 1st | 2nd | 3rd | 4th | Win & Pl |
|---|---|---|---|---|---|
| 5 | 5 | - | - | - | £524,445 |
| | 10/10 Lonc | 7f Gp1 2yo v soft | | | £176,982 |
| | 9/10 Donc | 6½f Cls2 2yo good | | | £193,267 |
| | 8/10 York | 6f Cls2 2yo good | | | £147,720 |
| | 7/10 Donc | 6f Cls4 2yo gd-fm | | | £3,238 |
| | 6/10 Ayr | 6f Cls5 Mdn 2yo gd-fm | | | £3,238 |

Unbeaten; won valuable sales races at York and Doncaster before taking step up into Group 1 company in his stride in Prix Jean-Luc Lagardere at Longchamp; looks sure to be suited by 1m and possibly further.

## 1244 Workforce
4 b c King's Best - Soviet Moon (Sadler's Wells)
Sir Michael Stoute    Juddmonte Farms Inc
**PLACINGS: 1/2151-**    **RPR 130+**

| Starts | 1st | 2nd | 3rd | 4th | Win & Pl |
|---|---|---|---|---|---|
| 5 | 3 | 1 | - | - | £2,856,900 |
| | 10/10 Lonc | 1m4f Gp1 v soft | | | £2,022,655 |
| | 6/10 Epsm | 1m4f Cls1 Gp1 3yo gd-fm | | | £771,504 |
| | 9/09 Gdwd | 7f Cls5 Mdn 2yo good | | | £3,562 |

Brilliant winner of Derby and Arc last season, thrashing good field by 7l at Epsom and holding off Japanese raider at Longchamp; clearly fragile and also beaten twice but hugely exciting on his day.

## 1245 Yaa Wayl (Ire)
4 b g Whipper - Lidanna (Nicholas)
Saeed Bin Suroor    Sheikh Ahmed Al Maktoum
**PLACINGS: 41242/1214103-90**    **RPR 115**

| Starts | 1st | 2nd | 3rd | 4th | Win & Pl |
|---|---|---|---|---|---|
| 14 | 4 | 3 | 1 | 3 | £72,389 |
| | 8/10 York | 7f Cls1 List gd-fm | | | £23,704 |
| | 7/10 Newb | 7f Cls3 gd-fm | | | £6,543 |
| 88 | 5/10 Ches | 7½f Cls2 84-98 3yo Hcap gd-sft | | | £14,193 |
| | 7/09 Thsk | 5f Cls5 Auct Mdn 2yo good | | | £4,274 |

Progressed steadily for Michael Jarvis over 7f last season, impressing when winning Listed race at York, although flopped when favourite to beat Delegator next time.

## 1246 Zacinto
5 b h Dansili - Ithaca (Distant View)
Sir Michael Stoute    K Abdulla
**PLACINGS: 12/1120/9455-**    **RPR 118**

| Starts | 1st | 2nd | 3rd | 4th | Win & Pl |
|---|---|---|---|---|---|
| 10 | 3 | 2 | | 1 | £205,574 |
| | 8/09 Gdwd | 1m Cls1 Gp2 good | | | £67,443 |
| | 8/09 Gdwd | 1m Cls1 List 3yo soft | | | £28,385 |
| | 7/08 Sand | 7f Cls4 Mdn 2yo gd-fm | | | £6,476 |

Bitterly disappointing last season having been terrific second in Queen Elizabeth II Stakes in 2009 but has dire record on good to firm or quicker and was fair fourth in Queen Anne Stakes on only start on favourable ground; worth trying at 1m2f.

## 1247 Zeitoper
4 br c Singspiel - Kazzia (Zinaad)
Mahmood Al Zarooni    Godolphin
**PLACINGS: 111/3**    **RPR 96**

| Starts | 1st | 2nd | 3rd | 4th | Win & Pl |
|---|---|---|---|---|---|
| 4 | 3 | | 1 | - | £59,185 |
| | 10/09 Lonc | 1m1f Gp3 2yo gd-sft | | | £38,835 |
| | 10/09 Epsm | 1m½f Cls3 2yo gd-fm | | | £7,477 |
| | 9/09 Sand | 1m Cls4 Mdn 2yo gd-fm | | | £5,181 |

Exciting juvenile in 2009 when completing hat-trick in Group 3 at Longchamp but missed all of last season through injury; proved he was over his problems when returning at Meydan this spring; smart middle-distance prospect.

## 1248 Zoffany (Ire)
3 b c Dansili - Tyranny (Machiavellian)
Aidan O'Brien (Ir)    M Tabor, D Smith & Mrs John Magnier
**PLACINGS: 1161113-**    **RPR 115+**

| Starts | 1st | 2nd | 3rd | 4th | Win & Pl |
|---|---|---|---|---|---|
| 7 | 5 | | 1 | - | £192,465 |
| | 8/10 Curr | 6f Gp1 2yo yield | | | £102,655 |
| | 7/10 Leop | 7f Gp3 2yo yield | | | £28,761 |
| | 7/10 Leop | 7f List 2yo yield | | | £23,009 |
| | 5/10 Naas | 6f 2yo good | | | £10,075 |
| | 4/10 Leop | 6f Mdn 2yo gd-fm | | | £10,686 |

Bounced back from disappointing sixth in Coventry Stakes to land quickfire hat-trick last summer, culminating with fine turn of foot to land Group 1 Phoenix Stakes; hated soft ground when third in National Stakes on final start; should stay 1m-1m2f.

## 1249 Zoowraa
3 b f Azamour - Beraysim (Lion Cavern)
Mahmood Al Zarooni    Sheikh Ahmed Al Maktoum
**PLACINGS: 11-**    **RPR 102+**

| Starts | 1st | 2nd | 3rd | 4th | Win & Pl |
|---|---|---|---|---|---|
| 2 | 2 | - | - | - | £17,874 |
| | 10/10 Newb | 7f Cls1 List 2yo gd-sft | | | £13,341 |
| | 10/10 Rdcr | 7f Cls4 Mdn 2yo gd-sft | | | £4,533 |

Unbeaten in two starts last season for Michael Jarvis, defying step up to Listed class at Doncaster last time; won well enough that day to enter 1,000 Guineas calculations but relatively small and not guaranteed to train on.

*Pen portraits written by Dylan Hill*

# STATISTICS

Statistical analysis of trainers' performances in 2010 by age of runner, time of year and race

# MICHAEL BELL
## NEWMARKET, SUFFOLK

| | No. of Hrs | Races Run | 1st | 2nd | 3rd | Unpl | Per cent | £1 Level Stake |
|---|---|---|---|---|---|---|---|---|
| 2-y-o | 38 | 119 | 12 | 18 | 11 | 78 | 10.1 | -40.81 |
| 3-y-o | 42 | 234 | 38 | 31 | 36 | 129 | 16.2 | -38.60 |
| 4-y-o+ | 12 | 53 | 4 | 9 | 8 | 31 | 7.5 | -31.26 |
| Totals | 92 | 406 | 54 | 58 | 55 | 238 | 13.3 | -110.67 |
| 2009 | 92 | 369 | 48 | 41 | 42 | 237 | 13.0 | -31.90 |
| 2008 | 94 | 476 | 72 | 55 | 58 | 288 | 15.1 | +21.42 |

### BY MONTH

| 2-y-o | W-R | Per cent | £1 Level Stake | 3-y-o | W-R | Per cent | £1 Level Stake |
|---|---|---|---|---|---|---|---|
| January | 0-0 | 0.0 | 0.00 | January | 2-2 | 100.0 | +5.00 |
| February | 0-0 | 0.0 | 0.00 | February | 0-4 | 0.0 | -4.00 |
| March | 0-0 | 0.0 | 0.00 | March | 2-13 | 15.4 | -9.95 |
| April | 0-0 | 0.0 | 0.00 | April | 9-37 | 24.3 | +18.73 |
| May | 1-6 | 16.7 | +3.00 | May | 5-42 | 11.9 | -23.84 |
| June | 2-11 | 18.2 | +2.44 | June | 3-34 | 8.8 | -21.92 |
| July | 2-20 | 10.0 | +1.00 | July | 2-22 | 9.1 | -13.50 |
| August | 2-18 | 11.1 | -4.00 | August | 7-26 | 26.9 | +12.50 |
| September | 4-25 | 16.0 | -6.25 | September | 6-28 | 21.4 | +5.38 |
| October | 1-32 | 3.1 | -30.00 | October | 1-20 | 5.0 | -14.00 |
| November | 0-6 | 0.0 | -6.00 | November | 1-3 | 33.3 | +10.00 |
| December | 0-1 | 0.0 | -1.00 | December | 0-3 | 0.0 | -3.00 |

| 4-y-o+ | W-R | Per cent | £1 Level Stake | Totals | W-R | Per cent | £1 Level Stake |
|---|---|---|---|---|---|---|---|
| January | 0-2 | 0.0 | -2.00 | January | 2-4 | 50.0 | +3.00 |
| February | 0-0 | 0.0 | 0.00 | February | 0-4 | 0.0 | -4.00 |
| March | 0-3 | 0.0 | -3.00 | March | 2-16 | 12.5 | -12.95 |
| April | 0-5 | 0.0 | -5.00 | April | 9-42 | 21.4 | +13.73 |
| May | 2-9 | 22.2 | -0.59 | May | 8-57 | 14.0 | -21.43 |
| June | 0-6 | 0.0 | -6.00 | June | 5-51 | 9.8 | -25.48 |
| July | 0-4 | 0.0 | -4.00 | July | 4-46 | 8.7 | -16.50 |
| August | 0-6 | 0.0 | -6.00 | August | 9-50 | 18.0 | +2.50 |
| September | 1-8 | 12.5 | -3.67 | September | 11-61 | 18.0 | -4.54 |
| October | 1-9 | 11.1 | 0.00 | October | 3-61 | 4.9 | -44.00 |
| November | 0-1 | 0.0 | -1.00 | November | 1-10 | 10.0 | +9.00 |
| December | 0-0 | 0.0 | 0.00 | December | 0-4 | 0.0 | -3.00 |

### DISTANCE

| 2-y-o | W-R | Per cent | £1 Level Stake | 3-y-o | W-R | Per cent | £1 Level Stake |
|---|---|---|---|---|---|---|---|
| 5f-6f | 6-41 | 14.6 | -10.31 | 5f-6f | 6-27 | 22.2 | -1.38 |
| 7f-8f | 6-78 | 7.7 | -30.50 | 7f-8f | 17-98 | 17.3 | -21.33 |
| 9f-13f | 0-0 | 0.0 | 0.00 | 9f-13f | 13-100 | 13.0 | -18.40 |
| 14f+ | 0-0 | 0.0 | 0.00 | 14f+ | 2-9 | 22.2 | +2.50 |

| 4-y-o+ | W-R | Per cent | £1 Level Stake | Totals | W-R | Per cent | £1 Level Stake |
|---|---|---|---|---|---|---|---|
| 5f-6f | 0-6 | 0.0 | -6.00 | 5f-6f | 12-74 | 16.2 | -17.69 |
| 7f-8f | 2-14 | 14.3 | -3.17 | 7f-8f | 25-190 | 13.2 | -55.00 |
| 9f-13f | 2-19 | 10.5 | -8.09 | 9f-13f | 15-119 | 12.6 | -26.49 |
| 14f+ | 0-14 | 0.0 | -14.00 | 14f+ | 2-23 | 8.7 | -11.50 |

### TYPE OF RACE

| Non-Handicaps | W-R | Per cent | £1 Level Stake | Handicaps | W-R | Per cent | £1 Level Stake |
|---|---|---|---|---|---|---|---|
| 2-y-o | 10-100 | 10.0 | -35.31 | 2-y-o | 2-19 | 10.5 | -5.50 |
| 3-y-o | 16-87 | 18.4 | -21.47 | 3-y-o | 22-147 | 15.0 | -17.13 |
| 4-y-o+ | 1-8 | 12.5 | +3.00 | 4-y-o+ | 3-45 | 6.7 | -25.17 |

### RACE CLASS / FIRST TIME OUT

| Class | W-R | Per cent | £1 Level Stake | | W-R | Per cent | £1 Level Stake |
|---|---|---|---|---|---|---|---|
| Class 1 | 1-27 | 3.7 | -25.09 | 2-y-o | 1-38 | 2.6 | -29.00 |
| Class 2 | 6-42 | 14.3 | +6.50 | 3-y-o | 9-42 | 21.4 | +13.13 |
| Class 3 | 5-35 | 14.3 | -6.13 | 4-y-o+ | 1-12 | 8.3 | -10.09 |
| Class 4 | 11-110 | 10.0 | -43.04 | | | | |
| Class 5 | 20-148 | 13.5 | -56.83 | Totals | 11-92 | 12.0 | -25.96 |
| Class 6 | 11-44 | 25.0 | +13.92 | | | | |
| Class 7 | 0-0 | 0.0 | 0.00 | | | | |

# MICK CHANNON
## WEST ILSLEY, BERKS

|  | No. of Hrs | Races Run | 1st | 2nd | 3rd | Unpl | Per cent | £1 Level Stake |
|---|---|---|---|---|---|---|---|---|
| 2-y-o | 77 | 446 | 47 | 75 | 61 | 262 | 10.5 | -162.13 |
| 3-y-o | 45 | 366 | 46 | 44 | 40 | 236 | 12.6 | -6.35 |
| 4-y-o+ | 21 | 164 | 8 | 22 | 17 | 117 | 4.9 | -112.27 |
| Totals | 143 | 976 | 101 | 141 | 118 | 615 | 10.3 | -280.75 |
| 2009 | 157 | 1119 | 108 | 131 | 144 | 732 | 9.7 | -88.15 |
| 2008 | 156 | 988 | 96 | 92 | 127 | 670 | 9.7 | -62.00 |

### BY MONTH

| 2-y-o | W-R | Per cent | £1 Level Stake | 3-y-o | W-R | Per cent | £1 Level Stake |
|---|---|---|---|---|---|---|---|
| January | 0-0 | 0.0 | 0.00 | January | 2-4 | 50.0 | +3.00 |
| February | 0-0 | 0.0 | 0.00 | February | 0-6 | 0.0 | -6.00 |
| March | 0-4 | 0.0 | -4.00 | March | 3-12 | 25.0 | +2.75 |
| April | 1-22 | 4.5 | -18.25 | April | 4-44 | 9.1 | -5.50 |
| May | 8-45 | 17.8 | -10.86 | May | 8-61 | 13.1 | -19.25 |
| June | 8-61 | 13.1 | -30.97 | June | 5-45 | 11.1 | -10.22 |
| July | 8-81 | 9.9 | -29.13 | July | 6-56 | 10.7 | -11.13 |
| August | 8-84 | 9.5 | -27.48 | August | 10-58 | 17.2 | +54.50 |
| September | 6-80 | 7.5 | -17.47 | September | 3-47 | 6.4 | -25.50 |
| October | 7-57 | 12.3 | -16.49 | October | 5-31 | 16.1 | +13.00 |
| November | 1-9 | 11.1 | -4.50 | November | 0-1 | 0.0 | -1.00 |
| December | 0-3 | 0.0 | -3.00 | December | 0-1 | 0.0 | -1.00 |

| 4-y-o+ | W-R | Per cent | £1 Level Stake | Totals | W-R | Per cent | £1 Level Stake |
|---|---|---|---|---|---|---|---|
| January | 0-6 | 0.0 | -6.00 | January | 2-10 | 20.0 | -3.00 |
| February | 0-6 | 0.0 | -6.00 | February | 0-12 | 0.0 | -12.00 |
| March | 1-5 | 20.0 | +2.00 | March | 4-21 | 19.0 | +0.75 |
| April | 0-22 | 0.0 | -22.00 | April | 5-88 | 5.7 | -45.75 |
| May | 3-34 | 8.8 | -14.00 | May | 19-140 | 13.6 | -44.11 |
| June | 2-31 | 6.5 | -14.50 | June | 15-137 | 10.9 | -55.69 |
| July | 0-24 | 0.0 | -24.00 | July | 14-161 | 8.7 | -64.26 |
| August | 2-18 | 11.1 | -9.77 | August | 20-160 | 12.5 | +17.25 |
| September | 0-10 | 0.0 | -10.00 | September | 9-137 | 6.6 | -52.97 |
| October | 0-7 | 0.0 | -7.00 | October | 12-95 | 12.6 | -10.49 |
| November | 0-1 | 0.0 | -1.00 | November | 1-11 | 9.1 | -2.00 |
| December | 0-0 | 0.0 | 0.00 | December | 0-4 | 0.0 | -1.00 |

### DISTANCE

| 2-y-o | W-R | Per cent | £1 Level Stake | 3-y-o | W-R | Per cent | £1 Level Stake |
|---|---|---|---|---|---|---|---|
| 5f-6f | 36-302 | 11.9 | -135.13 | 5f-6f | 18-121 | 14.9 | +23.38 |
| 7f-8f | 11-141 | 7.8 | -24.00 | 7f-8f | 18-156 | 11.5 | -12.54 |
| 9f-13f | 0-3 | 0.0 | -3.00 | 9f-13f | 8-80 | 10.0 | -38.68 |
| 14f+ | 0-0 | 0.0 | 0.00 | 14f+ | 2-9 | 22.2 | +21.50 |

| 4-y-o | W-R | Per cent | £1 Level Stake | Totals | W-R | Per cent | £1 Level Stake |
|---|---|---|---|---|---|---|---|
| 5f-6f | 4-65 | 6.2 | -35.00 | 5f-6f | 58-488 | 11.9 | -146.75 |
| 7f-8f | 2-43 | 4.7 | -30.50 | 7f-8f | 31-340 | 9.1 | -67.04 |
| 9f-13f | 2-43 | 4.7 | -33.77 | 9f-13f | 10-126 | 7.9 | -75.45 |
| 14f+ | 0-13 | 0.0 | -13.00 | 14f+ | 2-22 | 9.1 | +8.50 |

### TYPE OF RACE

| Non-Handicaps | W-R | Per cent | £1 Level Stake | Handicaps | W-R | Per cent | £1 Level Stake |
|---|---|---|---|---|---|---|---|
| 2-y-o | 39-329 | 11.9 | -96.73 | 2-y-o | 8-117 | 6.8 | -65.40 |
| 3-y-o | 17-108 | 15.7 | -28.72 | 3-y-o | 29-258 | 11.2 | +22.38 |
| 4-y-o+ | 1-27 | 3.7 | -18.00 | 4-y-o+ | 7-137 | 5.1 | -87.00 |

### RACE CLASS / FIRST TIME OUT

| RACE CLASS | W-R | Per cent | £1 Level Stake | FIRST TIME OUT | W-R | Per cent | £1 Level Stake |
|---|---|---|---|---|---|---|---|
| Class 1 | 6-75 | 8.0 | -8.50 | | | | |
| Class 2 | 6-82 | 7.3 | -20.47 | 2-y-o | 5-77 | 6.5 | -49.38 |
| Class 3 | 6-56 | 10.7 | -14.25 | 3-y-o | 5-45 | 11.1 | -0.75 |
| Class 4 | 16-207 | 7.7 | -100.31 | 4-y-o+ | 2-21 | 9.5 | -6.50 |
| Class 5 | 43-340 | 12.6 | -46.16 | Totals | 12-143 | 8.4 | -56.63 |
| Class 6 | 24-212 | 11.3 | -87.06 | | | | |
| Class 7 | 0-4 | 0.0 | -4.00 | | | | |

# ED DUNLOP
## NEWMARKET, SUFFOLK

|        | No. of Hrs | Races Run | 1st | 2nd | 3rd | Unpl | Per cent | £1 Level Stake |
|--------|-----------|-----------|-----|-----|-----|------|----------|----------------|
| 2-y-o  | 44        | 138       | 13  | 9   | 16  | 100  | 9.4      | -58.75         |
| 3-y-o  | 34        | 157       | 20  | 28  | 15  | 94   | 12.7     | -57.07         |
| 4-y-o+ | 13        | 52        | 6   | 12  | 5   | 29   | 11.5     | -22.87         |
| Totals | 91        | 347       | 39  | 49  | 36  | 223  | 11.2     | -138.69        |
| 2009   | 101       | 411       | 41  | 52  | 53  | 265  | 10.0     | -35.25         |
| 2008   | 102       | 423       | 44  | 43  | 43  | 289  | 10.4     | -38.77         |

## BY MONTH

| 2-y-o     | W-R   | Per cent | £1 Level Stake | 3-y-o     | W-R  | Per cent | £1 Level Stake |
|-----------|-------|----------|----------------|-----------|------|----------|----------------|
| January   | 0-0   | 0.0      | 0.00           | January   | 1-4  | 25.0     | -1.63          |
| February  | 0-0   | 0.0      | 0.00           | February  | 0-2  | 0.0      | -2.00          |
| March     | 0-0   | 0.0      | 0.00           | March     | 1-4  | 25.0     | -1.50          |
| April     | 0-0   | 0.0      | 0.00           | April     | 4-23 | 17.4     | -11.80         |
| May       | 0-5   | 0.0      | -5.00          | May       | 3-24 | 12.5     | -4.29          |
| June      | 0-8   | 0.0      | -8.00          | June      | 2-26 | 7.7      | -11.00         |
| July      | 2-21  | 9.5      | +9.00          | July      | 0-23 | 0.0      | -23.00         |
| August    | 4-18  | 22.2     | -5.88          | August    | 6-22 | 27.3     | -2.35          |
| September | 3-36  | 8.3      | -11.25         | September | 2-21 | 9.5      | +1.00          |
| October   | 1-28  | 3.6      | -25.63         | October   | 1-8  | 12.5     | -0.50          |
| November  | 2-16  | 12.5     | -8.25          | November  | 0-0  | 0.0      | 0.00           |
| December  | 1-6   | 16.7     | -3.75          | December  | 0-0  | 0.0      | 0.00           |

| 4-y-o+    | W-R  | Per cent | £1 Level Stake | Totals    | W-R   | Per cent | £1 Level Stake |
|-----------|------|----------|----------------|-----------|-------|----------|----------------|
| January   | 1-5  | 20.0     | -3.20          | January   | 2-9   | 22.2     | -4.83          |
| February  | 1-2  | 50.0     | +2.33          | February  | 1-4   | 25.0     | +0.33          |
| March     | 1-3  | 33.3     | +1.50          | March     | 2-7   | 28.6     | 0.00           |
| April     | 1-4  | 25.0     | +4.00          | April     | 5-27  | 18.5     | -7.80          |
| May       | 2-6  | 33.3     | +4.50          | May       | 5-35  | 14.3     | -4.79          |
| June      | 0-4  | 0.0      | -4.00          | June      | 2-38  | 5.3      | -23.00         |
| July      | 0-7  | 0.0      | -7.00          | July      | 2-51  | 3.9      | -21.00         |
| August    | 0-6  | 0.0      | -6.00          | August    | 10-46 | 21.7     | -14.23         |
| September | 0-10 | 0.0      | -10.00         | September | 5-67  | 7.5      | -20.25         |
| October   | 0-5  | 0.0      | -5.00          | October   | 2-41  | 4.9      | -31.13         |
| November  | 0-0  | 0.0      | 0.00           | November  | 2-16  | 12.5     | 0.00           |
| December  | 0-0  | 0.0      | 0.00           | December  | 1-6   | 16.7     | 0.00           |

## DISTANCE

| 2-y-o  | W-R  | Per cent | £1 Level Stake | 3-y-o  | W-R    | Per cent | £1 Level Stake |
|--------|------|----------|----------------|--------|--------|----------|----------------|
| 5f-6f  | 4-40 | 10.0     | -26.32         | 5f-6f  | 7-32   | 21.9     | -7.35          |
| 7f-8f  | 9-96 | 9.4      | -30.42         | 7f-8f  | 9-69   | 13.0     | -26.97         |
| 9f-13f | 0-2  | 0.0      | -2.00          | 9f-13f | 3-49   | 6.1      | -23.25         |
| 14f+   | 0-0  | 0.0      | 0.00           | 14f+   | 1-7    | 14.3     | +0.50          |

| 4-y-o+ | W-R  | Per cent | £1 Level Stake | Totals | W-R    | Per cent | £1 Level Stake |
|--------|------|----------|----------------|--------|--------|----------|----------------|
| 5f-6f  | 0-0  | 0.0      | 0.00           | 5f-6f  | 11-72  | 15.3     | -33.67         |
| 7f-8f  | 2-19 | 10.5     | -8.50          | 7f-8f  | 20-184 | 10.9     | -65.89         |
| 9f-13f | 4-29 | 13.8     | -10.37         | 9f-13f | 7-80   | 8.8      | -35.62         |
| 14f+   | 0-4  | 0.0      | -4.00          | 14f+   | 1-11   | 9.1      | -3.50          |

## TYPE OF RACE

| Non-Handicaps | | | | Handicaps | | | |
|--------|-------|----------|----------------|--------|------|----------|----------------|
|        | W-R   | Per cent | £1 Level Stake |        | W-R  | Per cent | £1 Level Stake |
| 2-y-o  | 9-110 | 8.2      | -61.00         | 2-y-o  | 4-28 | 14.3     | +2.25          |
| 3-y-o  | 8-61  | 13.1     | -21.07         | 3-y-o  | 12-96| 12.5     | -36.00         |
| 4-y-o+ | 1-9   | 11.1     | -4.00          | 4-y-o+ | 5-43 | 11.6     | -15.67         |

## RACE CLASS | FIRST TIME OUT

|         | W-R    | Per cent | £1 Level Stake |        | W-R  | Per cent | £1 Level Stake |
|---------|--------|----------|----------------|--------|------|----------|----------------|
| Class 1 | 4-22   | 18.2     | +9.70          | 2-y-o  | 3-44 | 6.8      | -9.00          |
| Class 2 | 2-24   | 8.3      | -1.00          | 3-y-o  | 6-34 | 17.6     | -7.43          |
| Class 3 | 2-26   | 7.7      | -18.63         | 4-y-o+ | 1-13 | 7.7      | -8.50          |
| Class 4 | 8-85   | 9.4      | -21.00         |        |      |          |                |
| Class 5 | 17-142 | 12.0     | -77.89         | Totals | 10-91| 11.0     | -24.93         |
| Class 6 | 6-49   | 12.2     | -30.87         |        |      |          |                |
| Class 7 | 0-0    | 0.0      | 0.00           |        |      |          |                |

# Statistics

# JOHN DUNLOP
## ARUNDEL, W SUSSEX

|  | No. of Hrs | Races Run | 1st | 2nd | 3rd | Unpl | Per cent | £1 Level Stake |
|---|---|---|---|---|---|---|---|---|
| 2-y-o | 38 | 113 | 8 | 8 | 8 | 89 | 7.1 | -53.88 |
| 3-y-o | 34 | 169 | 24 | 23 | 20 | 102 | 14.2 | -38.12 |
| 4-y-o+ | 7 | 33 | 6 | 3 | 3 | 21 | 18.2 | +16.75 |
| Totals | 79 | 315 | 38 | 34 | 31 | 212 | 12.1 | -75.25 |
| 2009 | 85 | 366 | 50 | 57 | 50 | 208 | 13.7 | -14.25 |
| 2008 | 107 | 454 | 37 | 38 | 48 | 331 | 8.1 | -38.00 |

## BY MONTH

| 2-y-o | W-R | Per cent | £1 Level Stake | 3-y-o | W-R | Per cent | £1 Level Stake |
|---|---|---|---|---|---|---|---|
| January | 0-0 | 0.0 | 0.00 | January | 0-0 | 0.0 | 0.00 |
| February | 0-0 | 0.0 | 0.00 | February | 0-0 | 0.0 | 0.00 |
| March | 0-0 | 0.0 | 0.00 | March | 0-0 | 0.0 | 0.00 |
| April | 0-0 | 0.0 | 0.00 | April | 3-21 | 14.3 | -7.09 |
| May | 0-8 | 0.0 | -8.00 | May | 6-32 | 18.8 | -3.00 |
| June | 2-9 | 22.2 | -5.13 | June | 3-26 | 11.5 | -14.15 |
| July | 0-18 | 0.0 | -18.00 | July | 2-24 | 8.3 | -13.13 |
| August | 1-19 | 5.3 | -15.25 | August | 2-20 | 10.0 | -11.75 |
| September | 4-33 | 12.1 | +9.50 | September | 4-23 | 17.4 | +1.50 |
| October | 1-26 | 3.8 | -17.00 | October | 3-19 | 15.8 | +10.75 |
| November | 0-0 | 0.0 | 0.00 | November | 1-4 | 25.0 | -1.25 |
| December | 0-0 | 0.0 | 0.00 | December | 0-0 | 0.0 | 0.00 |

| 4-y-o+ | W-R | Per cent | £1 Level Stake | Totals | W-R | Per cent | £1 Level Stake |
|---|---|---|---|---|---|---|---|
| January | 0-0 | 0.0 | 0.00 | January | 0-0 | 0.0 | 0.00 |
| February | 0-0 | 0.0 | 0.00 | February | 0-0 | 0.0 | 0.00 |
| March | 0-0 | 0.0 | 0.00 | March | 0-0 | 0.0 | 0.00 |
| April | 0-5 | 0.0 | -5.00 | April | 3-26 | 11.5 | -12.09 |
| May | 3-6 | 50.0 | +15.00 | May | 9-46 | 19.6 | +4.00 |
| June | 1-5 | 20.0 | -1.25 | June | 6-40 | 15.0 | -20.53 |
| July | 1-4 | 25.0 | +6.00 | July | 3-46 | 6.5 | -25.13 |
| August | 0-3 | 0.0 | -3.00 | August | 3-42 | 7.1 | -30.00 |
| September | 0-5 | 0.0 | -5.00 | September | 8-61 | 13.1 | +6.00 |
| October | 0-4 | 0.0 | -4.00 | October | 4-49 | 8.2 | -10.25 |
| November | 1-1 | 100.0 | +14.00 | November | 2-5 | 40.0 | +12.75 |
| December | 0-0 | 0.0 | 0.00 | December | 0-0 | 0.0 | 0.00 |

## DISTANCE

| 2-y-o | W-R | Per cent | £1 Level Stake | 3-y-o | W-R | Per cent | £1 Level Stake |
|---|---|---|---|---|---|---|---|
| 5f-6f | 1-41 | 2.4 | -39.50 | 5f-6f | 1-16 | 6.3 | -13.90 |
| 7f-8f | 7-71 | 9.9 | -13.38 | 7f-8f | 5-37 | 13.5 | -22.72 |
| 9f-13f | 0-1 | 0.0 | -1.00 | 9f-13f | 16-94 | 17.0 | +14.00 |
| 14f+ | 0-0 | 0.0 | 0.00 | 14f+ | 2-22 | 9.1 | -15.50 |

| 4-y-o+ | W-R | Per cent | £1 Level Stake | Totals | W-R | Per cent | £1 Level Stake |
|---|---|---|---|---|---|---|---|
| 5f-6f | 0-0 | 0.0 | 0.00 | 5f-6f | 2-57 | 3.5 | -53.40 |
| 7f-8f | 0-0 | 0.0 | 0.00 | 7f-8f | 12-108 | 11.1 | -36.10 |
| 9f-13f | 3-12 | 25.0 | +16.75 | 9f-13f | 19-107 | 17.8 | +29.75 |
| 14f+ | 3-21 | 14.3 | 0.00 | 14f+ | 5-43 | 11.6 | -15.50 |

## TYPE OF RACE

| Non-Handicaps | W-R | Per cent | £1 Level Stake | Handicaps | W-R | Per cent | £1 Level Stake |
|---|---|---|---|---|---|---|---|
| 2-y-o | 6-93 | 6.5 | -53.88 | 2-y-o | 2-20 | 10.0 | 0.00 |
| 3-y-o | 8-61 | 13.1 | -21.37 | 3-y-o | 16-108 | 14.8 | -16.75 |
| 4-y-o+ | 2-14 | 14.3 | +2.00 | 4-y-o+ | 4-19 | 21.1 | +14.7 |

## RACE CLASS / FIRST TIME OUT

| | W-R | Per cent | £1 Level Stake | | W-R | Per cent | £1 Level Stake |
|---|---|---|---|---|---|---|---|
| Class 1 | 3-28 | 10.7 | -10.09 | 2-y-o | 0-38 | 0.0 | -38.00 |
| Class 2 | 3-37 | 8.1 | -11.50 | 3-y-o | 5-34 | 14.7 | -10.09 |
| Class 3 | 5-27 | 18.5 | +19.00 | 4-y-o+ | 1-7 | 14.3 | -3.25 |
| Class 4 | 10-92 | 10.9 | -23.00 | | | | |
| Class 5 | 15-106 | 14.2 | -38.90 | Totals | 6-79 | 7.6 | -51.34 |
| Class 6 | 2-25 | 8.0 | -10.75 | | | | |
| Class 7 | 0-0 | 0.0 | 0.00 | | | | |

racingpost.com

# RICHARD FAHEY
## KIMPTON, HANTS

|       | No. of Hrs | Races Run | 1st | 2nd | 3rd | Unpl | Per cent | £1 Level Stake |
|-------|------------|-----------|-----|-----|-----|------|---------|----------------|
| 2-y-o | 72 | 336 | 75 | 36 | 39 | 184 | 22.3 | +68.56 |
| 3-y-o | 61 | 362 | 33 | 37 | 38 | 254 | 9.1 | -178.79 |
| 4-y-o+ | 92 | 658 | 73 | 70 | 78 | 436 | 11.1 | -163.31 |
| Totals | 225 | 1356 | 181 | 143 | 155 | 874 | 13.3 | -273.54 |
| 2009 | 186 | 1106 | 165 | 137 | 143 | 658 | 14.9 | +38.24 |
| 2008 | 169 | 971 | 113 | 116 | 95 | 640 | 11.6 | -200.47 |

### BY MONTH

| 2-y-o | W-R | Per cent | £1 Level Stake | 3-y-o | W-R | Per cent | £1 Level Stake |
|-------|-----|----------|----------------|-------|-----|----------|----------------|
| January | 0-0 | 0.0 | 0.00 | January | 1-5 | 20.0 | -3.27 |
| February | 0-0 | 0.0 | 0.00 | February | 2-7 | 28.6 | +1.25 |
| March | 3-5 | 60.0 | +7.45 | March | 1-9 | 11.1 | -6.13 |
| April | 3-12 | 25.0 | -2.52 | April | 3-32 | 9.4 | -21.88 |
| May | 4-18 | 22.2 | -5.25 | May | 7-67 | 10.4 | -30.55 |
| June | 11-41 | 26.8 | +10.82 | June | 5-46 | 10.9 | -25.09 |
| July | 15-57 | 26.3 | -4.41 | July | 2-42 | 4.8 | -30.13 |
| August | 11-65 | 16.9 | +21.60 | August | 3-45 | 6.7 | -22.00 |
| September | 11-57 | 19.3 | -2.75 | September | 5-42 | 11.9 | -12.00 |
| October | 5-41 | 12.2 | +4.50 | October | 2-36 | 5.6 | -22.00 |
| November | 9-25 | 36.0 | +32.63 | November | 0-18 | 0.0 | -18.00 |
| December | 3-15 | 20.0 | +6.50 | December | 2-13 | 15.4 | +11.00 |

| 4-y-o+ | W-R | Per cent | £1 Level Stake | Totals | W-R | Per cent | £1 Level Stake |
|--------|-----|----------|----------------|--------|-----|----------|----------------|
| January | 4-35 | 11.4 | -9.38 | January | 5-40 | 12.5 | -12.65 |
| February | 1-16 | 6.3 | -10.50 | February | 3-23 | 13.0 | -9.25 |
| March | 6-37 | 16.2 | +9.50 | March | 10-51 | 19.6 | +10.82 |
| April | 14-52 | 26.9 | +51.55 | April | 20-96 | 20.8 | +27.15 |
| May | 8-83 | 9.6 | -42.88 | May | 19-168 | 11.3 | -78.68 |
| June | 5-73 | 6.8 | -54.42 | June | 21-160 | 13.1 | -68.69 |
| July | 9-79 | 11.4 | -27.63 | July | 26-178 | 14.6 | -62.17 |
| August | 6-67 | 9.0 | -25.05 | August | 20-177 | 11.3 | -25.45 |
| September | 8-86 | 9.3 | -40.65 | September | 24-185 | 13.0 | -55.40 |
| October | 6-62 | 9.7 | +19.33 | October | 13-139 | 9.4 | +1.83 |
| November | 3-32 | 9.4 | -16.50 | November | 12-75 | 16.0 | -34.50 |
| December | 3-36 | 8.3 | -16.70 | December | 8-64 | 12.5 | -5.70 |

### DISTANCE

| 2-y-o | W-R | Per cent | £1 Level Stake | 3-y-o | W-R | Per cent | £1 Level Stake |
|-------|-----|----------|----------------|-------|-----|----------|----------------|
| 5f-6f | 56-234 | 23.9 | +61.53 | 5f-6f | 13-115 | 11.3 | -52.70 |
| 7f-8f | 19-101 | 18.8 | +8.03 | 7f-8f | 11-132 | 8.3 | -75.38 |
| 9f-13f | 0-1 | 0.0 | -1.00 | 9f-13f | 9-112 | 8.0 | -47.72 |
| 14f+ | 0-0 | 0.0 | 0.00 | 14f+ | 0-3 | 0.0 | -3.00 |

| 4-y-o+ | W-R | Per cent | £1 Level Stake | Totals | W-R | Per cent | £1 Level Stake |
|--------|-----|----------|----------------|--------|-----|----------|----------------|
| 5f-6f | 15-172 | 8.7 | -41.38 | 5f-6f | 84-521 | 16.1 | -32.55 |
| 7f-8f | 27-226 | 11.9 | -63.60 | 7f-8f | 57-459 | 12.4 | -130.95 |
| 9f-13f | 31-229 | 13.5 | -27.33 | 9f-13f | 40-342 | 11.7 | -76.05 |
| 14f+ | 0-31 | 0.0 | -31.00 | 14f+ | 0-34 | 0.0 | -34.00 |

### TYPE OF RACE

| Non-Handicaps | W-R | Per cent | £1 Level Stake | Handicaps | W-R | Per cent | £1 Level Stake |
|---------------|-----|----------|----------------|-----------|-----|----------|----------------|
| 2-y-o | 56-243 | 23.0 | +38.03 | 2-y-o | 19-93 | 20.4 | +30.53 |
| 3-y-o | 10-90 | 11.1 | -42.58 | 3-y-o | 23-272 | 8.5 | -136.22 |
| 4-y-o+ | 20-98 | 20.4 | +82.00 | 4-y-o+ | 53-560 | 9.5 | -132.42 |

### RACE CLASS | FIRST TIME OUT

| Race Class | W-R | Per cent | £1 Level Stake | First Time Out | W-R | Per cent | £1 Level Stake |
|------------|-----|----------|----------------|----------------|-----|----------|----------------|
| Class 1 | 4-65 | 6.2 | -33.50 | 2-y-o | 18-72 | 25.0 | +38.33 |
| Class 2 | 21-279 | 7.5 | -120.09 | 3-y-o | 8-61 | 13.1 | -33.81 |
| Class 3 | 21-178 | 11.8 | -44.92 | 4-y-o+ | 16-92 | 17.4 | +16.42 |
| Class 4 | 44-298 | 14.8 | -11.29 | | | | |
| Class 5 | 60-348 | 17.2 | -30.65 | Totals | 42-225 | 18.7 | +20.94 |
| Class 6 | 30-186 | 16.1 | -39.08 | | | | |
| Class 7 | 1-2 | 50.0 | +6.00 | | | | |

## Statistics

# RICHARD HANNON
## EAST EVERLEIGH, WILTS

|  | No. of Hrs | Races Run | 1st | 2nd | 3rd | Unpl | Per cent | £1 Level Stake |
|---|---|---|---|---|---|---|---|---|
| 2-y-o | 144 | 628 | 120 | 95 | 57 | 354 | 19.1 | -87.23 |
| 3-y-o | 90 | 510 | 68 | 79 | 63 | 299 | 13.3 | -70.57 |
| 4-y-o+ | 33 | 203 | 22 | 24 | 22 | 135 | 10.8 | -45.90 |
| Totals | 267 | 1341 | 210 | 198 | 142 | 788 | 15.7 | -203.70 |
| 2009 | 255 | 1371 | 188 | 163 | 156 | 861 | 13.7 | -48.46 |
| 2008 | 234 | 1406 | 189 | 181 | 143 | 891 | 13.4 | +12.8 |

### BY MONTH

| 2-y-o | W-R | Per cent | £1 Level Stake | 3-y-o | W-R | Per cent | £1 Level Stake |
|---|---|---|---|---|---|---|---|
| January | 0-0 | 0.0 | 0.00 | January | 1-6 | 16.7 | -4.56 |
| February | 0-0 | 0.0 | 0.00 | February | 2-8 | 25.0 | +7.00 |
| March | 1-1 | 100.0 | +3.50 | March | 4-18 | 22.2 | -4.59 |
| April | 10-21 | 47.6 | +15.00 | April | 8-56 | 14.3 | -11.31 |
| May | 15-61 | 24.6 | +17.32 | May | 14-97 | 14.4 | -5.04 |
| June | 15-70 | 21.4 | -6.90 | June | 16-88 | 18.2 | +31.45 |
| July | 29-104 | 27.9 | +12.99 | July | 10-72 | 13.9 | +0.87 |
| August | 15-105 | 14.3 | -48.46 | August | 5-58 | 8.6 | -26.00 |
| September | 21-134 | 15.7 | -25.08 | September | 5-50 | 10.0 | -24.39 |
| October | 12-91 | 13.2 | -18.37 | October | 2-40 | 5.0 | -30.00 |
| November | 1-26 | 3.8 | -23.90 | November | 0-12 | 0.0 | -12.00 |
| December | 1-15 | 6.7 | -13.33 | December | 1-5 | 20.0 | +8.00 |

| 4-y-o+ | W-R | Per cent | £1 Level Stake | Totals | W-R | Per cent | £1 Level Stake |
|---|---|---|---|---|---|---|---|
| January | 0-6 | 0.0 | -6.00 | January | 1-12 | 8.3 | -10.56 |
| February | 0-3 | 0.0 | -3.00 | February | 2-11 | 18.2 | +4.00 |
| March | 3-12 | 25.0 | +5.00 | March | 8-31 | 25.8 | +3.91 |
| April | 4-19 | 21.1 | -1.28 | April | 22-96 | 22.9 | +2.41 |
| May | 4-36 | 11.1 | -19.02 | May | 33-194 | 17.0 | -6.74 |
| June | 0-29 | 0.0 | -29.00 | June | 31-187 | 16.6 | -4.45 |
| July | 5-29 | 17.2 | +1.90 | July | 44-205 | 21.5 | +15.76 |
| August | 1-26 | 3.8 | -17.00 | August | 21-189 | 11.1 | -91.46 |
| September | 2-22 | 9.1 | -8.50 | September | 28-206 | 13.6 | -57.97 |
| October | 3-14 | 21.4 | +38.00 | October | 17-145 | 11.7 | -10.37 |
| November | 0-6 | 0.0 | -6.00 | November | 1-44 | 2.3 | -18.00 |
| December | 0-1 | 0.0 | -1.00 | December | 2-21 | 9.5 | +7.00 |

### DISTANCE

| 2-y-o | W-R | Per cent | £1 Level Stake | 3-y-o | W-R | Per cent | £1 Level Stake |
|---|---|---|---|---|---|---|---|
| 5f-6f | 75-358 | 20.9 | -43.41 | 5f-6f | 15-95 | 15.8 | +16.04 |
| 7f-8f | 45-262 | 17.2 | -35.82 | 7f-8f | 36-251 | 14.3 | -50.56 |
| 9f-13f | 0-8 | 0.0 | -8.00 | 9f-13f | 16-157 | 10.2 | -37.04 |
| 14f+ | 0-0 | 0.0 | 0.00 | 14f+ | 1-7 | 14.3 | +1.00 |

| 4-y-o | W-R | Per cent | £1 Level Stake | Totals | W-R | Per cent | £1 Level Stake |
|---|---|---|---|---|---|---|---|
| 5f-6f | 5-36 | 13.9 | -5.60 | 5f-6f | 95-489 | 19.4 | -32.97 |
| 7f-8f | 8-80 | 10.0 | -33.55 | 7f-8f | 89-593 | 15.0 | -119.93 |
| 9f-13f | 5-68 | 7.4 | -17.25 | 9f-13f | 21-233 | 9.0 | -62.29 |
| 14f+ | 4-19 | 21.1 | +10.50 | 14f+ | 5-26 | 19.2 | +11.50 |

### TYPE OF RACE

| Non-Handicaps | W-R | Per cent | £1 Level Stake | Handicaps | W-R | Per cent | £1 Level Stake |
|---|---|---|---|---|---|---|---|
| 2-y-o | 103-509 | 20.2 | -68.64 | 2-y-o | 17-119 | 14.3 | -18.58 |
| 3-y-o | 31-161 | 19.3 | +16.10 | 3-y-o | 37-349 | 10.6 | -86.66 |
| 4-y-o+ | 7-60 | 11.7 | 0.00 | 4-y-o+ | 15-143 | 10.5 | -6.25 |

### RACE CLASS | FIRST TIME OUT

|  | W-R | Per cent | £1 Level Stake |  | W-R | Per cent | £1 Level Stake |
|---|---|---|---|---|---|---|---|
| Class 1 | 23-148 | 15.5 | -17.39 | 2-y-o | 25-144 | 17.4 | -11.88 |
| Class 2 | 21-175 | 12.0 | -50.17 | 3-y-o | 18-90 | 20.0 | +67.55 |
| Class 3 | 21-114 | 18.4 | -1.92 | 4-y-o+ | 6-33 | 18.2 | +2.73 |
| Class 4 | 50-394 | 12.7 | -112.76 |  |  |  |  |
| Class 5 | 81-416 | 19.5 | +15.66 | Totals | 49-267 | 18.4 | +58.40 |
| Class 6 | 14-93 | 15.1 | -35.11 |  |  |  |  |
| Class 7 | 0-1 | 0.0 | -1.00 |  |  |  |  |

# BARRY HILLS
## LAMBOURN, BERKS

|  | No. of Hrs | Races Run | 1st | 2nd | 3rd | Unpl | Per cent | £1 Level Stake |
|---|---|---|---|---|---|---|---|---|
| 2-y-o | 63 | 179 | 23 | 23 | 21 | 112 | 12.8 | -53.91 |
| 3-y-o | 56 | 264 | 38 | 40 | 28 | 157 | 14.4 | -83.50 |
| 4-y-o+ | 14 | 80 | 9 | 14 | 3 | 53 | 11.3 | +0.58 |
| Totals | 133 | 523 | 70 | 77 | 52 | 322 | 13.4 | -136.83 |
| 2009 | 140 | 566 | 88 | 72 | 69 | 335 | 15.5 | -16.50 |
| 2008 | 151 | 625 | 70 | 73 | 69 | 413 | 11.2 | -36.00 |

### BY MONTH

| 2-y-o | W-R | Per cent | £1 Level Stake | 3-y-o | W-R | Per cent | £1 Level Stake |
|---|---|---|---|---|---|---|---|
| January | 0-0 | 0.0 | 0.00 | January | 0-3 | 0.0 | -3.00 |
| February | 0-0 | 0.0 | 0.00 | February | 3-8 | 37.5 | +3.25 |
| March | 0-2 | 0.0 | -2.00 | March | 1-10 | 10.0 | -7.63 |
| April | 0-3 | 0.0 | -3.00 | April | 4-27 | 14.8 | -11.67 |
| May | 1-11 | 9.1 | -9.60 | May | 7-43 | 16.3 | -8.52 |
| June | 2-8 | 25.0 | +2.41 | June | 8-48 | 16.7 | -14.77 |
| July | 8-29 | 27.6 | -1.36 | July | 5-35 | 14.3 | -16.13 |
| August | 1-33 | 3.0 | -30.25 | August | 4-35 | 11.4 | -10.90 |
| September | 5-46 | 10.9 | +6.78 | September | 1-31 | 3.2 | -27.75 |
| October | 5-34 | 14.7 | -10.90 | October | 4-21 | 19.0 | +14.50 |
| November | 1-13 | 7.7 | -6.00 | November | 1-3 | 33.3 | -0.90 |
| December | 0-0 | 0.0 | 0.00 | December | 0-0 | 0.0 | 0.00 |

| 4-y-o+ | W-R | Per cent | £1 Level Stake | Totals | W-R | Per cent | £1 Level Stake |
|---|---|---|---|---|---|---|---|
| January | 0-0 | 0.0 | 0.00 | January | 0-3 | 0.0 | -3.00 |
| February | 0-0 | 0.0 | 0.00 | February | 3-8 | 37.5 | +3.25 |
| March | 0-4 | 0.0 | -4.00 | March | 1-16 | 6.3 | -13.63 |
| April | 1-12 | 8.3 | -8.25 | April | 5-42 | 11.9 | -22.92 |
| May | 3-15 | 20.0 | +16.00 | May | 11-69 | 15.9 | -2.12 |
| June | 1-11 | 9.1 | -5.50 | June | 11-67 | 16.4 | -17.86 |
| July | 2-12 | 16.7 | +17.00 | July | 15-76 | 19.7 | -0.49 |
| August | 0-8 | 0.0 | -8.00 | August | 5-76 | 6.6 | -49.15 |
| September | 1-10 | 10.0 | -3.00 | September | 7-87 | 8.0 | -23.97 |
| October | 1-6 | 16.7 | -1.67 | October | 10-61 | 16.4 | +1.93 |
| November | 0-2 | 0.0 | -2.00 | November | 2-18 | 11.1 | -2.90 |
| December | 0-0 | 0.0 | 0.00 | December | 0-0 | 0.0 | 0.00 |

### DISTANCE

| 2-y-o | W-R | Per cent | £1 Level Stake | 3-y-o | W-R | Per cent | £1 Level Stake |
|---|---|---|---|---|---|---|---|
| 5f-6f | 12-91 | 13.2 | -49.30 | 5f-6f | 3-34 | 8.8 | -15.00 |
| 7f-8f | 11-88 | 12.5 | -4.62 | 7f-8f | 22-131 | 16.8 | -5.59 |
| 9f-13f | 0-0 | 0.0 | 0.00 | 9f-13f | 13-97 | 13.4 | -60.91 |
| 14f+ | 0-0 | 0.0 | 0.00 | 14f+ | 0-2 | 0.0 | -2.00 |

| 4-y-o | W-R | Per cent | £1 Level Stake | Totals | W-R | Per cent | £1 Level Stake |
|---|---|---|---|---|---|---|---|
| 5f-6f | 6-30 | 20.0 | +31.25 | 5f-6f | 21-155 | 13.5 | -33.05 |
| 7f-8f | 1-31 | 3.2 | -24.00 | 7f-8f | 34-250 | 13.6 | -34.21 |
| 9f-13f | 1-10 | 10.0 | -2.00 | 9f-13f | 14-107 | 13.1 | -62.91 |
| 14f+ | 1-9 | 11.1 | -4.67 | 14f+ | 1-11 | 9.1 | -6.67 |

### TYPE OF RACE

| Non-Handicaps | W-R | Per cent | £1 Level Stake | Handicaps | W-R | Per cent | £1 Level Stake |
|---|---|---|---|---|---|---|---|
| 2-y-o | 18-149 | 12.1 | -49.58 | 2-y-o | 5-30 | 16.7 | -4.33 |
| 3-y-o | 23-122 | 18.9 | -43.18 | 3-y-o | 15-142 | 10.6 | -40.32 |
| 4-y-o+ | 7-33 | 21.2 | +39.00 | 4-y-o+ | 2-47 | 4.3 | -19.00 |

### RACE CLASS

| | W-R | Per cent | £1 Level Stake |
|---|---|---|---|
| Class 1 | 10-71 | 14.1 | +3.58 |
| Class 2 | 6-86 | 7.0 | -37.25 |
| Class 3 | 6-65 | 9.2 | -25.83 |
| Class 4 | 14-147 | 9.5 | -72.52 |
| Class 5 | 34-143 | 23.8 | +6.18 |
| Class 6 | 0-11 | 0.0 | -11.00 |
| Class 7 | 0-0 | 0.0 | 0.00 |

### FIRST TIME OUT

| | W-R | Per cent | £1 Level Stake |
|---|---|---|---|
| 2-y-o | 4-63 | 6.3 | -16.50 |
| 3-y-o | 9-56 | 16.1 | -13.04 |
| 4-y-o+ | 1-14 | 7.1 | -10.25 |
| Totals | 14-133 | 10.5 | -39.79 |

## Statistics

# BRIAN MEEHAN
**MANTON, WILTS**

|  | No. of Hrs | Races Run | 1st | 2nd | 3rd | Unpl | Per cent | £1 Level Stake |
|---|---|---|---|---|---|---|---|---|
| 2-y-o | 74 | 255 | 36 | 19 | 25 | 175 | 14.1 | -36.02 |
| 3-y-o | 46 | 195 | 27 | 20 | 16 | 132 | 13.8 | +47.43 |
| 4-y-o+ | 23 | 130 | 10 | 13 | 12 | 95 | 7.7 | -38.75 |
| Totals | 143 | 580 | 73 | 52 | 53 | 402 | 12.6 | -27.34 |
| 2009 | 124 | 505 | 62 | 59 | 58 | 326 | 12.3 | +74.53 |
| 2008 | 141 | 598 | 72 | 60 | 43 | 422 | 12.0 | +17.08 |

### BY MONTH

| 2-y-o | W-R | Per cent | £1 Level Stake | 3-y-o | W-R | Per cent | £1 Level Stake |
|---|---|---|---|---|---|---|---|
| January | 0-0 | 0.0 | 0.00 | January | 0-0 | 0.0 | 0.00 |
| February | 0-0 | 0.0 | 0.00 | February | 0-6 | 0.0 | -6.00 |
| March | 0-0 | 0.0 | 0.00 | March | 0-6 | 0.0 | -6.00 |
| April | 0-1 | 0.0 | -1.00 | April | 4-24 | 16.7 | +28.00 |
| May | 1-11 | 9.1 | -7.00 | May | 4-33 | 12.1 | -16.05 |
| June | 2-12 | 16.7 | -6.67 | June | 4-35 | 11.4 | +20.50 |
| July | 8-40 | 20.0 | +8.03 | July | 8-27 | 29.6 | +21.13 |
| August | 7-50 | 14.0 | -28.02 | August | 3-24 | 12.5 | -10.25 |
| September | 10-79 | 12.7 | +11.40 | September | 1-15 | 6.7 | -10.00 |
| October | 7-52 | 13.5 | -4.67 | October | 2-18 | 11.1 | +31.00 |
| November | 1-8 | 12.5 | -6.09 | November | 1-5 | 20.0 | -2.90 |
| December | 0-2 | 0.0 | -2.00 | December | 0-2 | 0.0 | -2.00 |

| 4-y-o+ | W-R | Per cent | £1 Level Stake | Totals | W-R | Per cent | £1 Level Stake |
|---|---|---|---|---|---|---|---|
| January | 0-0 | 0.0 | 0.00 | January | 0-0 | 0.0 | 0.00 |
| February | 0-0 | 0.0 | 0.00 | February | 0-6 | 0.0 | -6.00 |
| March | 0-0 | 0.0 | 0.00 | March | 0-6 | 0.0 | -6.00 |
| April | 1-6 | 16.7 | 0.00 | April | 5-31 | 16.1 | +27.00 |
| May | 0-18 | 0.0 | -18.00 | May | 5-62 | 8.1 | -41.05 |
| June | 1-23 | 4.3 | -14.00 | June | 7-70 | 10.0 | -0.17 |
| July | 3-24 | 12.5 | +4.50 | July | 19-91 | 20.9 | +33.66 |
| August | 2-18 | 11.1 | -9.75 | August | 12-92 | 13.0 | -48.02 |
| September | 1-15 | 6.7 | -9.50 | September | 12-109 | 11.0 | -8.10 |
| October | 2-16 | 12.5 | +18.00 | October | 11-86 | 12.8 | +44.33 |
| November | 0-8 | 0.0 | -8.00 | November | 2-21 | 9.5 | -10.90 |
| December | 0-2 | 0.0 | -2.00 | December | 0-6 | 0.0 | -4.00 |

### DISTANCE

| 2-y-o | W-R | Per cent | £1 Level Stake | 3-y-o | W-R | Per cent | £1 Level Stake |
|---|---|---|---|---|---|---|---|
| 5f-6f | 17-104 | 16.3 | +8.18 | 5f-6f | 5-29 | 17.2 | +5.30 |
| 7f-8f | 18-146 | 12.3 | -45.70 | 7f-8f | 16-107 | 15.0 | +45.03 |
| 9f-13f | 1-5 | 20.0 | +1.50 | 9f-13f | 5-54 | 9.3 | -3.40 |
| 14f+ | 0-0 | 0.0 | 0.00 | 14f+ | 1-5 | 20.0 | +0.50 |

| 4-y-o+ | W-R | Per cent | £1 Level Stake | Totals | W-R | Per cent | £1 Level Stake |
|---|---|---|---|---|---|---|---|
| 5f-6f | 1-17 | 5.9 | -12.50 | 5f-6f | 23-150 | 15.3 | +0.98 |
| 7f-8f | 5-72 | 6.9 | -23.25 | 7f-8f | 39-325 | 12.0 | -23.92 |
| 9f-13f | 3-26 | 11.5 | -5.00 | 9f-13f | 9-85 | 10.6 | -6.90 |
| 14f+ | 1-15 | 6.7 | +2.00 | 14f+ | 2-20 | 10.0 | +2.50 |

### TYPE OF RACE

| Non-Handicaps | W-R | Per cent | £1 Level Stake | Handicaps | W-R | Per cent | £1 Level Stake |
|---|---|---|---|---|---|---|---|
| 2-y-o | 34-214 | 15.9 | -10.02 | 2-y-o | 2-41 | 4.9 | -26.00 |
| 3-y-o | 14-90 | 15.6 | +10.35 | 3-y-o | 13-105 | 12.4 | +37.08 |
| 4-y-o+ | 1-36 | 2.8 | -26.00 | 4-y-o+ | 9-94 | 9.6 | -8.25 |

### RACE CLASS | FIRST TIME OUT

|  | W-R | Per cent | £1 Level Stake |  | W-R | Per cent | £1 Level Stake |
|---|---|---|---|---|---|---|---|
| Class 1 | 8-61 | 13.1 | -14.57 | 2-y-o | 3-74 | 4.1 | -46.00 |
| Class 2 | 9-69 | 13.0 | +6.08 | 3-y-o | 4-46 | 8.7 | +6.00 |
| Class 3 | 9-39 | 23.1 | +32.53 | 4-y-o+ | 1-23 | 4.3 | -17.00 |
| Class 4 | 22-180 | 12.2 | +13.16 |  |  |  |  |
| Class 5 | 22-186 | 11.8 | -36.85 | Totals | 8-143 | 5.6 | -57.00 |
| Class 6 | 3-46 | 6.5 | -28.70 |  |  |  |  |
| Class 7 | 0-0 | 0.0 | 0.00 |  |  |  |  |

# DAVID NICHOLLS
## SESSAY, N YORKS

|       | No. of Hrs | Races Run | 1st | 2nd | 3rd | Unpl | Per cent | £1 Level Stake |
|-------|-----------|-----------|-----|-----|-----|------|---------|----------------|
| 2-y-o | 20 | 62 | 12 | 10 | 7 | 33 | 19.4 | -3.77 |
| 3-y-o | 31 | 134 | 19 | 18 | 20 | 77 | 14.2 | +2.65 |
| 4-y-o+ | 72 | 432 | 57 | 35 | 44 | 295 | 13.2 | -62.73 |
| Totals | 123 | 628 | 88 | 63 | 71 | 405 | 14.0 | -63.85 |
| 2009 | 113 | 687 | 84 | 74 | 64 | 463 | 12.2 | -92.77 |
| 2008 | 95 | 532 | 68 | 62 | 58 | 343 | 12.8 | +71.08 |

## BY MONTH

| 2-y-o | W-R | Per cent | £1 Level Stake | 3-y-o | W-R | Per cent | £1 Level Stake |
|-------|-----|----------|----------------|-------|-----|----------|----------------|
| January | 0-0 | 0.0 | 0.00 | January | 2-6 | 33.3 | +8.25 |
| February | 0-0 | 0.0 | 0.00 | February | 1-6 | 16.7 | +2.00 |
| March | 0-0 | 0.0 | 0.00 | March | 3-11 | 27.3 | -2.25 |
| April | 1-4 | 25.0 | +1.50 | April | 2-17 | 11.8 | +8.25 |
| May | 1-6 | 16.7 | +3.00 | May | 0-9 | 0.0 | -9.00 |
| June | 3-9 | 33.3 | +8.50 | June | 3-13 | 23.1 | +23.50 |
| July | 1-12 | 8.3 | -10.27 | July | 4-14 | 28.6 | +12.00 |
| August | 0-3 | 0.0 | -3.00 | August | 2-15 | 13.3 | -2.50 |
| September | 1-4 | 25.0 | +2.00 | September | 0-13 | 0.0 | -13.00 |
| October | 0-5 | 0.0 | -5.00 | October | 0-12 | 0.0 | -12.00 |
| November | 2-8 | 25.0 | -1.50 | November | 1-8 | 12.5 | -4.00 |
| December | 3-11 | 27.3 | +1.00 | December | 1-10 | 10.0 | -8.60 |

| 4-y-o+ | W-R | Per cent | £1 Level Stake | Totals | W-R | Per cent | £1 Level Stake |
|--------|-----|----------|----------------|--------|-----|----------|----------------|
| January | 0-5 | 0.0 | -5.00 | January | 2-11 | 18.2 | +3.25 |
| February | 1-3 | 33.3 | -0.25 | February | 2-9 | 22.2 | +1.75 |
| March | 3-20 | 15.0 | -4.13 | March | 6-31 | 19.4 | -6.38 |
| April | 8-43 | 18.6 | -5.75 | April | 11-64 | 17.2 | +4.00 |
| May | 10-74 | 13.5 | -18.10 | May | 11-89 | 12.4 | -24.10 |
| June | 7-64 | 10.9 | -39.00 | June | 13-86 | 15.1 | -7.00 |
| July | 6-62 | 9.7 | +20.75 | July | 11-88 | 12.5 | +22.48 |
| August | 7-49 | 14.3 | -1.83 | August | 9-67 | 13.4 | -7.33 |
| September | 6-46 | 13.0 | +2.00 | September | 7-63 | 11.1 | -9.00 |
| October | 1-27 | 3.7 | -23.00 | October | 1-44 | 2.3 | -40.00 |
| November | 4-13 | 30.8 | +11.58 | November | 7-29 | 24.1 | +7.58 |
| December | 4-26 | 15.4 | 0.00 | December | 8-47 | 17.0 | -8.60 |

## DISTANCE

| 2-y-o | W-R | Per cent | £1 Level Stake | 3-y-o | W-R | Per cent | £1 Level Stake |
|-------|-----|----------|----------------|-------|-----|----------|----------------|
| 5f-6f | 11-48 | 22.9 | +4.23 | 5f-6f | 14-81 | 17.3 | +26.65 |
| 7f-8f | 1-14 | 7.1 | -8.00 | 7f-8f | 5-50 | 10.0 | -21.00 |
| 9f-13f | 0-0 | 0.0 | 0.00 | 9f-13f | 0-3 | 0.0 | -3.00 |
| 14f+ | 0-0 | 0.0 | 0.00 | 14f+ | 0-0 | 0.0 | 0.00 |

| 4-y-o+ | W-R | Per cent | £1 Level Stake | Totals | W-R | Per cent | £1 Level Stake |
|--------|-----|----------|----------------|--------|-----|----------|----------------|
| 5f-6f | 29-234 | 12.4 | -21.84 | 5f-6f | 54-363 | 14.9 | +9.04 |
| 7f-8f | 20-143 | 14.0 | -33.75 | 7f-8f | 26-207 | 12.6 | -62.75 |
| 9f-13f | 8-55 | 14.5 | -7.13 | 9f-13f | 8-58 | 13.8 | -10.13 |
| 14f+ | 0-0 | 0.0 | 0.00 | 14f+ | 0-0 | 0.0 | 0.00 |

## TYPE OF RACE

| Non-Handicaps | W-R | Per cent | £1 Level Stake | Handicaps | W-R | Per cent | £1 Level Stake |
|---------------|-----|----------|----------------|-----------|-----|----------|----------------|
| 2-y-o | 8-44 | 18.2 | -3.77 | 2-y-o | 4-18 | 22.2 | 0.00 |
| 3-y-o | 10-61 | 16.4 | -7.85 | 3-y-o | 9-73 | 12.3 | +10.50 |
| 4-y-o+ | 29-104 | 27.9 | +134.00 | 4-y-o+ | 28-328 | 8.5 | -60.67 |

## RACE CLASS FIRST TIME OUT

|         | W-R | Per cent | £1 Level Stake |        | W-R | Per cent | £1 Level Stake |
|---------|-----|----------|----------------|--------|-----|----------|----------------|
| Class 1 | 3-28 | 10.7 | -6.00 | 2-y-o | 3-20 | 15.0 | +2.50 |
| Class 2 | 9-131 | 6.9 | -19.50 | 3-y-o | 8-31 | 25.8 | +43.75 |
| Class 3 | 8-84 | 9.5 | -4.00 | 4-y-o+ | 7-72 | 9.7 | -24.50 |
| Class 4 | 15-127 | 11.8 | -25.44 | | | | |
| Class 5 | 23-150 | 15.3 | -5.31 | Totals | 18-123 | 14.6 | +21.75 |
| Class 6 | 30-108 | 27.8 | -2.60 | | | | |
| Class 7 | 0-0 | 0.0 | 0.00 | | | | |

## Statistics

# JEREMY NOSEDA
## NEWMARKET, SUFFOLK

|        | No. of Hrs | Races Run | 1st | 2nd | 3rd | Unpl | Per cent | £1 Level Stake |
|--------|------------|-----------|-----|-----|-----|------|----------|----------------|
| 2-y-o  | 26         | 67        | 11  | 12  | 7   | 37   | 16.4     | -39.06         |
| 3-y-o  | 43         | 182       | 35  | 22  | 27  | 95   | 19.2     | -55.80         |
| 4-y-o+ | 19         | 79        | 9   | 15  | 9   | 46   | 11.4     | -28.18         |
| Totals | 88         | 328       | 55  | 49  | 43  | 178  | 16.8     | -123.04        |
| 2009   | 90         | 334       | 61  | 47  | 54  | 171  | 18.3     | +7.19          |
| 2008   | 84         | 285       | 61  | 34  | 30  | 160  | 21.4     | +5.21          |

### BY MONTH

| 2-y-o     | W-R  | Per cent | £1 Level Stake | 3-y-o     | W-R   | Per cent | £1 Level Stake |
|-----------|------|----------|----------------|-----------|-------|----------|----------------|
| January   | 0-0  | 0.0      | 0.00           | January   | 1-5   | 20.0     | -3.43          |
| February  | 0-0  | 0.0      | 0.00           | February  | 2-3   | 66.7     | +1.08          |
| March     | 0-0  | 0.0      | 0.00           | March     | 1-2   | 50.0     | -0.27          |
| April     | 0-0  | 0.0      | 0.00           | April     | 1-24  | 4.2      | -21.90         |
| May       | 1-6  | 16.7     | -4.67          | May       | 4-26  | 15.4     | -14.55         |
| June      | 1-5  | 20.0     | -3.64          | June      | 5-24  | 20.8     | -6.29          |
| July      | 1-5  | 20.0     | -2.00          | July      | 6-23  | 26.1     | -4.17          |
| August    | 1-8  | 12.5     | -5.75          | August    | 4-22  | 18.2     | -13.42         |
| September | 1-11 | 9.1      | -8.75          | September | 7-28  | 25.0     | +16.74         |
| October   | 4-21 | 19.0     | -9.59          | October   | 3-21  | 14.3     | -7.50          |
| November  | 2-8  | 25.0     | -1.67          | November  | 1-2   | 50.0     | -0.09          |
| December  | 0-3  | 0.0      | -3.00          | December  | 0-2   | 0.0      | -2.00          |

| 4-y-o+    | W-R   | Per cent | £1 Level Stake | Totals    | W-R    | Per cent | £1 Level Stake |
|-----------|-------|----------|----------------|-----------|--------|----------|----------------|
| January   | 0-3   | 0.0      | -3.00          | January   | 1-8    | 12.5     | -6.43          |
| February  | 0-1   | 0.0      | -1.00          | February  | 2-4    | 50.0     | +0.08          |
| March     | 0-0   | 0.0      | 0.00           | March     | 1-2    | 50.0     | -0.27          |
| April     | 0-3   | 0.0      | -3.00          | April     | 1-27   | 3.7      | -24.90         |
| May       | 0-6   | 0.0      | -6.00          | May       | 5-38   | 13.2     | -25.22         |
| June      | 2-15  | 13.3     | -2.50          | June      | 8-44   | 18.2     | -12.43         |
| July      | 2-15  | 13.3     | +1.91          | July      | 9-43   | 20.9     | -4.26          |
| August    | 1-7   | 14.3     | -3.00          | August    | 6-37   | 16.2     | -22.17         |
| September | 3-15  | 20.0     | -4.59          | September | 11-54  | 20.4     | +3.40          |
| October   | 0-11  | 0.0      | -11.00         | October   | 7-53   | 13.2     | -28.09         |
| November  | 1-1   | 100.0    | +6.00          | November  | 4-11   | 36.4     | +5.91          |
| December  | 0-2   | 0.0      | -2.00          | December  | 0-7    | 0.0      | -4.00          |

### DISTANCE

| 2-y-o  | W-R  | Per cent | £1 Level Stake | 3-y-o  | W-R    | Per cent | £1 Level Stake |
|--------|------|----------|----------------|--------|--------|----------|----------------|
| 5f-6f  | 6-30 | 20.0     | -15.30         | 5f-6f  | 9-23   | 39.1     | +19.69         |
| 7f-8f  | 5-36 | 13.9     | -22.76         | 7f-8f  | 13-91  | 14.3     | -55.66         |
| 9f-13f | 0-1  | 0.0      | -1.00          | 9f-13f | 11-60  | 18.3     | -19.20         |
| 14f+   | 0-0  | 0.0      | 0.00           | 14f+   | 2-8    | 25.0     | -0.63          |

| 4-y-o+ | W-R  | Per cent | £1 Level Stake | Totals | W-R    | Per cent | £1 Level Stake |
|--------|------|----------|----------------|--------|--------|----------|----------------|
| 5f-6f  | 3-19 | 15.8     | -3.00          | 5f-6f  | 18-72  | 25.0     | +1.39          |
| 7f-8f  | 3-36 | 8.3      | -25.18         | 7f-8f  | 21-163 | 12.9     | -103.60        |
| 9f-13f | 3-19 | 15.8     | +5.00          | 9f-13f | 14-80  | 17.5     | -15.20         |
| 14f+   | 0-5  | 0.0      | -5.00          | 14f+   | 2-13   | 15.4     | -5.63          |

### TYPE OF RACE

| Non-Handicaps | W-R    | Per cent | £1 Level Stake | Handicaps | W-R    | Per cent | £1 Level Stake |
|---------------|--------|----------|----------------|-----------|--------|----------|----------------|
| 2-y-o         | 11-60  | 18.3     | -32.06         | 2-y-o     | 0-7    | 0.0      | -7.00          |
| 3-y-o         | 18-105 | 17.1     | -54.55         | 3-y-o     | 17-77  | 22.1     | -1.25          |
| 4-y-o+        | 4-32   | 12.5     | +5.00          | 4-y-o+    | 5-47   | 10.6     | -24.09         |

### RACE CLASS

|         | W-R     | Per cent | £1 Level Stake |
|---------|---------|----------|----------------|
| Class 1 | 3-36    | 8.3      | -12.00         |
| Class 2 | 7-40    | 17.5     | +4.25          |
| Class 3 | 1-29    | 3.4      | -22.00         |
| Class 4 | 15-93   | 16.1     | -44.28         |
| Class 5 | 28-122  | 23.0     | -43.26         |
| Class 6 | 1-8     | 12.5     | -5.75          |
| Class 7 | 0-0     | 0.0      | 0.00           |

### FIRST TIME OUT

|        | W-R   | Per cent | £1 Level Stake |
|--------|-------|----------|----------------|
| 2-y-o  | 5-26  | 19.2     | -10.17         |
| 3-y-o  | 4-43  | 9.3      | -35.15         |
| 4-y-o+ | 2-19  | 10.5     | -6.50          |
| Totals | 11-88 | 12.5     | -51.82         |

## BRYAN SMART
### HAMBLETON, N YORKS

| | No. of Hrs | Races Run | 1st | 2nd | 3rd | Unpl | Per cent | £1 Level Stake |
|---|---|---|---|---|---|---|---|---|
| 2-y-o | 25 | 88 | 12 | 6 | 9 | 60 | 13.6 | -14.23 |
| 3-y-o | 25 | 120 | 16 | 11 | 17 | 76 | 13.3 | -55.47 |
| 4-y-o+ | 42 | 243 | 34 | 20 | 25 | 163 | 14.0 | +46.95 |
| Totals | 92 | 451 | 62 | 37 | 51 | 299 | 13.7 | -22.75 |
| 2009 | 108 | 483 | 51 | 59 | 67 | 306 | 10.6 | -78.25 |
| 2008 | 109 | 458 | 57 | 60 | 47 | 294 | 12.4 | -43.50 |

### BY MONTH

| 2-y-o | W-R | Per cent | £1 Level Stake | 3-y-o | W-R | Per cent | £1 Level Stake |
|---|---|---|---|---|---|---|---|
| January | 0-0 | 0.0 | 0.00 | January | 1-2 | 50.0 | 0.00 |
| February | 0-0 | 0.0 | 0.00 | February | 1-1 | 100.0 | +0.83 |
| March | 0-0 | 0.0 | 0.00 | March | 1-2 | 50.0 | +6.00 |
| April | 0-1 | 0.0 | -1.00 | April | 1-14 | 7.1 | -10.75 |
| May | 4-6 | 66.7 | +14.10 | May | 1-14 | 7.1 | -10.00 |
| June | 2-7 | 28.6 | -0.33 | June | 0-16 | 0.0 | -16.00 |
| July | 0-11 | 0.0 | -11.00 | July | 7-16 | 43.8 | +16.50 |
| August | 3-14 | 21.4 | +10.75 | August | 3-19 | 15.8 | -9.80 |
| September | 1-17 | 5.9 | -14.25 | September | 0-11 | 0.0 | -11.00 |
| October | 0-18 | 0.0 | -18.00 | October | 0-12 | 0.0 | -12.00 |
| November | 0-7 | 0.0 | -7.00 | November | 1-8 | 12.5 | -4.25 |
| December | 2-7 | 28.6 | +12.50 | December | 0-5 | 0.0 | -5.00 |

| 4-y-o+ | W-R | Per cent | £1 Level Stake | Totals | W-R | Per cent | £1 Level Stake |
|---|---|---|---|---|---|---|---|
| January | 7-26 | 26.9 | +10.50 | January | 8-28 | 28.6 | +10.50 |
| February | 4-23 | 17.4 | -1.93 | February | 5-24 | 20.8 | -1.10 |
| March | 0-15 | 0.0 | -15.00 | March | 1-17 | 5.9 | -9.00 |
| April | 5-22 | 22.7 | +15.38 | April | 6-37 | 16.2 | +3.63 |
| May | 1-20 | 5.0 | -10.00 | May | 6-40 | 15.0 | -5.90 |
| June | 3-18 | 16.7 | -7.25 | June | 5-41 | 12.2 | -23.58 |
| July | 2-27 | 7.4 | -15.00 | July | 9-54 | 16.7 | -9.50 |
| August | 4-30 | 13.3 | +14.00 | August | 10-63 | 15.9 | +14.95 |
| September | 3-24 | 12.5 | +27.00 | September | 4-52 | 7.7 | +1.75 |
| October | 2-19 | 10.5 | +19.00 | October | 2-49 | 4.1 | -11.00 |
| November | 1-13 | 7.7 | +4.00 | November | 2-28 | 7.1 | -0.25 |
| December | 2-6 | 33.3 | +6.25 | December | 4-18 | 22.2 | +1.25 |

### DISTANCE

| 2-y-o | W-R | Per cent | £1 Level Stake | 3-y-o | W-R | Per cent | £1 Level Stake |
|---|---|---|---|---|---|---|---|
| 5f-6f | 9-59 | 15.3 | -17.23 | 5f-6f | 9-46 | 19.6 | -17.79 |
| 7f-8f | 3-29 | 10.3 | +3.00 | 7f-8f | 6-60 | 10.0 | -25.29 |
| 9f-13f | 0-0 | 0.0 | 0.00 | 9f-13f | 1-14 | 7.1 | -12.39 |
| 14f+ | 0-0 | 0.0 | 0.00 | 14f+ | 0-0 | 0.0 | 0.00 |

| 4-y-o | W-R | Per cent | £1 Level Stake | Totals | W-R | Per cent | £1 Level Stake |
|---|---|---|---|---|---|---|---|
| 5f-6f | 21-140 | 15.0 | +40.32 | 5f-6f | 39-245 | 15.9 | +5.30 |
| 7f-8f | 12-84 | 14.3 | -8.38 | 7f-8f | 21-173 | 12.1 | -30.67 |
| 9f-13f | 1-15 | 6.7 | +19.00 | 9f-13f | 2-29 | 6.9 | +6.61 |
| 14f+ | 0-4 | 0.0 | -4.00 | 14f+ | 0-4 | 0.0 | -4.00 |

### TYPE OF RACE

| Non-Handicaps | W-R | Per cent | £1 Level Stake | Handicaps | W-R | Per cent | £1 Level Stake |
|---|---|---|---|---|---|---|---|
| 2-y-o | 10-69 | 14.5 | -14.73 | 2-y-o | 2-19 | 10.5 | +0.50 |
| 3-y-o | 7-47 | 14.9 | -22.93 | 3-y-o | 9-73 | 12.3 | -32.54 |
| 4-y-o+ | 5-46 | 10.9 | +25.00 | 4-y-o+ | 29-197 | 14.7 | +36.07 |

### RACE CLASS / FIRST TIME OUT

| | W-R | Per cent | £1 Level Stake | | W-R | Per cent | £1 Level Stake |
|---|---|---|---|---|---|---|---|
| Class 1 | 1-35 | 2.9 | -25.00 | 2-y-o | 2-25 | 8.0 | -18.00 |
| Class 2 | 5-30 | 16.7 | -8.76 | 3-y-o | 4-25 | 16.0 | -9.92 |
| Class 3 | 4-43 | 9.3 | +13.50 | 4-y-o+ | 7-42 | 16.7 | -1.50 |
| Class 4 | 11-87 | 12.6 | -19.88 | | | | |
| Class 5 | 24-160 | 15.0 | -48.62 | Totals | 13-92 | 14.1 | -29.42 |
| Class 6 | 17-91 | 18.7 | +71.00 | | | | |
| Class 7 | 0-5 | 0.0 | -5.00 | | | | |

# TOP TRAINERS: 2010

| Trainer | WINS-RUNS | %WINS | 2nd | 3rd | 4th | WIN £ | TOTAL £ | £1 STKE |
|---|---|---|---|---|---|---|---|---|
| Sir Michael Stoute | 68-410 | 17% | 73 | 56 | 52 | £2,232,303 | £2,980,338 | -108.89 |
| Richard Hannon | 166-1080 | 15% | 157 | 112 | 102 | £1,850,077 | £2,934,426 | -159.96 |
| Aidan O'Brien | 7-89 | 8% | 16 | 6 | 11 | £1,283,570 | £2,821,567 | -60.92 |
| Henry Cecil | 50-243 | 21% | 39 | 29 | 31 | £1,567,008 | £2,166,767 | -30.14 |
| Mark Johnston | 145-1095 | 13% | 115 | 126 | 108 | £1,424,959 | £2,072,205 | -275.79 |
| Richard Fahey | 143-1088 | 13% | 114 | 121 | 121 | £1,225,735 | £1,928,489 | -261.14 |
| Saeed Bin Suroor | 62-326 | 19% | 48 | 35 | 34 | £1,230,291 | £1,865,143 | -43.32 |
| John Gosden | 74-384 | 19% | 58 | 50 | 43 | £1,018,447 | £1,587,440 | +5.53 |
| Barry Hills | 65-459 | 14% | 72 | 47 | 53 | £840,886 | £1,432,868 | -88.56 |
| Mick Channon | 90-814 | 11% | 106 | 100 | 104 | £565,430 | £1,221,684 | -173.98 |
| Michael Jarvis | 64-283 | 23% | 51 | 38 | 25 | £695,877 | £1,163,966 | -8.94 |
| William Haggas | 46-279 | 16% | 36 | 25 | 25 | £882,458 | £1,099,565 | -62.73 |
| Brian Meehan | 60-453 | 13% | 40 | 40 | 53 | £628,336 | £1,067,125 | -35.00 |
| Andrew Balding | 50-376 | 13% | 39 | 51 | 39 | £593,085 | £969,907 | -13.67 |
| David Nicholls | 62-492 | 13% | 39 | 51 | 54 | £627,447 | £875,276 | -61.62 |
| Luca Cumani | 53-253 | 21% | 24 | 28 | 12 | £610,591 | £870,645 | +36.19 |
| Tim Easterby | 88-795 | 11% | 104 | 93 | 89 | £495,399 | £838,385 | -259.21 |
| Michael Bell | 38-313 | 12% | 48 | 42 | 22 | £473,189 | £759,001 | -88.69 |
| Jeremy Noseda | 40-242 | 17% | 34 | 30 | 32 | £377,112 | £707,031 | -79.55 |
| Kevin Ryan | 66-581 | 11% | 59 | 61 | 59 | £352,496 | £642,303 | -137.58 |
| Mahmood Al Zarooni | 34-234 | 15% | 36 | 43 | 21 | £264,756 | £593,153 | -23.20 |
| David Simcock | 33-265 | 12% | 40 | 38 | 36 | £354,774 | £588,858 | -59.07 |
| Ed Dunlop | 19-224 | 8% | 32 | 20 | 26 | £333,677 | £566,230 | -116.89 |
| Clive Cox | 18-240 | 8% | 33 | 37 | 27 | £283,738 | £528,139 | -36.29 |
| Henry Candy | 23-163 | 14% | 25 | 26 | 21 | £278,599 | £477,525 | -21.19 |
| John Dunlop | 37-301 | 12% | 33 | 27 | 28 | £330,560 | £471,776 | -63.99 |
| Ralph Beckett | 44-283 | 16% | 26 | 38 | 26 | £330,955 | £453,147 | +84.11 |
| Roger Charlton | 40-195 | 21% | 17 | 15 | 23 | £327,856 | £451,615 | +53.85 |
| Clive Brittain | 21-202 | 10% | 13 | 20 | 18 | £293,547 | £429,384 | +0.08 |
| Sir Mark Prescott | 39-148 | 26% | 25 | 21 | 14 | £323,092 | £427,639 | -7.86 |
| Paul Cole | 25-289 | 9% | 39 | 37 | 26 | £204,513 | £416,481 | -70.75 |
| Jim Goldie | 34-403 | 8% | 37 | 43 | 48 | £210,159 | £397,782 | -191.50 |
| Chris Wall | 25-192 | 13% | 28 | 20 | 27 | £259,173 | £395,963 | -13.48 |
| James Fanshawe | 15-131 | 11% | 24 | 18 | 8 | £121,951 | £380,316 | -43.33 |
| Hughie Morrison | 31-251 | 12% | 27 | 22 | 30 | £150,824 | £371,687 | -53.22 |
| David Barron | 34-250 | 14% | 26 | 25 | 25 | £250,593 | £368,227 | +30.53 |
| Bryan Smart | 41-319 | 13% | 24 | 36 | 35 | £204,315 | £357,518 | -46.66 |
| Michael Dods | 32-311 | 10% | 29 | 38 | 32 | £243,957 | £333,700 | -10.75 |
| Ed McMahon | 21-120 | 18% | 13 | 16 | 10 | £271,151 | £332,328 | -12.85 |
| Andre Fabre | 1-2 | 50% | 0 | 1 | 0 | £255,465 | £330,155 | +1.50 |
| David Evans | 45-568 | 8% | 54 | 65 | 45 | £186,162 | £316,477 | -180.89 |
| Walter Swinburn | 33-257 | 13% | 24 | 40 | 24 | £223,584 | £310,988 | -38.04 |
| David Elsworth | 19-170 | 11% | 24 | 20 | 17 | £179,888 | £307,146 | -28.13 |
| Alan Swinbank | 42-273 | 15% | 26 | 28 | 25 | £172,334 | £276,682 | +10.18 |
| William Knight | 22-157 | 14% | 16 | 20 | 20 | £174,295 | £259,169 | +57.60 |
| Tom Tate | 19-173 | 11% | 17 | 23 | 11 | £123,969 | £253,611 | -58.50 |
| James Given | 23-272 | 8% | 34 | 22 | 39 | £160,473 | £240,195 | -106.17 |
| Mikael Delzangles | 1-6 | 17% | 0 | 0 | 0 | £227,080 | £234,276 | +28.00 |
| Criquette Head-Maarek | 1-3 | 33% | 0 | 0 | 0 | £227,080 | £227,080 | +2.50 |
| Mark Tompkins | 19-239 | 8% | 19 | 22 | 33 | £158,283 | £222,657 | -81.79 |

*Figures for March 27 - November 6, 2010*

## TOP JOCKEYS: 2010

| Jockey | WINS-RUNS | %WINS | 2nd | 3rd | 4th | WIN £ | TOTAL £ | £1 STKE |
|---|---|---|---|---|---|---|---|---|
| Paul Hanagan | 205–1214 | 17% | 139 | 144 | 157 | £1,334,122 | £1,846,556 | -172.58 |
| Richard Hughes | 192–1098 | 17% | 171 | 123 | 113 | £2,087,294 | £3,169,420 | -231.26 |
| Kieren Fallon | 140–821 | 17% | 96 | 104 | 74 | £1,551,075 | £2,588,957 | -99.39 |
| Ryan Moore | 138–784 | 18% | 139 | 98 | 86 | £2,533,604 | £3,928,871 | -138.94 |
| Frankie Dettori | 123–541 | 23% | 73 | 70 | 57 | £2,283,288 | £3,205,484 | -66.94 |
| Joe Fanning | 120–895 | 13% | 109 | 95 | 105 | £523,442 | £921,934 | -200.22 |
| Jamie Spencer | 107–691 | 15% | 99 | 96 | 69 | £994,746 | £1,609,577 | -66.52 |
| Neil Callan | 106–822 | 13% | 106 | 91 | 96 | £511,531 | £970,896 | -223.52 |
| Seb Sanders | 102–759 | 13% | 80 | 90 | 71 | £599,862 | £868,259 | -255.37 |
| Jim Crowley | 101–857 | 12% | 92 | 82 | 95 | £717,148 | £970,334 | -58.02 |
| Tom Queally | 101–797 | 13% | 94 | 74 | 97 | £1,991,069 | £2,747,565 | +39.48 |
| George Baker | 101–677 | 15% | 88 | 64 | 56 | £387,250 | £636,099 | -110.31 |
| S De Sousa | 100–626 | 16% | 68 | 84 | 62 | £527,258 | £736,480 | -4.91 |
| William Buick | 99–584 | 17% | 78 | 64 | 61 | £1,237,628 | £1,830,623 | +5.28 |
| Steve Drowne | 96–787 | 12% | 72 | 79 | 78 | £431,203 | £717,836 | -174.46 |
| G Gibbons | 94–741 | 13% | 90 | 73 | 73 | £370,610 | £579,014 | +52.23 |
| Liam Keniry | 89–879 | 10% | 86 | 89 | 96 | £265,799 | £461,164 | -184.76 |
| Ted Durcan | 88–567 | 16% | 67 | 61 | 65 | £483,536 | £741,534 | -99.07 |
| Robert Winston | 86–744 | 12% | 102 | 79 | 92 | £449,767 | £717,746 | -256.78 |
| Tom Eaves | 81–906 | 9% | 71 | 86 | 95 | £376,674 | £623,254 | -234.75 |
| Chris Catlin | 80–1001 | 8% | 102 | 84 | 98 | £301,021 | £555,526 | -305.82 |
| Dane O'Neill | 80–856 | 9% | 109 | 87 | 108 | £370,639 | £693,021 | -162.45 |
| Jimmy Quinn | 77–894 | 9% | 81 | 95 | 112 | £313,662 | £549,510 | -276.73 |
| David Probert | 77–778 | 10% | 76 | 87 | 93 | £402,413 | £635,121 | -152.57 |
| Jimmy Fortune | 77–612 | 13% | 60 | 72 | 69 | £456,601 | £1,016,962 | -148.31 |
| P J McDonald | 76–647 | 12% | 58 | 62 | 75 | £271,904 | £421,186 | -29.26 |
| Phillip Makin | 75–769 | 10% | 74 | 109 | 104 | £417,143 | £614,435 | -208.11 |
| Shane Kelly | 74–685 | 11% | 84 | 84 | 75 | £282,844 | £482,669 | -177.95 |
| Adam Kirby | 73–636 | 11% | 64 | 83 | 64 | £329,606 | £548,528 | -124.51 |
| Hayley Turner | 72–752 | 10% | 91 | 80 | 62 | £400,579 | £665,860 | -279.56 |
| David Allan | 72–536 | 13% | 69 | 63 | 50 | £375,108 | £594,988 | -95.86 |
| Paul Mulrennan | 69–712 | 10% | 65 | 76 | 88 | £300,386 | £517,529 | -158.17 |
| Martin Dwyer | 68–478 | 14% | 60 | 47 | 45 | £403,381 | £738,150 | +138.55 |
| Luke Morris | 67–1000 | 7% | 103 | 122 | 98 | £286,111 | £499,385 | -252.57 |
| Eddie Ahern | 67–612 | 11% | 77 | 75 | 76 | £632,652 | £1,055,161 | -187.05 |
| Barry McHugh | 60–540 | 11% | 65 | 49 | 56 | £226,883 | £360,604 | -105.86 |
| Adrian Nicholls | 60–378 | 16% | 29 | 34 | 35 | £340,345 | £509,051 | -81.79 |
| Cathy Gannon | 59–607 | 10% | 58 | 57 | 67 | £166,139 | £261,993 | -70.39 |
| Kieren Fox | 58–541 | 11% | 70 | 60 | 57 | £160,625 | £246,233 | -29.16 |
| Fergus Sweeney | 57–683 | 8% | 60 | 72 | 78 | £214,576 | £357,225 | -103.27 |
| Richard Hills | 57–394 | 14% | 59 | 50 | 42 | £602,917 | £1,147,960 | -109.62 |
| Franny Norton | 55–626 | 9% | 66 | 59 | 67 | £298,533 | £474,399 | -61.72 |
| Ian Mongan | 55–441 | 12% | 43 | 62 | 39 | £268,767 | £363,080 | +100.98 |
| Greg Fairley | 54–486 | 11% | 59 | 56 | 49 | £270,265 | £436,728 | -143.51 |
| Stevie Donohoe | 53–475 | 11% | 48 | 38 | 37 | £176,467 | £262,535 | -85.07 |
| Pat Cosgrave | 52–496 | 10% | 47 | 44 | 43 | £371,327 | £627,268 | +20.26 |
| Martin Lane | 52–465 | 11% | 45 | 32 | 37 | £291,947 | £412,902 | -28.52 |
| William Carson | 51–498 | 10% | 49 | 54 | 42 | £123,038 | £251,030 | -64.97 |
| Pat Dobbs | 49–425 | 12% | 56 | 50 | 42 | £213,281 | £352,379 | -93.02 |
| Jack Mitchell | 49–380 | 13% | 47 | 36 | 35 | £225,753 | £346,433 | +13.10 |

*Figures for March 27 - November 6, 2010*

# TOP OWNERS: 2010

| Owner | WINS-RUNS | %WINS | 2nd | 3rd | 4th | WIN £ | TOTAL £ |
|---|---|---|---|---|---|---|---|
| Khalid Abdulla | 74–341 | 22% | 69 | 36 | 41 | £3,054,270 | £3,860,917 |
| Godolphin | 133–687 | 19% | 106 | 95 | 68 | £1,686,131 | £2,712,390 |
| Hamdan Bin Moh'med Al Maktoum | 108 692 | 16% | 89 | 81 | 68 | £1,047,811 | £1,472,816 |
| Hamdan Al Maktoum | 97–607 | 16% | 82 | 82 | 62 | £750,313 | £1,468,875 |
| Cheveley Park Stud | 36–199 | 18% | 30 | 22 | 31 | £745,282 | £979,065 |
| D Smith, Mrs J Magnier, M Tabor | 4–30 | 13% | 5 | 3 | 3 | £288,150 | £947,832 |
| Dr Marwan Koukash | 45–381 | 12% | 43 | 53 | 40 | £489,242 | £720,000 |
| Highclere (Adm. Rous) | 4–4 | 100% | 0 | 0 | 0 | £718,141 | £718,141 |
| Jaber Abdullah | 30–213 | 14% | 29 | 30 | 31 | £328,305 | £613,784 |
| Mrs J Magnier, M Tabor & D Smith | 4–27 | 15% | 2 | 2 | 3 | £445,420 | £595,436 |
| Tabor/Smith/Magnier/Massey | 2–5 | 40% | 1 | 0 | 0 | £482,545 | £544,645 |
| Saeed Manana | 41–296 | 14% | 24 | 31 | 28 | £363,020 | £530,386 |
| Sheikh Ahmed Al Maktoum | 43–140 | 31% | 19 | 12 | 17 | £393,811 | £506,564 |
| J C Smith | 29–182 | 16% | 29 | 19 | 18 | £222,303 | £441,032 |
| Mrs J Wood | 25–113 | 22% | 11 | 11 | 12 | £317,434 | £413,759 |
| Heffer Synd/Mrs Roy/Mrs Instance | 2–4 | 50% | 1 | 1 | 0 | £321,602 | £378,670 |
| Mrs Fitri Hay | 27–171 | 16% | 24 | 26 | 18 | £191,510 | £375,969 |
| M Tabor, D Smith & Mrs J Magnier | 2–19 | 11% | 3 | 1 | 6 | £171,729 | £368,940 |
| H R H Princess Haya Of Jordan | 36–185 | 19% | 19 | 22 | 17 | £223,742 | £351,320 |
| J Acheson | 5–22 | 23% | 4 | 3 | 0 | £237,556 | £350,502 |
| Frank Brady & The Cosmic Cases | 4–4 | 100% | 0 | 0 | 0 | £347,463 | £347,463 |
| Anamoine Limited | 2–10 | 20% | 3 | 0 | 1 | £231,823 | £326,594 |
| A D Spence | 16–142 | 11% | 15 | 13 | 13 | £211,774 | £324,544 |
| Rachel Hood and Robin Geffen | 1–2 | 50% | 0 | 1 | 0 | £283,850 | £291,389 |
| John Fretwell | 21–71 | 30% | 9 | 8 | 3 | £242,097 | £266,558 |
| Mrs R J Jacobs | 11–55 | 20% | 15 | 7 | 4 | £185,623 | £264,428 |
| Khalifa Dasmal | 8–82 | 10% | 8 | 6 | 13 | £183,399 | £245,309 |
| Tight Lines Partnership | 2–4 | 50% | 1 | 0 | 0 | £175,026 | £240,396 |
| The Queen | 13–108 | 12% | 24 | 10 | 12 | £103,700 | £237,487 |
| Mathieu Offenstadt | 1–3 | 33% | 0 | 0 | 0 | £227,080 | £234,276 |
| Sir Robert Ogden | 11–54 | 20% | 7 | 9 | 5 | £201,258 | £233,278 |
| The Calvera Partnership No 2 | 2–10 | 20% | 2 | 1 | 1 | £170,310 | £225,123 |
| Reg Bond | 16–110 | 15% | 13 | 15 | 11 | £183,647 | £221,782 |
| R J Arculli | 7–52 | 13% | 12 | 7 | 7 | £101,406 | £221,754 |
| Normandie Stud Ltd | 8–50 | 16% | 6 | 10 | 7 | £112,665 | £218,640 |
| M Channon | 12–124 | 10% | 15 | 14 | 16 | £40,959 | £209,959 |
| Shkh Sultan Bin Khalifa Al Nahyan | 9–64 | 14% | 15 | 9 | 4 | £152,900 | £206,651 |
| Ballymacoll Stud | 9–56 | 16% | 6 | 6 | 5 | £104,047 | £203,727 |
| Pearl Bloodstock Ltd | 10–39 | 26% | 7 | 2 | 3 | £132,128 | £197,888 |
| Highclere (Bahram) | 3–8 | 38% | 1 | 2 | 2 | £145,751 | £197,746 |
| John Manley | 1–12 | 8% | 2 | 0 | 1 | £36,901 | £195,820 |
| H R H Sultan Ahmad Shah | 6–72 | 8% | 8 | 6 | 6 | £53,004 | £188,091 |
| Shkh Moh'med Obaid Al Maktoum | 8–26 | 31% | 5 | 3 | 1 | £153,928 | £187,909 |
| Peter Harris | 19–133 | 14% | 14 | 24 | 13 | £129,891 | £184,322 |
| Jim McGrath | 8–42 | 19% | 5 | 8 | 0 | £83,844 | £177,673 |
| Magnier/Tabor/Smith/Denford Stud | 0–3 | — | 2 | 0 | 0 | £0 | £175,531 |
| M B Hawtin | 5–17 | 29% | 4 | 2 | 0 | £134,232 | £174,328 |
| Dab Hand Racing | 5–31 | 16% | 2 | 2 | 2 | £132,242 | £172,178 |
| Fittocks Stud | 11–25 | 44% | 2 | 4 | 2 | £160,573 | £168,096 |
| Malih Lahej Al Basti | 15–71 | 21% | 6 | 8 | 6 | £134,058 | £165,645 |

*Figures for March 27 - November 6, 2010*

# Guide to the Flat 2011

## FLAT FIXTURES: APRIL

| | | |
|---|---|---|
| 1 | Fri | Musselburgh, Wolverhampton (AW) |
| 2 | Sat | Doncaster, Kempton (AW) |
| 3 | Sun | Doncaster |
| 4 | Mon | Folkestone, Windsor |
| 5 | Tue | Kempton (AW), Pontefract |
| 6 | Wed | Beverley, Kempton (AW), Lingfield (AW), Nottingham |
| 7 | Thu | Kempton (AW), Ripon |
| 8 | Fri | Newcastle, Wolverhampton (AW) |
| 9 | Sat | Lingfield (AW), Thirsk, Wolverhampton (AW)* |
| 11 | Mon | Windsor*, Wolverhampton (AW) |
| 12 | Tue | Folkestone, Southwell (AW), Wolverhampton (AW) |
| 13 | Wed | Catterick, Kempton (AW)*, Newmarket |
| 14 | Thu | Beverley, Kempton (AW)*, Newmarket |
| 15 | Fri | Brighton*, Newbury, Wolverhampton (AW) |
| 16 | Sat | Doncaster*, Haydock*, Leicester, Newbury, Ripon |
| 18 | Mon | Redcar, Windsor* |
| 19 | Tue | Bath*, Pontefract, Southwell (AW), Wolverhampton (AW)* |
| 20 | Wed | Epsom, Kempton (AW)*, Newcastle*, Southwell (AW) |
| 21 | Thu | Folkestone |
| 23 | Sat | Musselburgh, Nottingham*, Sandown |
| 24 | Sun | Musselburgh, Sandown |
| 25 | Mon | Redcar, Warwick, Yarmouth |
| 26 | Tue | Lingfield (AW), Wolverhampton(AW)*, Yarmouth |
| 27 | Wed | Ascot, Kempton (AW)*, Newcastle*, Pontefract |
| 28 | Thu | Bath, Brighton* |
| 29 | Fri | Doncaster, Leicester |
| 30 | Sat | Doncaster*, Goodwood, Newmarket, Thirsk |

## MAY

| | | |
|---|---|---|
| 1 | Sun | Hamilton, Newmarket, Salisbury |
| 2 | Mon | Beverley, Chepstow, Kempton (AW), Warwick, Windsor |
| 3 | Tue | Bath, Catterick*, Newcastle |
| 4 | Wed | Chester, Southwell (AW) |
| 5 | Thu | Chester, Goodwood, Ffos Las* |
| 6 | Fri | Ascot*, Chester, Hamilton*, Lingfield, Nottingham, Ripon* |
| 7 | Sat | Ascot, Haydock, Lingfield, Nottingham, Thirsk*, Warwick* |
| 9 | Mon | Brighton, Redcar, Windsor*, Wolverhampton (AW) |
| 10 | Tue | Beverley, Southwell (AW)*, Warwick, Yarmouth |
| 11 | Wed | Kempton (AW)*, York |
| 12 | Thu | Newmarket*, Salisbury, York |
| 13 | Fri | Hamilton*, Newbury, Newcastle*, Newmarket, York |
| 14 | Sat | Doncaster*, Newbury, Newmarket, Thirsk |
| 15 | Sun | Ripon |
| 16 | Mon | Bath, Leicester*, Windsor* Wolverhampton (AW) |
| 17 | Tue | Brighton, Kempton (AW)*, Nottingham |
| 18 | Wed | Goodwood, Kempton (AW), Lingfield |
| 19 | Thu | Haydock, Salisbury* Sandown*, Southwell (AW) |
| 20 | Fri | Bath, Catterick*, Musselburgh*, Haydock, Yarmouth |
| 21 | Sat | Chester, Goodwood, Haydock, Lingfield*, Newbury*, York |
| 23 | Mon | Carlisle, Leicester, Thirsk*, Windsor* |
| 24 | Tue | Chepstow, Lingfield (AW), Ripon |
| 25 | Wed | Ayr, Beverley* |
| 26 | Thu | Ayr, Brighton, Folkestone, Newcastle*, Sandown* |
| 27 | Fri | Brighton, Haydock*, Newcastle, Newmarket, Pontefract* |
| 28 | Sat | Beverley, Catterick, Haydock, Newmarket |
| 29 | Sun | Nottingham |
| 30 | Mon | Carlisle, Chepstow, Goodwood, Leicester, Redcar |
| 31 | Tue | Leicester, Redcar, Yarmouth |

## JUNE

| | | |
|---|---|---|
| 1 | Wed | Kempton (AW)*, Nottingham, Ripon* |
| 2 | Thu | Hamilton, Lingfield, Sandown*, Southwell (AW) |
| 3 | Fri | Bath*, Catterick, Doncaster*, Musselburgh, Epsom, Goodwood* |
| 4 | Sat | Doncaster, Musselburgh, Epsom, Lingfield*, Newcastle* |
| 6 | Mon | Folkestone, Pontefract*, Windsor* |
| 7 | Tue | Redcar, Salisbury |
| 8 | Wed | Beverley, Hamilton*, Haydock, Kempton (AW)*, Yarmouth |
| 9 | Thu | Haydock*, Newbury, Nottingham, Yarmouth |
| 10 | Fri | Chepstow*, Goodwood*, Sandown, York |
| 11 | Sat | Bath, Chester, Leicester*, Lingfield*, Sandown, York |
| 12 | Sun | Doncaster, Salisbury |
| 13 | Mon | Carlisle, Warwick*, Windsor* |
| 14 | Tue | Ascot, Brighton*, Thirsk |
| 15 | Wed | Ascot, Hamilton, Kempton (AW)*, Ripon* |
| 16 | Thu | Ascot, Beverley*, Leicester*, Ripon, Warwick |
| 17 | Fri | Ascot, Ayr*, Musselburgh, Goodwood*, Newmarket*, Redcar |
| 18 | Sat | Ascot, Ayr, Haydock*, Lingfield*, Newmarket, Redcar |
| 19 | Sun | Pontefract |
| 20 | Mon | Chepstow*, Kempton (AW), Windsor*, Wolverhampton (AW) |
| 21 | Tue | Beverley, Brighton, Newbury* |
| 22 | Wed | Bath*, Carlisle, Kempton (AW)*, Salisbury |
| 23 | Thu | Hamilton*, Leicester*, Newcastle, Warwick |
| 24 | Fri | Chester*, Doncaster, Folkestone, Newcastle*, Newmarket* |
| 25 | Sat | Chester, Doncaster*, Lingfield*, Newcastle, Newmarket, Windsor |
| 26 | Sun | Salisbury, Windsor |
| 27 | Mon | Musselburgh*, Pontefract, Windsor*, Wolverhampton (AW) |
| 28 | Tue | Brighton, Hamilton, Southwell (AW)* |
| 29 | Wed | Catterick, Chepstow*, Kempton (AW)* |
| 30 | Thu | Epsom, Haydock, Newbury*, Yarmouth |

## JULY

| | | |
|---|---|---|
| 1 | Fri | Beverley*, Doncaster, Haydock*, Sandown, Warwick |

# Fixtures

| 2 | Sat | Beverley, Carlisle*, Haydock, Leicester, Nottingham*, Sandown |
|---|---|---|
| 3 | Sun | Ayr |
| 4 | Mon | Brighton, Ripon*, Windsor* |
| 5 | Tue | Pontefract, Southwell (AW)*, Wolverhampton (AW) |
| 6 | Wed | Bath, Catterick, Kempton (AW)*, Lingfield |
| 7 | Thu | Doncaster*, Epsom*, Folkestone, Newmarket, Warwick |
| 8 | Fri | Ascot, Chepstow*, Chester*, Newbury*, Newmarket, York |
| 9 | Sat | Ascot, Chester, Hamilton*, Newmarket, Salisbury*, York |
| 11 | Mon | Ayr, Windsor*, Wolverhampton(AW)*, Ffos Las |
| 12 | Tue | Beverley, Brighton, Southwell (AW)*, Yarmouth |
| 13 | Wed | Catterick, Lingfield, Sandown* |
| 14 | Thu | Bath*, Doncaster*, Epsom* Hamilton, Leicester |
| 15 | Fri | Hamilton*, Haydock, Newbury, Newmarket*, Nottingham, Pontefract* |
| 16 | Sat | Haydock*, Lingfield*, Newbury, Newmarket, Ripon |
| 17 | Sun | Redcar |
| 18 | Mon | Ayr, Beverley*, Windsor*, Yarmouth |
| 19 | Tue | Musselburgh, Southwell (AW)*, Yarmouth |
| 20 | Wed | Catterick, Leicester*, Lingfield (AW), Sandown* |
| 21 | Thu | Bath, Doncaster*, Epsom*, Folkestone*, Sandown |
| 22 | Fri | Ascot, Chepstow*, Newmarket*, Thirsk, York* |
| 23 | Sat | Ascot, Lingfield*, Newcastle, Newmarket, Salisbury*, York |
| 24 | Sun | Ascot, Carlisle, Pontefract |
| 25 | Mon | Ayr, Windsor*, Yarmouth |
| 26 | Tue | Beverley, Goodwood |
| 27 | Wed | Goodwood, Leicester*, Redcar, Sandown* |
| 28 | Thu | Epsom*, Goodwood, Nottingham, Ffos Las* |
| 29 | Fri | Bath*, Musselburgh*, Goodwood, Newmarket*, Thirsk |
| 30 | Sat | Doncaster, Goodwood, Hamilton*, Lingfield*, Newmarket, Thirsk |
| 31 | Sun | Chester, Newbury |

## AUGUST

| 1 | Mon | Carlisle*, Ripon, Windsor* |
|---|---|---|
| 2 | Tue | Bath, Catterick, Southwell (AW)*, Ffos Las* |
| 3 | Wed | Brighton, Kempton (AW)*, Newcastle, Pontefract, Yarmouth* |
| 4 | Thu | Brighton, Chepstow*, Folkestone*, Haydock, Sandown*, Yarmouth |
| 5 | Fri | Brighton, Haydock*, Lingfield (AW), Newmarket* |
| 6 | Sat | Ascot, Ayr*, Haydock, Lingfield*, Newmarket, Redcar |
| 7 | Sun | Leicester, Windsor |
| 8 | Mon | Lingfield, Thirsk*, Windsor*, Wolverhampton (AW) |
| 9 | Tue | Ayr, Nottingham*, Ffos Las* |
| 10 | Wed | Beverley, Kempton (AW)*, Salisbury, Wolverhampton (AW)*, Yarmouth |
| 11 | Thu | Beverley, Chepstow*, Goodwood*, Newmarket, Salisbury |
| 12 | Fri | Catterick*, Kempton (AW)*, Newbury, Newcastle, Newmarket*, Nottingham |
| 13 | Sat | Doncaster, Lingfield*, Newbury, Newmarket, Ripon |
| 14 | Sun | Pontefract |
| 15 | Mon | Kempton (AW), Thirsk, Windsor*, Yarmouth* |
| 16 | Tue | Brighton, Musselburgh, Kempton (AW)* |
| 17 | Wed | Carlisle, Folkestone*, Nottingham, York |
| 18 | Thu | Epsom*, Hamilton |
| 18 | Thu | Southwell (AW)*, York |
| 19 | Fri | Salisbury*, Sandown, Wolverhampton (AW)*, York |
| 20 | Sat | Bath*, Chester, Sandown, York |
| 21 | Sun | Folkestone |
| 22 | Mon | Hamilton, Kempton (AW), Windsor* |
| 23 | Tue | Leicester, Warwick*, Yarmouth* |
| 24 | Wed | Catterick, Chepstow, Kempton (AW)*, Wolverhampton (AW)* |
| 25 | Thu | Carlisle, Lingfield, Wolverhampton (AW)* |
| 26 | Fri | Brighton*, Ffos Las, Hamilton*, Newcastle*, Newmarket, Thirsk |
| 27 | Sat | Beverley, Goodwood, Newmarket, Redcar*, Windsor* |
| 28 | Sun | Beverley, Goodwood, Yarmouth |
| 29 | Mon | Chepstow, Epsom, Newcastle |
| 29 | Mon | Ripon, Warwick |
| 30 | Tue | Epsom, Goodwood, Ripon, Southwell (AW)*, Wolverhampton (AW)* |
| 31 | Wed | Bath, Carlisle*, Folkestone, Kempton (AW)* |

## SEPTEMBER

| 1 | Thu | Kempton (AW), Redcar, Salisbury |
|---|---|---|
| 2 | Fri | Brighton, Chepstow, Haydock, Kempton (AW)* |
| 3 | Sat | Ascot, Musselburgh, Haydock, Kempton (AW), Thirsk, Wolverhampton (AW)* |
| 4 | Sun | York |
| 5 | Mon | Bath, Newcastle |
| 6 | Tue | Leicester, Lingfield |
| 7 | Wed | Carlisle, Doncaster, Kempton (AW) |
| 8 | Thu | Chepstow, Doncaster, Epsom, Wolverhampton (AW) |
| 9 | Fri | Chester, Doncaster, Sandown, Wolverhampton (AW) |
| 10 | Sat | Bath, Chester, Doncaster, Goodwood, Kempton (AW) |
| 11 | Sun | Goodwood, Ffos Las |
| 12 | Mon | Brighton, Musselburgh, Kempton (AW) |
| 13 | Tue | Folkestone, Haydock, Yarmouth |
| 14 | Wed | Beverley, Kempton (AW), Sandown, Yarmouth |
| 15 | Thu | Ayr, Kempton (AW), Pontefract, Yarmouth |
| 16 | Fri | Ayr, Lingfield, Newbury, Wolverhampton (AW) |
| 17 | Sat | Ayr, Catterick, Newbury, Newmarket, Wolverhampton (AW)* |
| 18 | Sun | Hamilton |
| 19 | Mon | Hamilton, Kempton (AW), Leicester |
| 20 | Tue | Beverley, Folkestone |
| 21 | Wed | Goodwood, Kempton (AW), Redcar |
| 22 | Thu | Newmarket, Pontefract, Wolverhampton (AW) |
| 23 | Fri | Haydock, Newmarket, Wolverhampton (AW) |

racingpost.com

| | | |
|---|---|---|
| 24 | Sat | Chester, Haydock, Newmarket, Ripon, Wolverhampton (AW) |
| 25 | Sun | Musselburgh, Epsom |
| 26 | Mon | Bath, Hamilton, Ffos Las |
| 27 | Tue | Ayr, Chepstow |
| 28 | Wed | Kempton (AW), Newcastle, Nottingham, Salisbury |
| 29 | Thu | Kempton (AW), Warwick, Wolverhampton (AW) |
| 30 | Fri | Ascot, Wolverhampton (AW) |

## OCTOBER

| | | |
|---|---|---|
| 1 | Sat | Ascot, Newmarket, Redcar , Wolverhampton (AW)* |
| 3 | Mon | Pontefract, Warwick, Windsor |
| 4 | Tue | Catterick, Leicester, Southwell (AW) |
| 5 | Wed | Kempton (AW), Nottingham |
| 6 | Thu | Ayr, Wolverhampton (AW) |
| 7 | Fri | Wolverhampton(AW), York |
| 8 | Sat | Newmarket, Wolverhampton(AW), York |
| 9 | Sun | Goodwood |
| 10 | Mon | Salisbury, Windsor, Yarmouth |
| 11 | Tue | Leicester, Newcastle |
| 12 | Wed | Kempton (AW), Lingfield (AW), Nottingham |
| 13 | Thu | Brighton, Kempton (AW) |
| 14 | Fri | Haydock, Redcar, Wolverhampton (AW) |
| 15 | Sat | Ascot, Catterick, Wolverhampton (AW)* |
| 16 | Sun | Bath |
| 17 | Mon | Pontefract, Windsor |
| 18 | Tue | Lingfield (AW), Yarmouth |
| 19 | Wed | Kempton (AW) |
| 19 | Wed | Newmarket |
| 20 | Thu | Brighton |
| 20 | Thu | Wolverhampton (AW) |
| 21 | Fri | Doncaster, Newbury, Wolverhampton (AW) |
| 22 | Sat | Doncaster, Newbury, Wolverhampton (AW) |
| 24 | Mon | Leicester, Redcar, Southwell (AW) |
| 25 | Tue | Catterick, Yarmouth |
| 26 | Wed | Musselburgh, Kempton (AW), Nottingham |
| 27 | Thu | Kempton (AW), Lingfield (AW) |
| 28 | Fri | Newmarket, Wolverhampton (AW) |
| 29 | Sat | Ayr, Newmarket, Wolverhampton (AW)* |
| 31 | Mon | Wolverhampton (AW) |

## NOVEMBER

| | | |
|---|---|---|
| 1 | Tue | Kempton (AW), Redcar |
| 2 | Wed | Kempton (AW), Nottingham |
| 3 | Thu | Southwell (AW), Wolverhampton (AW) |
| 4 | Fri | Wolverhampton (AW), Ffos Las |
| 5 | Sat | Doncaster |
| 9 | Wed | Kempton (AW), Southwell (AW) |
| 10 | Thu | Kempton (AW), Southwell (AW) |
| 11 | Fri | Lingfield (AW), Wolverhampton (AW) |
| 12 | Sat | Lingfield (AW), Wolverhampton (AW)* |
| 14 | Mon | Wolverhampton (AW) |
| 15 | Tue | Southwell (AW) |
| 16 | Wed | Kempton (AW), Lingfield (AW) |
| 17 | Thu | Kempton (AW) |
| 18 | Fri | Kempton (AW), Wolverhampton (AW) |
| 19 | Sat | Lingfield (AW), Wolverhampton (AW)* |
| 22 | Tue | Southwell (AW) |
| 23 | Wed | Kempton (AW), Lingfield (AW) |
| 24 | Thu | Kempton (AW) |
| 25 | Fri | Wolverhampton (AW) |
| 26 | Sat | Wolverhampton (AW)* |
| 28 | Mon | Wolverhampton (AW) |
| 29 | Tue | Lingfield (AW) |
| 30 | Wed | Kempton (AW) |

## DECEMBER

| | | |
|---|---|---|
| 1 | Thu | Wolverhampton (AW) |
| 2 | Fri | Lingfield (AW), Wolverhampton (AW) |
| 3 | Sat | Wolverhampton (AW)* |
| 5 | Mon | Lingfield (AW) |
| 6 | Tue | Southwell (AW) |
| 7 | Wed | Kempton (AW), Lingfield (AW) |
| 8 | Thu | Kempton (AW) |
| 9 | Fri | Southwell (AW), Wolverhampton (AW) |
| 10 | Sat | Southwell (AW), Wolverhampton (AW)* |
| 11 | Sun | Southwell (AW) |
| 12 | Mon | Wolverhampton (AW) |
| 13 | Tue | Southwell (AW) |
| 14 | Wed | Kempton (AW), Lingfield (AW) |
| 15 | Thu | Kempton (AW), Southwell (AW) |
| 16 | Fri | Southwell (AW), Wolverhampton (AW) |
| 17 | Sat | Lingfield (AW) |
| 18 | Sun | Kempton (AW) |
| 19 | Mon | Wolverhampton (AW) |
| 20 | Tue | Kempton (AW) |
| 21 | Wed | Kempton (AW), Wolverhampton (AW) |
| 22 | Thu | Southwell (AW) |
| 26 | Mon | Wolverhampton (AW) |
| 27 | Tue | Southwell (AW) |
| 28 | Wed | Lingfield (AW), Wolverhampton (AW) |
| 29 | Thu | Kempton (AW), Southwell (AW) |
| 30 | Fri | Lingfield (AW), Wolverhampton (AW) |
| 31 | Sat | Lingfield (AW) |

*Denotes evening fixture

# INDEX OF HORSES

Abjer 113
Afsare 29, 113
Agony And Ecstasy 4-5
Air Traffic 12
Akdarena 113
Al Kazeem 23, 88
Al Zir 113
Alainmaar 88, 113
Alanza 72
Aldedash 12
Alexandros 113-114
All Time 12
Allied Powers 114
Aneedah 46
Anna Salai 38
Antara 35, 114
Arctic Cosmos 43, 47, 67, 114
Arizona Jewel 12
Arizona Run 78
Art History 54
Ashbrittle 5
Ashram 114
Astrophysical Jet 114
Autumn Blades 80
Aviate 114
Await The Dawn 115
Awzaan 51-52, 115
Azmeel 115

Bajan Tryst 97
Balthazar's Gift 115
Bated Breath 20, 116
Bauer 27
Beachfire 45
Behkabad 77, 116
Bethrah 116
Bewitched 116
Bible Belt 116
Bikini Babe 52, 54, 67
Biondetti 116-117
Blu Constellation 117
Blue Bunting 38, 117
Borderlescott 117
Bourne 28-29, 68
Brevity 117-118
Broox 118
Bullet Train 118
Bushman 118
Buzzword 118
Byword 118

Call To Reason 88
Campanologist 35, 118
Canford Cliffs 119
Cape Blanco 72, 74, 119
Cape Dollar 62, 119
Cape Of Dance 54
Caraboss 62
Carlton House 61-62, 68, 84, 119
Casamento 36, 70, 119
Casual Conquest 119
Caucus 44
Cavalryman 36, 120
Ceilidh House 4
Chabal 120
Charleston Lady 6
Chill 30

Chrysanthemum 120
Circumvent 120
Cirrus Des Aigles 120
Cityscape 20, 23, 66, 120
Claremont 120-121
Class Is Class 121
Clowance 22
Cochabamba 121
Conduct 60
Contredanse 30
Crown Counsel 54
Crown Prosecutor 121
Crystal Capella 60-61, 121
Crystal Etoile 62

Dalghar 121
Dandino 121-122
Dangerous Midge 122
Date With Destiny 122
Dealbata 76
Debussy 122
Deck Walk 23
Definightly 20-21, 23
Delegator 36, 122
Denton 80
Devastation 46, 68
Dick Turpin 122
Diescentric 15
Dinkum Diamond 122
Distant Memories 123
Doncaster Rover 123
Dordogne 53
Dream Ahead 84, 123
Dream Eater 123
Drunken Sailor 28
Dubai Prince 36, 123
Duff 123
Dunboyne Express 72, 124
Duncan 44, 124
Dux Scholar 62, 124

Echo Ridge 6
Elas Diamond 124
Eleanora Duse 61, 124
Electrolyser 124
Elrasheed 86
Elusive Pimpernel 124
Elzaam 125
Emerald Commander 125
Emiyna 86
Encore Une Annee 6-7
English Summer 52
Espirita 125
Exemplary 52
Exemplify 125

Face The Problem 125
Fair Trade 86
Falmouth Bay 53
Fame And Glory 72, 125
Famous Name 125-126
Farhh 38, 68
Federation 23
First Mohican 12
Flash Of Intuition 12
Flood Plain 46-47
Flying Cross 126

Footsteppy 78
Forte Dei Marmi 29, 30, 66, 126
Fox Hunt 52
Frankel 10, 15, 66, 69, 84, 96, 126
French Navy 36, 126
Fulgur 30
Fury 127

Galikova 77, 78
Genki 21-22
Gertrude Bell 45
Gile Na Greine 127
Gitano Hernando 127
Glass Harmonium 127
Glencadam Gold 12
Glor Na Mara 70, 127
Golden Lilac 78
Goldikova 77, 127

Handassa 72, 74, 128
Hanoverian Baron 80-81
Harris Tweed 128
Harrison George 128
Havant 62, 69, 84, 129
Head Space 129
Helleborine 76, 129
Hibaayeb 129
High Constable 22, 88
High Heeled 129
High Standing 130
Hillview Boy 81
History Note 96
Holberg 130
Hoof It 81-82
Hooray 85, 130
Hot Prospect 130
Hot Spice 96
Hung Parliament 130
Hurricane Higgins 53-54, 86

I Love Me 130
Indian Days 130-131
Inler 131
Invent 97
Irish Heartbeat 97
Ishbelle 7
Izzi Top 46

Jacqueline Quest 14, 131
Jan Vermeer 131
Janood 131
Joanna 131
Joshua Tree 131
Jukebox Jury 51, 132

Kansai Spirit 45
Katla 132
Kepler's Law 97
Keratiya 132
Khawlah 36-37
Khor Sheed 30, 132
King Gambit 133
King Of Wands 44-45, 132
King Torus 132
Kingdom Of Fife 132
Kingsfort 133
Kingsgate Native 133

racingpost.com 175

Kirthill 30
Kissable 72, 133
Kite Wood 133
Korithi 23

Laaheb 133
Labarinto 62
Laddie Poker Two 134
Ladies Are Forever 88-89, 134
Lady Of The Desert 134
Late Telegraph 12
Laughing Lashes 71-72, 134
Libranno 134
Life And Soul 82
Liliside 134
Lillie Langtry 134-135
Lily Of The Valley 77, 79, 135
Luminieux 79
Lyric Street 30

Mabait 135
Mahayogin 86-87
Maiguri 135
Main Aim 135
Majestic Bright 97
Man Of God 47
Manhaj 77, 78
Manifest 13-14, 135
Manighar 27
Mantoba 135
Maqaasid 46, 136
Margot Did 136
Markab 136
Masaya 136
Masked Marvel 46, 136
Master Of Hounds 70-71, 136
Mastery 35, 136-137
Matula 6
Maxios 76, 78
Medicean Man 82
Meeznah 137
Memory 137
Mendip 137
Meow 137
Midas Touch 137
Midday 12-13, 137
Millennium Star 12
Mirror Lake 138
Miss Diagnosis 7, 67
Mister Manannan 138
Misty For Me 71, 74, 85, 138
Mohedian Lady 30
Monterosso 36, 138
Moonlight Cloud 139
Moonyr 77
Moretta Blanche 5
Morning Charm 139
Motrice 139
Music Show 139
My Name Is Bond 139
Myplacelater 139

Namibian 54
Naqshabban 30, 66
Native Khan 139
Neebras 36
Never Forget 30
New Planet 140
Noble Citizen 82-83
Nouriya 61

Oasis Dancer 4
Oceanway 53
Opinion Poll 36, 140
Overdose 140
Pathfork 70, 74, 85, 140
Patkai 140
Penitent 140
Peter Martins 140-141
Picture Editor 10, 141
Planteur 77, 79, 141
Plumania 141
Poet's Voice 34, 141
Pontenuovo 23, 66, 69, 76, 141
Premio Loco 141
Presvis 27-28, 142
Prime Defender 142
Primevere 87
Prince Bishop 35, 142
Puff 4
Purple Moon 142

Raahin 62, 67
Rainbow Peak 143
Rainbow Springs 143
Rainbow View 46
Rainfall 36, 143
Ravindra 12
Recital 71, 74-75
Red Badge 143
Red Jazz 143
Redford 143
Redwood 143
Regal Parade 144
Remember When 144
Rerouted 144
Rewilding 34-35, 144
Rien Ne Vas Plus 62, 96
Rimth 145
Rio De La Plata 35, 38, 66, 145
Rite Of Passage 72, 75, 145
Roderic O'Conner 70-71, 75, 145
Royal Bench 146
Ruby Brook 6
Rumoush 146

Saamid 36, 146
Sadler's Risk 54, 67
Sahpresa 146
Sajjhaa 147
Salto 77, 147
Samuel 147
Sans Frontieres 147
Sarafina 77, 79, 147
Sea Lord 147-148
Sea Moon 62, 87, 148
Sea Of Heartbreak 21
Secrecy 148
Seelo 47
Seta 29-30, 148
Seville 148
Shakespearean 149
Sharedah 83
Shifting Star 83
Shimraan 149
Signor Verdi 87
Simon De Montfort 149
Sirius Prospect 89
Skysurfers 149
Slumber 87
Snow Fairy 149
So You Think 72, 75, 149

Society Rock 150
Sole Power 72, 75, 150
Son Vida 54
Soraaya 150
Specific Gravity 10, 12, 85, 89
Splash Point 36, 38, 66
Splendid Light 46, 47, 67
Sri Putra 150
St Nicholas Abbey 72, 151
State Opera 54, 69, 89
Stentorian 53
Strong Suit 151
Summit Surge 28, 151
Swiss Diva 151

Tactic 151
Taqleed 89
Tastahil 151
Tazahum 62
Tazeez 45, 152
Temple Meads 152
The Paddyman 152
Theology 152
Theyskens' Theory 152
Thistle Bird 23
Tiddliwinks 96-97
Timepiece 14-15, 152
Tin Horse 153
Titus Mills 153
Together 72, 153
Total Command 59-60
Treasury Devil 47
Triple Aspect 153
Tropical Treat 4, 7, 67
Twice Over 12, 153

Umseyat 47
Utley 45-46, 153
Utmost Respect 104-105

Vadamar 77
Varenar 153
Verdant 60
Vesuve 154
Viscount Nelson 154
Vita Nova 15, 66, 69, 89
Vulcanite 5

Waiter's Dream 154
Waseet 154
Western Prize 6, 69
Whispering Gallery 154
White Moonstone 37, 85, 154
Wiener Walzer 154-155
Wigmore Hall 155
Wild Wind 155
Wonder Of Wonders 155
Wootton Bassett 85, 155
Workforce 59, 62, 67, 155
World Domination 12

Yaa Wayl 155
Yaseer 87

Zacinto 156
Zaminast 75
Zeitoper 156
Zoffany 70, 156
Zoowraa 37-38, 156